CLAUDIUS CA

Image and Power in the Earl

The story of Claudius has often been told before. Ancient writers saw the emperor as the dupe of his wives and palace insiders; Robert Graves tried to rehabilitate him as a far shrewder, if still frustrated, politician. Josiah Osgood shifts the focus off the personality of Claudius and onto what his tumultuous years in power reveal about the developing political culture of the early Roman Empire. What precedents set by Augustus were followed? What had to be abandoned? How could a new emperor win the support of key elements of Roman society? This richly illustrated discussion draws on a range of newly discovered documents, exploring events that move far beyond the city of Rome and Italy to Egypt and Judea, Morocco and Britain. *Claudius Caesar* provides a new perspective not just on Claudius himself, but on all Roman emperors, the Roman Empire, and the nature of empires more generally.

JOSIAH OSGOOD is Professor of Classics at Georgetown University. His teaching and research touch many areas of Roman history and Latin literature, but focus especially on the late Roman Republic and early Empire. His first book, *Caesar's Legacy: Civil War and the Emergence of the Roman Empire* (Cambridge, 2006), examined the period after the assassination of Julius Caesar. Osgood has more recently published several articles on Caesar, as well as aspects of Roman family life and education. He is currently finishing a Latin textbook for intermediate and advanced students, *A Suetonius Reader*, and is also co-editing with Susanna Braund *A Companion to Persius and Juvenal*.

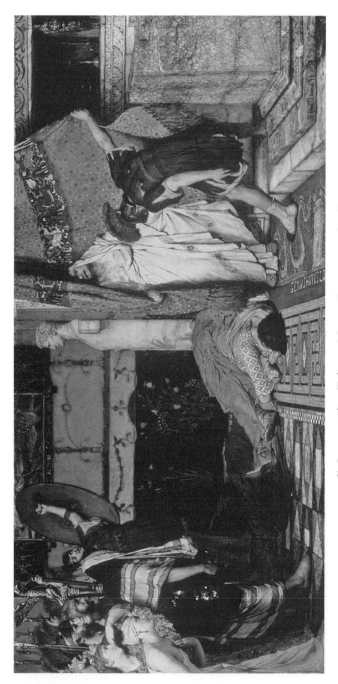

Sir Laurence Alma-Tadema, *A Roman Emperor* AD 41 (1871)

CLAUDIUS CAESAR

Image and Power in the Early Roman Empire

JOSIAH OSGOOD

Georgetown University

CAMBRIDGE
UNIVERSITY PRESS

CAMBRIDGE UNIVERSITY PRESS
Cambridge, New York, Melbourne, Madrid, Cape Town, Singapore,
São Paulo, Delhi, Dubai, Tokyo, Mexico City

Cambridge University Press
The Edinburgh Building, Cambridge CB2 8RU, UK

Published in the United States of America by Cambridge University Press, New York

www.cambridge.org
Information on this title: www.cambridge.org/9780521881814

First published 2011

Printed in the United Kingdom at the University Press, Cambridge

A catalog record for this publication is available from the British Library

Library of Congress Cataloging in Publication data
Osgood, Josiah, 1974–
Claudius Caesar : image and power in the early Roman empire / Josiah Osgood.
      p.   cm.
ISBN 978-0-521-88181-4 (hardback)
1. Claudius, Emperor of Rome, 10 B.C.–54 A.D.   2. Emperors – Rome – Biography.   3. Rome –
History – Claudius, 41–54.   4. Political culture – Rome.   5. Dystonia – Rome.   I. Title.
DG284.O84   2010
937′.07092 – dc22 [B]   2010035123

ISBN 978-0-521-88181-4 Hardback
ISBN 978-0-521-70825-8 Paperback

Contents

Illustrations

Maps and Tables

Acknowledgments

Working on *Claudius Caesar* more, and less, intensely over the last five years, I have incurred a number of debts, which I repay not only with this book but also sincerest gratitude. Many at Georgetown University, where I am honored to teach, have given much help. I thank especially my beloved colleagues in the Department of Classics for all their confidence in me, and our students for the stimulation they offer: Jack Carlson in particular kept me on my toes. I also thank Dean of the College Chet Gillis and Provost Jim O'Donnell, as well as Jane McAuliffe (formerly Dean of the College, and now President of Bryn Mawr College), for their generous support; and I thank the Graduate School of Georgetown University for research funding. The American Academy in Rome facilitated a research trip to Rome, and it was a great privilege to work in its superb library, now beautifully restored. I also express my gratitude to the staff of Lauinger Library at Georgetown for their unfailing help, and salute University Librarian Artemis Kirk for her heroic efforts on the Library's behalf. Finally, Yale University welcomed me back into its embrace in the spring of 2005 as a visiting fellow, and I thank old friends there (as well as new) for their help and hospitality, including Ann Hanson, John Matthews and Veronika Grimm, Kirk Swinehart, and Jay and Gordon Williams.

Michael Sharp at Cambridge University Press has once again supported my work, and I am grateful for his encouragement and advice. I also am greatly indebted to the various referees who commented on an early proposal for *Claudius Caesar* as well as a draft of the whole. They raised salutary concerns, and suggested ways to make this book more accessible. The Prologue, at the start, aims to give a short background sketch for those who may be less familiar with the field, while the bibliographic essays introducing each notes section, it is hoped, will help students of all sorts to pursue particular topics in greater depth. These essays also make clear the debt I owe to the army of scholars who, over the centuries, have assembled some of the fragmented evidence for Roman history and subjected it to careful interpretation. In Cambridge, Liz Hanlon, Laura Morris, and Rosina Di Marzo have helped shepherd a manuscript of many parts through production. I thank them, and my copy-editor, Anna Zaranko.

Without friends and family I cannot imagine how I would have sustained the inspiration and discipline needed to write this book. Let me thank especially Flagg Youngblood, who took over renovation of my house at a critical moment, to free me to complete final revisions; Carla Lukas, for her generosity and grace; Brad Boyd, for all the laughs; Maya Jasanoff, for always being there; and my parents Russell and Paula Osgood, and my siblings Mollie, Mike, and Iain, for all their love. And lastly, very special thanks to Adam Kemerer, who had to live with this book almost as much as I did, and did so with remarkable sympathy while always offering enthusiastic encouragement.

It was Adam who took me to see for the first time Henry Walters' collections of paintings in Baltimore, including Sir Lawrence Alma-Tadema's *A Roman Emperor AD 41* (1871), which so brilliantly encapsulates the theme of this book. In that painting is shown not one emperor, but three: Caligula lying dead, Claudius cowering behind a curtain, and, finally, Augustus, who, atop his blood-spattered herm, presides over the whole sordid scene. In 1917, Henry Walters purchased this canvas and added it to his father's collection, a notable piece of which was Gérôme's *The Death of Caesar* (1867), a dramatic depiction of an earlier and seemingly nobler assassination, without soldiers, but Senators, in pristine white togas, their swords raised high. Displayed together now in the Walters Art Gallery, the two works invite the viewer to reflect on how much the Roman world had changed from 44 BC to AD 41. For ten years I have been thinking almost daily about the history encapsulated by this extraordinary pair of paintings – and for all who encourage, or even just put up with, my eccentric interests, I am thankful.

Note on abbreviations

Ancient authors and their works are cited according to the abbreviations of S. Hornblower and A. Spawforth, eds., *The Oxford Classical Dictionary*, third edn (Oxford, 1996), with a few self-explanatory exceptions.

Modern reference works are also cited according to the abbreviations of *The Oxford Classical Dictionary*. Note in addition the following:

LTUR   E. Steinby, *Lexicon Topographicum Urbis Romae* (Rome, 1993–2000)

RPC   A. Burnett *et al.*, *Roman Provincial Coinage* (London, 1992–)

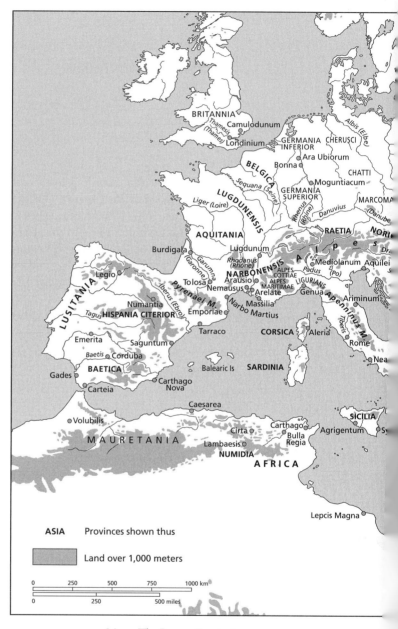

Map 1 The Roman Empire in AD 41

DACIANS

BASTARNAE

SARMATIANS

Borysthenes (Dnieper)

Sirmium

GETAE

Maeotis

CUM

MOESIA

Danuvius (Danube)

TAURI

Bosporus

THRACE

PONTUS EUXINUS
(Black Sea)

Hebrus

Sinope

Dyrrhachium

Byzantium

Nicomedia

BITHYNIA

PONTUS

Halys

nia

MACEDONIA

Thessalonica

Cyzicus

Nicaea

Ancyra

ARMENIA

disium

MYSIA

GALATIA

EPIRUS

THESSALY

AEGAEUM

Pergamum

CAPPADOCIA

Melitene

um

MARE

ASIA

Smyrna

Tyana

M.

Samosata

Delphi

ACHAEA

Chios

Ephesus

Taurus

CILICIA

Tigris

Dyme

Athens

Aphrodisias

Tarsus

Olympia

Corinth

Delos

PAMPHYLIA

ELOPONNESE

Argos

Cos

LYCIA

Antiochia

Sparta

SYRIA

Rhodes

Salamis

Euphrates

Cnossus

CYPRUS

CRETE

Caesarea

JUDEA

Cyrene

Jerusalem

Alexandria

ARABIA

CYRENE

Memphis

AEGYPTUS

Oxyrhynchus

Nilus

SINUS
ARABICUS

Prologue: The Roman Empire in AD 41

In AD 41, the Roman Empire had almost reached its maximum extent. It stretched from the Rhine and Danube in northern Europe to the Atlas Mountains of Morocco and the Sahara Desert, from the Atlantic coast in the west all the way to the Euphrates in the east. Romans were well aware of outlying lands – Britain; Germany, beyond the Rhine; fertile Mesopotamia, controlled by the neighboring Parthian Empire; even India, whose perfumes, spices, ivory, and gems were shipped to Rome each year – but Romans also liked to think they ruled the world. It is true the territory they controlled was vast, perhaps 3.5 million square kilometers.[1] But it was not in fact unparalleled: at just the same time, at the other end of Eurasia in the same temperate zone, the Han Dynasty of China ruled an empire of roughly the same size.[2] Rome's territory, though, was more spread out and consequently more prone to fragmentation, as later history shows; holding it together was a remarkable achievement.

Approximately sixty million souls lived within this empire, of astonishing diversity.[3] Traveling across it, one would have encountered different social customs – Egyptians, for instance, famously practiced brother–sister marriage, while Greeks still might seclude their wives from public life; Greek cities trained their young men in gymnasia where they exercised nude, Gallic chieftains now sent their children to Latin schools.[4] Greek one would have heard throughout the east, ever more Latin in the west, but myriad other tongues too: Punic dialects in North Africa and Spain, Celtic in northern Europe, Hebrew, Aramaic, and Syriac in the east.[5] Religious practice varied, with local gods cultivated almost everywhere. Worshiping their one shared God, with His lone Temple in Jerusalem, Jews, spread across the empire, were a notable minority population, perhaps numbering as many as four or five million.[6]

But wherever one went, two fundamental distinctions applied: that between slaves and free and, within the latter group, that between citizens of Rome and aliens.[7] Citizens were a minority – in a census taken in AD 14, about five million were counted, almost certainly including women and children – and a privileged minority: wherever they resided, they enjoyed legal protection from torture or execution on the spot by a provincial governor; and governors were to put citizens' interests ahead of those of all others.[8] Still, hierarchical as Rome was, within the group of citizens itself there were additional distinctions, enacted by law and enshrined by custom. The 600 or so members of the Senate and their families formed the top social class, and even within that there were divisions between the old patrician and other noble families, on the one hand, and new men, on the other, recruited from Italy, southern Gaul, and Spain. Senators still competed with one another, fiercely, for offices that they had held in the Republic: the quaestorship, the praetorship, the consulship at the top.[9] These offices still brought luster, even if their powers were now more circumscribed. Just below the Senatorial order, and replenishing it as needed, were equestrians, required to possess an estate of 400,000 sesterces; to them new and powerful posts in the imperial government were now available. And among the masses below these top orders, town councilors formed a privileged group, while a large group of manumitted slaves, the so-called freedmen and freedwomen, though often wildly successful economically, legally suffered some disadvantages.

The empire itself was divided up into several dozen jurisdictions, typically called "provinces."[10] Following an arrangement worked out after the end of the terrible civil wars of the late Republic, provinces would be ruled either by a legate chosen by the emperor from among the higher ranks of the Senate or by former consuls or praetors sent out for fixed terms of one year; the former group had control of virtually all the heavily militarized areas (and ultimately grew to have control of almost all troops, aside from some auxiliaries). One notable exception to this division was Egypt, ruled by an equestrian prefect appointed by the emperor himself. Sensitive areas on the edges of the empire – Thrace, for instance – could be ruled by native kings appointed by the emperor and ultimately answerable to him, but arrangements here were constantly evolving.

All provinces had miniscule numbers of officials: the governor and his few assistants, some slaves of the emperor, a handful of financial officers.[11] The Romans instead relied heavily on largely autonomous city governments to do the work of local governance for them, and also to collect taxes. Here there is a notable comparison to be made with Han China, where cities were run by low-level officials recruited from outside the territory in which they served.[12] Just as the empire, then, was a series of discrete provinces, a province itself was a collection of jurisdictions, each typically centered around a city. Cities managed their territories, saw to their own finances, ran the local markets, might even strike their own currency. Like individual men and women, they had statuses too: some had been founded as citizen colonies, with full Roman rights, while other, preexisting centers were made *municipia*, with full, or partial, rights; the great majority, though, were "foreign," most paying tribute, a fortunate few exempt. Cities might be close to one another, or scattered, and they ranged in size greatly – with Rome itself an extraordinary outlier, housing perhaps one million souls.[13] Alexandria was at most half that size, followed by the regional hubs of Carthage, Antioch, and Ephesus. Altogether there were perhaps close to 2,000 cities.

After the civil wars, Rome's first emperor, Augustus, reduced the swollen number of sixty legions to twenty-eight, and the number was further dropped to twenty-five after the terrible loss of three legions fighting under Quinctilius Varus in Germany in AD 9.[14] There it stayed – although by AD 41, two had most likely just been added, in preparation for an invasion of Britain contemplated by the emperor Caligula.[15] These legions, comprising about 150,000 citizens, formed a permanent standing army; they were supplemented with about as many men serving in auxiliary units (light infantry and cavalry), recruited from subject peoples of the empire, and sometimes commanded by their own tribal leaders. Arminius, chief of the German Cherusci – and mastermind of the Varan massacre of AD 9 – is a famous example. Altogether, then, there were about 300,000 serving, with major concentrations along the Rhine, in the Balkans, and in Syria.[16] The number could have been higher – but too many troops, too closely concentrated, might have threatened civil war again. And, even as it was, the army still represented by far the imperial government's largest expense; troops received not only yearly salaries, but also generous discharge bonuses, designed to keep them obedient in service, content afterwards. Fleets, again manned by non-citizen provincials, were stationed at Misenum, Ravenna, and in southern France. Also, an elite force of twelve Praetorian cohorts (each numbering probably around 500 men), guarded the emperor's life, normally residing within Rome, and commanded by two equestrian prefects appointed by the emperor. Very generous pay – much higher than that of legionaries – and large discharge bonuses again were to keep them loyal. A separate City prefect, a Senator, had three urban cohorts to help keep the peace in Rome.

All of these troops, their disposition, and their system of remuneration point to what was the paramount goal of the first emperor Augustus (and the chief reason his autocracy was accepted): the maintenance of peace in the empire after the horrific civil wars. Armed forces were needed to keep his own position secure, preventing would-be rivals from reigniting civil war. Armed forces were also kept up as a deterrent to unwelcome foreign intrusions – above all by the Parthians, who had breached the boundaries of the empire during the civil wars, causing great destruction, but also in Africa, for instance, where marauding tribes threatened the precious fields of grain.[17] In AD 41 itself, Sulpicius Galba, the governor of Upper Germany, was struggling with raids across the Rhine by the Chatti.[18] Almost as important, the armies and their commanders were also very clearly to watch over Rome's own subjects. Of Egypt's two legions, one was stationed in the outskirts of Alexandria, to keep an eye on that large and turbulent city.[19] The Rhine legions were a defense against Gauls as much as Germans.[20] And the troops in Syria intervened more than once in Judea, when tensions there rose.[21]

Governors played a key role also in the administration of justice, another paramount goal of the imperial government, one interlocked with the quest for peace.[22] Governors were regularly called in to settle boundary disputes between cities, or handle grievances of communities about their privileges and obligations. To varying degrees, governors even tried to dispense justice to individual provincials and citizens, traveling on a regular circuit around their province to hear from those they governed. Of course, protecting the privileged citizens was, at least in principle, an almost sacred responsibility. But governors might intervene too, for instance, if edicts of the emperor guaranteeing the privileges of specific groups such as veterans, doctors, or Jews were not being followed. Appeals could even be made to the governor on matters of local law, and occasionally the appeal could be referred to the emperor himself. The imperial government naturally oversaw the administration of justice in Rome itself, too, where some of the old Republican courts survived and the magistrates still gave judgments, even as the emperor, who could hear appeals, gradually took over, along with his staff, much of the responsibility. Augustus, according to his biographer Suetonius, sat as judge often into the night, lying on a couch on the tribunal, if he was unwell, or on a sickbed at home.[23]

Administration of all aspects of the City of Rome was in fact a third central task of the government, and this was an enormous operation, given just how many were crammed into it, packed into high and dangerous tenements.[24] No European city was so large, until London, in the age of industrialization. A substantial military presence helped – the Praetorians, the urban cohorts, and also watchmen to help fight fires. At the same time, a variety of amenities contributed to the peace, while adding to the emperor's prestige. Water was freely distributed, through the great system of aqueducts, three of which were built under Augustus.[25] There was a regular dole of free grain for citizens, given to perhaps a fifth of the City's population, and Augustus also appointed an equestrian prefect, to make sure there was an adequate food supply overall: well over 200,000 metric tons of wheat (the equivalent of 4 million sacks of 50 kilograms each) was required each year, most of which had to be brought on ships from overseas.[26] Spectacles were shown free: plays, gladiatorial matches, chariot-racing in the Circus, and beast hunts, the latter requiring importation of exotic animals, giraffes, tigers, panthers, and lions, sometimes hundreds at a time.[27] At the end of his life, the emperor Augustus boasted that he had given twenty-six beast hunts, at which 3,500 animals were killed.[28]

The scale of the government's activity was not unduly large – certainly, Rome took on no more than Han China – but given the empire's overall size, it required extensive effort. Gathering, organizing, and deploying resources was, then, a final key function of the imperial government. The whole operation rested on the collection of tribute.[29] Some goods of value were collected directly, some resources – precious metal mines, for instance, and stone quarries – controlled directly. But in a world where peasant agriculture was the chief economic activity, and the transportation of surpluses expensive, taxation of individuals was a necessity, on their land and also, more efficiently, on their heads. For this, it was necessary to inventory and count, and census-taking became a regular imperial practice, made famous forever by the census of Quirinius, in Judea, introduced portentously at the start of Luke's Gospel.[30] Collection itself was largely left to the leaders of local communities, who can only have undertaken the task in exchange for the ability to keep some of the local surplus for themselves. That actually happened in China, too, but in the Roman Empire much of that surplus was then used to adorn the cities with lavish buildings of stone, the ruins of which survive to this day.[31] As the existence of the poll tax suggests, taxes could be assessed at least partly in monetary terms, and that was possible in turn because the government also took as its responsibility the maintenance of a money supply on an unprecedented scale. From the central mint there were vast outputs, of coin theoretically worth the value of its content, whether gold, silver, bronze, or copper.

So much for the ambitions of the empire, but what of the obstacles to fulfilling them? Perhaps above all was the enemy of every vast empire of history: distance. Certain large, or remote, areas, within the boundaries of the empire or contiguous to it, simply could not be policed: deserts, mountain ranges, regions thickly forested. In them, outlaws might congregate, periodically breaking the peace elsewhere. Distance also posed difficulties in communication. Despite Rome's justly renowned roads, and the creation of a posting system under Augustus, which relied on the requisitioning of local communities' wagons and mules to speed messages along, it was quite hard to bring the average rate of travel by land much above fifty Roman miles per day.[32] From Rome to Antioch was about 2,500 Roman miles, and for a message to get there and back could easily take two months. And so, even if general policies could be set in Rome, by necessity men on the spot had to have a great deal of power. At the same time, considering the hierarchical nature of Roman society, the governor's high status, even the status of subordinate officials, easily overwhelmed that of all others: imperial government, then, could only really be as good as the men chosen to run it. While rights of appeal might exist, it would be hard for poor villagers, far from the governor's seat of justice, to exercise them.

Another set of limitations was financial.[33] If more tribute were to be extracted from the local communities, the government risked losing local support; raising indirect taxes was politically hard too; in the early empire, some of the most hateful memories of the civil wars concerned the exactions of the warlords.[34] There was no issuing of bonds, nor any "printing" of money, at least in our period – coinage was supposed to be pure. And unlike the Persian or Egyptian Empires, Rome seems not to have maintained reserves, at least by set policy. The result was not just a year-to-year struggle to match revenues with expenditures, but also the real difficulty of taking on major new commitments, including especially military operations – even if desired. In AD 14, following the death of Augustus, the troops in Pannonia and Lower Germany staged rebellions over their pay and terms of service – and the concessions they extracted were later rescinded by Tiberius.[35]

Other rebellions flared up in the years after Augustus' death, reflecting sometimes general dissatisfaction with Roman rule, more often unhappiness brought on by census-taking, tax-collection, or the imposition of military service. In Gaul, in AD 21, a rising took place, led by two Gallic nobles, the principal cause almost certainly economic distress.[36] There was also, under Tiberius, a full rising of the Musulamii in Africa, instigated by the Numidian Tacfarinas, a former auxiliary trooper who had deserted from the army and was raiding Roman territory.[37] At the start of AD 41 itself, the east was unsettled, with a recent crisis only narrowly averted in Judea, after Caligula had tried to convert the Temple of Jerusalem into an imperial shrine and install a colossal gold statue in the Holy of Holies.[38]

Such troubles were not in themselves grave enough to bring down the empire. The greatest immediate threat lay within the imperial government itself, for the government was, in a sense, divided. Fundamentally, it had two only slightly overlapping branches – the old, but still functioning *res publica*, on the one hand, represented above all by the Senators who still commanded most of the armies and, on the other, the emperor himself and his court, in which all manner of intrigues could blossom. For ideological reasons, Augustus had felt it desirable to keep the venerable old *res publica* alive – so obsessed were Romans with preserving their traditions – but power predominantly lay with him and the members of his court. And unlike Han China, in early imperial Rome, an ideology had not been fully worked out, and perhaps could not, that supported the political reality.[39] Augustus called himself *princeps*, an old Republican term that originally meant "first man" or "leader" and did not imply the holding of a transferable office.[40] His successors were not automatically accorded the authority that he had acquired.

And so, in the years following his death, all too easily resentments flared up over the way power was distributed, with a breakdown in relations between members of the Senate and the emperor in particular, which forced the people and the army to choose sides. Tiberius, Augustus' immediate successor, who was *princeps* from AD 14–37, tried to cooperate with the Senate initially, attending its debates, consulting it on matters he need not have. But it was unclear to Senators just how much they might say, and Tiberius found the tact required in dealing with them difficult to muster. Perhaps even worse, under Tiberius, Senators began more fully to use accusations of treason against the emperor as a way to persecute one another; after Tiberius himself retired from Rome to rule from the island of Capri, the situation grew worse still. Altogether, at least several dozen men were accused of treason. Disgruntled, demoralized, the Senate refused to vote Tiberius after his death the divine honors they had granted Augustus in AD 14.

Under Tiberius' successor, Caligula, relations between Senate and emperor deteriorated. Only twenty-four years old on his accession, Caligula had little practice in dealing with Senators, which fact alone, despite the euphoria over Tiberius' death, might have led to some mild resentment. But Caligula's subsequent behavior, perhaps best seen as a mixture of intemperate conceit and concerted effort to recast the emperor's rule as more akin to that of an eastern king, provoked outright hostility. Treason trials resumed, and in AD 39, Caligula claimed to have detected a conspiracy against him led by Cornelius Gaetulicus, the legate of Upper Germany, who was executed without trial; later in the year, perhaps also implicated in Gaetulicus' conspiracy, Aemilius Lepidus, the widower of Caligula's sister Drusilla, was put to death, while Caligula's own sisters, Julia Livilla and Julia Agrippina, accused of having been Lepidus' lovers, were exiled.[41] More executions followed. Though it was actually officers of his own Praetorian Guard who killed Caligula, Senators would in no way mourn the loss.

So it was that in AD 41, while the contours of the Roman Empire had already largely been set by Augustus, at its heart lay a key political weakness, exposed and amplified by more recent events. And to that weakness Claudius brought a new problem all his own.

Introduction: The problem of Claudius

Throughout his childhood and early adult years, Claudius never could have expected to become ruler of the Roman world. Born in 10 BC to Drusus, Augustus' stepson, and Antonia, Augustus' niece, he had not a drop of the first emperor's blood in him. But that was not his disqualification, for Claudius' own older brother, Germanicus, was considered a possible successor (Fig. 1). When, in AD 4, Augustus finally adopted Tiberius, gave him new powers, and made him his heir, he required Tiberius first to adopt Germanicus; both thereby gained the crucial name "Caesar" and entered the Julian family.[1] And after the premature death of Germanicus in AD 19, it was Germanicus' own young sons, including Gaius Caesar – otherwise known as Caligula – rather than Claudius, who came to be seen as possible successors to Tiberius.[2] The obstacle for Claudius was that as a child he suffered from a nervous disorder now diagnosed as dystonia – symptoms mentioned included irregular motor movements, a stammer, and drooling – and was thus deemed unsuitable for public life.[3] His own mother, it could be claimed, liked to call him "a freak of a man, not finished by Nature but only begun."[4] She, along with the rest of rest of the family, finally decided, when Germanicus was consul in AD 12, that Claudius was not to serve in any magistracy or to join the Senate. "The public," as Augustus wrote to his wife Livia at the time, "must not be given a chance of mocking him – and us."[5]

Claudius was given no experience of warfare, oratory, and the law, the staples of a Roman noble's education.[6] Excluded from the men's world, he spent his days in the household of his mother and his grandmother, Livia (his father had died when Claudius was still an infant).[7] The family ignored him, it is said, a tutor found who administered savage beatings.[8] The young man allegedly sought consolation in drinking and dicing; he also wrote voluminous histories, in Latin and Greek, on the age of Augustus and the antiquities of the Etruscans and the Carthaginians.[9] Only when Caligula succeeded Tiberius, in AD 37, did Claudius, now forty-five years old, join

Fig. 1 Portrait of Germanicus, from Gabii. Louvre, Paris.

the Senate when he briefly served as consul with Caligula.[10] Though the sudden promotion might have almost have seemed to be a joke – it certainly was an offense to custom – some signs of Claudius' disability apparently had abated with age. His biographer, Suetonius, claims that as emperor, Claudius was a man of some presence: he was "tall, well-built, handsome, with a fine head of white hair and a strong neck."[11]

Still, even shortly before Caligula's assassination in AD 41, the notion that Claudius might be proclaimed emperor – as he was, by the Praetorians – would have been unsettling. While the new Leader (to give the Latin word *princeps* one English equivalent[12]) was Caligula's kinsman and, more importantly, a member of the dynastic house established by Augustus, he had neither been adopted by any earlier emperor, nor shared many honors with them, nor (it seems) been named chief heir of any of them, the main formulas Augustus had established for promoting a smooth succession of power; he was neither a member of the Julian family nor a Caesar, as the other actual, or designated, successors of Augustus were.[13] Caligula, only twenty-eight years old, had left no clear plans at all for what was to happen.[14] Members of the Senate, appalled by the young man's final months of rule, contemplated a restoration of the Republic, or a candidate of more proven competence than Claudius. In Spain with three legions was C. Appius Junius Silanus, whose extra first name proclaimed ancestry in another branch of the Claudian clan; in Dalmatia, with two, L. Arruntius Camillus Scribonianus, descendant of Pompey, Sulla, and the Furius Camillus enshrined in the legendary history of Rome; in Upper Germany, with four or five, Ser. Sulpicius Galba, who did become emperor in AD 68.[15]

Threatened by men like this, and largely unprepared for rule, Claudius managed to hold onto power for nearly fourteen years and preserve the peace of Augustus across the vast empire. The shut-in scholar suddenly emerged, with energy, initiative, ideas. Ambitious projects were undertaken: Britain was to be annexed, a harbor built for Rome. Reforms were announced, opening up membership in the Senate, tightening Rome's finances. Claudius tirelessly held legal hearings, he issued floods of edicts. Yet along with such enterprises, the regime saw a number of casualties, including even Claudius' own wife, Messallina, who was put to death, without trial, apparently for conspiring against her husband.

The relationship between the shut-in scholar, steeped in the past, and the busy – but allegedly bloodthirsty – emperor has traditionally dominated the way Claudius' story has been told. In the eighteenth and nineteenth centuries, attitudes could be harsh. Edward Gibbon declared him the

Table 1 *The family of Augustus*

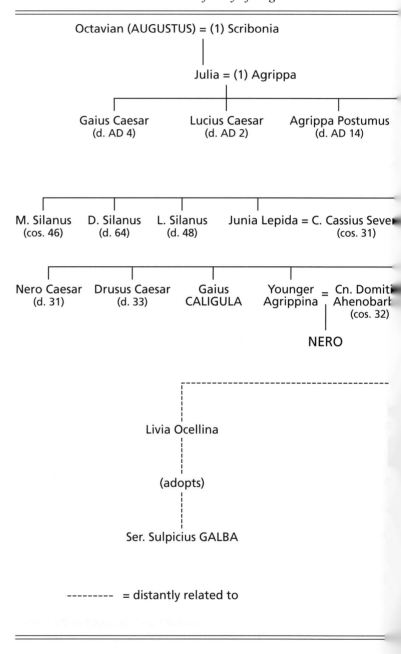

Octavian (AUGUSTUS) = (1) Scribonia

Julia = (1) Agrippa

Gaius Caesar   Lucius Caesar   Agrippa Postumus
(d. AD 4)   (d. AD 2)   (d. AD 14)

M. Silanus   D. Silanus   L. Silanus   Junia Lepida = C. Cassius Sever
(cos. 46)   (d. 64)   (d. 48)   (cos. 31)

Nero Caesar   Drusus Caesar   Gaius   Younger = Cn. Domiti
(d. 31)   (d. 33)   CALIGULA   Agrippina   Ahenobart
                                                      (cos. 32)

NERO

Livia Ocellina

(adopts)

Ser. Sulpicius GALBA

--------   = distantly related to

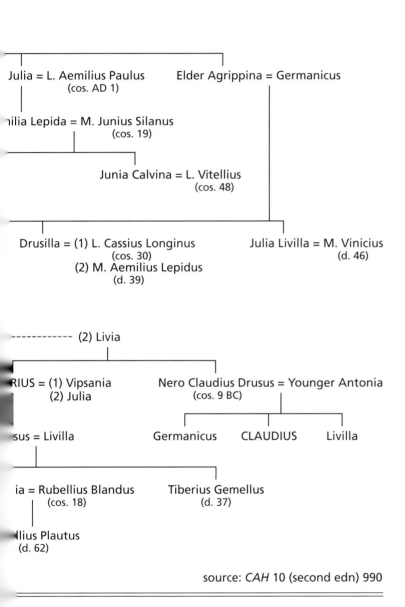

source: *CAH* 10 (second edn) 990

stupidest of emperors, while for Theodor Mommsen, "Claudius was mildly
deranged, an insignificant, even apolitical person."[16] There were no major
accomplishments to speak of, Mommsen claimed, aside from public works.
Far from ruling, he was ruled by others, his wives and former slaves; he was
a man "with no will of his own."[17] His main contribution to his principate
was paranoia. Mommsen concludes: "Claudius' regime is of little general
interest. As a person he is easiest of all Roman rulers to ridicule: it is hardly
even possible to deal with him seriously."[18]

William Smith's *Dictionary of Greek and Roman Biography and Mythology*
of 1849 was gentler. Claudius, to be sure, is criticized for "deficiency in
judgment, tact, and presence of mind."[19] But there is exculpation too. The
emperor's youthful illness is cited as a cause for intellectual deficiency; the
fear in which he lived in early years, it is argued, made him easy to exploit
after his accession; and it was the wives and freedmen who led him into
cruel acts, and stamped him with the name of tyrant. "If he had been left
alone," we are told, "or had been assisted by a sincere friend and adviser, his
government would have afforded little or no ground for complaint." Still,
the entry notes, Claudius "made several useful and beneficial legislative
enactments."

This sort of apologia was taken further in a 1916 dissertation, aptly
called *The Problem of Claudius*.[20] Examining the mixture of abilities and
weaknesses that the ancient sources present, its author concluded that
Claudius was born prematurely and suffered from infantile paralysis: this
brought on his physical problems. Further, any charge of grave mental
incapacity, such as Mommsen's, must go out the window; Claudius, it is
rightly argued, had intellectual ability. His nervousness and lack of control,
the author concludes, stemmed rather from brutal treatment in early life.
There is cogency to this view, even if Claudius' childhood ailment is now
diagnosed differently.

The problem, though, is that like Smith's entry, it still hews too closely
to not entirely reliable sources, above all Suetonius. Suetonius, who served
as a high-ranking official under the emperors Trajan and Hadrian, wrote
the only full biography of the emperor to survive from antiquity, part of
his innovative *Lives of the Caesars*. It uniquely recounts not just Claudius'
undertakings as emperor, but his whole early life as well as his personal
habits. The two other major sources, both annalistic histories written by
Senators, focus on Claudius only as Leader, and even then, thanks to the
vagaries of their manuscript traditions, each is incomplete: the *Annals* of
Suetonius' contemporary Tacitus is missing for the first seven years of
Claudius' reign (and all of Caligula's), while from Cassius Dio's epic work,

written still a century later, for this period it is often later excerpts or epitomes that survive.[21]

Suetonius seeks to portray Claudius as an inept and fearful man, pushed into a position for which he was ill-suited. Weak-minded, he disastrously relied on those around him and really wished to return to private life. Yet he could show remarkable cruelty. At least some of this unflattering depiction goes back to the very first accounts of Claudius, written after his death in AD 54. A short satire by Nero's tutor Seneca, *Apocolocyntosis*, probably composed that very year, condemns Claudius as a stupid yet savage ruler, as timid as a mouse.[22] An important historical work by Seneca's protégé, Fabius Rusticus, known to have been used by Tacitus, likely was similarly harsh.[23] Captious, too, one must suspect, was the now lost history of the consular Cluvius Rufus, which Tacitus esteemed.[24] Somewhat more balanced seems to have been yet another lost work of great importance, the history of Pliny the Elder, to judge by Pliny's references to Claudius in his extant encyclopedia.[25] There Pliny acknowledges the intellectual capacity and imperial accomplishments, but he also rebukes the influence and license granted to the wives and freedmen. There is Messallina's infamous contest with the prostitutes: in a twenty-four-hour match, she won with a score of twenty-five. Or the dining room that Callistus, "one of the freedmen of Claudius notorious for his power," built for himself with no fewer than thirty large columns of onyx.[26]

Suetonius himself supplies evidence that undercuts his own characterization of a feeble man, even as he tries to adhere to it. He may claim that the freedmen and wives dominated Claudius, but the first half of the biography details acts, often idiosyncratic, that seem to bear the stamp of a single personality – Claudius' own. As he worked through his sources, including perhaps the emperor's eight-book autobiography, Suetonius, it has been suggested, became aware that at least some of "The Problem of Claudius" had been exaggerated.[27] Whatever his physical difficulties, Claudius was not a totally weak-minded man; he showed, more than Tiberius or Caligula, energy in the practical business of government.

The question thus becomes how to explain the existence of so hostile a later tradition when evidence survives for a more positive view. Suetonius opts for a desperate solution. After crediting Claudius with a great deal through the early chapters of his biography, then, as he shifts discussion to the emperor's private life, he claims: "These acts and others too, and indeed almost his whole principate, he carried out not so much according to his own judgment as that of his wives and freedmen, nearly always being just what *they* found useful or desirable."[28] It is an unlikely, really impossible,

position. Even Tacitus and Cassius Dio (to judge by what does survive
of their work) can acknowledge some initiative on Claudius' part, though
their accounts, we shall see, still pose problems for a modern historian.

The difficulty now seems glaring. What awakened scholars to it was an
ever-growing collection of documents, preserved on papyri found in Egypt
or on bronze or stone from across the rest of the Roman Empire, which
demonstrated even more firmly the emperor's energy in governing. One
discovery was decisive. Around 1920, in the Fayum of Egypt, a substantial
cache of papers belonging to a tax-collector from the early Roman period
was illicitly excavated. Mostly registers of names, they attracted little interest
from Cairo dealers but finally found a buyer in Harold Idris Bell, Assistant
Keeper in the Department of Manuscripts in the British Museum.[29] On
the back of one of these registers, Bell discovered, copied in the hand of
the tax-collector, a transcript of an extensive letter written by Claudius
in the first year of his reign.[30] Even in those early and exciting days of
papyrology, it was the find of a lifetime – the equivalent, almost, of the
tomb of Tutankhamen.

Bell published his discovery, along with several other texts, in a lavish
volume of 1924, *Jews and Christians in Egypt*. The letter, a response to
an embassy from the Egyptian city of Alexandria to Claudius, dealt with
various matters, including a recent outbreak of violence between the Jewish
and Greek populations of the city. Though Claudius registers dissatisfaction
with the Jews, he also had a strong reproach for the Gentile community.
In Bell's translation: "Wherefore I conjure you yet once again that . . . the
Alexandrians show themselves forbearing and kindly toward the Jews who
for many years have dwelt in the same city, and offer no outrage to them in
the exercise of their traditional worship but permit them to observe their
customs."

As Bell noted, relations between the Jews of the Diaspora and the rest
of the Graeco-Roman world were a subject of debate in contemporary
scholarship, and not merely because of the typical problem of lack of good
evidence. Bell puts it delicately, but unmistakably: "Unfortunately, the
discussion, in modern as in ancient times, has not always been free from
racial or theological bias."[31] Max Radin was more explicit in a review of
Bell's work, writing: "a few German scholars have displayed in this matter
an irritation and emphasis which can only be a reflex of their disinclination
for the society of their Jewish contemporaries."[32]

The topicality of Claudius' letter helped bring it immediate renown,
and a flood of new publications ensued on the Jewish question (of the first
century AD).[33] But the document aroused tremendous interest too because

it cast new light on Claudius. Bell himself suggested: "The character of Claudius was a curious mixture, and included traits which made him, alike to contemporaries and to posterity, somewhat of a 'figure of fun'; but it is clear that his natural endowment... was good, and to the end one must recognize in him a solid base of character and commonsense." From the letter, Bell rightly says, "one would never suspect that Claudius was 'weak-minded.'"[34] Even if (say) a secretary had helped draft the letter, that would still reflect well on Claudius. After its discovery, the Suetonian portrait was never again to be accepted at face value.

Simple weak-mindedness had to go, and with it the emphasis on personal inadequacy. But questions remained. There was not just the most serious challenge of how to explain the divergence of contemporary evidence projecting a strong image of the emperor with the later figure of contempt. If Claudius had an able mind, one might wish to understand the relationship between his early scholarly endeavors and his vision of the principate. And at the same time, if Claudius had some positive intentions, whence the record of casualties? For if the *good* was to be credited to him, he would now have to take the stand for the *bad*: it could not all simply be pinned on wives or freedmen. In the wake of Bell's publication, two solutions were attempted.

The first belonged to a prodigy of historical scholarship, Arnaldo Momigliano, who by his twenty-sixth year had written three important monographs as well as over one hundred and fifty articles and reviews.[35] A student of the formidable historian of Greece and Rome Gaetano de Sanctis (who had himself immediately published an important paper in response to Bell's volume), Momigliano had followed de Sanctis to Rome from Turin and took over his classes after de Sanctis resigned rather than take an oath to the Fascist regime. Momigliano would later be deprived of his own professorship by the Racial Laws, but had won enough fame to seek refuge in Britain. Especially admired was a short study that he had written of Claudius, first published in 1932 and then translated into English in 1934 as *Claudius: The Emperor and His Achievement*. The title announces the book's iconoclastic approach, made possible by Bell's work. As the introduction states, "The past ten years have done more, perhaps, for Claudius, than any other figure of ancient history," and Momigliano then singles out the letter to the Alexandrians.[36]

Momigliano's early work, it has been noted, is memorable for etching sharp portraits of individuals caught in the latent contradictions of their age, or their position, unable to see a way out.[37] A study of Herod the Great, for instance, showed the King floating between the worlds of Rome and

Judea, trying to please both, blind to the impossibility of the task.[38] The study of Claudius is a sort of tragedy too: "how much of what happens in every age lies outside the control of men who may govern a state but cannot rule history," Momigliano announces. His hope, he says, is to penetrate Claudius' mind, "to follow in its...contradictions the painful process whereby the spirit of Republican Rome, apparently courted and fostered, vanished in the monarchical and cosmopolitan organization toward which the Empire was tending."[39]

This is the key that unlocks Momigliano's study. From Augustus, Claudius inherited a dilemma. The principate was supposed to draw inspiration from the institutions of the Republican past, and Claudius, as a historian, was attuned to that. Yet at the same time, Rome was now a world empire, and must try to dispense justice based on humanity to all its subjects, not just citizens. Claudius tried to uphold that justice – arrogating power to himself away from the Senate, as part of what Momigliano called a "policy of centralization" – even though this flew in the face of the old ways and would alienate members of the aristocracy. Momigliano concludes that Claudius fundamentally was unable to see this opposition "as a problem demanding to be solved," and therefore "perpetuated it and rendered it still more bitter."[40] In doing so, he created an opposition that he had to suppress; and Senators formed a view of him, reflected in the writings of Seneca, as "the monstrous combination of two contrasted traits – hypocritical reverence for tradition and autocratic license."[41] From this arose the hostility encountered in later (Senatorial) sources.

Largely independent of Momigliano, another account of Claudius emerged in the early 1930s, less profound but more widely influential: the pair of novels published months apart in 1934 by Robert Graves, *I, Claudius* and *Claudius the God*.[42] Imagining his two books as installments in a "secret history" written (in Greek) by the emperor as a counterpart to his official (Latin) autobiography, Graves memorably begins:

I Tiberius Claudius Drusus Nero Germanicus This-that-and-the-other (for I shall not trouble you yet with all my titles), who was once, and not so long ago either, known to my friends and associates as "Claudius the Idiot" or "That Claudius" or "Claudius the Stammerer" or "Clau-Clau-Claudius," or at best as "Poor Uncle Claudius" am now about to write this strange history of my life; starting from my earliest childhood and continuing year by year until I reach the fateful point of change where, some eight years ago, at the age of fifty-one, I suddenly found myself caught in what I may call the "golden predicament" from which I have never since become disentangled.[43]

Thus, at the start, one encounters Claudius trapped in a situation akin to what Momigliano saw too, a "golden predicament." Graves, it seems, came up with that formulation himself, for he records his debt to Momigliano only in his second novel, and had already begun planning the work in 1929. (Graves does, though, mention the letter to the Alexandrians in the preface to *I, Claudius*, and the original title page actually reproduced Claudius' name in the script of the papyrus [Fig. 2]). Indeed, there is a key difference between Graves and Momigliano: Claudius, in the fictional history, is cognizant of the circumstances in which he finds himself trapped, and sees it perhaps less as tragedy than satire. The "figure of fun" is not abandoned altogether, and indeed Graves struggles to incorporate as much of the Suetonian portrait as he can, but with some twists. Discrediting tales, especially of Claudius' early life, get explained as conscious exaggerations to survive. Others are sufficiently reworked by the gregarious – and self-avowedly forgetful – narrator so that the reader comes to find them less outrageous, or at least pleasingly ironic. The baneful influence of the wives, though, is accepted, and darkens the story.

But the fun aside, what exactly is the emperor's predicament? He would have it that he wished to be a good Republican, like his father Drusus the Elder and his grandfather, Livia's first husband, Tiberius Claudius Drusus. He claims that he was innocent of any desire to rule, and was thrust into the principate by the Praetorian Guard. He does not wish "to be branded as a clever opportunist who pretended to be a fool, lying low and biding his time until he got wind of a palace intrigue."[44] Graves' Claudius tries to absolve himself of that charge, but the fact remains that he did rule as First Man for nearly fourteen years. There just never was the right time to resign, he claims, and restore the Republic. Too much hard work had to be done first, to get Rome in order. Much as this Claudius detests Livia, as emperor he grows to appreciate her methodical, if devious, mind, which kept the "governmental system" running.[45]

Graves' conception of Claudius as would-be Republican has proved enduring, even subtly influencing the scholarly literature, though in fact it rests on little evidence.[46] But in other ways, from a historian's point of view at least, Graves accepts too readily the problematic, if entertaining, testimony of Suetonius (along with Tacitus and Cassius Dio). In having the courage to depreciate the later tradition, and focusing instead on problems posed by the development of the principate, Momigliano comes far closer to showing the situation Claudius faced. But to relegate the wives to "the dim background" of his study, as Momigliano does, leaves their role – and their key position in the later tradition – unexplained.[47] Further, the whole

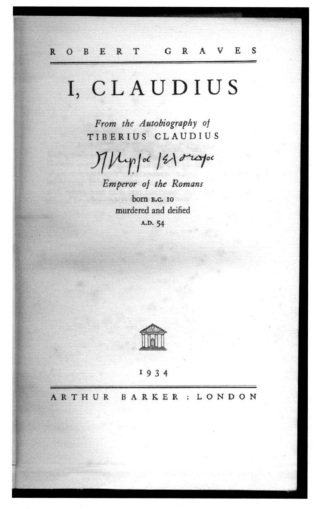

ROBERT GRAVES

I, CLAUDIUS

From the Autobiography of
TIBERIUS CLAUDIUS

Emperor of the Romans

born B.C. 10
murdered and deified
A.D. 54

1934

ARTHUR BARKER : LONDON

Fig. 2 Title page of *I, Claudius* by Robert Graves. Claudius' name appears in a Greek script, modeled on the letter to the Alexandrians preserved on papyrus.

notion of an increasingly "centralized" government is quite problematic.[48] There is no evidence for any major structural change in the government in this period – no evidence, for instance, that "Claudius was the first Emperor to organize a secretariat."[49] To have more immediate power over the subjects of its far-flung empire, the only choice for Rome in fact was to *decentralize* – to delegate more power to more men on the spot – and if anything Claudius seems to have made a few very modest steps in that

Fig. 3 Portrait of Livia, from the Fayum, Egypt. The wide dissemination of her portrait reflects Augustus' dynastic ambitions. Ny Carlsberg Glyptotek, Copenhagen.

direction. "Centralization" is not a helpful interpretation of Claudius' actions, or intentions.

This book argues against the view of earlier scholars that Claudius' problem was mental deficiency, and also against the view of Graves and Momigliano that the problem Claudius faced was any struggle within his mind. Indeed, Claudius' own inner thoughts are, historically speaking, less important than his actions, and hard to judge anyway. The paramount, in fact nearly insurmountable, problem for Claudius was rather that even if he belonged to the imperial house of Augustus, he was the first emperor of Rome whose selection might seem to rest on no authority whatever, save that of the Praetorian Guard (Figs. 3–4). He was not a great general, as Tiberius was; he was not a man of eloquence, as Tiberius and Caligula were. He was in no way a designate successor, and yet had no source of prestige other than his patently inferior position in the August House. In AD 41, when Caligula died, there was no established tradition of what to do;

Fig. 4 Portrait of Augustus, from the Fayum, Egypt, said to have been found with that of
Livia (Fig. 3). Ny Carlsberg Glyptotek, Copenhagen.

the political culture of the principate was still very much developing –
indeed, in a sense, it always was, but especially so now.[50] And the new
developments were not to everyone's liking.

The problem of Claudius, understood in this way, becomes not a puzzle
of biography, but a window for the historian onto this developing political
culture. Through his accession and years in power, we see how the principate was only gradually, and imperfectly, turned into an institution, with
an office that lay uneasily between hereditary monarch and elected magistrate. As Momigliano saw, because of the reverence for Rome's Republican
past, a truly typical monarchy, with fixed rules for succession, could never
be established. Sources of authority had to be developed otherwise, and
built on traditions already established in the Republic: wills, adoptions,
artistic imagery, building, religious ritual, military campaigning, and so
forth. Consent and support had to be elicited constantly from critical
groups across the empire, from the old Senate and People that met in
the city of Rome, to members of the towns of Italy, leading provincials,

and the armies stationed on the edge of empire as well as the Praetorian Guard.[51] The principate of Claudius was important for showing how this might be done by a man, unlike Tiberius or Caligula, little known to most of his subjects on his accession, in no way designated for power. It also dramatically demonstrated that the emerging monarchy was in an important sense a *military* monarch: however much other groups had to be cultivated, all emperors ruled most fundamentally at the behest of the armies.

As the principate was institutionalized, its monarchic features led to new experiments not just in ritual but also in establishing a court.[52] From the start, Augustus had relied for practical help in administering the empire on his own household, above all his slaves and freedmen, as well as members of his immediate family and friends from the top echelons of Roman society. In the years that followed, this court gained in prominence – and influence. Suddenly thrust into power, and with fewer allies in the Senate, Claudius was even more reliant on the slaves and freedmen he believed he could trust. He also had to demonstrate that after Caligula's disgrace, a new and lasting dynasty was being constructed, which led to innovative public roles for his wives in particular. These experiments were not entirely successful. For some, they caused resentment, leading Claudius' successors to articulate their courts differently, with administrative tasks shifted onto more explicitly defined officials. An even greater failure proved to be his effort to promote his own son, Britannicus, as successor; to put to rest troubles, after Messallina's fall, Claudius was forced to marry his own niece Julia Agrippina and adopt *her* son Nero, in whose veins the blood of Augustus flowed. The charismatic authority of the founder lingered on.

Finally, under Claudius another set of trends clarified themselves. As the old sovereignty of Senate and People of Rome gave way to a rule aimed to appeal to a larger band of society, provincials and citizens, despite their different statuses, were becoming more alike, both groups being subject to the same ultimate ruler. As the provinces rose in influence politically, the traditionally privileged position of Italy within the Roman empire inevitably declined. Further, as the dynamics of imperialism shifted, far less plunder from war was injected into the Italian economy. Whereas in the days of the Republic, Senators could enrich themselves with military campaigning, the old noble families that survived often had to live off their ever-dwindling estates. The large new fortunes to be seen belonged more to individuals dominant in the local economies of provinces, which might also export their products, not least to the city of Rome itself, for Rome did benefit greatly from the taxes and rents that flowed into the imperial coffers and were spent there. In embracing at least some of these trends, even as he resisted others, Claudius aroused further hostility.

Under Claudius, in myriad ways Roman society seemed to be, or was, in flux. The old nobility of Rome was being edged out; Italy was becoming more equal with the provinces; new fortunes were being amassed in unexpected quarters. Slaves, freedmen, and women of the court might seem to have more power than Senators; and they were winning property – if not prestige – as well. It was an age of real mobility, and, correspondingly, what sociologists call "status dissonance," the feeling that by some traditional criteria (especially power, property, and prestige) individuals rank high in society, by others low.[53] And what more palpable instance of status dissonance than Claudius himself, a stammerer whose word was now supreme, a fool made king? Feelings of status dissonance, sociologists explain, can be painful, unsettling even, and, perhaps for that reason, are also the stuff of satire.[54]

When the truest problem Claudius faced is better understood, the old conundrums start to find resolution: the divergences between the early scholar and later emperor, the record of bad as well as good, and, above all, the creation of so ridiculous, even satirical, a figure in the later tradition, including Tacitus and Dio. This book embraces that later tradition not as an objective representation of Claudius, but as evidence for understanding what Claudius signified in the eyes of his contemporaries and posterity, for that too can reveal something important about the development of the principate. To be sure, the writings of Suetonius, Tacitus, and Cassius Dio do demonstrably preserve genuine information concerning Claudius' administrative measures, and will be taken as doing so in the pages that follow. But, to get back to the reign of Claudius itself, the focus here will be as much as possible on more truly primary evidence – contemporary literary sources such as the writings of the Alexandrian Jew Philo, documents including the letter to the Alexandrians, and also, more originally, visual material including in particular sculpture and coins as well as architecture.

The aim here is not to write a biography of Claudius the man. The nature of the sources makes that task basically impossible. Indeed, over the decades, a consensus has emerged among historians that writing a true biography (in the modern sense) of almost any emperor is infeasible.[55] The fact is, like Claudius' own subjects, we are able to glimpse him most reliably on public occasions, or through his official pronouncements. Certainly, Suetonius, Tacitus, and Dio all give accounts, sometimes quite shocking, of what took place behind the scenes – the intrigues that followed the fall of Messallina, for example, or the circumstances of Claudius' own death; and there were a handful of insiders who might have known the truth about such affairs and preserved it; but all too often when it comes to the court's dealings, there are insoluble discrepancies between what the sources say, suggesting that the truth was not easily agreed on, or ascertained.[56] And even if the authorities later historians consulted did agree, they could all be misleading, if not outright wrong, so much blackening was there of some emperors' records after their death. Tacitus and Dio, to be fair, both explicitly acknowledge the problems involved in general terms and give their readers general warnings, but then show little hesitation time and again in offering a single reconstruction of events, when doubts might be entertained.[57] Modern scholars tend, rightly, to be skeptical of these reconstructions – for even where they do not rest on guesswork or historical imagination, they could still reflect later bias or even deliberate calumny. These reconstructions need not be dismissed out of hand, as if they were the sort of thing that could never happen; but they must be treated with caution.

More in favor, then, among scholars has been a sort of updated version of Suetonius, covering an emperor's background and early life, his accession and happenings in court (sometimes, it is true, with a fair amount of guesswork), and also broader aspects of his administration.[58] The two major studies of Claudius since Momigliano, by Vincent Scramuzza and more recently Barbara Levick, adapt this approach, the latter with greater finesse.[59] Her study firmly dismisses notions of Claudius the Republican or "centralizer" and illumines such subjects as "Finance and the Economy" or "Law, Justice, and the Stable Society." Levick's is an encyclopedic work, one which anyone interested in Claudius and the early empire will profitably refer to for years to come. But one limitation of such a thematic approach is that the interrelationship of events throughout Claudius' principate is sometimes hard to perceive – the ambitious invasion of Britain, for instance, of AD 43, is saved for one of the book's final chapters, even though it was connected to the circumstances of Claudius' accession.

Levick's approach, it should be noted, in many ways is in harmony with what is still the major synthetic interpretation of the role of the emperor in the Roman world, published by Fergus Millar in 1977. In this influential book, Millar famously took as his premise that "the emperor 'was' what the emperor did," and argued in consequence that the emperor's role had to be analyzed on the basis of his own actions.[60] What emerged was an essentially passive figure, who responded to his subjects much more than he initiated change himself. Roman emperors, Millar argued, had little scope for the active dissemination of "policy" or "propaganda." (And a corollary, for Millar, was that studying the rule of a single emperor in isolation would yield only limited results.[61]) On its own terms, such a model makes a great deal of sense: as seen above, Rome's resources, like those of other pre-industrial governments, were limited, and the empire's vast scale made decentralization of many aspects of governance necessary. (And a study of a single emperor will surely be successful only if contextualized properly.)

But there are also limitations to this approach.[62] To understand the role of the emperor in the Roman world, one has to recognize that in the eyes of many of his subjects, the emperor might *be* many things that he did not actually *do*. So focused is Millar on the workings of "government," he neglects the tremendous range of symbolic roles the emperor had to fill, not least the role of god. That is, for many of his subjects the emperor was more a symbol, almost a fiction, but a powerful fiction – one that could inspire individuals to modify their behavior. A study of the Roman emperor has to examine not just the words he sent back in response to petitions but the image he projected through statues that were replicated in cities and towns throughout his realm, set up and paid for by his own subjects. Granted, it was his subjects who erected such statues: but as the similarities between the statues show (as also the differences between the image of one emperor and the next), emperors and their immediate advisors must have taken an active role here too.[63]

And that leads to a second problem. While much of governance in the Roman empire was undeniably decentralized, that in no way obviated the need, in no way precluded the ability, to make decisions of consequence in the center.[64] By pursuing a diachronic analysis of various topics (e.g., "The Imperial Wealth" and "The Emperor at Work"), Millar, as he himself acknowledges, risks atomizing the principate and the *princeps* himself. One gains little sense of how a decision on one matter might affect another – of how (say) the gift of a costly donative to acknowledge the unexpected adoption of an heir could make an emperor reconsider the cost of a new military campaign. Emperors might have been limited in their resources, but that would only have made it all the more important for emperors to think strategically – to set priorities, even formulate what we could call policies. They had to, to survive in power. And when it came to ruling the provinces, emperors did not just have to react to the petitions of their subjects; the men they appointed to govern and the instructions given to them about such matters as the granting of citizenship rights and other privileges, or the promotion of cities and their adornment, or road-building, could, and did, over time affect the lives of thousands and thousands. Emperors were bound by the forces of history, and yet might shape history too, and could be aware of that great burden. Millar's book, ultimately, gives an imperfect sense of the exacting test it was to be the emperor of Rome.

And so this study has three chief goals. The first, most limited one is to retell the story of Claudius' principate itself. Structured more as a chronological narrative than a study that tidily splits up the various administrative roles of the emperor, this book seeks to explore the interrelationship of events across Claudius' years in power. It shows how Claudius and his subjects initially communicated, how they responded to one another in the years after accession, how (and why) the image of the emperor was changed in conjunction with events not always within his control. The focus is on Claudius, but also his subjects and their perception of him. Recently discovered evidence is exploited, to look at areas beyond Rome; and much excellent scholarship on the creation of the emperor's image is used to help retrieve Claudius' own contemporary image. This emphasis on image is a key divergence from Levick's *Claudius*.

A second, larger, goal is to use Claudius to think about the role of the Roman emperor more generally. A close examination of one principate helps, in particular, to challenge Millar's model of an essentially passive ruler. Claudius was not a passive ruler. If in some respects he did have to be reactive (as any government must), he also actively established priorities and made plans. The invasion of Britain, along with a strategically related set of decisions about the empire's boundaries, are enough to show that. And, through his own efforts, and in dialogue with his subjects, Claudius was able to construct an image of himself as a mighty ruler who stood for the strengthening of empire through hard work after years of perceived neglect by Tiberius and Caligula. Senators may have dismissed it, but we can be far less sure that everyone else did.

Other recent studies of individual emperors have turned to matters of image-making. One, for instance, shows how Nero drew on Greek mythology, and its reenactment on the theatrical stage, to shape an image of himself that enjoyed some success; another, on Commodus, uncovers the logic of that emperor's Herculean and gladiatorial posturing.[65] Works such as these will be the bricks and mortar that one day will allow a very different overarching interpretation of the Roman emperor to be constructed. Such an historical model will try to take account of, rather than dismiss as utterly eccentric, Nero's singing and Commodus' fighting – and it also has to try to explain Claudius' invasion of Britain, or the portraits that were disseminated of him.

Finally, to return to a point made above: once we apprehend how critical a moment it was when Caligula was assassinated and the whole legitimacy of imperial rule was thrown into question, the principate of Claudius can be used as an historical vantage point onto the development of the early imperial government as a whole, and this is the third goal here. These years point back to the government's troubled birth, in usurpation, and forward to its later maturity, when many provincials came to see it as theirs too. Failures there were, to some degree the fault of Claudius, even more the result of circumstances he could not control, as Momigliano divined. Yet with Claudius, thanks to his efforts and those of many of his subjects, the principate took an important step to becoming a more regular institution – the "social system" Millar so brilliantly, if only partially, describes in *The Emperor and the Roman World*.

But a "system" was not perfectly in place yet, as the events following Caligula's assassination showed. We turn back, then, to AD 41, as word of the new emperor's proclamation reached his subjects. They had questions. Claudius did too. How would he keep power? Who would help him, and who would stand in his way?

CHAPTER I

Claudius Caesar

On the twenty-fourth of January AD 41, the last day of the Palatine Games held each year in honor of Augustus, Caligula was assassinated by members of his Praetorian Guard.[1] Leaving the theater around lunchtime to enjoy a visit to the baths and inspect a choir of boys who were to sing that evening, he was caught, according to later reconstructions of the crime, in a deserted alleyway of the imperial grounds: the assassins, led by Cassius Chaerea, a burly Guard officer allegedly mocked by Caligula for his effeminate voice, each quickly struck a blow and then made their escape through another set of passages, leaving the corpse for the German Bodyguard to discover. Chaos immediately broke out. Reports of what happened spread through the palace, to the theater, and finally across Rome. The people gathered in panic in the Forum, while the consuls transfered the state treasuries to the Capitol and met with the Senate on and off through the next day. Gathered in the great Temple of Jupiter, they anxiously debated what to do, what Rome's future should be. Some hoped their old "freedom" might be restored; others made a bid for the principate themselves, such as M. Vinicius, husband of Julia Livilla, who was Caligula's sister and, more importantly, Augustus' great-great-granddaughter. Others still argued over the merits of rival claimants.

A decision was made for them elsewhere. On the outskirts of the City, in the well-fortified camp Tiberius had built for the Praetorian Guard, another meeting was taking place. Claudius, according to Suetonius' memorable account, was dragged there in terror, after an ordinary soldier discovered him cowering behind a curtain in a dark corner of the imperial property and hailed him as *imperator*.[2] As the Senate vacillated in the face of this unexpected development, and a crowd gathered outside its meeting clamoring for a ruler in Claudius, Claudius himself is said slowly, reluctantly, to have allowed the Praetorians to swear an oath in his name; Cassius Dio emphasizes that reluctance too.[3] And yet, a different version of events is suggested by the Jewish historian Josephus (Josephus, for reasons to be seen, had good reasons to give the assassination of Caligula a lavish treatment). By this account, after Caligula's death the Praetorians met and debated among themselves what course of action to take. Concluding that "when matters were still undecided, it was well to choose an emperor themselves," they proceeded to have Claudius abducted. The Senate, Josephus writes, resisted the choice just as long as they could, but when the military forces they did have abandoned them, capitulated.[4]

One may doubt it all came to pass in exactly either of these ways, one may even suspect that, while Chaerea and his colleagues performed the bloody deed, the high leadership of the Praetorians, prominent Senators, and just possibly Claudius himself, played some part in arranging Caligula's assassination – all might have felt they were in danger – and that they had a better plan for what was to happen than the chaos that actually ensued.[5] Yet Josephus is sure that the Senator Annius Vinicianus was an important ally of Chaerea, and Vinicianus, like Chaerea, seems to have been opposed to Claudius' succeeding Caligula. Perhaps, after the crime was committed, some of those in on it – perhaps, say, one of the Guard prefects, or perhaps even Claudius – betrayed their co-conspirators. There can be no certainty. But there can be little doubt that the Praetorians did accept Claudius as *imperator*, swear an oath of allegiance to him, and force the Senate to accept their acclamation. And there can be no doubt that, in the eyes of each other anyway, the cooperation of Claudius and the Praetorians was essential.

Claudius had no claim to be emperor deriving from personal prestige. He was not a great general or politician. Nor was there, at the moment Caligula fell dead, any legal basis for favoring him over another candidate. To be sure, Claudius was a member of the "August House" the first emperor had established and promoted as Rome's ruling dynasty. He was also, it might be remembered, brother of the beloved Germanicus in particular. But there were by now important traditions for recognizing a successor, and none could easily be invoked by Claudius. And so, whatever lay behind the events of January 24, AD 41, the chaos that ensued can also leave no doubt that Claudius' claim to the principate was a dubious one, most especially in the eyes of some Senators.

The Praetorians, it is rightly maintained, offered Claudius an invaluable military force, but what is less remarked is that they could lend him some legitimacy by an acclamation as *imperator*, an old title once awarded to victorious generals on the field, then adopted by Augustus as a first name, now coming to signify an emerging position of "emperor." Caligula, too, had almost certainly received such an acclamation from the Praetorians, before the Senate met to discuss his accession.[6] Now the Praetorians acted even in opposition to the Senate, because they were eager to stay in service – and because they were promised a large bounty by Claudius. They knew he would be especially beholden to them. For them, he was an excellent choice.

A new tradition had to be invented for the principate to survive. Effectively rendered impotent, at least temporarily, by the collusion of Claudius and the Praetorians, the Senate voted Claudius "all the remaining prerogatives of imperial power," and their wishes were duly enacted by the People in assembly.[7] The "prerogatives" should have included, ultimately:

(1) a bundle of legal powers, such as had been gradually accumulated by Augustus, including *imperium* over all those provinces with significant armies as well as in Italy itself and continuous tribunician power (which helped convey the permanence of the emperor's rule, and, counted yearly, could be used to date events in it);

(2) membership in all the major priestly colleges as well as the office of *pontifex maximus*;

(3) miscellaneous honors, most notably a garland of oak leaves, a traditional military decoration awarded for the saving of a citizen in battle, but now a symbol of the salvation the emperor represented for his fellow citizens (Augustus had received the decoration in 27 BC); and

(4) the names themselves: "Augustus" as well as "Caesar."

Caligula, it is inferred, received a similar grant, though not the name "Caesar" which he had already possessed along with "Julius"; Tiberius Caesar, by contrast, had shared most of the key powers (and some honors) with Augustus before Augustus' death, and gained the name "Augustus" through Augustus' will.[8] A secret of empire was out: a Caesar could be made other than a Julius. And, it could be asked, if Claudius could have this name – or title – why not somebody else?

These were decisions of great consequence. Yes, Augustus' vision of dynastic rule was affirmed, insomuch as Claudius more clearly than any other adult male belonged to the old "August House." But that is not why the Senate put their collective weight behind Claudius, giving him those magical, legitimizing names along with the other honors and powers. As their resistance shows, they were forced to, by the Praetorians. The only alternative was civil war, which they would not have been able to win with the forces they could muster in Rome, in January AD 41. Certainly, some Senators, loyal to the August House, might quickly have come to accept the new emperor. Yet, we shall see, a conspiracy that took shape the following year, the significance of which has not always been well understood, shows that not all did; some individuals might have voted to legitimize Claudius, and legitimacy their votes conveyed, but they viewed it all as a sham.

Claudius should have known as well as anybody that even after the votes of Senate and People, his position was still precarious. In the days and weeks that followed he executed two sets of policies to strengthen his relations with vital constituencies – the Senate and People of Rome, and the armies. In Rome, a particular concern was to try to make everyone forget, as much as possible, those awful two days when the future of the principate had been in question; it would also benefit Claudius to dissociate himself from Caligula, even blacken his memory, although to do so excessively might bring opprobrium on the emerging institution of the principate itself.

So it was that amnesty was granted to those Senators who had initially opposed Claudius, and vengeance was not sought against those who had mocked him before: there would be no long chain of reprisals. At the same time, it is said, Caligula's statues quietly started disappearing, taxes he had introduced were gradually remitted, pending cases of treason were disposed of, and exiles – including Caligula's own two sisters, Julia Livilla and Agrippina – were brought back.[9] Claudius completed work on an arch built in honor of Tiberius near the Theater of Pompey and also pointedly rededicated the Theater itself; though Tiberius had mostly finished repairs on this great monument after a devastating fire, Caligula had given him no credit in the dedicatory inscription, and also failed to mention Pompey; Claudius restored the names of Tiberius and Pompey, and added his own, thereby tacitly distancing himself from Caligula.[10]

The games held to celebrate the rededication afforded the new emperor a spectacular introduction to the people of Rome. Clad in the distinctive toga traditionally worn by a triumphing general, crowned in laurel, and perhaps holding a scepter capped by an ornamental eagle, he offered sacrifice at the shrines high in the rear of the auditorium, then slowly, in impressive silence, came down the tiers of seats to a raised platform in the orchestra from where he would preside.[11] The audience was to be stunned: it was a Claudius they had not seen before. Suetonius' report of this, and Claudius' many other spectacles seems credible; records were kept of them, and were researched by Suetonius not just for his imperial lives but his influential books on games, themselves a sign of the vital place of games in the political culture of imperial Rome.[12] Games were where the Leader showed his regard for the People, and the People in turn demonstrated their support for him. Claudius was to make ample use of them as a way to gain support.[13]

Table 2 *Distribution of legions on accession of Claudius*

Region	Titles	Commander
Lower Germany (4)	I Germanica V Alaudae XX XXI Rapax	P. Gabinius Secundus
Upper Germany (4)	II Augusta XIII Gemina XIV Gemina XVI Gallica	L. Livius Ocella, Ser. Sulpicius Galba
Africa (1)	III Augusta	uncertain
Egypt (2)	III Cyrenaica XXII Deiotariana	C. Vitrasius Pollio
Syria (4)	III Gallica VI Ferrata X Fretensis XII Fulminata	P. Petronius
Spain (3)	IV Macedonica VI Victrix X Gemina	C. Appius Junius Silanus
Moesia (2)	IV Scythica V Macedonica	P. Memmius Regulus
Dalmatia (2)	VII XI	L. Arruntius Camillus Scribonianus
Pannonia (3)	VIII Augusta IX Hispana XV Apollinaris	A. Plautius

Note: Two additional legions, XV Primigenia and XXII Primigenia, certainly in existence by AD 43, were most likely already formed by Caligula and were stationed in northern Europe in AD 41. See p. 87 below.

While the People's support was valuable, more crucial, ultimately, was that of the twenty-five or so legions stationed across the empire.[14] An independently minded commander might easily lead a rebellion, "especially the governors of large districts commanding large armies such as the Euphrates army in Syria," as a contemporary of Claudius remarked.[15] Even a mutiny spearheaded by the troops themselves could undermine an emperor's position, or at least distract him. The clear solution was for Claudius to do as he did with the Praetorians, and offer all of the troops substantial cash payments.[16] News of the bounty would reach them, it can

Fig. 5 *Aureus*, dated AD 41/2. The obverse shows the head of Claudius; the reverse an enforced wall enclosing the Praetorian Camp, in which a figure stands holding a standard, with the abbreviated legend, THE *IMPERATOR* RECEIVED. This figure may be a personification of good faith.

be surmised, just as they were asked to renew their oaths of loyalty in the name of the new emperor.

To help make at least some of the unanticipated payouts of this year the Roman mint produced a substantial emission of gold and silver coins, crudely estimated to make up a third of its entire production for the reign of Claudius.[17] The issue gives – and was designed to give – an excellent sense of the image Claudius was trying to project in these early months of rule, especially in Rome. It featured a portrait of Claudius in profile, at first depicted youthfully, despite his nearly fifty years, and a legend giving his new names "Caesar" and "Augustus" (e.g., Fig. 8). This connected him to his predecessors, and so bolstered his authority. At the same time, a more novel collection of reverse faces, exploiting the highly visual way in which Romans thought, reinforced two priorities of Claudius in AD 41: showing gratitude to the Praetorians for acclaiming him *imperator* and reconciliation with the Senate to avoid civil war (Figs. 5–9). The Praetorians received Claudius; Claudius in turn received them. The Augustan Peace was upheld – and along with it, Rome's dominance over the world – and rightly did the Senate award Claudius a crown of oak leaves: Claudius had shown regard for the lives of his fellow citizens.[18] And finally, his steadiness through the crisis of the late emperor's assassination was recognized with a goddess new to the coinage and, through her name, explicitly his own: the Constancy of Augustus.[19] Imperial rule – the rule of truly August Ones, who brought the

Fig. 6 *Aureus*, dated AD 41/2. The obverse shows the head of Claudius; the reverse Claudius shaking hands with a figure holding a standard, with the abbreviated legend, THE PRAETORIANS RECEIVED.

Fig. 7 *Aureus*, dated AD 41/2. The obverse shows the head of Claudius; the reverse the winged figure of Peace, with a staff, an attribute also associated with Concord and Good Fortune.

blessings of Peace – the coins suggested, even demonstrated, had survived Caligula.

All these beautiful gold and silver coins raise a fundamental question about Claudius' early days in power. The new emperor reportedly promised the Praetorian Guard a payment of 15,000 sesterces.[20] This was a staggering sum, five times their normal yearly pay, and far more substantial than the

Fig. 8 *Denarius*, dated AD 41/2. The obverse shows the head of Claudius; the reverse a garland of oak leaves encircling the abbreviated words BY DECREE OF THE SENATE, FOR SAVING CITIZENS. Note Claudius' youthful depiction, with fine facial features and a strong neck and chin.

Fig. 9 *Denarius*, dated AD 41/2. The obverse shows the head of Claudius; the reverse the figure of "Constancy of Augustus," seated on the curule chair of a magistrate.

bequests left to them by previous emperors and the sum paid by Caligula upon his accession.[21] While in a planned succession, the funds for such a donative might be set aside ahead of time, Claudius would have had suddenly to raise, or locate, the necessary 135 million sesterces (an amount equivalent to 20,000 pounds of gold).[22] And he apparently did so, at least in part, in the form of bullion, which was used to make the large new coin emission. But if he offered other troops handouts in the customary

Table 3 *Estimate of notional gross annual expenses for the early imperial government*

	(sesterces)
(1) army	
(a) salary costs	= 400,000,000
(b) discharge costs	= 50,000,000
(2) civilian employees	= 60,000,000
(3) grain distribution in Rome	= 60,000,000
(4) largesse and donatives to civilians and soldiers	= 16,000,000
(5) building	= 40,000,000
(6) other major expenses in emperor's name (household, gifts, games, etc.)	= 85,000,000
Total	= 711,000,000

Note: This tabulation is based primarily on data and estimates presented in Duncan-Jones (1994) 33–46, using the principates of Augustus and Tiberius in particular as a guide; see also Frank (1933–40) v.4–18. Some of these numbers are *quite* uncertain; several areas, especially (4)–(6), could fluctuate greatly from year to year, and (5)–(6) were probably lower under Tiberius in particular, leading to a currency crisis in AD 33 (Tac. *Ann.* 6.16–17) and, ultimately, a surplus (Suet. *Calig.* 37.3); finally, there were deductions from army pay to cover certain supplies, which might have been given in kind, hence lowering the amount of coin needed. The point of a tabulation such as this is to give a sense of likely orders of magnitude and proportionality.

proportion, he altogether owed around 800 million sesterces, about twice the cost of operating the army for a year, and perhaps nearly equivalent to the empire's annual intake of revenue.[23] Even if this sum is simply too high, a great deal, it seems, was required, and found. So the question is: how?

Here we come to another set of decisions Claudius had to make, veiled from public view at the time or at least not publicized in the same way that the relationship with the Praetorians (for instance) was, but crucial all the same for understanding his principate. While the votes of Senate and People might legitimize an emperor in the eyes of his subjects, seemingly giving him at a stroke the position his predecessors held, the true basis of the emperor's supremacy, going back to Augustus and his usurpation of power in civil war, was arms and the money to pay for them. To survive, the emperor needed to have control of the state's finances.[24]

And so, while the old treasury of Rome, based in the Temple of Saturn, still functioned, and another treasury created by Augustus funded military pensions – it was these that the consuls seized after Caligula's murder, suggesting that they might contain some funds – management of the empire's accounts overall ultimately lay with the emperor's personal staff. Tiberius made this perfectly clear when shortly after Augustus' death he had read out to the Senate a scroll that the late emperor had left for him written in his own hand.[25] A statement of Rome's resources, it listed the number of soldiers under arms and their locations, the amount of money in the treasury and the financial offices of the provinces, and the annual direct and indirect taxes owed along with sums outstanding. It made the nexus between arms and money clear. But it gave only an outline; all the details, Augustus wrote, could be had from slaves and freedmen whose names he supplied in a list at the end.

It was of the utmost importance, then, for Claudius, as soon as he left the Praetorian Camp in January AD 41, to gain control of the imperial property on the Palatine: it was there, more than in the Temple of Saturn, that he would find vital information about the empire. By private law, Caligula's house should have gone to Caligula's heirs – or, if he died intestate, to his sisters, since his daughter had been killed (along with his wife) shortly before his own death. By private law, Claudius had no claim at all, because he was not even a member of the Julian family. Yet, it could be said, the old house of Augustus, at least, had been made public property, and should be occupied by whoever was serving as *pontifex maximus*.[26] The matter might not have been discussed publicly (there is no record of doing so), but certainly Claudius knew he had to have the house – or, perhaps it is better to say, palace. Even if they underwent no physical transformation, it was with Claudius that the Palatine buildings irrevocably became a "Palace" that passed from one emperor to the next, regardless of his family name.

As important as the palace itself was its massive support staff, made up of current slaves or those manumitted, the so-called "freedpersons," who by law owed their former owner various services. Like the house, these too passed to Claudius, and then his successors, part of their patrimony whatever private law said. Caligula could make some claim to them on the basis of Tiberius' will (even though the will was nullified) and membership in the Julian family; Claudius, not a Julian, had no claim at all.[27] But pass they did to Claudius, as is shown by some of the thousands of epitaphs they left behind in collective burial grounds, texts which also reveal the bonds they formed with one another.[28] Living together and, once freed, marrying, they had children, some of whom were in service too; they also formed collective units (*collegia*), organizations that not only took care of one another but also frequently honored the emperor and his family. All this suggests that, like the Praetorians, at least some of these slaves and the freedmen in particular must have been eager enough for the Principate to continue, for their existence depended on it; their collective experience and cohesiveness, in turn, were of enormous help to Claudius. And so, again perhaps without even discussing the matter publicly, he simply assumed possession of his predecessors' staff – a crucial precedent for years to come.

For the slaves and freedmen handled a mind-boggling array of functions. The epitaphs fail to record the most menial tasks the staff must have performed (such as washing clothes or baking bread). But they do reveal a large number who took care of the imperial family, some ensuring their physical wellbeing and comfort (such as Ti. Iulius Secundus, an ear specialist, or the food taster Ti. Claudius Alcibiades or the litter-carrier for Claudius' son Britannicus, Ti. Claudius Quadratus), others helping them with wardrobe or grooming (e.g., Amoenus, jewel-keeper for Messallina or Paezusa, hairdresser for Claudius' daughter Octavia).[29] They also reveal a key group of individuals who controlled the imperial complex on the Palatine: footmen, stewards, guards, and an entire group of slaves who managed the emperor's bedroom. And they reveal that a small army too maintained the furnishings and decoration of the imperial buildings and gardens, where the emperor would meet with prominent members of Roman society at the customary morning salutation, or at recitations of literary works, or at dinners. It was on such occasions that he effectively held court: Augustus, in avoiding many of the explicit trappings of monarchy, had never actually called his house a court, but clearly on one level it was; but from around the time of Claudius, the Latin word *aula* (tellingly, a Greek borrowing), used previously to refer to the royal courts of the East, is attested in reference to Rome and the emperor.[30]

The slaves and freedmen did not just maintain a physical space that could be called a court; they also helped the emperor execute some of his most important duties in the court, and beyond. There were experts available to create all sorts of pageantry – a whole division, for instance, to handle wardrobe for the games the emperor gave.[31] There was a section *ab epistulis* which managed the emperor's correspondence, as the epitaph for the file-clerk Ti. Claudius Erastus shows.[32] There were individuals who helped with petitions and embassies.[33] Some slaves and freedmen *a studiis* dealt with the literary activities of the court.[34] Somewhat like a modern bureaucracy, the whole operation was really in the end still a household, ultimately in the control of Claudius, the new *paterfamilias*. This suited the emperor, insomuch as it gave him direct control over these important officers (for that is what some of them effectively were), but there was also a weakness: Claudius could not oversee everything himself, and yet the slaves and freedmen were, like their master, essentially beyond the reach of the law.[35]

Pageantry and the like certainly were important but, to be fair, the new emperor probably could have survived, at least for a time, without a Hermeros, superintendent of marbles, or Eutrapelus, record-keeper in the department of theatrical costumes.[36] The same could not be said for a final part of the staff, concealed within the palace and, indeed, spread across the empire, the slaves and freedmen who managed the paramount task, the maintenance of the imperial finances. Though much, for obvious reasons, was kept secret – the location, for instance, of reserves of coin or bullion that were accumulated separate from the state treasuries – it appears that there was a central bureau, on the Palatine, that handled the accounts overall and consulted with other officials in Rome as needed, as well as separate branches in the provinces, called *fisci*, which handled collection of taxes and disbursements of money (especially for the army); it made no sense to cart large amounts of coinage to Rome, only to ship them back, and taxes in kind might be redistributed locally. Two types of staff dominated: *tabularii* handled the accounts (and, when appropriate, communicated their results to the central bureau) while *dispensatores* had control of the money itself. This latter group kept the payments going as needed, and because their task was so vital, remained slaves throughout their period of service, although they enjoyed considerable privileges, for instance the use of their own slaves. Some of them did very well for themselves. Pliny in his encyclopedia fulminates against a fine example of "status dissonance," the slave Drusillianus, *dispensator* for Claudius in Nearer Spain, who earned the unflattering additional name "Rotundus"; he commissioned, Pliny claims, a silver service with dishes weighing 250 and even 500 pounds.[37]

However grotesque his platters might have been, Drusillianus and his office in Spain are a key to understanding the new emperor's initial success. As the slave's name shows, he once belonged to Caligula's sister, Drusilla, then at her death passed to Caligula, and finally to Claudius. There were others like him, Cinnamus, for instance, also once a slave of Drusilla, who died while still in servitude to Claudius and was buried by his concubine Secunda.[38] Kept on in service, these stewards, the accountants, and the others who dealt with finances supplied crucial experience in Claudius' first days of power. It must have been they who helped make the necessary arrangements for the donatives to be paid out. How the money was actually raised, or located, will always remain a secret. The likeliest guess is that despite the claims later historians made concerning Caligula's profligacy, something of the surplus the tight-fisted Tiberius had amassed remained, perhaps in the form of bullion received directly from the precious metal mines over which the emperors were coming to have a virtual monopoly.[39] Such bullion could easily enough have been converted into coinage. Not to be overlooked, either, are the gold crowns provincial assemblies likely would have sent to Claudius on his accession; Augustus claims that he refused no less than 35,000 (Roman) pounds of such offerings after his victory at the battle of Actium, the equivalent of around 150 million sesterces.[40]

Loyal as men like Drusillianus no doubt were, Claudius would have needed even more help. Here we are more in the dark, for while epitaphs can help repopulate the Palatine and (to a far lesser extent) the imperial *fisci*, they can never reveal with whom the inexperienced Claudius actually consulted when he arrived back to the imperial house from the Praetorian Camp. Some conjecture might not be entirely out of place and is necessary, to appreciate how the Roman empire worked – and survived.

While there were altogether hundreds of slaves and freedpersons in the imperial household, under Claudius' predecessors, a more select group of freedmen rose to positions of real influence, if not outright power.[41] They obviously knew a great deal, and so Caligula's most trusted freedmen would be a natural group for Claudius to turn to, except that, precisely because of their influence, they were reviled and might even have been thought a threat to the new emperor. And so, Claudius is said to have destroyed the sinister chamberlain of Caligula, Protogenes, along with the two ledgers he liked to carry around menacingly, the "Sword" and the "Dagger."[42] And the freedman Callistus, it is said, would have met a similar end, except for a story he came out with about saving Claudius' life despite being ordered by Caligula to poison him.[43] Such anecdotes may ultimately speak most to Caligula's posthumous memory, but some reshuffling of the staff must have been in order. While C. Julius Callistus did indeed continue to be an important member of Claudius' court, Claudius turned to other freedmen, and he relied on them more than his predecessors did, not just for the services that they provided but for counsel – Narcissus, for instance, who managed the correspondence; and Pallas, who managed the finances.[44]

A freedman of Claudius' recently deceased mother, Antonia, Pallas was a man not directly associated with Caligula's rule, but still familiar enough with the workings of the palace. He was also well-versed in matters of finance, as his own ever-growing fortune attested.[45] Pallas was the perfect choice, and he is a clue to where else Claudius turned for help. In these early days, one senses, quite a bit of Antonia's old household was reconstituted, her web of connections re-activated. Though it is Livia who has captured later imaginations, Antonia was no less a key figure in the August House and had, over her lifetime, cultivated dependants and allies from across the Roman world.[46] They ranged from the vassal princes of Rome she raised alongside her own children and grandchildren, including King Agrippa I of Judea, to versatile courtiers such as Lucius Vitellius and Valerius Asiaticus. These men, too, had skills which they were willing to share with a new and inexperienced emperor in exchange for renewed favor. Agrippa, who happened to be in Rome at the time of Caligula's assassination, allegedly intrigued on behalf of Claudius – which is one reason Josephus is so interested in the whole episode.[47]

But, one must imagine, others too appeared to offer their help, from beyond Antonia's old circle. One of these might be the extraordinary nonagenarian, Sex. Turannius: prefect of Egypt already in the last decade BC, he was in charge of the grain supply of Rome by the time Augustus died and, despite a brief and unhappy attempt to retire under Caligula, soldiered on in the post until at least AD 48, when he is said to have advised Claudius during the great crisis of that year.[48] Another was the enterprising Caecina Largus, owner of one of the finest houses in Rome, again said to have been on hand to help in AD 48, but also consul at the start of AD 42 with Claudius, surely a reward for help in the first months of power.[49] Men like this knew the secrets of empire.

Yet despite all the help he received, despite some months of apparent tranquility after the difficult accession, Claudius' situation deteriorated. Already before the year was out, Caligula's sister, Julia Livilla, just restored from exile, had to be banished again.[50] The official charge was adultery – and implicated in it was none other than Seneca, Claudius' later denouncer.[51] Cassius Dio, though, claims that the real motive was Messallina's anger that Julia had not flattered her enough, and that the young, and attractive, woman was spending too much time alone with uncle Claudius. This could all simply be a later, and inaccurate, reconstruction, reflecting Claudius' final marriage in AD 49 to his other niece, Agrippina, Julia Livilla's sister. One might suspect instead that this great-granddaughter of Augustus, married to Marcus Vinicius (a potential candidate for emperor), was trying to hatch a plot against the imperial couple – or at least she had come under suspicion for doing so. (Whether Seneca was entangled in that seems more dubious, given his later recall to Rome from Corsica, to where he was banished in 41.) There is no sure way to know. But one way or another, Julia Livilla's banishment was a crack in the façade of a stabilized dynastic rule that Claudius was trying to present in his early months of power.

The real trouble, though, in the view of Cassius Dio, began the following year with the death of C. Appius Silanus, who had shortly after Claudius' accession been recalled from his governorship in Spain to marry Messallina's mother, Domitia Lepida.[52] According to Dio, it was once again Messallina who masterminded the whole affair, this time resentful because Silanus refused to sleep with her: she had the freedman Narcissus invent a dream "that he had seen Claudius murdered by Silanus' own hand." Narcissus related the dream to Claudius early in the morning when the emperor was still in bed, Messallina took it up and emphasized its significance, and Silanus was put to death. Suetonius has a not dissimilar reconstruction (though according to him, Messallina also feigned a dream) and adds that Claudius did not hesitate to report to the Senate the execution of Silanus – carried out on the grounds of Narcissus' dream. It was, apparently, not the only occasion under Claudius that a plot was said to have been detected in such a manner.[53]

Yet Suetonius and Dio's accounts show that, later anyway, serious doubts could be entertained regarding Narcissus' dream. Their exact reconstructions, of course, may be wrong, resting more on guesswork, historical imagination, or calumny. More compelling is the view that one, or both, members of the imperial couple were suspicious of Silanus – hence the marriage to Lepida in the first place – and with their suspicions further aroused, had him eliminated: it would not have been out of place in a court that felt its survival at risk.[54] Silanus, an influential Senator and experienced commander, whose family had run into trouble with the August House before, could have caused problems for Claudius. Again, certainty is unattainable, but the more important point to recognize is that Senators, whatever they were told about the passing of Silanus or any dreams of particular members of Claudius' household, could not have been certain of what really happened either. It was not unreasonable to harbor dark suspicions. And yet if Claudius was dealing with a genuine threat, that need not have been conceded by his opponents. So it was that almost immediately after the emperor's own demise, Seneca could simply accuse him of murdering Silanus.[55]

Later in the year, it is much more certain, Claudius did face a real crisis, and took substantial public measures in response to it. The fullest account once more is that of Dio, who writes that after the death of Silanus, Annius Vinicianus, in company with others, was inspired to form a plot against

Claudius (and Dio mentions here that Annius had in fact been considered a candidate for emperor after Caligula's death).[56] Lacking any military force themselves, they got in touch with Furius Camillus Scribonianus, the governor of Dalmatia, "for Camillus was already making his own plans to revolt, especially because he had been thought of as emperor."[57] Senators and knights flocked to Annius but then it all went awry in Dalmatia: as Camillus talked of restoring the Republic, his soldiers decided to abandon him, and Camillus took his own life.

Much more briefly, Suetonius describes the abortive rebellion as a "civil war," but says that it was put down in only five days – again, when the legions deserted. He later adds that Camillus thought he could intimidate Claudius even without a fight, and sent him an abusive letter, telling him to give up power and take himself back into retirement. A third writer, Pliny the Younger, adds that the former consul Caecina Paetus had joined the plot of Scribonianus and was with him in Dalmatia when Scribonianus died; he was taken prisoner and sent to Rome for trial. His brave wife Arria, according to Pliny, begged the soldiers to let her accompany him. "Of course to a man of consular rank," she insisted, "you will grant him a few slaves to feed him, dress him, and put on his shoes; I will do all of this for him myself."[58] When her request was refused, she hired a small fishing boat, and it followed her husband's ship all the way to Italy.

Probably by the time Paetus and Arria reached Rome, an investigation had been launched by Claudius. However short-lived, the "civil war" had undermined his shaky claim to power; he was determined to find out, by the most exacting means it took, what had happened in Dalmatia, if others were involved. This inquisition, as much as the abortive rebellion itself, is fundamental for understanding Claudius' principate, yet both can only tentatively be pieced together, as follows. Scribonianus had been in Dalmatia with his family since around AD 40, an active governor who built up extra auxiliaries.[59] Hearing of Claudius' accession, he evidently was disgruntled with the choice, perhaps because he truly yearned for restoration of old Republican "freedom," perhaps because he believed the empire deserved somebody better than "Claudius Caesar," such as Silanus, Vinicianus, or even himself. But nothing could be done straightaway. Messages had to go back and forth to Rome, from one provincial commander to another. Eventually Paetus, with Arria, joined him, and plans were made, probably by late 41 (and so before Silanus' death).[60] Caligula had been removed: why not Claudius? Whatever his ultimate intentions, there could be little doubt of the guilt of Scribonianus on this score. Or of Paetus: allowed to kill himself in Rome, he wavered, until his wife, in a legendary moment, grabbed the sword, plunged it into herself, and said, "See, Paetus, it does not hurt."[61]

But were others involved? Anyone with relevant information was told to come forward: not just Senators, but their wives, freedmen, and slaves. Suspects were imprisoned, even, it is said, tortured. Pliny states that one person who volunteered evidence was the wife of Scribonianus, who had been with him in Dalmatia and in whose arms he died. The testimony gathered implicated a whole group of prominent individuals in Rome, most notably Annius Vinicianus, and also Q. Pomponius, the consul of AD 41, who, perhaps suffering along with his brother at the hands of Caligula, had argued for a restoration of "freedom" and opposed Claudius.[62]

The apparent collusion of Vinicianus and Pomponius, along with the timing of events in Dalmatia, strongly suggests that the whole rising, with its two wings in Rome and Dalmatia, must be seen as a response to the accession of Claudius in AD 41 and his early months in power as a whole rather than the death of Appius Silanus alone. Silanus himself might have been part of an early phase of it. The rising, ultimately, was an effort to complete what had only been started in AD 41: a full reassertion, after the death of Caligula, of the "freedom" of Senators, whether they used it to restore the old Republic or to choose their own Leader. It also challenged the legitimacy granted to the new emperor's accession by the Senate. And, appropriately enough for this variation on the events of January AD 41, the second challenge to Claudius failed because the legions in Dalmatia abandoned Scribonianus, and no others would join the cause. The donatives had done their work, and Claudius further showed his indebtedness when he gave Scribonianus' two legions fresh rewards and renamed them "Claudian, Loyal, and Patriotic."[63]

Yet even as the rising pointed back to AD 41, Claudius' inquisition had profound consequences for the rest of his principate. As is the way with such witch-hunts, denunciations started to pour in. Some, one can suppose, seized the opportunity to settle private scores, which is in part why the loyalty of Arria came to be remarked on so much. Even for the innocent, there could be hard choices: although last rites were denied to any found guilty (and their names were effaced from public monuments), a certain Cloatilla still buried her husband, who had been "among the rebels," and was put on trial for doing so. She managed to obtain a pardon from Claudius.[64] That act of mercy notwithstanding, it all added up to a grim sequence of trials, executions, and, no doubt, more than one act of treachery which, along with the earlier death of Silanus, wrecked any fair prospects Senators had for the new reign after its unsettling start.

Claudius probably erred in responding so repressively to a threat that, at least on the surface, evaporated quickly, for he at once lost his reputation for clemency and likely created even more simmering resentment. Nobody in Senatorial circles forgot the episode quickly. It was terrible in itself, and it also spoke more broadly to their dilemma under the principate. Anyone with a moral imagination might suddenly find himself, or herself, forced to decide whether personal liberty and loyalty to a family, or subservience to Caesar – even Claudius Caesar – was a greater good. The wife of Scribonianus and Vibia had made their choices, and individuals continued to reflect on them, even take inspiration. Yet Arria's heroics were not a model by which all might wish to live – or die.

CHAPTER 2

A statue in silver

In the Roman world, Alexandrians were as famous for their fractiousness as their erudition. In this teeming city of Egyptians, Greeks, and Jews, where shrines to Zeus sat next to synagogues and cats were considered sacred, Homeric scholars came to blows over the question of citizenship rights as easily as over obscure words in the *Odyssey*, philosophers argued, not just in their schools, but before the Roman prefect, and works of history made only the most thinly veiled allusions to present enmities. Take the Egyptian priest Chaeremon, an authority on hieroglyphics called to Rome in Claudius' reign to tutor the young Nero (he was expert in Stoic philosophy too).[1] In his version of the Exodus story, the Jews were a diseased lot banished by the Pharaoh Amenophis after a vision of Isis appeared to him in his sleep. Or consider Apion, author of a learned commentary on the lyric poet Alcaeus: he gets credit too for the first accusation of ritual murder on the part of the Jews, an eerie anticipation of the medieval blood libel.[2]

Chaeremon and Apion were contemporaries of the far more famous Philo, a philosopher who belonged to one of Alexandria's most prominent Jewish families.[3] Immersed in the thought of Plato, Pythagoras, and others, yet even more committed to the Scriptures of his faith, Philo wrote in an elegant Greek a long series of commentaries on the Torah, firmly convinced that Moses in his wisdom anticipated all of value in later philosophy. Other works survive, including a biography of Moses and a fascinating, if not entirely plausible, account of a community of Jews living in the hinterland of Alexandria who practiced an extreme asceticism. But for all his admiration of these hermits' contemplative life, even Philo was drawn at least once into Alexandria's turbulent affairs. When, in AD 38, a violent attack was launched against the city's Jews, culminating in a grim celebration of Caligula's birthday at which Jewish leaders were scourged in the Theater, Philo joined the embassy that afterwards sought redress from the emperor.[4]

His heart nearly broken by the persecution in Alexandria, Philo grew only more distraught when in Italy he learned of the emperor's plans to install a colossal golden statue of himself in the Temple at Jerusalem. There was apparently more personal anguish too, for Philo's fantastically rich brother, Alexander, seems to have run into some trouble with Caligula.[5] To offset his fears Philo had only his faith, which was vindicated when Cassius Chaerea's daggers took Caligula's life and left the Temple of the Most High God unscathed. Claudius released Alexander, whom he likely already knew, as Alexander had once managed some of Antonia's property. Like another of her men, Pallas, he could lend expertise to Claudius in his early days of power.[6]

So exceptional was this episode in Philo's experience, he decided to write a work equally exceptional in his massive corpus, an account, in five books, of the persecution of the Jews under Caligula and their final vindication with the accession of Claudius, called *On Virtues*.[7] A portion still survives, it seems clear, in an extant work called *The Embassy*, and shares in detail with the reader, Jewish or not, Philo's own explanation for his despair over Caligula's colossus – while also implicitly rebutting the sorts of allegations spread about by the likes of Apion.[8] Placing a graven image in the Temple, Philo explains, violated the Commandments which lay at the very heart of the Law handed down by Moses: Apion's claim that the Jews venerated the golden head of an ass was nonsense.[9] Further, Jews across the Mediterranean felt affection, as well as awe, for the Temple; they regularly sent it gifts and tried to visit it (as Philo did, at least once); polytheist Greeks and Romans admired it too, and offered sacrifices in its outer courts.[10] On the Temple, Philo says, "which shines everywhere like the sun, east and west look with admiration."[11] A third reason for everyone's shock, including (according to Philo) the governor of Syria who had to carry out Caligula's orders, lay in the emperor's abrupt departure from the zealous protection Augustus and Tiberius had offered to the Jews.[12]

Not only would Augustus never have dreamt of installing a statue in the Temple, even more importantly he showed full understanding when the Jews refused to honor him with images in their other places of worship. During his forty-three years of rule, the Alexandrian Jews "did not make a single dedication on his behalf in the synagogues – not a statue, not a carving, not a painting."[13] This in a world where everyone else was voting him honors equal to those of the Olympians, not just statues but temples and arches, sacred precincts and porticoes! Alexandria itself boasted a resplendent Temple of Augustus, built on high ground near the Great Harbor, for in this city Caesar was above all a protector of sailors.[14] Unlike the synagogues, Philo acknowledges, "it is full of dedications such as nowhere else, and is surrounded by paintings, statues, gold, and silver all around."[15] Jews might offer an inscription or a gilt shield, but nothing more, as was clearly shown in AD 38. As part of the unrest of that year, the persecutors of the Jews installed images of Caligula in some city synagogues (while burning others); in the largest and most famous, they also placed a flaking bronze statue of a four-horse chariot dragged from the Gymnasium.[16] To the Romans, they could point out that they were only creating shrines for the emperor's cult.

The desecrated synagogues of Alexandria, and the fragments of Philo's *On Virtues*, haunting previews of so much to come in Jewish history, also offer a good vantage point onto a distinctive practice of the Roman Empire. Philo, while he may well be misleading in his explanation for the outbreak of violence in Alexandria, was not exaggerating much to suggest that synagogues were about the only public spaces in Alexandria that lacked imperial images. Already under Augustus, statues of the emperor were put up simply everywhere across Italy and the provinces: in sanctuaries and temples, of course, but also army camps and governors' residences; in libraries and theaters, baths, circuses, and gymnasia; in public squares and the meeting halls of town councils; on honorary columns, inscribed pillars, triumphal arches, and city gates.[17] For a wide array of viewers, statues reflected and created the emperor's standing – for civilians and soldiers, citizens and provincials, easterners with ancient traditions of anthropomorphic art and westerners who might be new to it. Portraits of Augustus marked him as a man of honor, philanthropist, and military victor; as a friend of athletes and artists and patron of intellectuals; as a witness to oaths, a hero, even a god, who might literally offer sanctuary.

Individual statues had served all of these functions before, in the Roman world; but never until Augustus, not even with Alexander the Great, had the image of one man been so thoroughly disseminated, never before had it taken on so many meanings as this one now did.[18] Statuary proved to be a crucial means by which Augustus and his subjects articulated his own utterly new position, of the greatest use because statues are highly visible, "legible" to those who cannot actually read, and, as unique artistic commissions, able to show something about those they honor and also those who pay for them. While Augustus and his family did commission a handful of statues for themselves in public places, or might suggest to friends in the Senate a plan for doing so, the overwhelming majority (as Philo rightly suggests) were set up for them by others.[19] This does not mean that local workshops failed to take cues from Rome; in fact, Augustus and his family seem to have made available likenesses of their portrait features – which, by an old convention in Roman art, were thought to lie only in the head, not the body as a whole.[20] After all, portraits would (normally anyway) have the greatest impact if they were instantly recognizable. And so Augustus' likenesses, though strongly classicizing, also show idiosyncratic features such as his jug ears (Fig. 4). Yet through variations in carving technique, the material used, the type of body attached to the head, and the placement of the statue and the inscription that might accompany it, individuals were able to fashion a great range of statues to serve their needs. Though artists worked painstakingly, and modern scholars gruelingly reconstruct the lost models, the whole system was admirably free. This is why Philo's account of Caligula's colossus could speak to a polytheist too: the emperor was not supposed to give orders to set up his statue.

Because the first emperors and, even more, their subjects had made such ample and varied use of statues – Augustus even touches on the subject in the *Achievements* he composed to adorn his mausoleum in Rome – Claudius after his accession had to decide what his practice would be.[21] With Augustus' precedents before him and the memory of Philo's delegation still fresh (to say nothing of King Agrippa's presence in Rome), the choices might seem obvious, and to some extent Claudius made the obvious choices. Yet insecure in his power, the first Caesar not a Julius, Claudius shrewdly took the opportunity to send new, as well as familiar, messages to his subjects not only through the statues he had erected of himself, but also through those statues he created of other members of the August House, those he declined, and those he removed. Heeding the messages, Claudius' new subjects sent their own back, either in images that he might actually see or through verbal descriptions given by ambassadors or in letters. Yet many of their statues probably remained unknown to him: statues were a way local communities spoke to themselves too. Statues are sometimes called *signa* in Latin, and suggestively so; positioned in the thousands, even the millions, across the Roman empire, these "signs" were markers that helped order existence, asserting the power of Rome and the emperor, precisely because their power was limited.[22] Making plans for the erection of new statues was a useful way for individuals to come to terms with political change: to put them up was to suggest that imperial power would endure.[23]

In Rome itself, according to Cassius Dio (likely relying ultimately on the record of Senate proceedings), of the statues voted by Senate and People Claudius accepted only three, one in silver, one in bronze, and one in marble. "All such expenditures," he declared, "are pointless and furthermore lead to great waste and trouble for the City."[24] A marble statue could be had for 5,000 sesterces, paltry from the government's point of view (though substantial to ordinary citizens who might contemplate erecting a monument for a beloved patron or a deceased relative).[25] Claudius' refusal of any statues in gold, on the other hand, did represent real savings: one set up for Augustus in his Forum by the province of Baetica weighed (its base certifies) one hundred (Roman) pounds, the equivalent of 400,000 sesterces.[26] The new emperor was aiming, through his choice, to underscore his concern for the people's welfare; he did not wish to seem tyrannical or even too kinglike; he would be *civilis*, a citizens' emperor. And to make this concern even clearer, he complained that too many statues overall were going up in Rome, and ruled several years later that unless the Senate decided otherwise, honorific dedications would be reserved for those who had built or repaired some public work.[27]

But Claudius himself could be sparing because he knew that private individuals and groups would set up plenty of images for him in Rome. Inscriptions reveal what can only be a small portion of these, for instance the marble statue that was erected (perhaps along with a statue of his wife Messallina) in January AD 42 by the group of bronze instrumentalists who played throughout the year at religious ceremonies.[28] They placed their commission in a newly built shrine along with previous dedications to Augustus and Tiberius, while omitting, tellingly, Caligula. The construction work seems to account for the year it took for the statue to go up, though there may be other reasons: a hesitation to see whether Claudius would succeed or delays in procuring a statue from the busy workshops of Rome. The workshops were busy, not just because Claudius was a new emperor, but also because he had been shut out of public life so thoroughly by his family that few individuals or groups had bothered to erect his statue before.[29]

Some portraits of Claudius, it is true, already did exist, and, according to the most persuasive interpretations of the evidence, likely were based on a model that depicted him as a youth with strong neck and chin, fine facial features, and a thick cap of hair that reached down the back of his head (Fig. 10). This type, usually called "Kassel" after a bust in the Kunstsammlungen there, shows great variation, in part because these heads often turn out to be re-carved portraits of Caligula, in part because Claudius himself was so unknown (Fig. 11).[30] The portrait in Kassel itself, with its austere classicism, partially assimilates Claudius to Augustus. While workshops continued to employ this type at least early in Claudius' reign – which

Fig. 10 Portrait of Claudius. This portrait gives the name for the "Kassel type," Claudius'
early portrait style. Staatliche Kunstsammlungen, Kassel.

would account for the surviving examples of it – in the year of his accession the emperor's artists (again, according to modern reconstructions)
created a new model that boldly departed from the agelessness of portraits
of Augustus and his successors.[31] Not named after any one specimen, since
many faithful reproductions survive, this type is best apprehended through
portraits such as those in Braunschweig and Copenhagen, as well as the state
coinage (Figs. 12–14).[32] Here Claudius is depicted with a lined forehead,
knitted brow, bags under his eyes, creases from his nose to mouth, and a
double chin: a man in middle age rather than an eternal youth. More than

Fig. 11 Head of the emperor Claudius, refashioned from an earlier representation of
Caligula, from Ocriculum. The head is about 0.75 m in height, and so would have
belonged to a colossal statue, too expensive to throw out. Vatican Museums, Rome.

Augustus' portraits, it resembles the face of a real person – not that it need
have been entirely true to life.

What might such a portrait mean to those who saw it? Some have been
tempted to regard its vigorous realism as a calculated return to the style of
portraiture in favor just before Augustus – it would appeal "to just those
citizens who had Republican sympathies."[33] The problem with such a view
(leaving aside the question of how many viewers did have Republican
sympathies at this point) is the hair, always a key part of a Roman portrait.

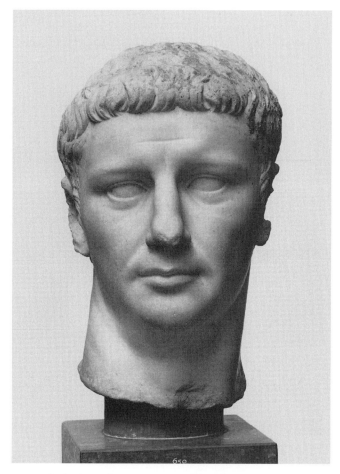

Fig. 12 Portrait of Claudius. This portrait exemplifies the main type of Claudius' portrait
style. Ny Carlsberg Glyptotek, Copenhagen.

While the tough-bitten men in the earlier veristic style notoriously have
very little of it or even none, Claudius boasts a gloriously full cap that
puts him firmly in the line of rulers following Augustus. It is a necessary
complement to the facial features: this portrait is saying not that Claudius
is a Republican, but that he is Leader – albeit of a different sort. Precisely
because Claudius had minimal experience, this new image suggests just
the opposite, and so marks a contrast with the portraiture of Caligula. It
suggests to the viewer that the new emperor, nearly fifty years old, would
be steady, where his predecessor had been erratic. In its fascinating mixture

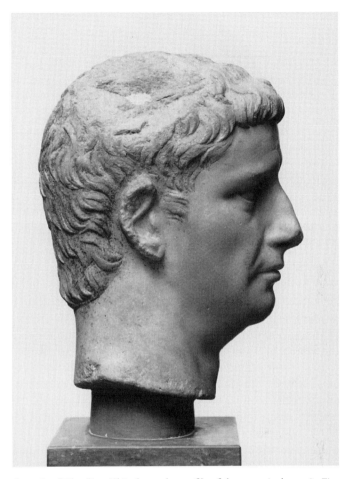

Fig. 13 Portrait of Claudius. This shows the profile of the portrait shown in Fig. 12. Ny Carlsberg Glyptotek, Copenhagen.

of features it emblematizes the virtue new to Claudius and announces on his coins: THE CONSTANCY OF AUGUSTUS.[34]

Claudius' decisions regarding portraits were not limited to his own; in his first uncertain months of power he also manipulated the images of other members of the August House to strengthen his position. The strategy was twofold. On the one hand, though he decided not to have Caligula's memory condemned by the Senate (as Antony's had been after his defeat by Augustus), he did have statues of his predecessor removed, a step that

Fig. 14 *Aureus*, dated AD 43/4. The obverse here shows the head of Claudius in
his main portrait type, with the double chin and signs of aging especially prominent
in comparison to Fig. 8.

others – including, it seems, the bronze instrumentalists – followed, as
the archeological record amply shows.[35] Like Claudius' own portrait, this
served to mark a break with Caligula without unduly undermining the
emerging institution of the principate. On the other hand, by creating or
displaying images of his own immediate forebears, and by acknowledging
them in other ways, Claudius affirmed his relation to other members of
the imperial house.[36] In doing so, he was aiming to surmount a second
vulnerability, perhaps even graver than his lack of experience: the assiduous
neglect the rest of the imperial family had shown him throughout his early
life.[37]

Since his own connection to Augustus, founder of the whole dynasty, lay
through Livia, Augustus' wife, and Antonia, Augustus' niece, it made good
sense for Claudius to honor both of these women, in conjunction with
Augustus. For Antonia, Claudius arranged to have her image displayed on
a carriage at Circus games to be held annually on her birthday, and her title
of Augusta was to be confirmed, associating her with Augustus, in whose
cult she had been a priestess.[38] Coins issued in the first year of Claudius'
reign further acknowledged her position, including one series that link her
image to *Constantia*: Claudius, it would seem, derived his constancy from
her (Figs. 15–16).[39]

Even more spectacularly, Livia was officially acknowledged to be a goddess, Diva Augusta.[40] Consort of Divus Augustus, she would now share her
husband's temple lying between the Capitoline and Palatine Hills, where
Claudius installed an image of her seated on a throne, crowned, with heads

Fig. 15 *Denarius*, c. AD 41. The obverse shows the head of Claudius' mother Antonia; the reverse the figure of "Constancy of Augustus" holding a torch and cornucopiae.

Fig. 16 *Aureus*, c. AD 41. The obverse shows the head of Antonia; the reverse two torches and the legend PRIESTESS OF THE DIVINE AUGUSTUS.

of grain in her right hand and in her left a torch (Fig. 17).[41] The consecration took place in AD 42 on January 17 (her wedding anniversary), in a ceremony that must have been visually impressive.[42] It, or anyway something like it, is depicted on a partially preserved relief from the city of Rome thought to have been sculpted under Claudius.[43] On it, moving towards the leg of what should be the throne of a seated deity, is a procession of magistrates with lictors, followed by three sacrificial animals – a bull, a steer, and a

Fig. 17 *Dupondius*, c. AD 42. The obverse shows the head of the Divine Augustus; the reverse a seated Livia ("Diva Augusta"), holding ears of grain. The image of Livia likely reflects the cult statue created for her in the Temple of Augustus in Rome.

heifer – accompanied by attendants (Fig. 18). Musicians, including trumpeters, are scattered through the group, emphasizing the aural element of the sacrificial procession (and for us recalling the dedication of the instrumentalists). Then come several figures in tunics (Fig. 19), three of them carrying statues of the *genius* (guardian spirit) of the emperor and his *lares* (household deities), followed by another group, in togas, including perhaps the emperor himself. The emperor's *genius* was venerated, along with his *lares*, on analogy with the traditional cult of the *genius* of each individual head of household in Rome.

It is the tunicate group with the statuettes in particular which has suggested a relationship with Livia's consecration, for just five days before that event, Claudius was officially made "Father of the Fatherland" by vote of Senate and People; at that time, it has been hypothesized, the *genius* of the new "Father" was officially introduced into the state religion.[44] The *genius* would receive a bull in a sacrifice, while, as is otherwise attested, Divus Augustus and Diva Augusta a steer and heifer respectively: the Brethren of the Fields, a college of twelve priests in which some of Rome's most illustrious men served, are known to have yearly commemorated Livia's consecration with a heifer to her and bull to Augustus.[45] While, without more evidence, a definite interpretation of the relief is impossible, it still helps to make a broader point. Statues such as that of Diva Augusta or Antonia Augusta, far from being isolated works of art, were incorporated into more elaborate forms of display and even drama – such as Circus

Fig. 18 Relief depicting a sacrificial procession, from an unknown monument in Rome, detail. Prominent here are three trumpet-players and the three sacrificial animals, a bull, steer, and heifer. Vatican Museums, Rome.

Fig. 19 Relief depicting a sacrificial procession, from the same unknown monument in
Rome, detail. The three figures in tunics carry statuettes of two *lares* and a togate *genius*
(on the left). Vatican Museums, Rome.

processions or the ceremony of consecration – which helped to animate
and endow them with a rich array of meanings.

   Though fewer statues seem to have been involved, Claudius emphasized
two other members of his immediate family. The beloved Germanicus,
whom the Senate and Tiberius had honored with effusion after his death,
Claudius inventively celebrated by traveling to Naples and entering in a
festival there a Greek comedy Germanicus had written.[46] Claudius thus
showed himself as fluent in Greek and admiring of Greek culture, a true
heir to his brother. The memory of Drusus, their father, dead for nearly fifty

Fig. 20 *Aureus*, c. AD 41. The obverse shows the head of Claudius' father Drusus; the reverse a triumphal arch surmounted by an equestrian statue between two trophies and the legend OVER THE GERMANS. The Senate voted Drusus a marble arch with trophies on the Via Appia in recognition of his military exploits (Suet. *Claud.* 1.3).

years, was revived with Circus games on his birthday, as well as coins that alluded to his military successes in the north; it was for these victories that Claudius, like his brother, received the new name "Germanicus" (Fig. 20).[47] While celebrations of "Diva Augusta" and "Antonia Augusta" patently linked Claudius to Augustus, recalling his own father, who was born and died a Claudius, they also promoted the Claudians as a family fit to rule Rome in their own name. Fortuitously timed successes in Germany that year, including recovery of the military eagle that still remained in enemy hands after Varus' disaster in AD 9, further helped the new emperor in making a claim on his father's memory.[48]

The significance Claudius placed on Drusus has further been illustrated by the inscribed marble fragments of a monument discovered during excavations in the 1920s along the Via dell'Impresa in modern Rome.[49] Inscriptions on these fragments reveal that the monument was constructed by Tiberius in AD 22, and then, having fallen into disrepair, refurbished by Claudius between 41 and AD 43. In its new configuration, it included statues (identified by inscription) of Claudius' father Drusus, and also, if a partial restoration is trusted, ANTONIA AUGUSTA, MOTHER OF TI. CLAUDIUS CAESAR AUGUSTUS GERMANICUS. Tiberius' original monument, it has been argued, was constructed in conjunction with the award of tribunician power to his ill-starred son Drusus, an occasion accompanied by a series of honors awarded by the Senate, including

(Tacitus says) statues, altars, shrines, and arches.[50] Further, given its location within 100 meters from the Altar of August Peace, and given an additional piece of inscriptional evidence, the monument in question (the speculation continues) might have been an Altar of August Pietas.[51] If so – and indeed, even if not – Claudius, in restoring it, was underscoring his own *pietas*, or loyalty, to his family (and thus his place within it) while also promoting in particular his father Drusus (and probably Antonia).

Claudius' efforts to assert squarely his own and his immediate family's place within the August House, while banishing Caligula, enjoyed at least some success, especially in the eyes of Italians, as several independent commissions demonstrate. In the old Etruscan town of Rusellae, the town council decided to include several new images in an apsidal building where they honored the ruling family of Rome.[52] Retaining a few portraits set up in the Augustan period and several more from the reign of Caligula, they added a pair of colossal enthroned statues of the deified Augustus and the deified Livia, the latter wearing a diadem as she surely did in her new temple in Rome. Caligula himself was removed, to make way for a statue of Claudius. The head of the murdered emperor was, it has been surmised, put into storage since it was carved (likely later) into a second portrait of his successor.[53] Neither Claudius nor his agents were likely to have told the people of Rusellae what to do; rather, they simply observed what was happening in the capital and themselves created at least a partial reflection of it – which, nonetheless, still bolstered Claudius' image and suggested a continuity between him and the founder of the dynasty.

Likewise, in Ravenna an altar was built almost certainly in the Claudian period (presumably commissioned by the town councilors), which again was a local reflection of measures undertaken at Rome.[54] Only two portions of its decorative reliefs are preserved. One shows a sacrificial bull conducted by three laureate attendants, behind whom are three additional figures, one obscured by the head of an ax (Fig. 21). The victim may well be intended for the divine Augustus, since the late emperor appears prominently in the other extant piece, half nude, crowned in oak, his foot atop a globe (Fig. 22). Next to him is a similarly deified Livia, cast in the guise of Venus Genetrix, and beyond her are, according to the most persuasive interpretation, Germanicus, Drusus, and a seated woman who should be Antonia.[55] Figures clearly stood to Augustus' left too, who, according to the same interpretation, likely would have been Claudius, along with his wife and children (and possibly Tiberius too, Livia's other son). The whole relief, then, would have visualized the August House as it was construed under Claudius: Augustus himself in the center as the founder (with his

Fig. 21 Fragment of a frieze from an altar erected in Ravenna, depicting a sacrificial bull conducted by three attendants wearing laurel garlands. Museo Nazionale, Ravenna.

importance signalized by his slightly greater stature), along with the newly deified Livia, and then the rest of Claudius' most significant relatives.

Yet the Ravenna altar was hardly a copy of a work now lost in Rome, but rather its own creative commission. The relief of Augustus and the other members of his house stylistically has no contemporaneous counterpart in the City; with their statuesque poses, the figures on it are in fact closer to the members of a portrait cycle such as that at Rusellae, except that the

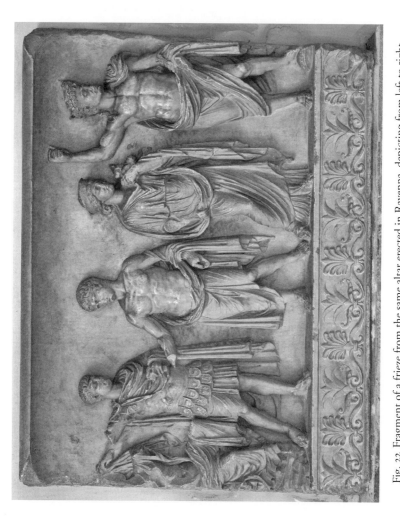

Fig. 22 Fragment of a frieze from the same altar erected in Ravenna, depicting from left to right members of the August House, identifiable as Antonia, Drusus, Germanicus, Livia, and Augustus. Museo Nazionale, Ravenna.

artist here can fix more permanently the relations between those depicted. Indeed, the sculpture almost seems to suggest that for the Ravennans, the members of Augustus' house were more like statues than gods or mortals. Distinctive, too, is the rendering of Germanicus as a god (assuming it is he shown), despite his never receiving official deification: not only is he partially nude like Augustus, a star sits over his brow. Local needs always influenced statue commissions, making them more meaningful to their intended audience. Whatever his official iconography in Rome, some individuals clearly saw Germanicus as godlike.[56]

When, exactly, the council of Rusellae added the new statues to their previously existing cycle and the Ravennans constructed their altar remains unknown.[57] They can only suggest some ultimate acceptance of Claudius and his dynastic claims. Yet enough statue bases of Claudius are datable (like that from the shrine of the bronze instrumentalists) to suggest that his portrait did not go up immediately everywhere. True, some images were dedicated in the first year of his reign; but there were many more in the second, and still quite a few in the third.[58] It took time for town councils, groups like the instrumentalists, and individuals to absorb the news of his accession and consider what they would do. Some, at least, would petition the emperor for permission to erect his image, a shrewd way of showing him their loyalty, but also another source of delay. The conversations dedicators had with each other or with the emperor are largely lost; we often know only the official details: that the town council of Sestinum dedicated a statue of Claudius in AD 42; that the "Senate and People of Lanuvium" did the same; that Roman citizens living in Moguntiacum in Upper Germany who dealt in leather goods dedicated a statue in AD 43; or that in the same year Roman citizens who did business in the province of Asia also dedicated a statue, its erection overseen by a tribune of the Thirteenth Legion.[59] But with one set of dedicators a great deal can be said, an exceptional group but illuminating all the same.

Upon learning of Caligula's assassination, some of the Jews in Alexandria, still seething at the persecutions of AD 38, took the chance for revenge, armed themselves and perhaps other Jews from farther away, and went on a violent spree, until the prefect could stop the violence.[60] Shortly afterwards, in spring of 41, a group of twelve envoys representing the Greeks of Alexandria, among them the priest Chaeremon, arrived in Italy to explain their side of the story, ask for the right to form a senate, and offer Claudius a whole array of honors, including many statues. At least one separate Jewish embassy also made a presentation – needless to say, without the same extravagant offers. Claudius sent his response to all the Alexandrians, Greeks and Jews, as a letter, which the prefect Aemilius Rectus ordered to be read out and distributed.[61] While more will be said later on the embassies, and also the matter of ruler cult, here Claudius' famous letter to the Alexandrians is of interest for offering clear evidence of how statues were functioning for the Greeks of this city, as well as Claudius.[62]

At their meeting with Claudius, the envoys expressed the Alexandrians' desire to erect a series of statues. There were to be (1) images of Claudius and his family in several places of the city; (2) two golden statues, one of the "Claudian August Peace" that would go up in Rome, the other to be carried in processions in Alexandria; and (3) four-horse chariots at the entrances to Egypt (including the lighthouse island of Alexandria).[63] Other honors were offered (e.g., special celebration of Claudius' birthday as an "August day") and permission was even sought to build a temple for the new emperor and establish a high priest for his cult. The Alexandrians were thus acknowledging Claudius as the full successor to Augustus and pledging their loyalty to him in the strongest terms.

According to his letter, Claudius refused to be deified, "not wishing to be arrogant to the people of my own time."[64] Yet he did accept all of the statues of himself and his family, explaining that "I see . . . that you were eager to set up everywhere memorials of your piety towards my house." The emperor clearly suggests that statues to him will forge the link he needs with his predecessors – even as the letter asserts that link more than once, too, by referring to "my house" or "my family." The other statues he also approved, only balking at the gold statue in Rome (since again "it seemed too arrogant") until won over by one of the delegates, Balbillus – likely the same Balbillus who was active in the Alexandrian Museum and interested in Egyptian antiquities.[65] Apparently Claudius felt it more acceptable for provincials to commission a work in this precious metal. Still, the message of the letter is largely in tune with the other steps Claudius took. Eager to insert himself squarely into the August House, he wished still to suggest a sense of balance; it was, once again, his constancy shining through.

The letter parades that constancy elsewhere, not least in its final pronouncement on the larger situation in Alexandria, which reads almost like a verbal complement to Claudius' accession portrait. After deferring the request for the new senate, he speaks forthrightly about the recent situation:

As to who was responsible for the riot and civil strife in respect of the Jews (or rather, if I am to speak the truth, the war): although your envoys, particularly Dionysius, son of Theon, put your case energetically, I was unwilling to conduct a detailed investigation, but am storing up within me unremitting anger against those who started it again. And I tell you once and for all, that unless you stop this disastrous and stubborn anger against each other, I shall be compelled to show what a benevolent Leader can be when moved to justifiable anger. Therefore, once again I ask that the Alexandrians behave gently and benevolently toward the Jews, who for many years have inhabited the same city, that they not dishonor any customs relating to the worship of their god, and that instead they allow the Jews to keep their ways which were guaranteed in the time of the divine Augustus and which I too have guaranteed after hearing both sides.

Ideas of anger and benevolence appear again and again throughout these words; the Alexandrians and the emperor alike are capable of both, the difference being that the emperor's anger is "justifiable." His normal disposition is more placid, as will become clear (Claudius promises) should the Alexandrians reach peace too: "If both sides desist from these ways and are willing to live with gentleness and benevolence for one another, I for my part will exercise the foremost care for the city, as one falling to me from the forefathers of my house." Fully in control of his passions, stern when he must be, at heart benign, and mindful of the best traditions of his family: this is a depiction of Claudius as he wanted to be seen that reinforces the messages of the statues.

The Alexandrian embassy of 41 and the honors they pledged were hardly typical, and Claudius' elaborate response equally unusual, but they still point to larger truths. Statues were a way Romans – including the emperor and his subjects – made public statements. In the aftermath of Caligula's assassination, they buttressed the new emperor's position, whether erected by him or (as in most instances) by others; destruction, removal, or repositioning of other statues lent further support. Yet if statues affirmed the rule of Claudius and a continuity of imperial power, they generally did so locally. Rome provided models, but only models, models that could be freely adapted. The commissions of Alexandria, like the group at Rusellae or the altar from Ravenna, exemplify the variety. Yet the Alexandrian example reveals that statues outside Rome were, at least at times, built for the emperor's benefit too. To show their loyalty, individuals and groups might take measures to ensure that he knew of their efforts.

Most zealous in establishing ties with the unfamiliar Claudius in the months after Caligula's death were those who, like the Praetorian Guard and the palace staff, had something to lose if the principate were abolished – individuals such as the bronze instrumentalists, or the Jews who, whatever Caligula's aberrations, still depended on the old ruling of Augustus for their freedom to worship throughout the empire. Determined to see the new emperor succeed, they busily found ways to honor him, by erecting statues or, as Philo did, setting to work on his account of Caligula's persecutions (which probably ended with a celebration of Claudius' fair handling of the Jews and perhaps a record of further time in Rome).[66] Thus they helped him secure his position, making it that much harder for the disgruntled Scribonianus and his followers to succeed. Winning over the army might have been paramount for Claudius, but there was support to be gained from other quarters. As Caligula's own rule showed, statues alone were hardly sufficient to guarantee the emperor's authority, but in the visual culture of the Roman world they were indispensable all the same.

Even as Scribonianus was secretly plotting in Dalmatia, and Vinicianus in Rome, Claudius was presented with a parade of embassies like that of the Alexandrians assuring him of the loyalty of a remarkably diverse range of individuals across the provinces. Yet for all this, despite the statues, and the legitimacy conferred by votes of Senate and People, the aura given off by rituals and costume notwithstanding, as Claudius thought about his long-dead father he had to consider whether something more were needed to secure his authority. Was there a way to achieve greater prestige, to become a man of distinction?

CHAPTER 3

Imperial favors

In the world of the Hellenistic kings, as Greek civilization spread through Egypt, the Levant, Asia Minor, and beyond, actors, musicians, and impresarios found themselves in ever greater demand. The royal court might require entertainment for its feasts, religious sanctuaries needed competitors for long-established games, and cities would seek dancers, choruses, flautists, and lyre-players for new local festivals to be held in their newly built theaters. Keenly aware of the demand, and eager to organize their schedule more efficiently, the performers organized themselves into a series of local guilds, called the "Artists of Dionysus." At first they obtained special privileges from those for whom they performed, but later were installed in separate settlements, dependent on a larger town but exempted from military service and taxes and allowed to elect their own leadership and worship their own gods.[1]

Sometimes clashing with each other, the Artists, whose reputation was not unlike that of film stars today, ultimately formed a worldwide organization. Perhaps not coincidentally, they did so just as Augustus was solidifying his control of the entire Mediterranean world at the end of the civil wars. Claudius' grandfather, Antony, took the crucial first step when, in 32 BC, on the eve of the battle of Actium, he summoned the Artists from at least several guilds to winter with him and Cleopatra on Samos. "While almost all the world around was filled with sighs and lamentations," Plutarch writes, "a single island for many days echoed with flutes and stringed instruments, theaters were packed, and choirs were competing with one another."[2] The performers were rewarded with the city of Priene as their new home and, one may guess, a further range of privileges.[3]

Less than two years later, after Antony's defeat, Augustus had to confirm or cancel all of his former colleague's measures. The gift of Priene, it seems, was revoked, but Augustus still was eager to preserve and strengthen the nascent worldwide organization. It made sense for the regional guilds to collaborate and for the Artists to be able to move freely through the empire unencumbered. Augustus knew, furthermore, that with the establishment of joint cults in honor of him and Rome, it was prudent to encourage the entertainers who would perform at the associated festivals.[4] Such celebrations, costing him nothing directly, underscored his power and Rome's, encouraged loyalty in its own right, and at the same time pointed out added benefits that loyalty brought. So it was that he affirmed a series of privileges which (to judge by later documents) included again exemption from military service and most taxation.[5]

When Claudius came to power, the worldwide guild of Artists had to wonder what the new ruler would mean for them. Would the invaluable privileges endure? The question might have seemed more pressing now than it had when Tiberius and Caligula had acceded. Claudius was neither a Julius nor a Caesar and, despite his nearly fifty years, not well known to his new subjects either. Far worse, news of Caligula's assassination might well have raised the specter of civil war: Caesar's assassination, in 44 BC, had plunged the whole Roman world into a crisis memories of which would have been all too alive among the Artists. And so they sent to Rome an embassy of at least four men.

Such missions could entail great expense – often covered by the ambassadors themselves – and a considerable investment of time.[6] Not only was there the difficulty of getting to Italy; once there, the envoys might face considerable delays in seeing the emperor. The Leader was constantly moving around, constantly busy. Philo claims that after the disturbances in Alexandria in AD 38 he and the other Jews first had to wait some time to gain a brief audience with Caligula in Rome, then followed him to a villa on the Bay of Naples, and finally returned to Rome where they were heard a second time, but only as Caligula walked through the Gardens of Maecenas and Lamia inspecting his properties.[7] Whether or not that was typical, Claudius had a hectic round of engagements: presiding over judicial hearings, holding meetings of the Senate, giving shows in the Circus. Even when he was free, the emperor's staff controlled access: they too were a hurdle. Philo maintains that under Caligula one of them readily took bribes and showed great bias.[8] Embassies, though, offered opportunities as well: a chance to visit Rome's literary salons and libraries, even to impress the emperor sufficiently to enter his service. Claudius Balbillus, on record as an envoy from Alexandria in AD 41, is likely the same Claudius Balbillus who served not only as head of the Museum of that city (a post appointed by the emperor) but as an officer of embassies who also traveled with Claudius to Britain.[9]

How the haughty Artists passed their time in Rome remains unknown, but Claudius' response, addressed to the worldwide group, reveals their request: "On the one hand, I permit you to erect images, in which way we are shown piety with the appropriate honor; on the other, I preserve the rights and privileges granted by the Divine Augustus." They asked, then, not only for their old privileges to be upheld but also if they could erect statues in Claudius' honor. That he should reiterate his affirmative response in a letter is a crucial detail too: he was supplying documentary evidence of his benefaction that the Artists could later use, something Augustus, apparently, did not, but which now seemed desirable.[10] The Artists affirmed the emperor's position, the emperor confirmed theirs.

So it seems at first, but the power dynamics were actually more complex. In his letter, Claudius takes care to mention by name the ambassadors: "The envoys were . . ." Of the five men whose names are clearly preserved, four were called Claudius (Claudius Epagathus, Claudius Dionysius, and so forth), suggesting that they were honored with citizenship by the emperor himself, perhaps in recognition of the effort they took to come to Rome. And even regardless of that, simply by naming them in his response, the emperor memorialized their participation in a successful embassy. That alone enhanced their own position within the guild (likely already important). It too was an honor, worth having in its own right, but also because it might translate into more concrete power. The envoys affirmed the emperor's position, the emperor confirmed theirs.

Claudius, the envoys, and the worldwide guild of Artists in their dealings with one another exemplify another way in which the new emperor secured his position, and thus help show how the Roman empire held itself together in AD 41, despite crisis in Rome. As its inhabitants learned of the alarming news of Caligula's assassination and his replacement by Claudius, they, no less than Claudius, had to make decisions, especially anybody who had secured special benefits from the new emperor's predecessors. The leadership of such groups, concentrated in the eastern half of the empire, tended to employ a double strategy: on the one hand, they asked Claudius to uphold favors conferred upon them earlier, and, on the other, offered acknowledgments of the new ruler. They were trying to secure relations with Claudius, but also their own position within their part of the world, which depended on the imperial order. For their own reasons, then, they eagerly enriched their communities not just with statues of the new emperor, but games in his honor, festivals, arches, and so forth. At the start of the new reign, as additional examples will show, Claudius and Rome's subjects, looking back to the founder Augustus and his measures, reenacted the birth of the empire, knitting it together anew as they exchanged favors with one another.

There certainly was some of that feeling at a meeting that took place in AD 41 of the Commonalty of Greeks living in the province of Asia.[11] This council, established well before the time of Augustus to communicate its members' interests to Rome, became far more prominent and powerful when it assumed administration of the joint cult of Rome and Augustus just after the civil wars.[12] Initially based in Pergamum, where a great temple was built, it organized, in addition to the cult of the two deities, a regular festival with contests that drew participants from afar, and also a celebration of Augustus' birthday, at which a hymn was chanted in the emperor's honor by a group of perhaps several dozen hymnodists. These singers, hailing from throughout Asia but based in Pergamum, were funded – in an arrangement approved by Augustus – by a tax imposed throughout the province. Individual cities, such as Ephesus, might elect to sponsor their own choirs too, but, as an edict of Claudius' own proconsul in Asia shows, they were only required to pay for the Pergamene group.[13] Yet expenses grew over time, as the hymnodists added more festivals to their calendar to honor additional members of the imperial family.

At the Commonalty's meeting in AD 41, on a proposal of Anaxagoras, High Priest of Asia, the group decided to praise a new undertaking of the hymnodists. The hymnodists, meeting on the birthday of Tiberius (November 16), which had become part of their regular calendar of events, had decided on that day to make hymns to the "August House" and offer sacrifices to all the "August Gods"; a feast was held as well.[14] All this was a way for them to link the new emperor Claudius to his predecessors, above all Augustus but also Tiberius (while passing over Caligula). The hymnodists' wellbeing really did depend on the survival of the August Gods in Rome, whoever might fall into that number. The Commonalty, in turn, wished to praise the hymnodists, because for them too "there [was] need . . . to make clear their piety to the August House."

The new honors for Claudius and the Commonalty's decree are only known through a monument, with very fragmentary inscriptions, set up in the city of Hypaipa (near Ephesus) by some of the hymnodists, rather than the Commonalty itself. It appears that after their meeting, the Commonalty sent a copy of their decree to Claudius, presumably in the hands of envoys, and that he responded with a letter that approved the new celebration, while also (one must guess) affirming the precious financial privileges of the hymnodists (only the very opening of Claudius' letter survives). Learning of the letter, the hymnodists then decided to vote at a later meeting in Pergamum a decree of their own, concerning "the rights and privileges given to them." Individual members of the organization, such as those from Hypaipa, then had a copy of this decree posted, along with Claudius' letter and the earlier decree of the Commonalty. The whole dossier thus advertised the upholding of their privileges. If those were canceled, they would lose everything – and it was not unreasonable for them to think that some towns might be all too eager to cease paying their share of the choir's ever-growing budget. As with the Artists, a group that enjoyed a mutually beneficial relationship with previous emperors starting with Augustus stepped forward and, in exchange for an affirmation of their status, helped Claudius secure his own position, along with Roman rule, in the province of Asia.

Much the same happened on Thasos, a large independent island in the north Aegean, once rich in timber and precious metals, now more reliant on its export of fine wines.[15] For this community, too, the accession of a new emperor was a revisiting of the end of the civil wars: having lost their independence under Antony, because of support given to the assassins of Caesar, the Thasians regained it with Augustus. Would they stay free under Claudius, Antony's grandson? An embassy was sent off with a decree voted by the council, and fragments of Claudius' response survive on a stone along with letters from a governor of Thrace and the emperor Nero. It shows the now familiar pattern: addressed to the "magistrates, council, and people of the Thasians," it politely declines the offer of a temple, "considering it to be right for the gods alone, though I permit the other honors, which suit the best Leaders." These presumably included statues. And then: "And I uphold for you, in accordance with the decrees of the divine Augustus, all of the privileges issuing from him." Finally, in conclusion: "Those who gave me the decree were . . . " A fragmentary list follows. Though the Thasians were not officially subject to Rome, Claudius clearly was eager to retain their loyalty, as they could lend valuable assistance if trouble should arise in nearby Thrace, an area of frequent unrest.

The Artists, the hymnodists, and the Thasians were just several of a much larger group who appeared before Claudius in the early months and years of his reign, known only through the survival of papyri or inscriptions. Parading before the emperor when he had time to hear them, one after another, asking for their privileges to be affirmed, they offered to him and to his staff (who might have drafted at least the more routine responses sent back) a personal introduction to Rome's empire, at least in the east, and the measures worked out, largely by Augustus, to govern it. In upholding these,

Claudius kept the empire together and established himself as its ruler; in turn, he achieved further recognition from those he helped, back in their own communities. Whether Claudius canceled any benefits – something, to be sure, extant evidence would less likely reflect – seems dubious.

Revealing as these examples are, one might wish to ask further questions that they cannot themselves answer. Just how many embassies did come upon his accession to ask about their privileges? Had they all come before, on Caligula's accession in particular? Suetonius seems to imply so, when he states that after the principate of Tiberius, "favors (*beneficia*) granted by previous emperors" were not regarded as valid, unless confirmed by the new Caesar.[16] This may be less a statement of strictly enforced practice than theoretical possibility.[17] But a story told by Philo shows that by the time of Claudius, the practice of sending embassies to the emperor about privileges upon accession in particular was well and widely understood; it was probably fairly regular, then, if not in fact always required.

After Caligula came to power, Philo tells us, the Jews of Alexandria passed a decree bestowing on the emperor "all possible honors, as permitted by our laws," doubtless hoping, in return, for an affirmation of their privileges.[18] The prefect of Egypt, Avillius Flaccus, denying the Jews' request to present the decree in person, promised he would forward a copy of it instead. Philo and the others might have been happy enough with that arrangement, for they would be spared the burden of travel, yet felt confident that anything sent by the governor with urgency was read by the emperor. But Flaccus, biased against the Jews (or so Philo says), in fact kept the decree to himself, "so that we alone of all people under the sun might be considered hostile."[19] Only when King Agrippa came to Egypt and learned of the problem did he forward the decree, also including apologies for the delay, "showing that we had not been slow to learn the duty of piety towards the house which was our benefactor, but that we had from the very beginning been eager to show it."[20] In exchange for the favors granted by the August House, even Philo clearly acknowledges, Caligula was owed a pledge of loyalty; failure to provide one, he claims, was almost a form of treason.

Philo may, in blackening Caligula (and Avillius Flaccus), be guilty of some distortion. But his suggestion that it was already regular for a new emperor to hear embassies on his accession concerning the retention of favors seems confirmed not only by epigraphic evidence for two such embassies at the start of Caligula's reign – from a league of Greek cities and from Assos, in Asia Minor – but also by a recently discovered decree from the Thracian town of Maroneia.[21] It established, in Claudius' principate, a procedure whereby an embassy would be ready at any moment to speak to the emperor (referred to by the title "Augustus") about the town's privileges. (These had, apparently, recently been in jeopardy – probably because of the Roman annexation of Thrace – but an embassy to Claudius secured them.) According to the new arrangement, those interested in serving as envoys had to apply in writing and swear an oath regulating their conduct; only successful applicants could have their names included in the (sealed) decree that would be sent to the emperor. Once in Rome, the envoys were to make sure they greeted the emperor (generically called "divine Augustus Caesar") on behalf of the city; express joy that he and his house, along with the Roman people, were thriving; and cite the claims of Thasos before they made their actual request. False embassy and the accepting of bribes were explicitly prohibited – suggesting that ambassadors sometimes took the chance to serve their own interests, rather than those of their community.

And so, despite the very real urgency of AD 41, embassies might have been essentially routine by the accession of Claudius – as the principate was institutionalized, in other words, so were embassies to the *princeps* – with communities well advised to undertake them, to preserve their prerogatives. (It may also be, we shall see, that embassies were sent to recognize the new emperor, even when there was not a major question of privileges to settle.[22]) But to say all this still will not settle how many there were. One can recognize, at least, that it was a rather efficient system for the emperor to communicate with his new subjects – at least from his point of view. If he spent, let us suppose, an average of fifteen minutes with each group, then 1,000 embassies could have been heard over 250 hours, or about sixty-four half-days of four hours. Spread over a year, that was manageable. And to play with numbers further: if each of those 1,000 embassies relayed their experience back to a group (say) of 1,000, Claudius was thereby introduced to one million of his subjects, and if each group built five statues for him, he gained 5,000 statues. This was remarkable publicity, and it cost Claudius nothing in financial terms. For the communities involved, of course, expenses could mount. It is not, then, entirely surprising to be told that several decades later, Titus simply decreed on his accession that all of his predecessors' benefactions were to be upheld without specific petition, and Titus' successors did the same.[23] Claudius' own patient hearing of the embassies and his affirmative responses to them were a crucial step in that direction – just as the letters he and successors wrote were coming to be recognized as a full-fledged type of law.

But Claudius' work was, retrospectively, more important than that for another reason – which will account for another feature of the evidence. If

Caligula did hear so many embassies on his accession, why is there a less copious record of them? The answer would seem to be that in later periods, when a group wished to trace the history of its special privileges, it might look back to Augustus, who initially granted them, and to Claudius, who specifically confirmed them at a moment when everything seemed so up in the air. Additionally, given their posthumous memory, Caligula and Nero hardly made attractive authorities to cite. From this perspective, Claudius takes on special importance as a bridge between Augustus and the Flavian dynasty that established itself in the aftermath of Nero's fall.

If Philo's testimony along with the new Thracian decree shows that the embassies of the Artists, the hymnodists, and the Thasians were typical, Philo also makes clear that there could be variations on the basic theme: Philo's Jewish community did not offer the same honors in AD 37 as gentiles, a governor served (or was supposed to have served) as intermediary between emperor and subject. Other episodes point to that variety. It was not always so simple a matter as provincials securing their own privileges and acknowledging the emperor in turn. The emperor could, in exchange for a benefaction confirmed, ask for something extra from a provincial community; a provincial community could, after establishing their loyalty early in the reign, later ask for a favor, or might even seek additional privileges with the accession of the new emperor.

Given Caligula's own record, it was not surprising that Claudius and the Jews had more complex diplomatic relations in AD 41.[24] During his first year in power, the emperor made two important decisions to help soothe high feelings in Judea itself and among the Jewish communities of the Diaspora across the Mediterranean. First, he restored Judea from Roman control to his friend and childhood acquaintance Agrippa. Known chiefly through the pages of the Jewish historian Josephus, where he appears suspiciously like a typical Diaspora hero, blessed with good luck and a deep capacity for intrigue, Agrippa undeniably had steadily managed to secure ever more power for himself. Brought to Rome around the age of five by his mother Berenice, a friend of Antonia, Agrippa grew up there and only returned to Judea in his late twenties, when it had been annexed as a Roman province. On Tiberius' death, Caligula granted Agrippa a royal crown and gave him, in phases, portions of Syria held by Rome or by other rulers under Rome's thumb, though not Judea itself. Yet despite these grants, and with his eye on the greater prize, Agrippa is said to have lent Claudius aid immediately following Caligula's assassination. In keeping with his perspective, Josephus probably inflates the episode, but Cassius Dio too acknowledges Agrippa's help: as the grandson of Herod the Great, and from his own recent experiences, Agrippa knew more than a little about imposing kings on a people involuntarily.[25]

Agrippa could also help Claudius navigate relations with his Jewish subjects after the damage done by Caligula. Evidence survives depicting him in consultation with Claudius on the matter.[26] And so it might have been on his advice that Claudius expelled from Rome in AD 41 some apparently troublesome Jews – perhaps early worshippers of Christ (in the Acts of the Apostles, let it be recalled, Agrippa appears as an early persecutor of the church).[27] In exchange for whatever favors or advice he lent, he was entrusted with a fully restored kingdom of Judea, as large as that of his grandfather; and his brother, also named Herod, received some territory. The grants were celebrated with great fanfare in Rome: the brothers received the insignia of Roman magistrates.[28]

Claudius's second major decision was to issue an edict confirming the religious freedom (i.e., the right to live according to their Law) that Diaspora Jews had enjoyed since Augustus. He did so, he says, not in response to any embassy, but the requests of Agrippa and his brother. "It is right," he added, obliquely rebuking his predecessor, "that Jews throughout the whole world under our control should also observe their ancestral customs without hindrance." Josephus, who preserves a copy of the edict – or what purports to be a copy of it – includes it in his history, along with numerous other documents, because it was a notable benefaction for the Jewish people.[29] According to its text, Claudius wished it posted through the cities and towns of the empire "for at least thirty days in a place where it can be read completely from the ground." So again, a written document is of more value than a verbal response. But because this benefaction did not respond to any embassy as such, it varies the formulas previously examined. No present affirmation of loyalty is cited, but rather the Jews' past record. Ambassadors are not mentioned, but rather Agrippa and Herod, whose authority can thus be buttressed. And finally, insomuch as Claudius is supplying the Jews with a favor unrequited by present displays of loyalty, he feels freer to ask them for something in return: whatever their law says, the Jews must show more tolerance of polytheist religion. "And I bid them now," Claudius says, recognizing the privileges he has given, "to avail themselves of this kindness of mine in a more reasonable spirit and not to discount the religious feelings of other peoples."

To what might Claudius have been referring in making such a request? Perhaps the troublesome behavior (as he saw it) of the early Christians in Rome, at least in part. More obviously, the Jews of Alexandria. After

Caligula's accession, they had seized the chance to take vengeance on their Greek neighbors, perhaps even bringing in allies from as far away as Syria.[30] It was understandable, but, from the Roman point of view, unacceptable. In the letter he wrote to the Alexandrians, published in the fall of AD 41, Claudius, while again affirming the traditional religious freedom of the Jews, and excoriating the Greek community for their own recent atrocities, also has a strong rebuke for the Jews. He warns them not to invite Jews from Syria or Egypt, "thus compelling me to form greater suspicions." He continues: "otherwise by all means I will move against them just as if they were awakening some common plague for the inhabited world."[31] (The reference to worldwide plague suggests that troubles in Rome and Alexandria were linked, in Claudius' mind, if not in reality.) Like the Greeks of Alexandria, the city's Jews must show more appreciation for the ways of their neighbors. So again, in the letter, Claudius is taking the chance in making a benefaction to ask for something in return, though with the Alexandrian Jews he is harsher.

The tone of the letter may help to resolve an old scholarly problem. In his *Jewish Antiquities*, Josephus includes, along with the "worldwide" edict quoted above, an edict of Claudius issued to the Jews in Alexandria.[32] It begins thus:

I have been aware from the start that the Jews in Alexandria, called Alexandrians, were fellow colonizers with the Alexandrians from the earliest times and received from the kings equal civic rights, as has been made perfectly clear from the documents which they have and the edicts.

Some have tried to argue that this text, which takes a far more uniformly generous view of the Alexandrian Jews, and which gives so elaborate a history of their privileges, was an earlier proclamation, distinct from the letter preserved on papyrus.[33] More persuasive, for reasons of chronology (as well as Ockham's razor), is the view that Josephus' text here condenses the portion of the letter relevant to the Jews, and alters its tone and contents considerably (a revision that also entailed some recasting of the "worldwide" edict mentioned above).[34] Since Josephus' version goes on to attack the "great folly and madness" of Caligula, it has been suggested that the re-writing may be owed to none other than Philo himself, for inclusion in the final book of his *On Virtues*, a probable source for Josephus.[35]

Whoever was responsible, the alteration, if that is what it is, would perversely underscore how closely an emperor's original words would need to be examined if a dispute arose. Further, the appeal to previous "documents" in Josephus' edict neatly suggests the care an emperor in particular would have to take in investigating so thorny a situation as the Alexandrian problem. Documents could, potentially, be faked. (Indeed, according to a fascinating few paragraphs in Tacitus, under Tiberius an investigation was held in the Senate concerning asylum rights for the temples of Asia Minor, because they were being claimed on dubious if not downright fraudulent grounds, and those legations who had their privileges affirmed were to affix a record of that in bronze in their sanctuaries.[36]) There was a potentially seamy underside to the documents embassies might generate.

While the Jews would have been interested in immediate restoration of privileges undermined by Caligula, other communities acknowledged Claudius because they knew they might wish to ask for a special favor later, or simply establish a diplomatic relationship. (This is why, even after imperial benefits were to be confirmed automatically at the start of a new reign, the parade of envoys still continued.) So, early in Claudius' reign, the leadership of Delphi acknowledged the new emperor, in part, of course, because his predecessors had offered special benefits to the Pythian Apollo, his temple, and his games. In their vast sanctuary, already crammed with statues, the Delphians added one more of Claudius in 42 and another in 46; it was one of these, or a possible third statue of the emperor, that acted as a witness, along with a statue of Apollo, to various legal acts that private individuals chose to undertake in the sanctuary.[37] The loyalty had its reward, when, in AD 52, the city's leaders needed the emperor's help in a dispute, the details of which remain uncertain, since only part of Claudius' response is preserved, inscribed on a stone in the sanctuary. He begins by remarking, "For a long time I have been of good will towards the city of the Delphians . . . and well-disposed from the beginning, and I have always protected the worship of Pythian Apollo."[38] The emperor has shown favor to them, because they earlier had shown favor to him.

Even more clearly, the Artists of Dionysus, after their initial embassy following Claudius' accession, decided several years later to ask for additional privileges – what, precisely, is unknown.[39] The emperor was unprepared to grant them, at least immediately; but again, his response shows they had emphasized their own earlier acknowledgment of him. "I am pleased that you have remembered what I granted," he writes, "when I confirmed the rights given by the August Ones before me and by the Senate, and I will try to increase these, for you are piously disposed towards my House." As with the other letters and edicts, the didactic element is prominent: the emperor is advertising the rewards of loyalty, even if he could offer the Artists no favors straightaway. He did at least try to promote the envoy: "Marcus

Valerius Junianus, of my own household, presented this to me, and I praise him for being so well-disposed towards you." It was all the more important to do so, precisely because the Artists had not been immediately successful in their request.

If additional benefits could be requested later, why not at Claudius' accession? At least two embassies tried that, neither with great success, suggesting that it was better to wait. Yet the two embassies, representing the Greeks and Jews from Alexandria, to come back to that by now familiar situation one last time, may have thought their claims special, given the turmoil of the last few years.[40] They may even have suggested that their requests, if granted, would restore stability to the city. The Greeks had several favors to ask, most relatively minor, concerning citizenship rights, a new procedure for selecting the officials of the temple of the Divine Augustus, and a reduction in the length of time magistrates served. Claudius easily consented to these, while also upholding "all the other (privileges) granted to you by the Leaders before me and the kings and prefects." To their boldest request, that the city be given its own senate, he responded by pointing out there was no precedent under the earlier emperors, it did not suit his interests, and the prefect Aemilius Rectus would need to research the matter thoroughly. It was a cagey dodge, yet forthcoming about the basic principle of all such diplomacy in the early empire: both parties, in fact, had to derive a real benefit from new arrangements. Claudius already had the loyalty of the Alexandrians, as their extensive plans to recognize him showed.

So it was with the Jewish embassy too, who sought enhanced status within Alexandria, including the ability to participate in gymnastic contests in the city. To them Claudius was firm: "On the other hand, I order the Jews directly not to waste their labor vying for anything more than they had before, nor, as if they lived in two cities, to send out two embassies in future, something never done before, nor to force their way into the games of the gymnasiarch or cosmete."[41] They already had significant benefits, which the emperor had done the great favor of confirming. What more was he to gain by rewarding them additionally? Clearly he thought, and probably correctly, that such an innovation would do nothing to ease tensions in the city. And so he left them with the warning not to stir up further trouble, their traditional privileges affirmed.

Alexandria, a port of inestimable value because of the grain crops it shipped out each year in massive vessels to Rome, necessarily demanded the new emperor's attention. Yet Claudius personally heard envoys from less important communities and groups, such as the hymnodists. All that can be named are from the eastern half of the empire, and this is something of a surprise. To be sure, many of these communities had been established hundreds and hundreds of years earlier, benefited from a long apprenticeship to Roman rule under the Hellenistic kings to whom embassies were also sent, and gave their leading men the advantage of a solid training in the rhetorical arts. But what about the provinces of the west? How, if at all, would they establish ties with the emperor? Did they send embassies?

Here is not the place to explore the west completely, but looking at Africa in the first years of Claudius' reign begins to provide some answers.[42] The Roman province itself, when Claudius acceded, comprised two distinct regions, the small coastal belt of Tripolitania (in modern Libya), rich in olive orchards, and, to the west, separated by a desert, the eastern portion of the Maghreb (roughly Tunisia and eastern Algeria), which enjoys heavy winter rainfalls. The vast region of Mauretania, further west still, would soon join the empire, as two provinces, once unrest that had broken out under Caligula was settled.[43] Rome depended heavily on the older territories for its wheat and olive oil; after the civil war he fought with the Pompeians, Caesar is said to have boasted to the inhabitants of Rome that Africa could yield a yearly tribute of one million liters of oil and 8,000 tons of grain.[44] Such taxes continued into the empire and were required of most Roman citizens living in Africa, as well as provincials. To insure their regular delivery, the land had to be protected from marauding tribesmen living in the hills to the south. One legion (the Third Augustan) was permanently stationed in the province, and was aided by a far larger force of auxiliaries recruited from the native population. While the province as a whole was governed by a proconsul sent out by the Senate (in principle chosen by lot, but in reality often by the emperor), a legate answerable only to the emperor actually commanded the troops. The related burdens of surrendering their land, paying taxes, and serving in the army caused resentment, culminating in a full-scale rebellion during the reign of Tiberius spearheaded by the Musulami, a tribe of Numidians, which was only suppressed with some difficulty. (Under Claudius, there would be renewed troubles with this tribe.[45])

Q. Marcius Barea Soranus, chosen proconsul of Africa for 41, was keenly aware of all this as he set out for his province.[46] Little good was said of the place: it was mostly viewed as still primitive, despite years of Roman rule. A geographer writing under Claudius described it thus:

The shores are occupied by inhabitants with customs very much like our own, except that some differ in language and the ancestral gods they keep a cult for and worship in the traditional way. In neighboring areas no cities are located, but there are dwelling-places, which are called *mapalia*. Their way of life is rough and lacks refinements. The leading men are dressed in coarse woolen cloaks, the common people in the skins of wild and domestic animals. Sleeping and dining take place on the ground. Dishes are made of wood or bark. Their drink is milk and the juice of berries, their food usually the flesh of wild animals – since they spare their flocks, as much as possible, because that is their only wealth. Those living in the interior, in an even more uncivilized way, wander around following their flocks, and when the flocks have been led away by pasturage, so they move themselves and their huts, and when day ends there they pass the night.[47]

While modern scholars are quick to point out the stereotypes that inform the ethnography here, there is at least a kernel of truth to Pomponius Mela's account. Aside from Carthage (where the governor resided) and the other coastal settlements, along with a few major towns (e.g., the old Numidian centers of Thugga and Cirta) and a handful of more recent Roman colonies inland, the rest of the province was small villages and hilltop forts, as well as constantly shifting semi-nomadic tribes none too keen to see lands they had long relied on seized by the occupiers. To understand it all, Soranus did not have the benefit of modern maps. He had, instead, a long list of colonies and towns recording each community's status and tax burdens.[48]

One sign that northern Africa was a very different place from, say, Asia Minor was that very few statues, relatively, went up of the imperial family under the early emperors. From the reign of Claudius (according to a recent count) there are ten, compared to thirty-one from Greece, and forty-six from Asia.[49] This is not just an accident of preservation; African statue bases do survive in far greater numbers from the second century AD (e.g., twenty-four under Trajan, fifty-two under Hadrian) according to the same count.[50] In the early empire, those statues that did go up concentrate in the coastal areas and the few major inland cities – as Pomponius Mela might have predicted. In significant parts of the province, it mattered less that there was a new emperor.

Here, more than in the east, the communities that acknowledged the new emperor did so because they were eager to *become* a more visible part of the Roman world, one that would impress the governor, if not a distant Claudius too.[51] Some of their members were already citizens, even from longtime Roman families, others – perhaps from wealthy old Punic families – aspiring for the franchise. In Tripolitania, a statue went up for Claudius in his second year of power in the small town of Zian, where an elegant new forum was being built; and also, in the more bustling city of Leptis Magna, an arch.[52] In Leptis too there was a monument for the August Gods, paid for by Iddibal Tapapius, the son of Mago, from a prominent local family whose names patently betray Punic ancestry.[53] To the west along the coast, the people of Hippo Regius, an ancient Carthaginian city, set up a statue to Claudius, also honoring Soranus as the town's patron.[54] At Cirta, established as a colony by Augustus, a priestess of the newly deified Livia paid for a monument for the goddess, while in Thugga an arch erected for Caligula had its inscription re-carved to honor Claudius.[55]

This in fact was quite a spate of activity, far more significant (it appears) than what took place in Gaul or Spain in the same years. Africa, under the first years of Claudius, may have been different because Soranus was more actively rewarding loyalty to the new emperor and Rome than his counterparts elsewhere.[56] During his two terms in office, as the inscriptions show, he was on hand to dedicate the statue of Claudius that went up in Zian, in Tripolitania. He dedicated the monument to the divine Livia in Cirta. He dedicated Iddibal Tapapius' offering to the August Gods. He dedicated the Arch to Claudius in Lepcis. He was honored, along with Claudius, in Hippo Regius as the town's patron. He was patron of Lepcis Magna too.[57] From the inscriptions emerges a powerful impression of this man otherwise unknown, traveling for two years throughout his province, from Carthage to Tripolitania to Cirta and back, encouraging the erection of monuments to the new emperor and the emperor's deified relatives, even as he took care of his other duties too.

While Soranus himself, then, might not have been entirely a typical figure, his proconsulship reveals all the same how strong ties came to be established between Rome and the developing western provinces: by local initiative, which was encouraged, and rewarded, by local Roman authorities. This was still an exchange of favors – but on a more local level. All the same, it is quite likely that more established communities, like the colony of Carthage, or even Cirta, sent embassies to Rome on the accession of Claudius – to offer congratulations to the new emperor, if not discuss in any detail privileges with him (and communities in the east may have done the same).[58] Colonies and *municipia* are known to have had procedures for appointing ambassadors, and ambassadors are attested in Rome at critical moments for the August House – the death of Germanicus in AD 19, for instance.[59] Their service would not find commemoration akin to that of those more flamboyant envoys of the east, Chaeremon, Balbillus, Theon, and all the rest. But recognition almost certainly should be given to these nameless men too, for their efforts also helped to keep the empire together.

CHAPTER 4

Subduing the ocean

When in his early years of power Claudius looked back to precedents set by Augustus, he could take guidance not only from documents left behind by the first emperor, but also splendid monuments throughout the city of Rome. Most dazzling was the August Forum, a large colonnaded square paved in brilliant white marble from Carrara, at the rear of which rose the great Temple of Mars the Avenger.[1] Paid for, as Augustus gladly acknowledged, by the spoils of war, the Forum was a celebration, in stone, of the empire's unparalleled military achievements, culminating with those of Augustus and his family.[2] The temple housed, in addition to a cult statue of the god, the legionary standards that Crassus and Antony had lost to Parthia and Augustus had won back, while in the piazza in front stood a statue of the first emperor in a triumphal chariot, dedicated by the Senate; there was also an inscribed list of all the territories Rome had subjugated under his leadership.[3]

It was the function of the Forum's two long porticoes, packed with sculpture, to tell the story of Rome's growth to the present time, from small beginnings to domination of the world, from Aeneas to his descendant Augustus. On the northern side stood the Trojan founder, weighed down by his father Anchises and leading his son, along with the kings who followed him and other members of the Julian clan; on the southern was Romulus, with a spear and spoils he had won from the Etruscan king, Acro. In niches down the southern colonnade Augustus included statues of men who had contributed most to the growth of Rome, especially through war; many were clad in the dress of the *triumphator*, the military victor who paraded by chariot in a great procession from the outskirts of Rome to the Temple of Jupiter on the Capitoline. A brief inscription identified each honoree, while a larger plaque listed his accomplishments, focusing on the martial. Some of these inscriptions survive, along with others from Italian and provincial towns modeled on them. A typical example:

84

L. Aemilius Paulus, son of Lucius, twice consul, censor, interrex, praetor, curule aedile, quaestor, thrice tribune of the soldiers, augur. He subdued and triumphed over the Ligurians in his first consulship. He was made consul a second time by the people to wage war against King Perseus. He destroyed the king's forces in the ten days in which he reached Macedonia, and captured the king with his children.[4]

Members of Augustus' own family were included in the northern colon-nade, even if not strictly Julians, but (it would seem) received just one briefer inscription. A fragment remains of the bare record for Claudius' father: "Claudius Drusus Germanicus, son of Tiberius, consul, urban prae-tor, quaestor, augur, *imperator* in Germany."[5] The words conceal one of Rome's great losses, the unexpected and nerve-racking death of Drusus at age thirty while on campaign in the north. A hero of the people, this stepson of Augustus, as Claudius' biographer puts it, "was the first of the Roman generals to sail through the Northern Ocean," and, after having moved beyond the Rhine, campaigned all the way to the Elbe before he fell from his horse and was fatally wounded.[6] Claudius' early mentor in history, Livy, though he lived and wrote several decades longer, chose to end his great account of Rome with this sad episode, a moment of conquest tempered with a worrying note of loss, a poignant juxtaposition worthy of Vergil.[7]

Drusus' death foreshadowed (as Livy might have been implying) a greater bereavement, the destruction in AD 9 of three legions by the German leader Arminius, a massacre that must have prompted Augustus to reassess all his plans for expansion beyond the Rhine.[8] In the notes he left after his death enumerating the state's resources, it is reported, he included a recommen-dation to keep the empire within its current boundaries (including the Rhine).[9] Yet the Forum, dedicated in 2 BC and standing for all to see, seemed to urge a more grandiose future for Rome; with its programmatic mixture of cosmic, moral, and political messages, Augustus' great square was not merely a statement of world conquest but also a summons to further achievement. Those dispatched on commands abroad, a law announced, would ceremonially start from the Forum; the Senate would hold votes concerning the award of triumphs there; and the victors, along with any who received triumphal honors (in lieu of a full triumph), would join the ranks of those already honored with statues in the colonnades.[10] By 2 BC it was clear that triumphs, even most commands, would be reserved only for members of the imperial family, which meant that its younger members in particular were to live up to the legacy of past conquest – beginning with Augustus' adopted son Gaius, who was dispatched to Parthia directly after the dedication of the Temple of Mars the Avenger.[11] As Augustus later explained, he built his Forum "so that both he, while he lived, and the leaders of ensuing ages should be made by citizens to conform with the lives of those men as if it were their model."[12]

The solemn record of *Achievements* Augustus had inscribed after his death on pillars in front of his gigantic mausoleum also hardly seemed to admonish restraint. True, Augustus occasionally explains that he chose not to annex a territory, or that he achieved an objective through diplomacy rather than arms.[13] Granted, he celebrates the peace that befell much of the world in his time (albeit after war) and can envision Rome as fundamentally secure.[14] But again and again, in a style reminiscent of the eulogies of his Forum, he boasts of his conquests and parades their value to the people: "I extended the boundaries of all those provinces of the Roman people on whose borders were peoples not subject to our rule ... I added Egypt to the empire of the Roman people ... the Pannonian peoples, whom an army of the Roman people never approached before I was the Leader, I brought under the rule of the Roman people through the agency of Tiberius Nero, who was then my stepson and legate; and I extended the boundaries of Illyricum to the banks of the river Danube."[15] A paltry general himself, unlike his great foe Antony, Augustus still found it necessary to pose at the end of his life as a conqueror.

War answered the cries of the ancestral voices, subduing not just peoples on the edge of empire but critics back home. It helped affirm the Romans' identity as a military people, and an imperial people. It gave its generals prestige. Yet it came at great financial cost. It could lead to unthinkable disaster. It could throw up a commander to rival the Leader. And it might seem to conflict with Augustus' own celebration of peace. With Augustus' *Achievements* on the one hand, and his final recommendation, on the other, in mind, emperors afterwards would have to balance the need and desire for imperial and personal prestige with the price of war, real or perceived.[16]

In his fifty-fifth year when he succeeded Augustus in AD 14, Tiberius already had an impressive record of generalships, alluded to by Augustus himself in the *Achievements*.[17] His military valor thus established, the tight-fisted Tiberius was free to heed Augustus' official advice, and avoided potentially expensive wars of conquest in those edges of the world not yet subdued by Rome (not least Germany, where Drusus' son and Claudius' brother Germanicus was campaigning, doubtless hoping to match his father's achievements). Throughout his long principate, Tiberius annexed only Cappadocia and Commagene, when their respective kings, already under Rome's thumb, died.[18]

Caligula, by contrast, only twenty-four years at his accession, had nothing to boast of and saw an opportunity early in his reign to annex at least part of Britain: diplomacy and trade had gradually been bringing its peoples more fully into the Roman world, turmoil among them had increased recently, and the elderly King Cunobelin of the powerful Catuvellauni was approaching death.[19] While a thirst for glory would have been Caligula's chief motive – he wanted to win some of the glory his father Germanicus enjoyed even in death – a war on this scale required careful planning. Rome would not want to face a simultaneous attack from any of the German peoples, the principal foe of the north – and, an equally grave threat, the emperor would not want to face a rebellion from the Rhine legions themselves, or inhabitants of Gaul. Although Caligula's visit to Gaul and Germany in AD 39 and 40 seems, like his creation of two additional legions, to have been part of the preparations, in the end he decided not to attempt a Channel crossing in the latter year, perhaps because his soldiers were reluctant, perhaps because of lingering worries about the Germans, perhaps because he felt that he had to go back to Rome.[20]

Three years later Claudius launched the war that would carve from out of Britain a new province of the Roman Empire.[21] The purpose, whether entirely perceived or not, was essentially that of Caligula: to undertake a great war of conquest – one, no less, begun, but not finished, by Julius Caesar himself – and thereby establish Claudius' reputation for posterity and secure a stronger image for himself, as ruler of the world, among the soldiers, their commanders, Senators back in Rome, citizens more generally, and provincials. It was an attempt to gain a more charismatic authority. After the conspiracy of Scribonianus, its desirability seemed all the greater. At the same time, Claudius could point out that the situation in Britain was worsening, though that was to a large degree Rome's fault. Cunobelin had finally died, the sons who succeeded him, Caratacus and Togodumnus, were growing defiant, and in the meantime another king, Verica, had fled and, Claudius said, begged Rome to take up arms in vengeance.[22]

Careful to avoid repeating Caligula's errors, Claudius decided to spend as little time as possible away from Rome. He would join the campaign only briefly, getting credit, like the Aemilius Paulus of Augustus' Forum, for completing a war, or one phase of it. With luck, he might even drag back Caratacus and Togodumnus to display in a triumph. Yet since even a quick appearance in Britain entailed a month of travel on either end, and given the slowness of communication, the emperor would have to designate somebody to handle his affairs in Rome. Augustus had favored for moments like this men such as the smooth Maecenas, who shied away from the limelight, but was loyal and utterly ruthless when needed.

Now it seemed desirable to choose somebody more noticeably involved in public affairs, and so Claudius looked to Lucius Vitellius, an adroit courtier whom the emperor called "friend" but really relied on as a sort of chief minister.[23] From an obscure family of backwoods Italy, Vitellius had seen his father serve as steward of Augustus' property, while he himself became consul under Tiberius and then expertly governed Syria, where he had to face more than one diplomatic crisis. Faithfully administering an oath of loyalty in Jerusalem where he found himself when news of Caligula's accession reached the East, after Caligula's death he made his services available to the new Leader. A later source alleges that he approached Claudius through Messallina and the freedmen, even going so far as to remove the former's shoe, caress, and kiss it, while placing golden images of the latter in his household shrine.[24] To survive and flourish in a new court, some type of obsequiousness was necessary, but it was also Vitellius' connections and knowledge of foreign affairs that recommended him: his influence easily exceeded that of any other Senatorial "friend" Claudius could consult.

At the start of AD 43 Vitellius was to share a second consulship with Claudius – an unmistakable signal of his importance – and would direct affairs when both of them stepped down at the end of February and Claudius later departed. The pair of new men chosen as replacements – in middle age, and well tested, like other new men consuls – could be counted on to cause no trouble: Palpellius Hister, from Illyricum at the edge of Italy, and the opulent Pedanius Secundus, from Barcino (modern Barcelona).[25] Only the gods seemed unwilling to cooperate: a night owl had ominously flown into the Temple of Jupiter Greatest and Best on the Capitoline. Not to be deterred by this dreadful prodigy, Claudius had the whole city purified on March 7.[26]

No screeching owl, not even the gods, were going to impede the careful plan. Operations on the Rhine underway at Claudius' accession, culminating in the notable recapture of the last legionary eagle lost in AD 9 to Arminius, had conveniently reached their conclusion and were duly celebrated in Rome.[27] It thus became possible to reallocate forces more strategically. Though four legions (along with auxiliaries) were deemed necessary for the invasion, Claudius chose neither to incur the expense of raising new divisions, nor to send fresh recruits across the Channel. Instead, he selected from the Upper Rhine the Second Augusta and Twentieth Valeria, from the Lower Rhine the Fourteenth Gemina, and from

Pannonia – over a thousand miles from Britain – the Ninth Hispana, all accustomed to fighting in conditions judged similar to those on the island.[28] The Rhine forces, though, vital to the security of the empire, would have to be replenished immediately, with the Fourth Macedonica, sent from Spain, and Caligula's two new legions. The latter, quite shrewdly, were paired with more experienced troops in the double garrisons of Vetera and Moguntiacum. These movements show that while the military resources of an emperor were limited, he could redeploy them to carry out an ambitious plan that was to have significant consequences.[29]

Shrewd with his use of legions, Claudius took no chances with his commanders either. In charge of the expedition was Aulus Plautius, a capable general, loyal to Claudius, related through his mother to Vitellius, and without pretensions to imperial power.[30] He had already proved his worth, in the first years of the reign, as the emperor's governor in Pannonia.[31] Under him served an impressive group of officers, who would benefit from their participation in the campaign: T. Flavius Sabinus, a new man who came from a rich family of businessmen in Reate, in the old Sabine territory; his brother (and the future emperor), T. Flavius Vespasianus, previously in command of a legion in Upper Germany and a protégé of Vitellius; and C. Hosidius Geta, brother of one of Claudius' commanders in Mauretania.[32] The enigmatic Cn. Sentius Saturninus also participated actively, according to one source; certainly he won triumphal honors, including a statue in Augustus' Forum.[33] Consul in 41, he had initially opposed Claudius after Caligula's death but apparently then switched his mind and lent valuable support.[34] Perhaps he was simply part of the large group of Senators who joined Claudius when he set out to join the expedition, men brought out of respect – or fear.[35] For, so soon after Scribonianus' rebellion, the emperor could hardly be free of apprehension. And in fact, the historical record for AD 43 indicates that one equestrian was thrown from the Tarpeian Rock for plotting against the emperor.[36] Also, a second Julia, this time daughter of Claudius' late sister Livilla, was eliminated, denounced by the fearsome prosecutor Suillius Rufus (though for what is unknown).[37] Tacitus represents Suillius as claiming, later in life, to have been acting on behalf of Claudius and Messallina. Perhaps Julia had been up to something, or at least there were grounds for believing so.

Assembled by spring of 43, Plautius' troops, staring at the grey waters before them, observing the Atlantic tides, and fearful of campaigning "outside of the known world," at first refused to make the crossing – or so writes Cassius Dio, the lone and inadequate source for the details of the campaign.[38] With Claudius not yet due to appear, his freedman Narcissus (Dio continues) was sent ahead – the troops most likely were at Boulogne – and urged them on from Plautius' tribunal. Outrage giving way to laughter, the panic subsided. The tale at least reveals something of later attitudes to Claudius' freedmen, and also of the place Britain occupied in the Roman imagination. One way or another, Plautius did manage to cross over, beat the enemy back to the Thames, and secure a crossing there. Yet despite his early successes (including the death of Togodumnus), Plautius proceeded no further, waiting for Claudius, probably in accord with a previously formed plan, despite what Dio says.[39] The emperor would lead the final assault on the Catuvellaunian capital at Camulodunum (Colchester).

Claudius had surely already left Rome by the time the invasion was underway.[40] His entourage was substantial, numbering not just the large group of Senators, but also a detachment of the Praetorian Guard under Rufrius Pollio, selected members of his staff (including his physician Xenophon), and Lucius Silanus and the young Cn. Pompeius Magnus, the husband and fiancé respectively of his two daughters, both prominent aristocrats whom the emperor was promoting, as he made efforts to shape a new dynasty.[41]

As the large party made its way, it aroused a great deal of interest, at least in some quarters. Evidence survives for a number of vows made to the gods – usually pledges to put up a statue of the deity, in exchange for the emperor's safety, his return, and a victory in Britain. The individuals who offered them, such as A. Vicirius Proculus, military tribune and priest of Augustus in Rusellae, and Caecilia Secunda in Narbonne, had to have been of means to afford a statue; others may have made more modest undertakings, no traces of which survive.[42] All of these vows but one were fulfilled in Rome, Italy, and southern France, suggesting that individuals here were more interested in the incipient campaign. But it does seem quite possible that the campaign was officially advertised – perhaps through dissemination of a report of vows undertaken by the consuls, Vitellius and Claudius himself, or the Senate, which could have served as a model for others.[43] For tellingly, there is also a record of a vow undertaken faraway in a city of the east, Pisidian Antioch. A colony of Augustus, settled with veterans in 25 BC, it produced Senators and equestrians already in the first century, and by Claudius' day boasted an enormous imperial sanctuary in which sat a triumphal arch celebrating Augustus' victory over the nearby Pisidians and a copy of the emperor's *Achievements* was displayed.[44] A prominent equestrian of the colony, C. Caristanius Fronto Caesianus Iullus, who had served decades earlier as military tribune of the Twelfth Legion in Syria and prefect of an auxiliary cohort, made a vow, along with his sons, for

Claudius' wellbeing, offering in exchange sacrifices, a statue of the emperor, games for the youth, and a beast hunt.[45]

The vows would be paid – the Antiochenes treated to their very Roman beast hunt – because Claudius' expedition, limited as it was, went well, as he would recall with pride the rest of his life. If Dio can be trusted: the emperor, crossing the Ocean even with elephants, met up with Plautius, defeated the enemy beyond the Thames, and moved onto Camulodunum, which, poorly defended, quickly fell.[46] A number of kings came over to the Romans at this point, including perhaps even a ruler from the Orkneys (though not Caratacus, who regrouped in the west), and Claudius was hailed *imperator* several times.[47] Though the Romans still had much to accomplish in the following years (including the capture of Caratacus), Claudius himself, perhaps after only sixteen days on the island, began the journey back to Rome, sending ahead Silanus and Pompeius with a report of his victory, doubtless in the traditional form of wooden tablets decorated with laurel.[48]

The emperor returned at a more leisurely pace, stopping, it is recorded, by Ravenna, where, in a vast ship, he sailed out the Po into the Adriatic Sea, to advertise his conquest of Ocean.[49] (He might also have taken the chance to tour newly reorganized military installations along the Rhine and Danube, perhaps even following the route of the great Alpine road, the Via Claudia Augusta, to be completed in AD 46.[50]) Whatever difficulties remained for Plautius, the emperor could boast that an impressive victory had been achieved under his auspices, one that shored up his image, putting him in a line with Caesar and Augustus (and later expansionists such as Domitian and Trajan). But, the initial victory achieved, it comes time to ask more fully: whom, in particular, did Claudius wish to impress, how would he make his success known, and, basking in its luster, would he take the chance to emphasize new messages about himself?

Upon receiving the report conveyed by Silanus and Pompeius, the Senate immediately voted Claudius honors, perhaps agreed upon beforehand.[51] They decided to award him a triumph and (probably in fulfillment of a vow) establish annual games to perpetuate memory of his victory; arches were to be erected, one in Rome and one in Gaul from where he had set out; Claudius and his infant son were both given the extra honorary name "Britannicus" (though Claudius did not use it in his official titulature); and Messallina was granted the right on formal occasions to sit with the Vestals at games and to use a special carriage, privileges that had previously been granted to Augustus' wife Livia.[52] It was not, then, just Claudius' victory that was being celebrated, but also his own emerging dynasty.

The staging of the triumph itself in AD 44, the first celebrated by a ruling emperor since Augustus, featured several innovations, again drawing attention not only to the conquest of Britain but also the imperial house.[53] While Claudius rode, according to custom, in the victor's chariot, he was followed (it is said) by all those Senators who had fought with him and were given triumphal honors, as well as Messallina, on her newly awarded *carpentum*. The Praetorian prefect Rufrius Pollio, awarded a statue, also likely appeared with his men, along with at least a handful of equestrian officers and soldiers. Placards no doubt advertised, in traditional manner, the exploits of the campaign, the numbers involved, the geography of Britain, yet they also mentioned the weight of gold crowns that flowed in from the provinces in honor of the emperor.[54] Towards the end of the celebration, the emperor, like Julius Caesar before him, ascended the steps of the Temple of Jupiter Greatest and Best on his knees, but was attended by Silanus and Pompeius. Governors of the provinces were invited, along with exiles Claudius restored to Rome.[55]

Celebrations held afterwards featured the usual spectacles, along with extra horse races, beast hunts, athletic contests, and Pyrrhic dances performed by boys summoned from Asia. The association of stage actors, with Claudius' permission, also held a separate festival. It may have been at this time, too, that the emperor, presiding in a military cloak, staged on the Campus Martius an elaborate reenactment of the sack of Camulodunum and the surrender of the British kings.[56]

Further lavish celebrations punctuated the rest of Claudius' reign, making the conquest of Britain the emperor's signal accomplishment. In 45, separate games were held in Rome in fulfillment of a vow made by Claudius himself – similar to those of Vicirius Proculus in Rusellae and Caristianius Fronto in Pisidian Antioch – and to mark them, the free men of the City of Rome received largesse said to have been worth at least 300 sesterces apiece (which would yield a total cost of at least 45 million sesterces, perhaps quite a bit more); Silanus and Pompeius helped preside over the distribution.[57] In 47, Aulus Plautius paraded through Rome in an ovation (a sort of lesser triumph), with Claudius at his side.[58] And in 51, the wily Caratacus, after a long campaign against the Romans, was betrayed along with his wife, daughter, and brothers, by Cartimandua, queen of the Brigantes, and sent to the City, where, Tacitus reports:

The people were summoned as if to a distinguished spectacle; the Praetorian cohorts stood under arms on the level ground which lies before their camp. Then, as his royal clients filed by, the roundels, neck-rings, and everything that the king had acquired in foreign wars were paraded, and then his brothers, spouse, and daughter, and finally the man himself displayed. The prayers of the others were unworthy of them, owing to their dread; but not Caratacus, who was seeking no pity with downcast look or language.[59]

Tacitus goes on to give Caratacus a short but splendid speech, obviously invented; but surely Claudius planned for this pageant to culminate in his sparing of the king, who dutifully thanked the emperor and also his new wife, Agrippina, each perched atop a dais. It was, Tacitus represents several Senators later saying, all rather like the capture of Syphax by Scipio, or Perseus by Paulus, several centuries before – except that in an earlier age, the distinguished prisoners would have been executed.

To provide a more lasting commemoration of the victory, Claudius consented to several new monuments too. Very early in his reign, the emperor had focused his efforts on retrospection, looking back, for the prestige they enjoyed, to Livia and Augustus, Antonia and Drusus.[60] He also restored or completed several projects initiated under Tiberius, for instance the probable monument to Pietas Augusta and the refurbishment of the Theater of Pompey.[61] Now Rome was also to take heed of Claudius' own achievements and the emperor's living family. To the gable of the principal entrance of his Palatine house, next to Augustus' crown of oak leaves, was affixed a naval crown, normally awarded to the first soldier to board an enemy ship during battle, now transformed to signify that "Ocean had been crossed and, as it were, subdued."[62] Statues went up in the Forum of Augustus of the men who had won triumphal ornaments, perhaps of Claudius too.[63] But most important was the Senate's arch.[64]

Through its ensemble of large billboard-style text and statuary, and because it could be positioned in the most traversed parts of the City, an arch was an excellent way to broadcast messages to the people of Rome.[65] By tradition, this peculiarly Roman form of monument had advertised an individual's military achievements; in imperial times it was adapted to exalt the ruling dynasty as a whole, living and dead. In AD 19, for instance, after the death of Germanicus, a decree was passed stipulating a marble arch in the Circus Flaminius, near statues of Divus Augustus and "the August House" (most likely Tiberius, Livia, Germanicus, and Tiberius' son Drusus); on its top were to be a statue of the deceased in a triumphal chariot, along with other members of his family (including even Claudius), and images of defeated Germans were also to be included.[66] The Senate decree contained the text of the arch's dedicatory inscription, which listed some of Germanicus' exploits on behalf of the Roman people – clearing Germans out of Gaul, for instance, and recovering military standards.

Claudius' own monument was also certainly quite elaborate, but unfortunately presents a number of difficulties for scholars. Beginning in the Renaissance, excavations unearthed marble fragments of what was clearly the Britannic victory arch, and also revealed that it spanned the busy Via Flaminia, the main road out of Rome to the north.[67] The Senate likely voted a location here, not just for its prominence, but to link it with an arch to Claudius' father on the Via Appia.[68] With that road leading to the south, the two monuments formed a neat pair. What is more, the arch was actually incorporated into the arcade of the Aqua Virgo that brought water across the Campus Martius; a visitor to Rome, from the north, would be greeted by this impressive façade screening the City, with Claudius' arch providing a formal entrance.[69]

Now the arch probably should have been completed in AD 46, as Claudius performed repairs on the Aqua Virgo that year – adding a further layer of significance to the Senate's monument – and coinage from this year onwards depicts a British arch as well, and visually links it to that of Drusus (Fig. 24).[70] But the monument we can detect dates to AD 51, at least according to its massive dedicatory inscription, part of which is preserved (Fig. 23), celebrating Claudius' victory over the British kings and, it seems, the Roman people's control for the first time over people beyond the Ocean.[71] Reliefs complemented this message of imperial achievement, apparently depicting Claudius' triumphal parade of AD 44 – or perhaps the ceremony of AD 51 (Fig. 25). For it may be that an arch did go up in 46 or shortly afterwards, exactly where this later structure was found; and if, like that for Germanicus, the arch featured members of the imperial house, after Messallina's disgrace in 48 it would have been redesigned because of the sanctions the Senate imposed on her memory.[72]

The Senate, to add further conjectures here, may have honored Claudius with another monument, unknown to literary sources and an even greater puzzle to students of Roman topography. At the start of the sixteenth century, several large pieces of a substantial marble monument turned up which, when re-assembled, were seen to depict scenes of a sacrifice being performed with two temples dominating the background, the Temple of the Great Mother on the Palatine and (separately) the Temple of Mars the Avenger in the Forum of Augustus (Figs. 26–27); also visible are scenes of a procession attended by men in togas and laurel, and a child carrying a statuette of a *lar*. Further fragments emerged later, showing that all belonged to a monument quite similar in form to the famous Altar of Augustan Peace,

Fig. 23 Fragment of the dedicatory inscription from the Arch of Claudius. For the restoration of the full text, see Appendix to Chapter 4. Capitoline Museums, Rome.

but their technique and style suggest a Claudian date.[73] Since the earlier altar was voted in commemoration of Augustus' homecoming from time abroad, it may be that the Claudian monument celebrates that emperor's safe return from Britain.

The large reliefs, according to this proposal, would depict a celebration carried out in fulfillment of vows made before Claudius' departure

Fig. 24 *Aureus*, dated AD 46/7. The obverse shows the head of Claudius; the reverse a victory arch surmounted by an equestrian statue base between two trophies, similar to that on coins commemorating Claudius' father, Drusus (Fig. 20).

(perhaps those of the Senate, or Claudius, or both). Its culminating point would have been a sacrifice of bulls to Mars the Avenger and the emperor's *genius* in front of the Temple of Mars the Avenger.[74] The altar itself, then – perhaps named for August *felicitas* or *spes* – would represent a more permanent form of thanksgiving, mirroring the relationship of the victory arch to the triumph. And like the arch, it took on further meaning yet by its relationship to earlier monuments of imperial Rome. Indeed, its own relief sculpture, whatever its context, whatever its date, almost seems to suggest that important buildings of Augustan Rome themselves functioned as protagonists in later imperial ceremonies. Claudius, as seen, was able to use Augustan monuments to his advantage, by including new statues in the great August Forum, for example.

A further reason to suppose that the return from Britain could be the correct context for this monument is the handsome youth standing in the middle of one of the relief fragments (Fig. 28). Attention is clearly focused on him, and he is visually marked out by his *apex*, the spiked cap that was the distinctive headgear of a Roman *flamen*. While there was more than one of these priests in service in Claudian Rome, this figure must be of great importance, and is perhaps to be identified with Junius Silanus, the *flamen* of Augustus, who was also betrothed to Claudius' daughter and accompanied the emperor to Britain.[75] It was he, along with Pompeius, who brought back Claudius' report of the expedition's success to Rome. Destined to meet a terrible end in AD 48, Silanus is not known through other portraits, so the identification must remain speculative.

Fig. 25 Fragment of a relief, identified as belonging to the Britannic arch of Claudius. The scene depicted may be the triumph of 44 AD or perhaps the display of Caratacus in AD 51. The heads of the figures in the foreground are modern restorations, but the military costume suggests that they may be Praetorians (additionally, the eagle might be compared to that seen in the Praetorian Camp in Fig. 5). Louvre, Paris.

The honorary decree, the pageantry, and the monuments (however many there were), all consented to by Claudius if not of his own planning, enhanced the emperor's image, above all in the City of Rome itself. They showed him to be in the mold of Augustus, presiding over the empire's expansion through war, even if not actually a great general himself. And like

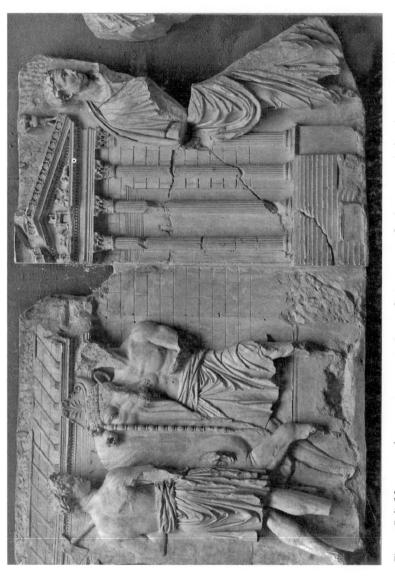

Fig. 26 Relief from an unknown monument in Rome, depicting a sacrificial procession before the Temple of the Great Mother on the Palatine. Cast from the original pieces, Villa Medici, Rome.

Fig. 27 Relief from an unknown monument in Rome, depicting a scene of sacrifice before the Temple of Mars the Avenger in the August Forum. Cast from the original pieces, Villa Medici, Rome.

Fig. 28 Relief from an unknown monument in Rome, showing a young man wearing an
apex, the distinctive spiked headgear of a *flamen*. Villa Medici, Rome.

Augustus, this was an emperor who showed clemency too. While Rome
was evidently superior to the strange peoples beyond Ocean, and could
celebrate conquest as it had in the days of the Republic, Claudius in the
end spared Caratacus, as he had some of his own exiled countrymen in AD
44: all were under his sway in this new cosmos. Conquest need not be so
violent as it was in another age; after all, the arch boasted that Claudius

prevailed "without any loss of blood" (on the Roman side, to be sure). At the same time, everything proclaimed, this was an emperor constructing a new house. Claudius need not look back as much as he did at the start of his reign: he could now promote his wife, his son "Britannicus," and his sons-in-law.[76] The appearance of Messallina at the triumph, in particular, was a great innovation. Distinctive too, and understandable, was the prominence both in AD 44 and 51 of the Praetorians, Claudius' partners in power.

If all of this was focused on the City of Rome, it was hardly surprising: the City had long been, and would long remain, the principal stage for such celebrations. The provinces, however much their ruling classes now identified with Rome, still existed for the benefit of the Roman people, not for the benefit of themselves (though of course, within the provinces, there existed exceptional communities, most notably citizen colonies). This was made clear by the primary way in which emperors, including Claudius, expected provincial subjects to celebrate a great military victory. From the time of Augustus, in accord with a custom long familiar in the East, they were obliged to offer, in exchange for the benefactions reported to them, gold crowns to the emperor.[77] Effectively a tax, though represented as a voluntary gift, the crowns perhaps irked provincials, but did also present an occasion to display loyalty to Rome. A council might decide, for instance, to send an unusually large gift, as those of Further Spain and Gaul are said to have for the British triumph.[78] And so in this manner Claudius made his victory known across his empire, gaining from it an influx of precious metal that along with booty might have contributed to a large emission of coins from the mint in AD 46, on which appeared, fittingly, the British victory arch.[79]

Yet what did Claudius' subjects, in Rome and the provinces, actually think of all the fanfare? Panegyrical literature of the time reflected at least something of the official celebration. The Spanish geographer Pomponius Mela, writing in the early 40s a description of the world, region by region, found an obvious way to praise the emperor:

What sort of place Britain is and what sort of peoples it produces will soon be told of more surely and on the basis of greater exploration. For, behold, the greatest of Leaders is opening it up after it has been closed so long, the conqueror of peoples not only unconquered but not even known at all.[80]

Languishing in Corsica after his banishment for involvement with Julia Livilla's adultery, Seneca mentions the "opening" of Britain too, but understandably also remarks on a different aspect of the triumph: "May he pacify Germany, open up Britain, and celebrate both his father's triumphs and new ones! And his clemency, which among his virtues holds the chief place, gives promise that I too will be a spectator of these."[81] Even more elaborate than these references is a series of anonymous epigrams, the so-called *Praise of Caesar*, arguably written for performance in conjunction with the triumph itself or else an offshoot of such a tradition.[82]

The adulation was, at least on Seneca's part, probably insincere. Soon after Claudius' death, in the sharp pamphlet called *Apocolocyntosis*, the former exile calculatedly undermined his own earlier praise. A crowd, in the Forum, intones in anapests the emperor's achievements: "That man ordered the Britons beyond the shores of the known sea and the blue-shielded Brigantes to offer their necks to Roman fetters and Ocean himself to tremble before the new authority of the Roman axe."[83] Yet as the rest of the song, and the satire as a whole, make clear, the flattery here is empty. Claudius, we hear in the very same song, could settle lawsuits as quickly as anyone, "only hearing one side, often not either."[84] These wicked verses, an effort to transmogrify Seneca's own earlier flattery, also undercut the sort of hack poetry seen in the *Praise of Caesar*.

It is true Seneca wrote his wicked satire only after Claudius' death. But the campaign, including the emperor's own crossing to Britain, probably never could have won over his most determined critics. For them, Claudius Caesar was still a fraud, a stammering fool who should never have been selected Leader, and they could tartly note with Suetonius: "He made just one campaign, and a slight one at that."[85] Some Senators who voted honors for Claudius may well have laughed privately, hopeful of playing a joke on posterity: Aemilius Paulus indeed! Yet, and this matters a great deal, at least some of those outside court circles, inclined to accept a physically distant Claudius and identify his power with the might of Rome, viewed the emperor's campaign more positively. Leaving aside all those who made vows in AD 43 and afterwards fulfilled them, we can identify two groups above all who saw the war as a source of pride. As with statues or embassies, looking at the praise they bestowed fills out the picture of Claudius' empire. One needs to move beyond the views of insiders in Rome.

First, for the Roman army and its officers, success in Britain repre-sented the greatest exploit in several decades. Monuments put up in honor of officers who served under Claudius show that these men would be quick to disagree with the bookish Suetonius – and justifiably, given the danger and difficulties they had faced. P. Anicius Maximus, for instance, an equestrian from Pisidian Antioch (where Caristanius orchestrated his elaborate celebrations), received a statue whose inscription recorded his time as camp-prefect in the Second Augustan Legion and also the decorations he won from Claudius for the "British war," an assault crown and a parade spear.[86] According to another statue base, erected around AD 64, C. Gavius Silvanus – an officer in the Praetorian Guard who would be implicated in the conspiracy against Nero of AD 65 – was "decorated by the deified Claudius in the British war, with necklets, bracelets, and roundels."[87] Even after the emperor's death, the honor of his grant seemed worth mentioning. Vettius Valens, while a Praetorian, won the same honors, again in the "British war."[88] These and similar inscriptions underscore an attitude lost in the literary sources: for some, Suetonius' insignificant campaign was a mark of honor, and the late Claudius' name not an embarrassment.

Second, communities or organizations in the provinces that felt close to Rome (or whose leaders did) could see the victory as theirs too. The Roman citizens of Cyzicus, along with the native community, established a victory arch for Claudius.[89] In Corinth, a citizen colony like Pisidian Antioch, a cult of "Victoria Britannica" was created, an early priest of whom was a military tribune of the Sixth Legion Hispaniensis.[90] And the mint-masters of Caesarea in Cappadocia, whose coinage showed unusually close affinities with official issues from Rome, honored Claudius' success with didrachms showing the emperor in a triumphal chariot.[91] But more impressive than any of these records is the relief sculpture from Aphrodisias, in Asia Minor, which shows the emperor, bare-chested like a god, on the verge of slaying a partially nude woman labeled as "Britannia" (Fig. 29).[92] A variation on statue groups of Achilles and the Amazon queen Penthesilea, this panel, just one of over a hundred in the town's imperial sanctuary, powerfully reconfigures the emperor's victory in a way quite foreign to official monuments in Rome. More violent, this image of conquest is sexually charged too, suggesting that for the Aphrodisians it was a kind of fantasy.

Yet with their close ties to Rome, it was certainly a part of history also. An old temple-town, Aphrodisias had shrewdly used its cult of Venus to impress Julius Caesar and then Augustus, who traced their ancestry through Aeneas back to the goddess.[93] In gratitude for the special privileges it received, the town in turn honored the ruling family of Rome with the unusually lavish sanctuary, paid for by two leading families.[94] Construction on it lasted many years, probably from the reigns of Tiberius through Nero, showing

Fig. 29 Relief from the Sebasteion at Aphrodisias, depicting Claudius and Britannia (both figures are identified by an inscription on the relief's base).

that the Aphrodisians were ready enough to accept Claudius as successor to the Julians. Both through its architectural plan (inspired by Augustus' Forum in Rome) and its sculptural program (which combined scenes of Greek mythology with reliefs of Claudius and the other emperors), the complex proclaimed that for this community, at least, Rome's world was starting to become theirs.

A visitor could only have been dazzled. Fronted with a massive two-story gate graced with statues of the imperial family and their mythical progenitors, the sanctuary opened from the street into a long paved area flanked on either side by tall and ornately decorated porticoes, with Doric, Ionic, and Corinthian orders in their first, second, and third stories respectively. At the far end, raised on a podium reached by a flight of stairs, sat the imperial temple. Walking towards it, looking up at the porticoes, one would have glimpsed on their upper levels the relief panels, marvelously blending, on the southern side, such stories as Leda and the Swan and Bellerephon and Pegasus with Romulus and Remus and Claudius Subduing Britain. On the north were allegorical figures, personifying time and place, and also peoples and provinces conquered by Augustus: Day and Ocean, for instance, along with Bosporans, Bessi, Dacians, and Dardanians, and the like.

It was all so eerily like Rome, and yet so different too. Here there was the fascination with cataloguing the defeated, and the idea that the empire was equivalent to the cosmos. Yet here was also a cult for the living emperor. The grand square, in imitating the Forum of Augustus, spoke to how Rome saw provincials, yet as an imperial sanctuary, spoke to how provincials saw Rome. It was a unique hybrid, a harbinger of a more cosmopolitan world to come. When provincials could celebrate the conquest of Britain, they were starting to become Roman too. But a full synthesis was still far off. Too many Romans, if not Claudius himself, still saw the massive empire, with all its people and places, solely as a means to self-enrichment.

APPENDIX: THE DEDICATORY INSCRIPTION FOR THE BRITANNIC VICTORY ARCH

Four discontinuous fragments of the dedicatory inscription are known, though only one now survives, the famous piece in the Capitoline Museums in Rome (Fig. 23). A great deal of the text must be restored by conjecture, represented here in square brackets. What follows is essentially the version proposed by Alföldy at *CIL* 6.40416, with an English translation of the whole.

Ti. Clau[dio Drusus f. Cai]sari / Augu[sto Germani]co / pontific[i maxim. trib. potes]tat. XI, / cos. V, im[p. XXII (?) cens(ori), patri pa]triai / senatus po[pulusque] Ro[manus, q]uod / reges Brit[annorum] XI [diebus paucis sine] / ulla iactu[ra devicerit et regna eorum] / gentesque b[arbaras trans Oceanum sitas] / primus in dici[onem populi Romani redegerit.]

For Tiberius Claudius Caesar Augustus Germanicus, son of Drusus, pontifex maximus, with tribunician power for the eleventh time, consul for the fifth time, *imperator* for the twenty-second time, censor, father of the fatherland, the Senate and People of Rome, because he conquered 11 kings of Britain in a few days without any loss and he was the first to bring the kingdoms and barbarian peoples beyond the Ocean under the rule of the Roman people.

In making the supplements, Alföldy relies on the fragmentary inscription from the Arch of Cyzicus (above, p. 103), which reads in part *devi[ctori regum XI] Britanniae* and also Suet. *Claud.* 17.2: *sine ullo proelio aut sanguine intra paucissimos dies parte insulae in deditionem recepta . . . Romam rediit.*

CHAPTER 5

Lists of peoples and places

Like other imperial peoples, Romans had a taste for geography. The enterprise was hardly scientific – not a rigorous delineation of the earth's surface, but rather a tendency to collect information that mirrored the acquisition of an empire. Geographic knowledge was, in its literary form, a growing catalogue of peoples and places under Roman sway, the distances that separated them, and the most noticeable features of the landscape: rivers, lakes, and mountains.[1] There was particular interest, too, in the edges of the world – or rather the Roman world – and what lay beyond, for these furnished an opportunity to describe colorful, if not downright freakish and frightening peoples, who reinforced civilized society's identity. Writers of such ethnographies sought guidance in a literary tradition going back to Homer and Herodotus more than in on-the-ground investigation.[2] They favored myths and marvels over first-hand anthropology. And while some Greeks did write longer, more scientific treatises on the subject, Latin authors first used geography and ethnography as an ornamental digression in historical writing.[3] This grew into a separate exercise with Seneca's short works on Egypt and India (followed by Tacitus' *Germania*).[4] As for more exhaustive efforts, Agrippa produced some geographic notes in conjunction with a large map he was preparing for display in Rome, but it was only under Claudius that Pomponius Mela attempted a full account of the known world, in three volumes. The task, he notes slyly at the start, using geographical language, "was blocked by obstacles and not capable of producing eloquence."[5]

The geographic books of Pliny the Elder's *Natural History*, written a generation after Claudius' principate, illuminate the whole tradition.[6] Quite typical is his description of Mauretania, in North Africa, largely ruled as an independent kingdom in the early empire but also home to several colonies of Roman citizens:

Twenty-five miles from Tingis, on the shore of the Ocean, is a colony of Augustus, Julia Constantia Zulil, which is exempt from the control of the kings and required to submit to the jurisdiction of Baetica. Thirty-five miles from it is a colony established by Claudius Caesar, Lixus, about which altogether the most fantastic tales are told by the old writers: this was the site of the palace of Antaeus, the fight with Hercules, and the gardens of the Hesperides... forty miles from Lixus in the interior, is another colony of Augustus, Babba, called Julia on the Plains, and seventy-five miles further, a third, Banasa, which has the second name of Valentia. Thirty-five miles from Banasa is the town of Volubile, equally distant from either sea. On the shore, fifty miles from Lixus, is the river Sububus, flowing by the colony of Banasa, a fine river available for navigation. The same number of miles from it is the town of Sala, situated on the river of the same name, on the very edge of the desert, and beset by herds of elephants, but much more seriously by the Autoteles tribe, through whom lies the route to Atlas, subject of altogether the most fantastic stories of all the mountains of Africa.

It is reported to rise into the sky out of the middle of the sands, rugged, covered with crags on the side facing towards the coast of the Ocean to which it has given its name, but to be shady, covered with woods, and watered by gushing springs on the side facing Africa, with all kinds of fruits springing up of their own accord such that pleasure is never lacking satisfaction. None of its inhabitants, it is said, are to be seen during the day, and all is silent with a dread like that of the desert; a speechless awe steals in on the minds of those who approach it, and also a dread of the peak that rises above the clouds and into the vicinity of the moon's path.[7]

The prosaic listing of people and places, along with Roman administrative details (some of them patently out of date by Pliny's day), sits side by side here with myths of old and the thrilling fantasia on Atlas, investing *imperium* with awe. The empire reaches the limits not just of the known, but seemingly the knowable. Mela is less grandiose, and in some ways less obviously Roman – indeed, it has been suggested that he departs from the Roman tradition in order to praise the ancient Phoenician civilization of his homeland in southern Spain – but he still has similarities with Pliny, who used Mela as a source.[8] There are in Mela's work bizarre borderlands – Scythians who eat the corpses of their parents at funerals, ants the size of dogs in India.[9] Contained within, threatening to burst his treatise, are what Mela explicitly terms "names of peoples and places."[10]

But it was not just in books that the people of Rome were exposed to geography. They could find it everywhere – in triumphs, games, maps in temples and other monuments, and dispatches of victorious generals from abroad trimmed with laurel. Again the emphasis was often on myths or marvels. Victorious generals might display unusual flora at their triumphs, the aediles regularly exhibited exotic animals – talking parrots or leopards, crocodiles and hippopotamuses – until the emperors usurped the privilege.[11] In the Republic, a painted map of Italy adorned the Temple of Earth; under Augustus, fittingly, Agrippa's map of the world went up, and was complemented by the list of subjected territories in the August Forum.[12] Campaigns often drew attention to far-off locales: it was Caesar who provoked interest in Britain with his dispatches and commentaries, and Augustus' grandson Gaius in Arabia when he journeyed east in 2 BC.[13] Through all this, and more, denizens of Rome might feel that their city did encompass the world: *urbs* and *orbs* were, as their names suggested, really one.

In his early years of power, Claudius aimed to reinvigorate that feeling, strong in the late Republic and under Augustus, weakened by the lack of campaigning under Tiberius and that emperor's withdrawal to Capri and the failures of Caligula (though Caligula probably was aiming for something of it too). The quest was politically expedient, but it also likely owed something to Claudius' own intellectual passions. Pliny supplies most of what can be known of these interests, for he pays the emperor (under whom his careers both as military officer and writer began) the compliment of citing his scholarship more than once, and, to judge from these references, the concerns were conventional enough.[14] Claudius offered opinions on the dimensions of Lake Maerotis south of Alexandria and the size of Armenia; he weighed in on the distance between the Black Sea and the Caspian.[15] He also described how the Tigris and Arsanias Rivers flowed together in flood season, without their waters intermingling.[16] He claimed that a hippocentaur was born and died the same day in Thessaly, and he remarked on the bratum wood for which people sent to the Elymaei, in western Iran: it had an agreeable scent when burnt, and the Parthians sprinkled its leaves into their drinks.[17]

Once emperor, Claudius could share his enthusiasms with an indulgent people craving spectacle. A hippocentaur was triumphantly brought from Egypt, suspiciously preserved in honey.[18] A freakishly tall Arabian was put on display.[19] Gladiators were made to fight elephants single-handedly, while a new method of capturing lions was imported from Gaetulia.[20] Four tigers were exhibited in a cage at once, surpassing the previous record.[21] And, in AD 47, the eight-hundredth year of Rome's founding, a phoenix was displayed in the old voting place.[22] Sacred to the Sun, with a fantastic longevity, this bird of fable was supposed to appear only in a Great Year. But what could be greater than Rome's anniversary? Here Claudius may have gone too far: Pliny records that nobody would doubt that the phoenix was a fake.

More authentic, presumably, were the captives at Claudius' British triumph and Plautius' ovation in AD 49.[23] At these ceremonies, and the re-enacted surrender of the kings and the fall of Camulodunum, a new world was opening up before the eyes of Rome. As Mela said of Britain: "behold, the greatest of Leaders is opening it up after it has been closed so long, the conqueror of peoples not only unconquered but not even known at all."[24] Whether most Romans really wished to know the Britons better is questionable, but Mela does express an ideal of Claudius' principate, which went back to the last generations of the Republic and Augustus. New lands should bravely be opened, and all of them, becoming less strange, knit finally into one peaceful whole. As Seneca in his tragedy *Medea* has the chorus sing, reflecting on the suffering of the Argonauts: "Nowadays the sea has yielded and endures all laws... any little rowboat wanders over the deep. Every boundary is removed, and cities have established their walls in new lands. A world allowing full passage has left nothing where it once had been."[25] Though he would have put it differently, Claudius shared the underlying sentiment: it is no accident that an enterprising freedman who traded in India, apparently blown off course during a voyage, helped to arrange for four envoys from Ceylon to appear before the emperor and describe their island.[26]

The conquest of Britain represented Claudius' most spectacular effort at enlarging Rome's geographic grasp, but it was not the only one. Immediately upon accession, he had to decide what to do with Mauretania. Caligula had already marked out the region for annexation, when, returning from his unimpressive northern campaign, he executed its ruler (and his cousin) Ptolemy.[27] A rebellion, staged by men loyal to the dead king, afterwards broke out, and had just been put down when Claudius gained the principate. In the chaos, though, it appears that neighboring nomads and *montagnards*, whom Ptolemy and his father, the scholarly King Juba, had held in check only with difficulty, made fresh incursions into the old kingdom. And it might also be that tribes who had joined in the rebellion did not give up so easily. With nobody from Juba's family left to rule, and with Romans living in Mauretania endangered, Claudius decided to persist with the annexation, and sent first the ex-praetor Suetonius Paulinus and then, in AD 42, Hosidius Geta.[28] The two would have not only to suppress the hostile Moors, but also to learn more about a region still imperfectly known.

The tasks were real enough, but back in the Rome of Claudius they could take on a greater, almost spiritual meaning, as Paulinus' own account of his governorship showed. Known only through Pliny, who consulted it firsthand, it might have been published under Claudius, but even if not, likely overlapped with dispatches Paulinus sent the Senate already in AD 41.[29] Insomuch as one can judge from Pliny, the commander dwelt on

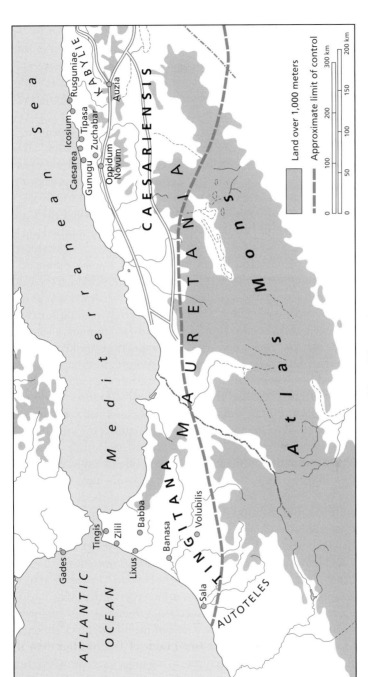

Map 2 Mauretania

his experience in crossing the imposing Atlas range. As one of the edges
of the known world, this, as seen, was a subject of myth and legend,
and Herodotus' description, in particular, echoed through the ages: "It is
narrow and a complete circle, and it is said to be so high that the peaks are
not able to be seen, because in summer and winter the clouds never leave
it. This, the natives say, is the Pillar of the Sky."[30]

"Suetonius Paulinus," Pliny tells us, explicitly echoing his source, "was
the first of the Roman commanders to cross the Atlas range and advance
some miles beyond it."[31] He gave some details very different from the
tradition: not of year-long clouds, but deep snow drifts conspicuous even
in summer on its peaks, a ten-day march to the river Ger, the black dust
deserts in between, and a previously unknown people called the Canarii.
Once again, the opening up of new Roman territory opened up new
geographic knowledge also: as territory becomes Roman, it becomes less
strange, a list of peoples and places, separated by known distances. But
not all the ethnographer's flourishes are gone: Paulinus claimed the Canarii
shared the diet of dogs (hence their name) and he described forests of
remarkably tall trees, with glossy timber, oppressively scented leaves, and,
on the leaves, a thin downy floss that could be spun into something
like silk. Its practical value aside, Paulinus' expedition spoke to the order
Romans imagined themselves imposing on the world. It certainly impressed
Claudius: Paulinus was rewarded with a consulship soon afterwards.[32]

The glory of conquest was duly emphasized. Claudius accepted triumphal decorations for the initial success in Mauretania, and through the
rest of his principate eagerly racked up acclamations for victories across
the world and boasted more than once of expanding Rome's empire.[33] He
liked to dwell primarily on Britain. Military exploits, especially one only
previously attempted by Julius Caesar, could magnify him, and thereby (it
might have been hoped) forefend criticism. Yet it was the Roman tradition
not just to fight, but to impose order, and Augustus, in particular, along
with his poets, had made much of the peace he brought, or promised to
bring, across the world.[34] Peace, they knew, is sometimes harder to achieve
than war, and imposing order the harder part of an annexation.[35] It required
thinking that overlapped with, but also went beyond, the sort seen in Pliny
and Pomponius Mela. Cataloguing was only a part of the task.

In Mauretania, Paulinus and his successors, much as they might vaunt
of the crossing of Atlas, had to face a nest of problems, beyond the struggle with local tribes. The peoples and places of the territory had to be
enumerated, to be sure. Like the empire as a whole, a new province fundamentally was a collection of peoples and places, each of which would have a

precise status and corresponding fiscal responsibility.[36] Provinces were not, in Roman thinking, vast open spaces to be dominated in their entirety. It was organized communities that could pay taxes which counted. Yet along with that went another consideration: these communities had to be protected. If a territory were to be taken over, Romans had to be able to move armies through it. Often, existing communication networks could be reinforced, but a frequent feature of Roman annexations was construction of new roads, used for military purposes – but also a dramatic symbol of Roman authority imposed on the landscape.[37] To ensure the peace, strong local allies needed to be identified, and awards granted to them. And an overall administrative structure had to be set.

It was all especially challenging in Mauretania because the kingdom comprised two distinct parts, connected by water rather than land, and even then only tenuously. In the west, a region anchored by Tingis (modern Tangier, at the Strait of Gibraltar) was cordoned off by the Atlas and Rif mountains and was generally reached from southern Spain; in the east, a second region, centered on Juba's old capital at Caesarea, was typically reached from further east.[38] Claudius' solution, ultimately, was to create two separate provinces, Mauretania Tingitana and Caesariensis, each administered by an equestrian procurator he appointed. Further, he established new military colonies in strategic locations (Lixus, for instance), reinforced several of Augustus' earlier colonies (including Tingis), and elevated the status of several native communities to the rank of *municipium*.[39] Among these last was Volubilis, which, nestled in the foothills of the Atlas, marked one vertex of the triangle of land the Romans intended to hold in Tingitana. (The triangle's other two vertices were Tingis and Sala, and it is no coincidence that the great cities of later Moroccan history are situated at roughly the same three points of this triangle: Tangier, Rabat, and – near Volubilis – Fez.) Volubilis had suffered in the war after Ptolemy's death, and its leading man, Valerius Severus, the son of Bostar, had commanded auxiliary troops on the Roman side.[40] Traveling to Rome to meet with Claudius, Severus also secured citizenship for his men, the right to contract a legal marriage with a local woman, and immunity from taxes for ten years. In all this, Claudius showed himself to be very much the successor of Augustus, who himself founded a dozen or so colonies in the Mauretanias and also colonies elsewhere in the empire, to help pacify unstable regions.[41]

Full pacification would not, as it happened, be achieved in Mauretania, just as it could not in other areas of the empire, especially those contiguous with mountains. Still, Claudius' effort is significant. After forty years, the

Augustan scheme of creating colonies and awarding citizenship to crucial allies was being revived. That the revival should be credited to Claudius and his advisors in Rome, and not merely his men on the spot, crucial as their input must have been, is clear, not only from Severus' trip to the City, but because there were similar developments elsewhere in the empire around the same time. To leave aside Britain, early in his reign, the emperor would annex, in addition to Mauretania, Lycia, Thrace, and Judea as new provinces. At first sight, it may seem that Claudius was, high-handedly, grabbing whatever he could, eager to burnish his reputation.[42]

Clearly, with Britain, the quest for glory was a motive, but an examination of his other acquisitions will reveal a different pattern. Much as Romans might like to imagine the outermost edges of the world coming under their sway, this was not an emperor bent on expansion, or annexation, at all costs. There were limits, and a rational strategy overall, if not the Grand Strategy of modern policymakers. Claudius did not recklessly fight wars of conquest against other neighbors of the empire, in Germany, Dacia, or Parthia, as some of his successors would. He also was, in principle, ready to rely on friendly kings such as Agrippa to rule regions on the edges of the empire. After all, at the start of his principate, he ceded some of Rome's territories to Agrippa, while also confirming an array of other rulers appointed by Caligula (Caligula had favored the use of these so-called client rulers more than Tiberius).[43] But when he judged the security of the empire and her citizens to be threatened, he was willing to annex directly, and he also favored, in these regions, creation of new colonies and building of roads, and appointment of administrators directly answerable to him.

His vigilance might have owed something to the circumstances of his unexpected accession. In that first year, the last thing he needed was riots or rebellions to put down – riots or rebellions might require redeploying other legions, which could open the way for potentially greater threats. As he said to the Alexandrians, "And I tell you once and for all, that unless you stop this disastrous and stubborn anger against each other, I shall be compelled to show what a benevolent Leader can be when moved to justifiable anger."[44] Yet in the annexations of Lycia, Thrace, and Judea, Claudius showed a tenacity that seems to transcend the dictates of political necessity alone. As his principate took shape, he could start to show his own priorities, and an attention to security was one of them. He was no longer indulging in scholarly flights of fancy or merely putting on a good show, but thinking about the empire strategically as well. From the point of view of Rome – and that is the view dominant in the available evidence, analyzed here – his measures were acceptable, welcome, and largely of lasting value. Only his decisions regarding Judea were, despite his best intentions, to provoke criticism – and ultimately, for the Jewish people, a great tragedy – but largely after his own rule ended.

A mountainous region of modern southwest Turkey, whose difficult terrain physically isolated its communities, yet also inspired them to come together in a federated League that was long recognized by the Romans, Lycia has in modern times been difficult of access too. Only in the last few decades has there been a rich harvest of inscriptions that cast much new light on the region. Especially remarkable are two lengthy texts from the otherwise unremarkable town of Oenoanda, one concerning the creation of an artistic festival by a local citizen in AD 125, the other the literary work of a local Epicurean philosopher.[45] Cultural pursuits, it has been suggested, relieved the tedium of life in these secluded towns, which took greatest pride in being the homeland of the Homeric heroes Sarpedon and Glaucus.[46] A later Roman governor, Licinius Mucianus, when putting together a book of marvels encountered on his travels through the east, mentioned that he could read in a temple a letter of Sarpedon written from Troy – on paper![47] (Mucianus, who during the principate of Claudius had retreated to Asia after a quarrel with the emperor, certainly had an indulgent side to him; he is known to have admired the oysters of Cyzicus on the Propontis and the wine of Maroneia, in Thrace, "which was black in color, with a strong bouquet, and enriched by age."[48]) Other Lycian curiosities were regularly shown to visitors. Mucianus himself also described an extraordinary plane-tree with a hollow cavity measuring 81 feet across in which he could dine with eighteen members of his retinue. Its branches were as big as trees, its shadows covered a field; one tree seemed to be like a whole grotto, he said.[49] And there were to be seen, according to Pliny the Elder (perhaps drawing on Mucianus), a statue that consumed human flesh, both living and dead, and fish in a spring of Apollo at Myra that gave oracular responses when summoned by a pipe.[50]

For such marvels the province's first governor, Q. Veranius, likely had less time. A stiff and proud Italian, whose family had like so many others come to prominence under Augustus and steadily risen through its loyal service to the August House, he made a name for himself as a military man: his connection to literature is a manual on generalship dedicated to him by the Greek writer Onasander.[51] Veranius' identity as first governor was only revealed by the identification of a large, though fragmentary, inscribed marble slab in Rome as his epitaph.[52] But now from Lycia an extraordinary

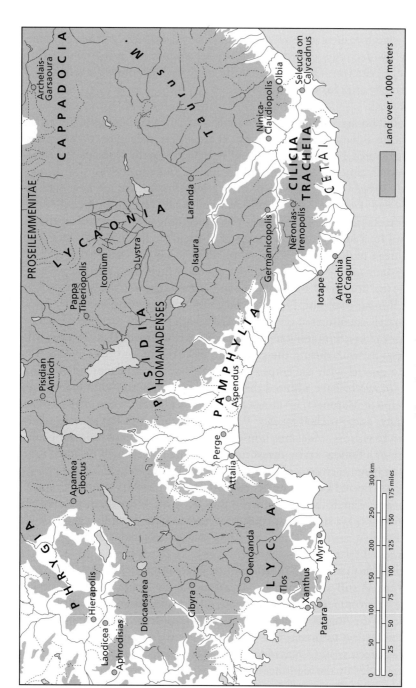

Map 3 Lycia and environs

Land over 1,000 meters

set of monuments has been recovered documenting his governorship, and allowing the annexation of the province to be understood in far more detail; these include:

(1) statue bases for Veranius and other members of his family;

(2) a stele with a decree of Veranius, in which he announces that Tryphon, a public slave of the city of Tlos, has been flogged for accepting into the city archives documents that did not meet Veranius' exacting standards;

(3) pieces of what was originally a square pillar, erected in the city of Patara overlooking the ancient harbor; the monument stood over five meters tall, and perhaps supported an equestrian statue of Claudius; it bore an inscription in honor of the emperor along with a list of roads built in Lycia under Veranius' supervision with the distances between pairs of cities on them; and

(4) an honorific altar, quite tall, from one such road, commemorating Claudius, as it says, "out of thanks for the peace and the building of roads."[53]

One can suppose that there were other altars like this on the other roads. Statue bases also survive for Claudius and his family that went up, at least one with Veranius' explicit support, and the dedicatory inscriptions of a temple to the August Gods, again with Veranius' support.[54]

Literary sources, while silent on Veranius' activities, do mention the background of the annexation.[55] Violent civil unrest, we are told, broke out, Roman citizens were killed, and Claudius proceeded (probably in AD 42) to hold an investigation before the Senate, at which representatives of the League which ruled Lycia were held to account. When one of the Lycian envoys failed to understand a question put to him in Latin, he lost his Roman citizenship. After the inquiry, a decree was likely passed, subsequently ratified by the People, adding the territory to the provinces for which Claudius was responsible. Some scholars had thought the civil unrest to be an empty pretext, but it is now evident that the Lycians, at least officially, recognized this version of events.[56] On the great monument from Patara they celebrate their concord, and remark that they are "freed from faction, lawlessness, and brigandage."[57]

When the inquiry was completed, Veranius was sent out as Claudius' legate to oversee the annexation. He was to govern Lycia for five years, attaching it to the territory of neighboring Pamphylia, which he also would rule. Re-establishment of peace was the first task, which meant not only restoring harmony among the Lycians themselves and disposing them to Roman rule, but also suppressing the banditry that had (as was so typical) cropped up during the unrest. Veranius tried to retain local institutions as much as possible: the old League would stay in place and still mint its beautiful silver coinage, though the coins now honored the emperor.[58] Nonetheless, a charter for the province had to be set (dealing with fiscal arrangements, for instance) and a new council was created, similar to those other provinces had, to communicate with Rome. The monument from Patara celebrates the new councilors, apparently chosen by Veranius himself. The councilors also separately dedicated a statue of Claudius, "the most present savior god" for his "divine foresight."[59] The decree issued by Veranius on the slave Tryphon of Tlos further reveals the marriage of old and new: while the old city archive was still functioning, the records containing "interpolations and erasures" were not to be tolerated by a Roman, for whom legal documents had to be kept pristine. The text also strikingly shows the way the governor wished to represent himself to Rome's new subjects:

> Tryphon, public slave of the city of Tlos, has been taught neither by my edicts nor threats nor even by the punishment of slaves who have committed the same wrongs, that he must not admit (into the city archive) official documents which contain interpolations and erasures. I led him to understand my displeasure against people like him by having him flogged and with this demonstration I made it clear that if he again ignores my edict about public records, it will not be with a beating but by exacting the supreme penalty from him that I will make the rest of the public slaves forget their past neglect. As for Apollonius, son of Diopeithes, from Patara, who brought Tryphon to justice, let him receive from the city of Tlos, through the appointed treasurers, 300 drachmas; for that is the amount of reward I have set for those who have brought public slaves to justice.[60]

Punishments are threatened, but also rewards (funded by the Lycians themselves) dangled before the reader's eye.

Along with dispensing justice, survey and road-building were vital to Veranius' mission. The Pataran monument is especially revealing, for with its detailed enumeration of no fewer than fifty-two communities and the distances between them, it shows the diligence with which Veranius surveyed his new territory and built (or, one might guess, in some instances re-built) roads for it. It suggests too his cooperation with the new local leaders of Lycia in advertising the benefits of Roman rule to the local communities. Indeed, the Pataran monument, the altars on the roads, and the roads themselves together made a powerful and coordinated assertion of the new tranquility. Veranius' roads, it should be added, were not just in Lycia; he built a road out of Lycia to the important city of Cibyra in neighboring Asia, and a road entirely in Asia itself, from Cibyra to Laodicea.[61] A separate inscription from Cibyra also reveals that he presided over other construction there, "in accordance with the instructions of Claudius."[62]

The epitaph from Rome suggests that these were city walls.[63] Claudius likely issued these instructions in response to a visit he received from Philagrus, a leading citizen of Cibyra, who made at least four embassies altogether to the emperors over his lifetime.[64] Certainly, as a result of one of them, Claudius had removed a minor official from Cibyra who was requisitioning grain from the townspeople inequitably. Veranius himself perhaps saw to the dismissal, for Philagrus was certainly in touch with Veranius too. It was Veranius who ultimately gave him citizenship.

The activity in Cibyra points to a larger reality of provincial administration, namely that the man on the spot might deal with affairs technically not within the boundary of his province. This was all the truer during an annexation. It was important to link the newly annexed territory to the north. In fact, Veranius did not just intervene in Cibrya. It seems, to judge by his partially extant epitaph from Rome, that he fought a campaign against some of the Tracheote Cilicians, in territory next to his province but not yet subjected to Roman rule. This would have made good sense if, as seems likely, Veranius had already been entrusted with some troops from Syria (they had fought on other occasions in this region).[65] For Veranius, it was a splendid opportunity: he could boast of an exploit in mountain warfare, which would recommend him for a governorship of Britain years later.[66]

Examined in the light of all the epigraphic evidence, the annexation of Lycia becomes a much more substantial enterprise. There was an active program of road-building (or refurbishment) with the new altars alongside them, construction of public works in neighboring Cibyra, attention to the public archives, establishment of a new council and councilors, and campaigning in Cilicia. To be sure, it remains quite unclear what local populations actually felt about losing their long-held independence. One key aspect of the operation, the new fiscal arrangements, is largely shielded from our view: that would not be something to emphasize in the monuments. What is evident, though, is how thoroughly Claudius and his man Veranius undertook their task. And what is astonishing is the extensive use made of monuments – whether statues of Veranius or Claudius, or the column from Patara and the altars on the roads, or even the roads themselves – to bring together Rome and Lycia, to put a new imprint on the old landscape, and to establish a lasting rule.

Judea's annexation is known through entirely different evidence: the parallel histories of Josephus, *Jewish War* and *Jewish Antiquities*. Since the death of Herod the Great in 4 BC, Rome had struggled to find the best way to maintain peace in this part of the world, which was critical above all because of its proximity to the rival empire of the Parthians, with whom Romans clashed repeatedly, especially northwards, where the Tigris and Euphrates lead into Armenia.[67] While unrest in Judea might not itself directly threaten Rome, Romans could remember that to suppress the rebellion that did break out after Herod's death, the governor of Syria had to commit all of the troops at his disposal, and that left Rome exposed. By AD 6, Judea was put under direct Roman rule, but the prefects in charge, including most notoriously Pontius Pilate, had trouble maintaining stability. Roman annexations (as in Mauretania) frequently met with some resistance, but here the problems were exacerbated on the one hand by insensitivity on the part of the occupiers to Jewish religion, and on the other the antipathy to foreign occupiers that was so enshrined in Jewish tradition. Caligula's actions in AD 40 had only inflamed feelings further.[68]

By the time of Claudius' accession, several portions of Herod's old kingdom had in fact been restored to Agrippa by Caligula – who, as seen, favored the use of such client rulers – and Claudius gave him what was effectively the final and most important part, Judea itself, including Jerusalem with the all-important Temple.[69] The hope was that Agrippa, raised in Rome but Jewish, would be able to satisfy the Jewish people while staying loyal to Rome. To judge by Josephus' narratives, he apparently enjoyed some success in keeping the peace internally, satisfying his Jewish subjects and also winning over the gentiles of his kingdom.[70] But, from a Roman point of view, there were unsettling aspects of his administration. First, his plan to strengthen the walls of Jerusalem aroused the suspicions of the governor of Syria, Vibius Marsus, who immediately wrote to Claudius, and Claudius, "suspecting revolt," required Agrippa to stop – even from a distance, the emperor was able to show his usual vigilance. Then, too, there was the meeting Marsus stumbled upon in Tiberias in Galilee, at which Agrippa had assembled five of his fellow client kings, the rulers of Commagene, Emesa, Lesser Armenia, and Pontus, as well as his brother Herod.[71] This too, Josephus says, aroused Marsus' suspicions. Agrippa, it was known, was also undertaking marriage alliances with at least several of these men – his daughter Drusilla, for instance, was engaged to Epiphanes, son of the king of Commagene.[72] It would have been unthinkable for Agrippa to launch rebellion against Rome; the fear, rather, was that Agrippa and his fellow kings, growing more powerful in alliance, might somehow upset Rome's very tenuous peace with the Parthian Empire, a much greater threat. A wall in Jerusalem surely did not portend plans for rebellion on Agrippa's part either; but it could suggest brewing internal unrest in Judea.

It had not helped matters that some time after Claudius' accession, a group of young men in the old Phoenician city of Dora, now part of the Roman province of Syria, had brought a statue of Claudius and placed it in the local synagogue, leading Agrippa to complain to Petronius, Marsus' predecessor.[73] Josephus quotes an edict issued by Petronius on this occasion, which delivers a stinging rebuke to the gentile miscreants:

> Some of your number have had such mad audacity as to disobey the published edict of Claudius Caesar Augustus Germanicus on allowing the Jews to uphold their ancestral customs; and they have done the very reverse in preventing the Jews from having a synagogue by transferring into it a statue of Caesar; they are breaking the law not only in respect to the Jews but also in respect to the emperor, whose statue was better placed in his own shrine than in that of another.[74]

Given the prominent reference here to another document included by Josephus which was perhaps at least lightly edited, one may suspect that this too is not in fact a *verbatim* transcript; it may even be that the episode at Dora involved some sort of Jewish retaliation against the gentiles that Josephus, or his source (perhaps Philo), has suppressed.[75]

That could help account for the decision Claudius made, on the death of Agrippa probably in late AD 43, to take Judea back as a Roman province, even though Agrippa did have a teenage son who might have succeeded him.[76] The hope that Agrippa, or a Jewish king, could bring a peace satisfactory to Rome was, in the end, delusive. The old kingdom would now be ruled by procurators directly in the service of Claudius, the first of whom was Cuspius Fadus. Upon arrival, says Josephus, he immediately displayed his will to maintain order.[77] Jewish inhabitants of the city of Peraea, at war with their neighbors, were punished with the death of one of their leaders and the exile of two others. Fadus' decision to take the vestments of the High Priest into Roman custody revealed total lack of appreciation for Jewish feelings, but, in conjunction with the new governor of Syria, he allowed an embassy to travel to Rome to discuss the matter with Claudius. On the advice of Vitellius, Claudius sensibly ruled to restore the vestments, and entrusted some of the late Agrippa's religious authority to his brother, including the ability to appoint the High Priests of the Temple.[78]

Fadus' successor was Tiberius Julius Alexander, son of Philo's brother Alexander.[79] In addition to repaying favors he owed this prominent Alexandrian family, Claudius probably hoped that in Alexander he would find an administrator with deeper understanding of Judaism.[80] The decision was a typical Roman blunder in this area: as an apostate, Alexander actually only stirred up even greater hostility. So the way to the Great Rebellion of the Jews that was to break out in AD 66 was being paved. Claudius tried to bring stability to the regions with his procurators. He also established a new veteran colony at Ptolemais (the main point of entry into Judea from the north) and probably began a road that would run from it to the major Syrian city of Antioch.[81] Yet despite all his efforts, as later events would show, the restoration of Judea to a Jewish king followed so soon afterwards by its sudden return to direct Roman rule ultimately proved a poor decision. It raised hopes, only to dash them.

Finally, we come to Thrace, the least understood of the annexations because it is barely documented.[82] The few scraps of evidence seem to point to the now familiar pattern. A vast area, bounded by the Danube, the Black Sea, the Sea of Marmara, the Aegean, and, to the west, the pass of Succi in the Rhodope mountains – and now comprising modern Bulgaria and parts of Romania, Turkey, and Greece – the kingdom of Thrace was critical to Rome above all because the main land route from Italy to the east, going from Aquileia to Emona (modern Ljubljana), from Emona down the Save past Sirmium and beyond Naissus, and from there by way of Serdica (modern Sofia) to Byzantium, passed through it. Also, on its stability the security of the Roman province of Macedonia in particular depended; it offered vast reserves of manpower and material resources on which the Romans relied; and goods from further afield entering the empire here were subject to lucrative customs. The country of the Moesi, on the Lower Danube, had been taken over by Augustus and joined with Macedonia, while the rest of Thrace stayed in the hand of client kings who, unfortunately, had a tendency to intrigue against each other matched only by the house of Herod in Judea.[83] Their dominance was far from perfect: Tacitus gives a fearful description of an uprising in AD 26 put down only with some difficulty by Poppaeus Sabinus, who governed Moesia for the extraordinary span of twenty-four years.[84]

On his accession, Claudius had confirmed Caligula's appointee to the throne, King Rhoemetalces, who had been raised in Rome along with two brothers who, sensibly, were assigned to other territories (Pontus and Lesser Armenia).[85] But in AD 44, Claudius did break up the unified Balkan command formed by Tiberius, encompassing Greece, Macedonia, and Moesia: Greece and Macedonia would be governed by Senate appointees, while Moesia would have a consular legate appointed directly by Claudius.[86] The intention, apparently, was to focus energy on shoring up defenses along the Danube, which was perceived to be a significant boundary, across which

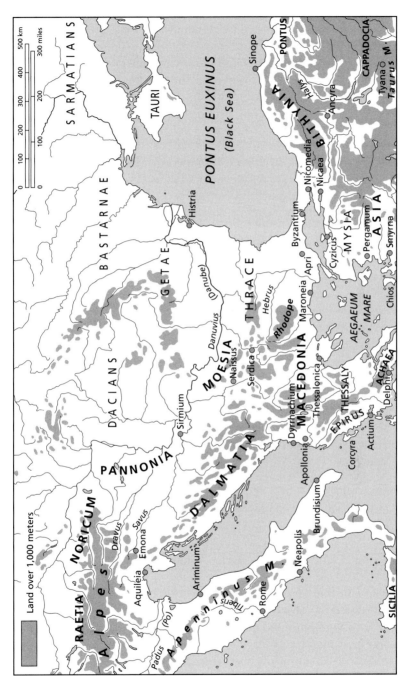

Map 4 Thrace and environs

Dacians and Sarmatians threatened. Around this time, a full legion was transferred from Pannonia.[87] And, according to several exceptionally brief sources, it was also just around this time – and perhaps closely related to this development – that unrest broke out in Thrace, after King Rhoemetalces fell dead at the hands of his wife.[88]

Whether a cause of Claudius' rearrangement of the Balkan command, or a consequence, such bloodbaths could not be allowed to continue; they threatened to destabilize the whole region. The capable Didius Gallus, from a family of eastern Italy that also rose up under Augustus, had been given the Moesian command and, to restore order in Thrace, he had to fight a fairly substantial campaign, apparently involving two of his legions.[89] Annexation ensued. Once again, a procurator directly answerable to Claudius would govern the province. The old Thracian system of administration by districts was retained, while coastal cities (including, probably, Maroneia) fought to retain their privileges; the Greek cities along the Thracian coast of the Black Sea, where the poet Ovid had spent his exile, were joined to Moesia, and an inscription shows how one of them, Histria, struggled as new taxes were imposed.[90] Meanwhile, following the annexation, a colony was created at Apri and there was road-building, with construction of military highways with resting-posts leading through the Haemus mountains to the legionary bases in Moesia.[91]

Developments set in motion by Claudius would prove to be of lasting significance. After the proclamation of Vespasian in July of AD 69 in Judea, the new emperor's indispensable ally Licinius Mucianus – the same man who authored *Mirabilia*, but now showing his far less indulgent side – was able to march 18,000 troops overland from Syria to Italy, reaching his goal before year's end.[92] En route, he peeled off one legion to suppress an incursion of the Dacians, brought on by the earlier departure of the Danubian legions for Italy. That Mucianus was able to achieve what he did – admittedly in a civil war – owed a great deal to the tightening of Rome's grip on Thrace, through the building of roads.[93]

As emperor, Claudius had to make a whole set of decisions concerning the borderlands of his realm. Romans tended to think of their empire as having specific boundaries, beyond which a less civilized world lurked; yet an ideal existed too of moving those boundaries forward, adding peoples and places to the empire and making the whole world known and at peace. Claudius most significantly tried to show his respect for this old ideal with his invasion of Britain, while Suetonius Paulinus promoted his campaign in Mauretania as a similar enterprise.

Yet as the planning for the British war showed, an emperor had to think carefully, even strategically it is fair to say, about allocating his limited resources: any re-deployment in one area had to be considered in relation to the rest. It would have been precipitous to change everything at once. For Claudius, the top priority quickly came to be Britain – and this shaped his strategy for the empire's boundaries as a whole. Where possible, he maintained client rulers in favor of direct annexation. It was only the specific situations of Lycia, Judea, and Thrace that led him to place these regions in the hands of his own legates or procurators, not some mad scheme of grabbing whatever he could. He was aiming to maintain tranquility, for the empire and its citizens in particular. In doing so, he revived the old Augustan scheme of establishing citizen colonies in provincial territories and awarding local allies with citizenship. A consistent policy can be discerned here, it is also fair to say, even in spite of sometimes wretched documentation. And, it can be added, he left a lasting imprint, for good and also for ill, on the territories he dealt with, including most obviously Britain, but also Mauretania, Lycia, Judea, and Thrace. Development of the lower Danube, in particular, was to prove of great importance for the rest of imperial Roman history. It is true, circumstances beyond Claudius' control forced him to make decisions he might otherwise have not, but that does not render him the "essentially passive" figure the Roman emperor is said to have been. Rather, at least in this area, the emperor was a figure both of action and reaction.

CHAPTER 6

Caesar-lovers

What did a new emperor mean for his subjects in the provinces? Was he for them a "passive" figure? Is this how they viewed him? Writing of the accession of Caligula in AD 37, Philo claims that not just Rome and Italy, but people of Asia and Europe rejoiced:

> For they all were thrilled with him as they had been with none of the emperors coming before, not because they were hoping to obtain and enjoy benefits as individuals and communities, but because they believed that they now possessed a complete measure of good fortune, with happiness attending it. At any rate, there was nothing to be seen throughout the cities but altars, victims, sacrifices, people in white clothes, garlanded and cheerful, showing their goodwill by their joyous faces, banquets, festivals, musical competitions, horse-races, revels, night-celebrations to the music of flutes and the lyre, enjoyment, recreation, holidays, and every kind of pleasure appealing to every sense.[1]

It is an exuberant picture, of people celebrating even before they had confirmed their privileges by embassies or correspondence. But one immediately asks: how much of it is true? Is this just a rhetorical counterpart to the attack on Caligula that will follow? The language here is not dissimilar to that found in a decree issued by the city of Assos, in Asia Minor, celebrating Caligula's accession.[2] And yet, even if the account is rhetorical, the language formulaic, one still might wonder: why in his imagination should Philo place the emphasis on *public* celebrations?

To test Philo and see what an emperor actually did mean to his subjects, unique evidence is available for two parts of the empire's fringe, Egypt and Judea (the latter after its re-annexation in AD 44). For Egypt it is papyri preserved in the country's dry sands and for Judea the detailed histories of Josephus as well as the books of the New Testament. Examination of these will reveal that the emperor typically did not take much direct initiative in the day-to-day government of a province; the emperor did not even intervene in a time of famine perceived to be worldwide. Given his limited resources, and the distances involved, this is not at all surprising. Officials

126

would receive general directions before setting out from Rome, but then were to a large degree on their own – and there were not that many of them to go around. Lack of conspicuous involvement also shielded the emperor from disgruntlement with Roman rule on the part of provincials. To local administrators were directed complaints, and also therefore a good deal of the hostility.

The limitations of his involvement would, at first glance, seem to point to a highly passive role for the emperor.[3] And a corollary would be that the accession of a new emperor such as Claudius, at least structurally, should matter little: the emperor's role with most of his distant subjects was still bound to be a matter of reaction more than anything else. Taxes still were due, whoever was in charge in Rome. Yet the paradox is that precisely because of his lack of regular, direct involvement, the emperor himself had the opportunity to intervene directly in sometimes detailed matters, and when he did so even his "reactions" seemed all the more powerful. He might provide relief after an earthquake, for instance, or pronounce judgment in a dispute between individuals or communities. He could free a city of its tax obligations, or endow it with walls or a building, or ban a religious practice.[4] The emperor was distant but could suddenly seem present and potent, exactly like a god – "manifest" (*epiphanes*) as Greek inscriptions sometimes put it.[5] Further, even if he did intervene little, as the head of the Roman world he could be credited with the peace that had basically, for the first (and only) time in history fallen across the Mediterranean, from Spain to Syria. Under the emperors, and sometimes with their direct help, cities developed, roads were built, citizenship spread. Peace with prosperity, there was no arguing, was a mighty achievement.

All this helps to explain a practice still very much developing under Claudius, the worship of emperors as gods or the honoring of them with godlike honors. It had begun with Augustus, but just as the emperors' role was being institutionalized at Rome, provincials too were institutionalizing their cults in recognition of the fact that emperors were acquiring an authority based more on a heritable position than personal accomplishments. Cult was a way to understand, and articulate, the power of a new emperor such as Claudius.[6] And once one takes cult into view – Philo's victims, sacrifices, and people in white clothes – the emperor suddenly seems much more visible in the lives of his subjects. The cult helps to explain how he held onto the power that he did have.

To turn first to Judea after its re-annexation by Claudius: Josephus' narrative, especially in *Jewish Antiquities*, reveals a clear and consistent pattern in how administration of the province worked.[7] Judea was ruled on a day-to-day basis by a procurator, appointed by the emperor, who typically resided (with most of his soldiers) at the old palace of Herod in Caesarea on the coast. A permanent garrison of one cohort was also maintained in Jerusalem, in the fortress Antonia overlooking the Temple court, scene of frequent unrest. The procurator's paramount task was to maintain order, using military force and dispensing justice as needed; he also helped to oversee collection of taxes. Normally he handled the major problems that came up, as in the following episodes, all recounted by Josephus:

(1) when one Theudas, a self-styled prophet, gathered a crowd of follow-
    ers and began marching down to the Jordan River, asserting that at his
    command the waters would part, Cuspius Fadus, Claudius' first procu-
    rator, broke up the group with a squadron of cavalry, and Theudas was
    beheaded; although Josephus does not state this, Fadus' fear, perhaps
    justified, would have been that Theudas was, in the aftermath of re-
    annexation, spearheading rebellion against Rome;[8]
(2) under Fadus' successor, Alexander, the sons of Judas the Galilean (who
    had earlier tried to stir up rebellion against Rome) were put on trial,
    condemned, and crucified: Josephus again omits the alleged crime but
    it is not hard to guess;[9]
(3) later still, under Ventidius Cumanus, during celebration of the Passover
    a Roman soldier on guard duty on the outskirts of the Temple exposed
    himself; Cumanus was criticized for his handling of the situation, and
    in response called in further forces who routed the crowd of worshipers,
    leading (Josephus claims) to 20,000 deaths (or more) in a stampede;[10]
(4) and finally, when an imperial slave named Stephanus was killed on
    the road from Jersualem, Cumanus ordered soldiers to plunder the
    neighboring villages and bring their leading men to him in chains; one
    of the soldiers, having found a copy of the Torah during the looting,
    tore it up in full public view; a delegation of Jews went to Cumanus to
    complain, who punished the perpetrator with death.[11]

In all these episodes, it was clearly the procurator who was in charge.

Occasionally, much more unusually, matters reached a higher level of authority according to Josephus. In the earlier period of direct Roman rule of Judea initiated by Augustus, the vestments of the High Priest, once entrusted to the king, had been taken into custody by Roman officials. This unpopular decision was reversed in AD 36 by Lucius Vitellius, then serving as governor of Syria, who turned the vestments over to the Temple priests.[12] Upon his arrival, Fadus ordered them to be taken into custody again.[13] The Jewish leaders, presumably thinking back to Vitellius' decision, went to Fadus and also Longinus, the governor of Syria who had come to Jerusalem, to ask them to reconsider the decision, or at least to allow an appeal to Claudius on the matter. An embassy to Rome was authorized. Claudius was favorable to their request, and issued a letter in response, which Josephus quotes. In it the emperor acknowledged the precedent of Vitellius, "that excellent man whom I hold in the highest esteem."[14] He also noted that he was writing separately to Cuspius Fadus.

A few years later, some Galilean Jews, passing through Samaria on their way to a festival in Jerusalem, were murdered in a Samaritan village.[15] The Galilean leaders beseeched Ventidius Cumanus to punish the perpetrators of the crime, but he refused, having been bribed by the Samaritans (according to Josephus in *Antiquities*). The Jews then took matters into their own hands, forming an armed band and massacring inhabitants of the Samaritan villages; Cumanus struck back at them. Meanwhile, Samaritan envoys had gone to Ummidius Quadratus, governor of Syria, to accuse the Jews of robbery and of showing contempt to the Romans, while a Jewish delegation also appeared to accuse the Samaritans – and Cumanus. Quadratus then carried out a strict investigation in Samaria. Ringleaders of both sides were sent to Rome along with Cumanus, and Claudius there decided that the Samaritan leaders should be executed and Cumanus removed from office, to be replaced by Felix, brother of Claudius' powerful freedman, Pallas. In Josephus' elaborate account, the imperial freedmen, friends of Claudius, his wife Agrippina, and young Agrippa II all tried to influence the emperor before he held the hearing and issued his ruling.

Insomuch as it was Quadratus who referred this whole matter to Claudius, one can see why the emperor might be viewed as essentially passive; but the story of Claudius' hearing is also remarkable for showing just how involved an emperor, far away in Rome, could choose to become in provincial affairs. Or at least, it shows that it was quite possible to *envision* Claudius as becoming closely involved in these affairs. Josephus' narrative as a whole, while it may in its effort to paint the Jews in the best light be guilty of some distortions, helps to define the emperor's power. If one defines this power as the possession of full control over the daily lives of his subjects, then obviously the emperor's power was practically non-existent. But power can also be significant when it is viewed merely as the *ability* to act or produce an effect; that can be enough to coerce. Claudius, like Caligula before him, most certainly had this ability to intervene in the lives of his subjects – the episode with the colossus in the Temple spectacularly showed that – and did on occasion determine their fates. To say otherwise would be to deny the experience of Roman rule Judea knew under Claudius and beyond. The procurators mattered, the governor of Syria mattered, but so did the emperor (who also, after all, picked them).

Some confirmation for Josephus' conception of the layering of Roman power is supplied by the contemporaneous Acts of the Apostles, above all in its culminating episode.[16] Upon Paul's return to Jerusalem after his last missionary journey, he entered the Temple, according to Acts, with other Jews, all purified.[17] But, in a pattern familiar to the reader of the narrative, Paul's opponents decided to cause trouble for him, and claimed he had brought Greeks into the Temple and violated the law. A crowd gathered, Paul was dragged out of the Temple, and word of the disturbance reached the tribune of the cohort on duty, who with his soldiers detained Paul and took him to the Antonia fortress; he subsequently ordered Paul examined by flogging. Then, in a stunning moment, and the turning-point for the rest of the narrative, Paul says to a centurion standing by: "Is it legal for you to flog a Roman citizen who is not condemned?"[18] The centurion goes to the tribune, and the tribune, after questioning Paul, and being told that Paul was in fact a citizen, simply responds, "It cost me a large sum of money to get my citizenship."[19] Here is a hint of venality – and an acknowledgment of the value of Roman citizenship in the provinces. Citizenship, this exchange between soldier and accused shows, brought rights a provincial did not have.

After making his revelation, Acts continues, Paul was released and brought to a hearing before the chief priests and council of Jerusalem. Centering as it did on Paul's alleged admission of foreigners into the inner court of the Temple, this should have been a matter for them to settle.[20] But, after passions flared up at the hearing, the tribune on duty, growing fearful for the citizen's life, took Paul back into custody at the barracks, where, that same night, the Lord appeared to Paul in a vision and commanded him to "bear witness also in Rome."[21] The narrative is moving inexorably to the distant, but powerful, center. Paul was then moved to Caesarea, where he was to be given a hearing by the procurator Felix, called simply the "governor"; and with Paul was sent a letter, written by the tribune, whose name is slyly revealed to be Claudius Lysias, suggesting that the citizenship he bought came from the emperor or (perhaps more likely) one of his agents.[22] Felix duly held the hearing, but ultimately left the matter unresolved in the hope of a bribe from Paul – another hint of venality. The successor of Felix under Nero, Porcius Festus, upon taking office immediately looked into the matter after being contacted by the Jewish enemies of Paul and convened a hearing at which the Jews could not prove their charges. "Wishing to do the Jews a favor," Festus then asked if Paul wished to be tried in Jerusalem: the implication is that he should have dismissed the case, protecting Paul's rights as a citizen.[23] Because he did not, Paul famously exercised his right of appeal to the tribunal of the emperor.

"You have appealed to the emperor: to the emperor you will go."[24] Paul can appeal in the narrative of Acts because he is a Roman citizen. The episode hardly shows, as is sometimes said, that an unimportant provincial could be presumed to enjoy the ability to exercise the right.[25] It is a key part of the literary drama of Acts to have Paul's struggle – and, by implication, the question of Christianity's legality – go up the layers of authority, from the centurion on duty in the Temple in Jerusalem, to the procurator in Caesarea, to the emperor in Rome. For this to happen, Paul had to be a citizen – otherwise he would be sure to suffer the same fate as Christ. Throughout Acts, Paul has been vindicated by other prominent Roman officials, notably Sergius Paulus, proconsul of Crete and Cyprus (who probably supplied the historical Paul with his Roman name), and Seneca's brother Junius Gallio, proconsul of Achaea.[26] Roman officials are not concerned with any threat posed by Christianity – even if subordinate figures are not always cast in the best light. Acts shows the emperor as unimportant in day-to-day life in the eastern empire, but then, suddenly, supremely significant at the end because of his *ability* to intervene in a very specific matter. If that power had not existed for him, or at least were not perceived to exist, the text would lose its force. Notoriously, though, Acts ends with Paul in Rome awaiting trial, with no final judgment given (by Nero). Paul's fate – and the future of Christianity – is to be left up in the air. The unresolved ending, whatever its explanation, almost seems to underscore the emperor's ultimate power – or to try to suggest that there may be a more important power yet.

The emperor's normal lack of involvement in provincial affairs, the crucial backdrop for the ending of Acts, is highlighted by an earlier episode in the text. At a meeting of Christian leaders in Antioch, in Syria, prophets from Jerusalem arrived, and "one of them named Agabus stood up and predicted by the Spirit that there would be a severe famine over all the world."[27] The narrator immediately adds a confirmatory "and this took place under the reign of Claudius," but leaves the gap in time between the prophecy and the famine unspecified. What is clear is the immediate response: "The disciples determined that according to their ability, each would send relief to the believers living in Judea."[28] That is, a sort of relief fund was created. While there are (at a minimum) chronological problems with the episode as presented, through it the author of Acts points to two real issues. First, there was a terrible shortage of food in Judea under Claudius, memories of which must have been all too real.[29] And second, neither emperor nor even the local Roman authorities did anything to deal with it. That was beyond the perceived responsibilities of the Roman government, at least in this period for this place.

The famine is known because Josephus mentions it during his narrative for the reign of Claudius, in the midst of his long digression on the ruling house of Adiabene (a vassal kingdom of the Parthian empire) which decided to embrace Judaism.[30] Queen Helena, a convert, like her son Izates, went to Jerusalem to worship in the Temple, Josephus reports, and "her arrival was very beneficial for the people of Jerusalem, for at that time famine was pressing down on their city and many were perishing, from a lack of money." Helena sent some of her agents to Alexandria to buy grain (evidently available for large sums) and others to Cyprus to bring back a cargo of dried figs. Upon their return, the queen lost no time in distributing the provisions "among the needy." Izates, Josephus adds, also sent money. Helena's charity is significant because unlike (say) the distribution of food in the city of Rome, according to which only citizens received aid, the Queen's plan was tied to need.

Whatever the truth of Acts about the relief fund from Antioch – Josephus obviously says nothing of it – Paul's own authentic letters show that organizing a collection from Christian converts for the church in Jerusalem was a major concern of his later in life. In Romans he explains that he will visit the west and the church in Rome, but first must return to Judea, "for Macedonia and Achaea have been pleased to share their resources with the poor among the saints at Jerusalem."[31] So, as with Helena's relief, this was aid based on need. Paul may tell the Romans that the Macedonians and Achaeans gave gladly, but his letters to the Corinthians suggest there were some problems. There he explains how the collection was to operate: "You should follow the directions I gave the churches of Galatia. On the first day of every week, each of you is to put aside and save whatever you earn, so that collections need not be taken when I come. And when I arrive, you will send any whom you approve with letters to take your gift to Jerusalem."[32] But he also says, "each of you must give as you have made up your mind, not reluctantly or under compulsion."[33]

While Jews had been in the habit of sending tribute to the Temple, and Paul's collection clearly owes something to that practice, the sending of a contribution with envoys and a letter could also remind one of embassies to the emperor in Rome (offering, say, a gold crown). Paul's collection, like Helena's relief, is important for underscoring the qualified role of the emperor in provincial affairs. Relief funds for his distant subjects, even in a time of famine, presumably seemed beyond his means, or at least unimportant – whereas not feeding the city of Rome could mean rebellion at his front door. Yet Paul's collection raises another, deeper question. If the emperor did not have the resources to give alms, but another group did, what would be the consequences?

The only other evidence that can show with much detail what an emperor, and the layers of government below him, meant to a provincial population is papyri from Egypt. These largely confirm the pattern found in Josephus and Acts, although understandably there are differences. The papyri have a more specific connection with the Judean evidence, too, because famine occurred in Egypt at roughly the same time; though in Egypt it was due to a specific and localized cause, high Nile flooding, the coincidence may have led to the perception of worldwide famine alluded to in Acts.[34] For our period, Egypt, or at least Alexandria, is also exceptionally illustrated by Philo, who overlaps with Josephus in his depiction of the emperor's power.[35] But here we will turn away from Philo and Alexandria to two sets of documents from the time of Claudius that throw light on Roman administration outside the chief city.

To understand these, a sketch of the most basic features of the Roman government is first necessary.[36] Whereas Judea had a relatively simple system of rule under the procurator, in Egypt, with its exceptional ecology and economy, the Romans inherited from the Ptolemies (and modified) a scheme which itself had even earlier Pharaonic roots. After Augustus' annexation of the province, an equestrian prefect, appointed directly by the emperor, ruled Egypt from Alexandria, taking over the old administrative functions of the king (the symbolic functions, by contrast, were more typically filled by the emperor). The prefect relied on subordinate officials in Alexandria (who managed, for instance, the great old temples or the imperial estates), and he also appointed *epistrategoi* in charge of the three main divisions of Egypt. Those divisions were further subdivided into nomes (or counties), each with its own governor, a *strategos*, and his assistant "royal scribe," both local, rather than Roman, officials. Nomes were further subdivided into toparchies (each with a toparch), and toparchies into villages (each with its own leaders and also a secretary). Through the elaborate structure, the manifold taxes of the province – along with information on the taxpayers – passed from the individual villages all the way up to the prefect himself, who resided primarily in Alexandria but who also toured at least Lower Egypt periodically to hold legal hearings.

Our first set of documents is the personal papers of the Egyptian Tryphon, a weaver from the nome capital of Oxyrhynchus, born in AD 8/9.[37] Oxyrhynchus, a city of perhaps 20,000 located in Middle Egypt, took its name from Greek settlers in recognition of its sacred animal, the "sharp-nosed" fish that earlier Egyptian inhabitants worshiped.[38] In Roman times, weaving was an important business in this crowded city, perhaps even its economic mainstay. Weavers operated independent workshops, employing members of their own family or hired workers; a special tax was placed on them. According to a census declaration of around AD 12, Tryphon's 64-year-old grandfather at that time headed an extended household including three adult sons (one of them Tryphon's father), and all the adult men were weavers – as would be Tryphon, his brother, and ultimately Typhon's two sons.[39] By AD 36, Tryphon's father must have been dead, as Tryphon was functioning as his mother's guardian. She lived on until at least AD 44. In that year, Tryphon's brother deserted Oxyrhynchus, leaving unpaid taxes: the mother informed the authorities, to escape liability, swearing an oath in the name of Claudius that she was stating the truth.[40]

Tryphon himself was first married to Demetrous, who deserted him by AD 37 probably after only a few years of marriage.[41] On May 22 of that year, he made what was effectively a marriage contract with a new wife, Seraeus, a woman with whom he was already living "without a contract."[42] According to the agreement, Seraeus lent Tryphon forty gold drachmas in cash and thirty-two drachmas in valuables (including a pair of gold earrings): this was a sort of dowry which had to be returned if the pair separated. Seraeus was pregnant at the time; only six weeks later, Demetrous reappeared with her mother and attacked Seraeus, leading her to miscarry. Or so Tryphon complained to the *strategos* through a written petition that survives among Tryphon's papers.[43] Tryphon himself was illiterate, at least in Greek, the language of government in Egypt, but the petition shows that access to literacy was essential for a provincial to exercise even his most basic right of appeal to the local official. That, in turn, might have meant hiring, at some expense, a professional scribe.[44]

These were not the end of the family's troubles. Probably in 46, a son, Apion, was born to Tryphon and Seraeus. (The date is suggested by a horoscope found among Tryphon's papers.[45]) After weaning him, Seraeus undertook the nursing of another child, implying that the family was short of money. This second child was a foundling, abandoned by his mother, and taken up by one Pesouris to raise as a slave. Again among Tryphon's papers was found a copy of the minutes of a hearing held by Claudius

Pasion, *strategos* of Oxyrhynchus.[46] According to the document, Pesouris claimed that Seraeus' own child had died, and she was trying now to pass the foundling off as her own; Seraeus, for her part, insisted that the foundling had died, and that Pesouris was trying now to steal *her* child. Faced with this dispute, Claudius Pasion ruled: "Since from its appearance the child seems to be of Seraeus, if she and her husband will sign a sworn affidavit that the slave child entrusted to her by Pesouris has died, it seems to me appropriate, in accordance with the rulings of our lord prefect, that provided she pays back the money she received, she should have her own child." Pesouris, though, apparently refused to abide by Pasion's ruling, because another document survives in the dossier, a petition from Tryphon addressed to the prefect of Egypt himself, Vergilius Capito, reporting Pesouris' obstinacy and claiming that Tryphon was, in consequence, unable to complete his work.[47]

Capito's response, if any, remains unknown – no sign of one was found among Tryphon's papers – but it was not Tryphon's last brush with the authorities. A petition survives from around AD 50, again to the *strategos* Claudius Pasion, reporting a theft.[48] And not long afterwards Tryphon claimed that because of failing eyesight he should be released from tax obligations. To do this, he had to travel 250 miles to Alexandria for an examination and certification (in duplicate) that he was affected by cataracts.[49] According to Tryphon's certificate, Vergilius Capito himself authorized the exemption, signaling its value. From all the documents, one sees that the official who typically mattered when a prosperous city-dweller's affairs took a turn for the worse was a local official, the *strategos*; in exceptional circumstances, it was the prefect; never the emperor. Yet Claudius, and the other emperors, were not unknown to Tryphon: they appear in the documents to date them, Tryphon's mother swore an oath by Claudius, and, perhaps more significantly, days mentioned in the texts are regularly classified as "Augustal." After Claudius' death, a separate papyrus shows, preparations were made in Oxyrhynchus to celebrate Nero's accession by the wearing of wreaths and sacrifice of oxen.[50]

The second archive complements Tryphon's, for it comes from a much smaller Fayum village, Philadelphia, in the Arsinoite nome, and it contains the papers (well over a hundred) of an official, Nemesion, son of Zoilos, collector of taxes assessed on individuals in the village.[51] It was Nemesion who copied in his own hand the letter Claudius sent to the Alexandrians in AD 41, showing that he certainly took interest in the new emperor and his rulings.[52] To be sure, it was a ruling concerned with Alexandria. And in fact, the other papyri from Egypt that significantly document the emperors' doings are typically focused on matters of direct concern to Egypt – the record of an embassy from Alexandria to Augustus in Rome in AD 12/13, for instance, or the copy of two edicts issued by Tiberius' representative Germanicus during his visit to Alexandria in AD 19.[53] Such documents show that who the emperor was mattered, again because of occasional, though effective, intervention in provincial affairs.

Even for the official Nemesion, the unsurprising truth is that on a day-to-day level it was the lower levels of the administrative structure that mattered. The daybooks of the collections he made suggest that typically he and his subordinate made the rounds of their village household by household, with useful information derived from the census provided to them by the village scribes. Occasionally, they would travel to other villages in the neighborhood, to the nome capital, even to Alexandria and Nicopolis on the Mediterranean, to collect payments from villagers registered in Philadelphia but not living in the village. Nemesion, it has been suggested, worked hard to collect the moneys owed to Rome.[54] He employed armed guards as he made his rounds. He also cultivated connections with local authorities. A letter from Heracleides, the village scribe, to Nemesion, advises him to send vine-cuttings to the secretary of the *strategos* of the Arsinoite nome: the two were effectively trying to bribe a subordinate figure in the administration of the district.[55]

Only in a very serious situation did Nemesion look higher for real assistance. Following an excessive Nile inundation – mentioned even by Pliny the Elder – in later summer of AD 45, crops failed and agricultural output fell for several years subsequently, leading to severe distress throughout the countryside.[56] Debts started to pile up among poor villagers, the worst effects of which only set in several years later. Nemesion's accounts reveal a growing number in arrears, and a substantial dip in the number of taxpayers: some had fled the village, while others probably simply died of malnutrition. Despite the gravity of the disaster, the prefect, through his subordinates, apparently showed no mercy and demanded from Nemesion and his counterparts the past arrears. But the delinquent taxpayers simply were not to be found. Among Nemesion's papers is a petition that he and five other collectors of poll taxes from the Arsinoite nome wrote to Tiberius Claudius Balbillus, prefect of Egypt at the start of Nero's reign (though an earlier protégé of Claudius).[57] They report:

The once numerous inhabitants of the aforesaid villages have now declined to a few, because some have withdrawn through lack of means, while others have died without heirs; and because of this, there is danger that because of impoverishment we shall abandon the collectorship. Turning to you for these reasons, with a view not to abandoning the collectorship, we request you, the savior and benefactor of all, to write, if you think fit, to the *strategos* of the *nome*, Asianus, to keep us free from molestation and to await your decision at the assize of the upper division, so that we may receive your beneficence.

Nemesion and his colleagues' apparent solution to their problem was to threaten, to the prefect, that they would withdraw their services – rather as the villagers had withdrawn themselves from the tax rolls. Obviously their effort to influence their own *strategos* failed, and like Tryphon in his dispute with Pesouris, they exceptionally took the matter to the highest level of authority in the province, who is addressed in the petition in suitably awesome language, typical of that used for the emperor himself. Even as the economy of Egypt was unraveling after ecological disaster – as villagers died and ran away from debt, and officials threatened to resign – the emperor (now Nero) still apparently absented himself from direct involvement in the matter. Even a high-ranking provincial like Nemesion had no way, or reason, to reach him or Rome.

We might seem, despite the garlands and oxen for Nero's accession, to be far away from Philo's account of Caligula's accession. Now, after Josephus, Acts, and the papyri, the world seems much more insecure, even sordid in places: citizenship sold, justice thwarted, governors or their subordinates bribed. But all that, of course, can help to show once more that if an emperor did intervene, it was spectacular. It shows why fantasies could attach to him. Through the combination of his limited involvement but real power, the emperor could almost seem a god. There were few day-to-day complaints to bring to his attention, as there were to a procurator or *strategos*. He was beyond the reach of petty bribes. Yet, we must remember, Judea and Egypt, as valuable as their evidence is, were not entirely typical. In Judea Jews and their Roman rulers had a strained relationship because of a difficulty in understanding, or tolerating, one another's religions – and the overlapping jurisdiction of the procurator and legate of Syria was a further anomalous source of tension; in Egypt, the Romans inherited, preserved, and enforced an unusually elaborate system of taxation, created because of the extraordinary agricultural resources of the region; and villages did not have the same autonomy that cities elsewhere typically enjoyed. In other provinces, perhaps, complaints may have been fewer. To Rome and the emperors, it might even be said, was owed some sense of security across the Mediterranean.

Whether viewed as a force for good or for ill, or perhaps both, emperors were, throughout the empire, worshiped as gods, or at least given honors more typically reserved for gods. By the accession of Claudius the practice was more fully established in the east, where it had antecedents under the Hellenistic kings, and was flourishing in Greece and Asia Minor in particular. The evidence is abundant enough to allow developments to be traced.[58] Here only a brief survey of it, and only for the latter region, will be offered.[59] This is enough to illustrate, from a different perspective, what yet another group of provincials understood the role of their (new) emperor to be. At the same time, since cults for the ruler helped reinforce, even create, his power, we can also acknowledge here how they helped Claudius, and Rome, win loyalty from imperial subjects. With Claudius, cults were becoming institutionalized in a manner that mirrored the institutionalization of the principate itself.

Already in 29 BC the province of Asia as a whole established at Pergamum a Temple of Rome and Augustus, with a High Priest of Rome and Augustus who officiated at an annual festival there.[60] A second temple was created under Tiberius for that emperor, Livia, and the Senate; there was a long fight over which city could actually contain it, but Smyrna carried the day.[61] Under Caligula, plans were made for a temple honoring that emperor alone (without Rome or the Senate) at Miletus.[62] This apparent highhandedness on Caligula's part may help explain why there is no record for any temple being built for Claudius: it might have seemed prudent to him to decline any such offers. Yet it also appears that already by around AD 40, the title of the priests for the temples at both Pergamum and Smyrna had been switched to "High Priest of Asia."[63] Neither would remain a priest specifically of Augustus or Tiberius and Livia. The way was thus paved for each new emperor, including Claudius, to be honored along with predecessors. Hence, in AD 41, the hymnodists who had been established to celebrate Augustus were now to hymn the August House and perform sacrifice to the August Gods, and the provincial council applauded their effort, because they too thought it appropriate to show piety to the August House.[64] By downplaying priesthoods for individual emperors, and emphasizing instead the continuity, even eternity, of the August House with its August Gods, the province was refining its rituals in parallel with what was happening in Rome.

The same trend is visible in the manifold cults individual communities of Asia maintained for members of the imperial house. To be sure, on the island of Cos, just off the coast of Asia Minor, an inscription reveals a temple dedicated to Claudius.[65] But elsewhere stood temples for the "August Ones" (*Augusti*) or the like, which could incorporate each individual who bore that title, even other members of the imperial house.[66] A coin of

Hierapolis from the Claudian period shows a temple with the legend "to the family of the Augusti"; on the epistyle of a small temple from Sidyma, in Lycia, is the inscription "To the August Gods, saviors, under Quintus Veranius, propraetorian legate of Tiberius Claudius Caesar Augustus"; the great imperial complex in Aphrodisias, which saw a major building phase under Claudius, was dedicated to "Aphrodite, the August Gods, and the People."[67] Priests specifically for Claudius are attested, but also now of the August Gods.[68] And so too for festivals.[69]

If temples were starting to stand for the continuity of the August Gods, statues could more easily be set up for the new emperor to mark him as a god or godlike. From Arneae in Lycia a base has been found for Messallina, Britannicus, and Claudius "god manifest"; at Acmonia, in Phrygia, a base for Britannicus, "son of New Zeus Claudius Caesar Augustus."[70] Examples could be multiplied. Yet statue bases too reflect the trend of institutionalization. At Cys, in Caria, a statue for Claudius, "savior and benefactor of all mankind," was set up by Euphranes, priest of divine Augustus, whose many contributions to the town are celebrated: he sold goods below marked price during an emergency and he offered "sacrifices to the gods and to the Augusti for the endurance and health of their house for all eternity."[71] The inscription shows perfectly how a leading citizen, identifying the ruling power of Rome as the guarantors of peace and prosperity, made a physically distant Claudius a visible presence in the life of his community. Claudius might not have intervened directly in the affairs of Cys, but that he then could be honored in this way shows – and helped to create – his power. A similar conjunction is found in another, partially preserved, inscription from Aezani honoring a local whose townsmen, "having learned of my zeal for the August family and my service to the country in all things," honored him with a priesthood of the Augusti as well as August Providence.[72]

For a historian, such evidence can illustrate how the emperor's power was viewed, but it must be urged once more that these pieces of evidence are also themselves fragments of a wide range of cult activities that helped to create that power in the first place. Collectively, cult activities played an important role in uniting the emperor, and Rome, with their subjects. This would not have been lost on Claudius because, as with his statues, in matters of cult too he had to make decisions, especially after his accession. Indeed, the two, as was already seen, often went hand in hand. While some communities might have worshiped him without his knowledge, others, such as the island of Thasos, asked to build him a temple, which Claudius declined, he explained, "considering it to be right for the gods alone, though

I permit the other honors, which suit the best Leaders."[73] In that comment must lurk the notion that as the imperial office became established, each holder of it would be judged on whether he had handled divine honors appropriately. Caligula, in particular, might have set some bad precedents, consenting to a temple that honored himself alone in Miletus, for instance, and perhaps overzealously encouraging cult honors privately in the city of Rome.[74] To all, Claudius refused divine honors; in Rome, in particular, he would be adamant that there was no explicit sign of them in public. Divine honors could, from a Roman's perspective, be a mark of provincial standing.

Yet if cult was a useful way for provincials to express, even to make sense, of their relationship with the emperor and to articulate his power, the fact was that for Romans and Italians it was too. If in Rome Claudius strictly forbade public worship of himself as a god, he might (as seen) still have allowed cult of his *genius*.[75] Very important too was the deification of his grandmother Livia.[76] Augustus had been deified after his death – which is to say, the Senate acknowledged that upon death, he had ascended into the heavens where he would live an immortal life, and that because of his merits should receive a cult.[77] Neither Tiberius nor Caligula was deified, and Caligula, it might have been felt, had acted entirely inappropriately in insisting that the Senate deify his sister Drusilla, after a Senator swore that he had seen her ascend to heaven.[78] She hardly had the achievements to match Augustus. With Livia now recognized as Diva Augusta, a second, seemingly more reputable, precedent was set for consecration. Was Claudius to become a god too? And, linked as he was to gods like Livia and Augustus, was Claudius already partly a god himself? That would seem to be the implication of a pair of bronze statues found together in Herculaneum, at least one of which was put up in AD 48 or 49 in the basilica at Herculaneum by a soldier of the thirteenth urban cohort (Figs. 30–31).[79] One of the pair depicts Augustus with divine attributes – the scepter and thunderbolt of Jupiter, and the hip-mantle that was the usual costume of senior male gods. The other, that known to be dedicated by the soldier, shows Claudius fully nude: he is not, it would seem, as ruler of the world, a god yet, but in more ways than one he is close to one.[80] The juxtaposition conveys a message not just about a familial relation but also divinity and power.

Even during his lifetime, it is clear, some citizens must have viewed Claudius as at least *like* a god, thanks to the power that he held. While statues of the emperor that went up in Rome usually represented him

Fig. 30 Statue of Claudius set up in the basilica of Herculaneum by a bequest of a soldier in the Urban cohorts, who also stipulated that four sesterces be distributed to each member of the town at a dedicatory ceremony. Archeological Museum, Naples.

Fig. 31 Statue of Augustus set up in the basilica of Herculaneum. Archeological
Museum, Naples.

in a toga, or perhaps military garb, outside Rome, in the towns of Italy,
Claudius, like his imperial predecessors, could be represented partially
nude, with the attributes of a god.[81] Some show him enthroned, wearing
only a hip-mantle, perhaps with the attributes of Jupiter such as an eagle
or a spear. Apparently during his own principate, a variation on this type
also became popular – a portrait of the emperor standing, partially nude,

again with the attributes of Jupiter.[82] An especially stunning example is the famous portrait from Lanuvium, with its marvelous juxtaposition of Claudius' standard facial features, the youthful and muscular body of a god, and Jupiter's eagle and scepter (Fig. 32).[83] Such a portrait effectively makes Claudius similar to a god, without going so far as to say explicitly that he was one.

A contemporary work of Latin literature also modulates Claudius' identity in such a way, engagingly blurring the boundaries between man and god – and also provincial and citizen. This is the consolation Seneca wrote from exile on Corsica to Claudius' freedman, Polybius, who had recently lost his brother. Like the earlier consolation Seneca addressed to his mother Helvia, this short work doubles as a sort of consolation for Seneca himself – whose exile is akin to death – but it also takes on a third function: Seneca was seeking through it a pardon and permission to return to Rome. The writer, in urging Polybius not to be distracted from his own literary endeavors or his duties at court, makes the plea unmistakable:

So many thousands of men must be given audiences, so many petitions disposed of; so great is the heap of business, emanating from every part of the world, that must be carefully weighed so that it may be brought to the attention of the most illustrious Leader in proper order. You, I say, may not weep; so that you may be able to listen to the many who are weeping – in order that you may dry the tears of those who are in danger and are longing to succeed in obtaining pity from Caesar's clemency, it is your own tears that you must dry.[84]

According to Seneca's exhortations, Polybius is to become a reflection of Claudius himself, similarly diligent in the execution of his imperial duties, a never-ending and unrelenting task (or so Seneca represents it).[85]

Thus, within the frame of advising Polybius to stay focused on serving his master, Seneca can celebrate Claudius too, while asking him for clemency. Three features of the panegyric are especially noticeable. First, according to it Claudius really is responsible for the whole world, of which he is the center. Caesar is like Atlas; and "his watchfulness guards all men's sleep, his toil all men's ease, his industry all men's pleasures, his work all men's vacations."[86] Seneca sums it up with a typical flourish: "From the moment when Caesar dedicated himself to the world, he robbed himself of himself."[87] Second, in governing the earth, Claudius has shown the wisdom of prevailing by benefactions rather than armed force. Caesar is a balm for wounds, a source of kindness and favor. The sight, even the thought, of him is a comfort: "Lift yourself up, and every time that tears well up in your eyes, direct them on Caesar; with the sight of the greatness

Fig. 32 Statue of Claudius, in the guise of Jupiter, from the theater at Lanuvium.
Vatican Museums, Rome.

and splendor of his divinity will they be dried."[88] This means, third, that Claudius is a god, or soon to become one: "May gods and goddesses lend him to the earth long!" Seneca prays. "May he rival the deeds of divine Augustus, surpass his years! So long as he shall be among mortals, let him learn that nothing of his house is mortal!"[89]

An explicit contrast with Caligula then follows:

Allow him to heal the human race, that has long been weakened and ill, allow him to restore and return all things to their place which the madness of the preceding Leader has shaken! May this sun, which has shone brightly on a world plunged into the abyss and sunk in darkness, always shine! May he pacify Germany, open up Britain, and celebrate both his father's triumphs and new ones![90]

Reading such a passage, one is tempted to dismiss the whole work as gross flattery. But through the references to Caligula throughout the work, there is a less sycophantic undercurrent. Seneca is bringing up the question of apotheosis. While Caligula, Seneca says, in his mad inconstancy, might have decreed temples for his sister, Claudius can only show himself to be a god through his positive achievements.[91]

Gods were worshipped in Greece and Rome not simply to avert disaster but because they were thought to bring blessings. Did they never do so, they perhaps would have been of less appeal to their acolytes. In articulating Claudius' power as akin to that of a god, Seneca is, in a sense, acting more like a provincial (or at least an Italian community outside Rome); but in dangling the promise of deification, he is more like a Senator back in Rome. Senators, more constantly affected by the emperor's rulings, ultimately had more basis to judge him than far-off provincials did. For them, consecration came after death, not on accession. For some, it would never come at all; the illusion could not exist. A pious Jew like Philo could never countenance cult-like worship of a living ruler. Christians would not be able to either.

Jews, and then Christians, were left out of this key practice of the Roman Empire. Yet there were new proselytes to Judaism, and then converts to Christianity too.[92] In part, at least, those who pursued a new faith likely already in some way have felt left out. They might have sought the strong moral code that Judaism offered. They might, falling between the cracks of society, have found community in a church that at least on the surface paid less respect to the traditional hierarchy of Roman society. These developments were beyond Claudius' ken, even to a large extent beyond his time. Yet however limited his role actually was in the lives of his subjects, Claudius, we will see, expressed the idea that the emperor needed to serve communal needs, and not merely satisfy his own individual whims. He himself might not have been looking for his subjects' love, but a good emperor was one who tried to command at least their loyalty. To do so required never-ending vigilance. It was not an easy or enviable task.

CHAPTER 7

The eight-hundredth year of Rome

With the year AD 47 our conception of Claudius can deepen for two reasons. The first is accidental: it is now that the richly detailed *Annals* of Tacitus resumes, continuing to the death of Claudius and on through the first eleven years of Nero's principate. The second is more deeply rooted in history: in AD 47, Rome celebrated her eight hundredth anniversary, and, to mark the centennial, the emperor staged an elaborate set of celebrations and took the opportunity to reflect, publicly, on Rome's past and future. Avowing as his goal Rome's continued survival and success, announcing that he would revive or strengthen obsolete or obsolescent customs and also establish new ones, Claudius, while he found in Augustus a precedent for such behavior, was able to reveal something of his own priorities, even his own personality. Through the celebrations, and other events of this time that aroused Tacitus' interest, one gets closer to Claudius himself – and the problems that he faced as well as his depiction in the later tradition.

To begin with Tacitus: according to the historian, by AD 47 Claudius' wife Messallina was resolved to destroy Poppaea Sabina, one of Rome's finest-looking women, who, though married, had usurped Messallina's place in the affections of the versatile dancer Mnester.[1] By AD 47 Messallina also had her eye on the finest gardens in Rome, those of the legendary Lucullus on the Pincian Hill, now owned by a rich and athletic Senator from southern Gaul, Valerius Asiaticus, who was overseeing improvements to them. Ingeniously fulfilling both ambitions at once, Messallina hurled the experienced accuser Suillius against Poppaea *and* Asiaticus – with a charge that together they had violated Augustus' law against adultery – and she also brought in young Britannicus' tutor, Sosibius, who was to warn Claudius to beware of might and wealth that were dangerous to emperors. Asiaticus, Sosibius claimed, had led the plot against Caligula and gloried in it afterwards; his renown had grown even stronger since; he was soon to travel to the German armies; he could spearhead an uprising among his brethren back in Gaul!

As the denunciations mounted, Claudius sent the Praetorian prefect Crispinus with a detachment of troops after Asiaticus, who was discovered at the resort of Baiae, clapped into chains, and brought to Rome. There was no trial in the Senate; "he was heard in the imperial bedroom, in the presence of Messallina." Suillius accused him of corrupting soldiers, of adultery with Poppaea, of physical softness. Asiaticus replied with a defense, moving Claudius deeply, eliciting tears from Messallina, but the latter swiftly left the room and warned Vitellius not to allow the accused to slip off. As she frightened Poppaea into suicide, Vitellius, with his own set of tears now on display, persuaded Claudius that Asiaticus should be allowed to take his life too – his guilt now simply being assumed. Exercising one last time, bathing, dining in good spirits, Valerius then slit open his veins, but not before taking care to move his pyre lest its flames destroy the trees of his beloved gardens. "So great was his calm to the end."

Aside from the deaths of Poppaea and Asiaticus, the rest of this lurid tale might be questioned. Was Asiaticus plotting against Claudius? Or was that charge really only a screen for Messallina's pettier motives? And would Claudius himself have had no interest in the gardens? "Gardens" such as Asiaticus' often in reality were vast estates, not only with ample facilities for recreation, but also lucrative agricultural enterprises, all sitting atop land worth a fortune; the construction of two major new aqueducts in the 40s which could supply them with additional water would only have increased their value.[2] And then one also has to wonder: who of the surviving parties – Suillius or Sosibius, Messallina or Vitellius, or Claudius himself – supplied Tacitus, or any historian before him, with a reliable report of what happened? Cassius Dio offers a different version, involving a trumped-up accusation by a soldier.[3] Suetonius is simply silent. Much was surely mysterious about the affair from the start, with Senators likely forced to reconstruct the last days of their colleague much as historians have been since.[4]

Some facts were known about this self-assertive man. Asiaticus *was* fantastically rich: he possessed not just vast domains in Gaul and the gardens in Rome (which passed into imperial control) but also, as papyri show, estates in Egypt.[5] He had achieved real political success: in AD 45 he enjoyed a second consulship at the start of the year, a signal honor, and his wife was Lollia Saturnina, granddaughter of one of the most prominent men of Augustan Rome.[6] And he had also taken a leading role at least in the aftermath of Caligula's assassination, exulting in the whole affair, while perhaps intriguing to become Leader himself.[7] "Might and wealth," arms and money: that, in the end, was the underlying basis of Claudius' power, as it had been of Augustus'. It could be for a rival too – if not Asiaticus himself, somebody supported by him.

All this the Senators knew, though presumably they were told something else – perhaps, say, that Asiaticus and Poppaea had been guilty of adultery. That, so good-looking a man, he had given himself over to other men too. That he had been tampering with some troops. That, on learning of the danger from a vigilant Sosibius, Claudius sent Crispinus to bring him to Rome, and that Claudius had investigated the threat, or perhaps still was, when Asiaticus took his own life; a trial before the Senate was no longer possible – or necessary. It might not have been the first time the Senate was fed such a story. In fact, it all seems rather similar to what they were told about Appius Silanus back in AD 42.[8] The Senators must have been told something. Tacitus reports that they awarded Crispinus a large sum of money and the insignia of a praetor, and (on Vitellius' motion) Sosibius also a large sum, which should be true, assuming that the notice derives ultimately from the official record of the Senate.[9] Certainly, later in the year, in a speech before the Senate Claudius fulminated against a Senator and consular whom he refuses to name, calling him only a "bandit" and a "wrestling school prodigy."[10] It must have been Asiaticus.

Senators blindly loyal to Claudius would have celebrated the aversion of the alleged danger. But surely at least some found the episode unnerving. A colleague had gone to his death without a trial before them. The emperor's protection seemed to override all other values. The Leader, as Tacitus puts it, seemed to be "drawing to himself all the functions of laws and magistrates."[11] If Valerius could be thrown into chains by the Praetorian prefect, who would be next?

Nor, to add to the anxiety, was the fall of Valerius Asiaticus an isolated episode. The trauma of AD 41, when members of the Senate impugned Claudius' authority, seemed to replay itself again and again. Above all there had been the abortive rising of AD 42, and the death of Silanus earlier that year.[12] But others whom Claudius had tried to win over were removed from the scene – or at least are reported to have been. M. Vinicius, who put himself forward as a candidate for the principate in AD 41, and who won a second consulship in 45 with Asiaticus, died the following year in circumstances that, at least later, aroused suspicion (his wife, Caligula's sister Julia Livilla, had already been eliminated in AD 41); Cassius Dio blames Messallina once more.[13] And also that year, Asinius Gallus was banished, on grounds of conspiracy, and along with him was accused Statilius Corvinus, consul of the previous year.[14] Claudius' own son-in-law, Pompeius Magnus, was said to have been killed when caught in the

arms of a male lover, and his parents perished with him (while Claudia
Antonia was then married to Messallina's half-brother Faustus Sulla).[15]
Perhaps this prominent family, with its illustrious ancestors, was judged a
threat to the prospects of Britannicus, or even to Claudius himself; however
it was, their end cannot have been entirely comforting to all members of
the Senate.[16]

Further, as if the fall of Asiaticus were not dispiriting enough, Tacitus
jolts readers even more by recounting immediately after it a debate in the
Senate allegedly brought on by a series of prosecutions recently launched by
none other than . . . Suillius.[17] With no guarantee of fair legal proceedings,
it was obvious, men like him stood to reap huge sums for what might
effectively be judicial murder; for the right sum, he would bring down
anyone's enemy. According to Tacitus, the consul elect, C. Silius, bravely
decided to revive the old Cincian law, which prohibited financial award
to advocates. Its effectiveness had waned over the years, even despite an
effort of Augustus to strengthen it in 17 BC.[18] A debate ensued – furnishing
Tacitus a chance to compose a fine speech for the doomed Silius – and was
resolved by a decision of Claudius which did not end all compensation but
set a limit of a paltry 10,000 sesterces.

Tacitus' account of the measure itself should be reliable, not only because
of the Augustan precedent – indeed, Claudius might have shown more initiative in this matter than Tacitus allows – but also since there are other
indications that Claudius aimed to display a concern for handling legal
matters properly.[19] For cases over which he had jurisdiction himself, it is
recorded by Suetonius and Dio, he ruled that if for any reason a defendant
failed to appear at the scheduled hearing, he would automatically decide
against him: proceedings would not be allowed to drag on.[20] He fastidi-
ously observed this policy, it was said, and Suetonius elsewhere mentions
four occasions where Claudius actually refused to hear a party even when
present: it is hard to know whether this happened, or whether these are
anecdotes that reflect the strict enforcement of this same policy.[21] Effi-
ciency, it seems, was a high priority: Claudius is also said personally to have
eliminated the normal recess period in the court schedule, allowing more
trials.[22]

It is these measures, in part, which have allowed a speech preserved
on papyrus to be identified as remarks Claudius made before the Senate
concerning not cases he heard, but trials in the courts of the praetors.[23]
These, too, were being dragged out, as prosecutors, aiming to cause trouble
for innocent parties, issued baseless charges and then delayed their *own*
appearance in court. "I think . . . I have noticed astonishing tricks on the

part of those engaged in lawsuits," the speaker says – and the style here, as elsewhere in the speech, is a further, convincing argument that this is Claudius. In the speech, Claudius (assuming that it is he), then makes several proposals to ameliorate the supposed problem: the Senate should lower the minimum age of jury service; require jurors who have not settled a case to meet into the recess period of the court; and let the praetor charge with calumny a prosecutor who fails to appear without a proper excuse when summoned for trial. "I cannot tolerate at all the tyranny of the prosecutors," explodes Claudius. The solutions will be of some help but he believes more will be needed: "I know that litigants acting in untoward ways will not lack numerous subterfuges against which, I hope, we will invent remedies."

Was Claudius aiming for justice, or not? Could imperial government even reliably guarantee justice? Tacitus raises those questions exactly at the point where his account of Claudius begins – and they emerge from other evidence too, which as it accumulates makes the problem even more acute. They will not be settled immediately here, because they connect to larger paradoxes of Claudius' position that become clearer when more of his principate is examined: if the emperor's position was of dubious legitimacy, he could more easily be challenged, and responding to the challenge in ways that seemed highhanded – so that he could survive – he only made matters worse. And as the emperor tried, even conscientiously, to solve perceived problems with imperial government and its dispensation of justice, and boasted of it, he might in the eyes of Senators only further lower opinion of himself and the emerging institution of principate: he would be a hypocrite, his desire for justice a sham.

Not for everyone, though, was all dark in AD 47. Rome was a society of more than Senators, and it was, after all, now in its 800th year, an extraordinary achievement.[24] There could be hope for the future, as the empire was once again expanding its reach: it was in this year that the hero of Britain, Aulus Plautius, returned and paraded through Rome in a victory celebration with Claudius at his side.[25] A statue, no doubt, went up in the Forum of Augustus.[26]

Even more spectacularly, Claudius revived the Centennial Games that, of emperors, only Augustus before him had staged.[27] The festival, whose origins were a subject of controversy among antiquarians already in ancient times, was perhaps first celebrated in 249 BC, during the dark days of war with Carthage. In accord with the Sibylline Books, it followed Greek ritual and was tinged with dread: sacrifices were offered to Dis Pater (that is,

Pluto) and his wife Proserpina, deities who had not been worshipped in
Rome before, but now, in a time of war, were to be appeased with dark
victims, at night, in a spot by the Tiber River thought to be connected to
the Underworld. The Games were held a hundred years later, in 149 BC (or
so some maintained), and again, belatedly, in 17 BC: Augustus argued that
the College of Fifteen Priests, in charge of the festival, should employ a new
calculation to achieve a centennial in this year.[28] And that was not the only
change: in a new Sibylline oracle that conveniently had turned up, a whole
new ceremony was outlined.[29] Over three days, and three nights, Augustus
and Agrippa made night-time offerings, not to the old dark deities but
to the Fates, the Goddesses of Childbirth, and Mother Earth, and they
also sacrificed, by day, to Jupiter, to Juno, to Apollo and Diana. And at
the completion of the sacrifices to Apollo and Diana, which took place on
the Palatine outside the great Temple of Apollo that adjoined the house of
Augustus, a hymn, specially commissioned from the poet Horace, was sung
by twenty-seven boys and twenty-seven girls, celebrating a bright future,
including future celebrations of the Games.

An inscription set up to commemorate Augustus' festival preserves the
prayer that accompanied the sacrifices, and the prayer further helps recapture the nature of the revived festival.[30] To the deities invoked, the officiant
declared:

I ask and pray that you increase the authority and majesty of the Roman people,
the Quirites, in war and at home; that you preserve always the Latin name, and
that you bestow everlasting safety, victory, and good health on the Roman people,
the Quirites; that you favor the Roman people, the Quirites, and the legions of the
Roman people, the Quirites; that you keep safe the state of the Roman people, the
Quirites; that you be willingly well-disposed to the Roman people, the Quirites,
to the college of the fifteen, to me, my house, and household.

The emphasis here on Rome's imperial achievement is a typical Augustan
theme. As with the festival as a whole, it sprang not just from pride in the
past (including the recent recovery of the standards lost by Crassus to the
Parthians), but also hope for the future, not least the future of Augustus'
House. By 17 BC, Agrippa was married to Augustus' daughter Julia, the
two had given birth to two sons, and the sons, Gaius and Lucius, had been
adopted by Augustus as a sign that one day they might rule Rome.[31]

In the history of Rome he wrote in his early life, Claudius had (according
to Suetonius) credited Augustus with holding the Games at the correct
time – suggesting at least an antiquarian's interest in the ceremony – but
now, in AD 47, he had to argue that the first emperor had been led astray.[32]
And as emperor now himself, he could. Still, this made for a good joke,

Fig. 33 *Denarius*, c. 17 BC. The reverse of this coin, minted in conjunction with Augustus' celebration of the Centennial Games, shows a herald wearing a full-length robe and feathered headdress.

especially when, as custom dictated, heralds clad in an archaic costume went round the City summoning every man to witness the festival, "which he had never seen, and would never see again" (Fig. 33).[33] Even some of the performers who participated in the festival, it was claimed, had appeared in Augustus' celebrations before![34] But Claudius was willing to risk such derision and invested great effort into the whole event, going so far as to have what was alleged to be a phoenix displayed in Rome's old voting place.[35]

Particularly lavish games, one can guess, were held in the Circus. A record for one remarkable chariot race survives (at which the charioteer of the Whites was thrown at the start, but his team still went on to victory), but Claudius spent heavily on the Circus throughout his principate: he covered its starting stalls in marble, gilded its turning posts, built new seating for the Senators.[36] There are records of unusual spectacles in it, including a display of Thessalian horsemen who were to drive wild bulls around its track, then leap onto them and bring them to the ground. Panthers were shown, which were hunted down by a squadron of Praetorian Guardsmen on horseback led by their prefect.[37] Spectacle reflected for the people of Rome the empire's reach – and with it the emperor's.[38]

But there was another side to Claudius' decision to hold Centennial Games, which went beyond Thessalian horsemen or panthers, and also beyond his own personal antiquarian interests, and again looked back to Augustus. Augustus' Games had coincided with, and were to help promote, a number of legislative reforms which promised a better future for Rome through a strengthening of the community's morals, among them the infamous law that criminalized adultery and also a law designed to promote marriage among citizens and increase the birth rate.[39] As Augustus himself put it in his *Achievements:* "By new laws passed on my proposal I brought back into use many exemplary practices of our ancestors which were already fading away in our time and in many areas I myself left exemplary practices for posterity to imitate."[40] So, too, was Claudius busy with legislative reform in AD 47, and to underscore the point he revived, and himself held with Vitellius, the old Republican office of censor, which nobody had held since 22 BC, when two prominent citizens filled the post.[41] (In AD 47 Vitellius also served in a third consulship, an honor not bestowed on anyone save an emperor since Marcus Agrippa.[42])

In the past, the censors' chief duty had been the conduct of a census of Roman citizens, but as the census itself ended with a ritual purification of the city, censors were also in charge of improving the moral health of the community.[43] They might do so by lowering the status of disreputable citizens, reviving lapsed religious ceremonies, giving a speech on pressing social problems, or issuing edicts limiting licentious behavior. Censors also had been in charge of contracting major public buildings and saw to it that division between public and private boundaries were enforced; encroaching on state funds or lands – these too were grave moral infringements.

Claudius took on all aspects of the position, doggedly carrying them out with his unfailing helpmate Vitellius at his side and also, at times, the full Senate. In summarizing Claudius' measures as a whole, Suetonius comments: "In matters of religious ritual and both civil and military practice, and of the standing of all the orders both at home and abroad, he either corrected various practices or reinstated those which had fallen into disuse, or else instituted new arrangements."[44] The echo of Augustus' *Achievements* is suggestive: it was surely Augustus who served as the chief inspiration for all of what happened in AD 47, not just the Centennial Games. To make pronouncements on matters moral, religious, legal, architectural, and linguistic was a way Augustus wrested authority from the old Republican nobility; for Claudius to do so was also a way to try to strengthen his own position.[45] To be censor elevated Claudius over his peers in the Senate. And yet, at least some of Claudius' enactments, it seems clear, also reflected his own early efforts as an antiquarian scholar. Something of Claudius' own personality was emerging.

Tacitus is the main source for the censorial enactments, and, while he is probably fundamentally reliable, first should come primary documents which more patently capture the public image of Claudius at this time. One is a Senate decree passed on a proposal of the emperor in September AD 47 that penalized individuals who purchased buildings only to tear them down in order to make a profit.[46] In typical fashion, the rationale for the ruling is set out at the start, and it is the most revealing portion of the text:

Since the providence of the best Leader has seen also to the buildings of our city and of all of Italy for eternity, which he has helped not only by his most august precept but also by his own example; and since it suits the good fortune of the era (*saeculum*) that is upon us to take care of both public and private structures in the degree proper to each; and since all should refrain from the most bloody form of business and not introduce a sight incompatible with peaceful conditions through the destruction of town and country houses, it is the will of the Senate . . .

There was apparently an old tradition of the Senate regulating the demolition of houses in Rome, in order to preserve the housing stock sufficiently for the City's needs.[47] But that seems less to be the concern here; rather, the anxiety is that in tearing down Rome's structures – in redeveloping property as Valerius Asiaticus might have been, with the goal of making money – one might almost be suggesting, unpatriotically, that the City was *not* worth preserving. In this age of "good fortune" which upholds the promise of an eternal Rome, the Senate proclaims, the emperor seeks to maintain all buildings, for Rome and Italy, public and private.

Similar regard for the City – and expressed distaste for allegedly immoral conduct – is shown by another document, a boundary marker set up to reclaim public land in Rome that had falsely been claimed as private.[48] With succinct authority it states: "Tiberius Claudius Caesar Augustus Germancius . . . and Lucius Vitellius, censors, by Senate decree restored to the state, after judicial inquiry, through due form of law, areas which were in the possession of private persons through pillars and columns." This marker was just one of a series – another recently has turned up, which confirmed holdings of the prominent family of the Volusii Saturnini.[49] Together, they suggest that Claudius arranged for a thorough review of the census of all Roman properties first undertaken by Augustus.[50] And collectively, the stones themselves would have made an impressive statement across the city of Rome, asserting, like the Senate decree, nothing less than the emperor's direct control over private property.

When we turn to Tacitus there are again measures undertaken in conjunction with the Senate, others by Claudius alone. Claudius in "stern edicts" rebuked the people of Rome for abusing those of high standing, including the consular Pomponius Secundus: upholding Rome's system of status had traditionally been important for a censor.[51] He passed a law trying to stop the "savagery" of creditors – a rather Claudian expression – who were lending money to young men against money they stood to inherit.[52] And he also put before the Senate a motion concerning the *haruspices*, "so that the oldest art in Italy should not fade away through slackness."[53] These soothsayers, hailing from the leading Etruscan cities, had long given advice on the appeasement of the gods after portentous events but were being consulted less and less in an age of greater peace in Italy. Their learning risked being forgotten. "Everything of course," Tacitus reports Claudius as saying, "was flourishing at the moment, yet thanks should be given for this kindness of the gods so that sacred rites cultivated in uncertain times were not consigned to oblivion during prosperous ones." In alluding to present tranquility Tacitus undoubtedly is setting up the great storm of Messallina's fall that was about to break, but to judge from the Senate decree on buildings which Claudius proposed, the gist of Claudius' remarks on this occasion is accurately reproduced (they would have been preserved in the minutes of the Senate for later consultation).[54] It is hardly improbable that the Senate (as Tacitus also notes) voted that the college of pontiffs – of which, of course, Claudius was the head – should turn their attention to the whole matter. At the old Etruscan city of Caere remains of a monument were found with reliefs of figures personifying three other Etruscan cities, Vetulonia, Vulci, and Tarquinii (and there originally would have been more, including Caere), along with a large seated statue of Claudius himself (Fig. 34); the Etruscan cities, no doubt, were eager to express their gratitude.[55]

Even if his remarks on the *haruspices* chime well with other themes of the year, it would be hard to maintain that Claudius' interest in Etruscan antiquities played no role in his concern.[56] The histories Claudius wrote were hardly swept under the carpet when he became emperor. When the Museum in Alexandria was expanded with an addition named after him, it was also decided that *Antiquities of the Etruscans* (in twenty books) along with *Antiquities of the Carthaginians* (in eight) were to be recited publicly each year.[57] The early scholarship certainly guided another enactment Tacitus describes, the addition of three letters to the Roman alphabet.[58] Claudius had already written a book advocating this measure before becoming emperor.[59] Alphabets, he could point out, had grown over time – just as Rome had – and could be become better yet. Now, as emperor, he had the power to try to make it come true. Inscriptions survive with two of the new letters, including the boundary stone described above reclaiming

Fig. 34 Statue of Claudius, seated, from the theater in Caere. Vatican Museums, Rome.

public land: the use of the new letter in it further marked Claudius' impact on Rome.[60]

Yet the reform did not prove lasting. Perhaps as risible then as it has seemed to commentators since, it suggests a tendency on Claudius' part, of which more will be seen later, to let his learning distract him from more pressing concerns. That was a feature of his personality shaped by the early years of long study, and there was more chance for it to express itself the more secure Claudius felt. In AD 41, it would have been unthinkable; in 47, he felt ready to attempt more idiosyncratic measures, measures which show that he was not simply slavishly imitating Augustus, and that he likely felt some confidence.

Not to be underestimated, amid all the enactments, was the execution of the census itself. It was a breathtaking accomplishment. A census had last been undertaken in AD 13/14 by Augustus and Tiberius (though they did not actually serve as censors). According to the *Achievements*, 4,937,000 citizens were recorded.[61] Procedures had by that time been established to register new citizens – crucial because of the privileges, as well as responsibilities, citizenship brought – and from this perspective, a census no longer was necessary.[62] But it is not clear that anybody knew how many citizens there actually were, and, while practically speaking it might not have mattered, it could have great symbolic value, because of the old idea that Rome's citizens were her greatest resource. Indeed, Claudius himself publicly stated that the purpose of the census was to note down "our resources."[63] As the number of citizens grew, so, it could be thought, did Rome's might; to quantify was to give a measure of strength. By the end of Claudius' census, according to Tacitus, 5,984,072 citizens had been registered – a substantial increase over the previous record or any record of the sort (though not necessarily impossible).[64] When Germanicus, in a visit to Egypt, looked on the ruins of Thebes, Tacitus writes, a priest, interpreting the hieroglyphs for him, reported that 700,000 men of military age had once lived there.[65] Rome easily surpassed that.

The census-taking had other resonances. First, the actual administration of it also suggested the dramatic capability of Rome, and of the emperor who presided over it. Simply to count up 5,984,072 individuals was a stupendous feat for a pre-industrial society. Claudius boasted of the difficulty of the task in a speech before the Senate in AD 47, but it is a papyrus from Egypt which shows that it really was undertaken across the empire.[66] This remarkable document is a copy, produced from the official record kept in Latin, of a declaration made before an unknown Roman magistrate in Egypt for the Claudian census; according to it, Pompeius Niger, a discharged soldier of the Twenty-second Legion, declared himself and his sons as citizens, and registered property worth altogether 1,250 Roman sesterces. (As in earlier censuses, a property assessment evidently had to be given, because it determined legal status.) But the text's interest does not end there: in his declaration, Pompeius stated that he owed his and his sons' citizenship to a grant of the emperor, made shortly after Pompeius' discharge from legionary service in AD 44. This, like the census itself, points to a larger interest in citizenship on Claudius' part, to which we will turn shortly. Here it is more important to imagine the act of perhaps several million men across the empire registering with the appropriate official their status along with that of their family members and also their property. Results would then have been sent on to Rome.

Second, while the census-taking was indeed empire-wide, it culminated in a time-honored religious ceremony in Rome, the lustration. The lustration was a ritual purification of the city that aimed to keep evil out, guard what was within, and mark a new beginning.[67] The tradition had been that one of the censors, chosen by lot, processed around the sacred boundary of the city, accompanied by torches and three sacrificial animals – a pig, sheep, and bull – and then offered the animals to Mars. It was a visually impressive event, and is likely depicted on two partially extant reliefs from an unknown monument of the City, which may in fact specifically commemorate the Claudian census.[68] One, better preserved, shows a togate and veiled figure (heavily restored) sacrificing at a fruit-laden altar, with the pig, sheep, and bull behind him ready for sacrifice; a second altar is also visible, with a pair of laurel trees (Fig. 35). The other fragment, showing a bull, seems to represent a parallel procession. The style shows the monument to be imperial in date, and even if (as has been argued) it commemorates the census of Tiberius and Augustus, it could suggest that both Claudius and Vitellius officiated at the lustration which followed their census. Whatever its context, it certainly lent prominence to the ceremony.

The lustration points to two others revivals of Claudius in which ancient ceremonies took on new meanings. Both are from AD 49 but extended the logic of the censorship. In that year, it was agreed to re-establish the augury of Well-being, an old rite in which at a time of peace the augurs were to inquire of Jupiter whether it was right to ask for prosperity for the Roman people.[69] Though Tacitus' notice is obscure, the Claudian innovation seems to have been to institute the ritual on a more permanent basis. Much clearer is Claudius' extension of the *pomerium*, the sacred boundary of Rome which effectively marked the point where a general could assume command of his troops.[70] Said to have been established by Romulus himself, it was then extended by King Servius Tullius and (within historical memory) Sulla, each time marking the acquisition of new territory by Rome in Italy. For Claudius, the new territory now seems to have been not in Italy but Britain, and despite objections by some antiquarians, he carried out the rite anyway, bestowing on it a new meaning and, at the same time, echoing a theme of his censorship, the increase of the Roman people. It became a specific

Fig. 35 Part of a relief from an unknown monument in Rome, depicting a scene of sacrifice at a fruit-laden altar. The three sacrificial animals are the pig, sheep, and bull of the *suovetaurilia*, suggesting that the scene represents completion of a *lustrum*. Louvre, Paris.

power of subsequent emperors to make further changes as appropriate, and the power was exercised at least once: this was a more lasting reform than the attempt to revise the alphabet.[71] Tacitus reports that the boundaries Claudius laid down were easy to make out even in his own day, and indeed a number of boundary stones have turned up, on which could be read, along with a sequencing number, a standard inscription (featuring one new Claudian letter):

Tiberius Claudius Caesar Augustus Germanicus, son of Drusus, pontifex maximus, with tribuncian power for the ninth time, imperator for the sixteenth time, consul for the fourth, censor, father of the fatherland, after the boundaries of the Roman people were expanded, has extended and delimited the *pomerium*.[72]

The language clearly echoes the celebrations of AD 47 and 48, with the stone giving the spirit of the age a more permanent form (Fig. 36). If, as has been suspected, Claudius' *pomerium* overlapped with an extant portion of the old Servian Wall, that was a further aspect of its monumental aspect.[73]

The census celebrated Rome's growth, and it also drew attention to the value Claudius placed on citizenship and status. Here, Claudius can be said to have had what can be called a policy, and an explicit one at that, which involved action as well as reaction. For him, citizenship, and other distinctions of status too, were not just a series of privileges but were also to be seen as a responsibility, and should be awarded to those who had served and strengthened Rome. Claudius was therefore willing to grant citizenship to individuals or even groups, as again Augustus most notably had before him, though Tiberius and Caligula likely did too, if the number of citizens recorded for the census of AD 47/48 is to be believed.[74]

One area of clear interest, for instance, was the province, Noricum, in the eastern Alps and south of the Danube, a rich recruiting ground for the armies.[75] As part of a substantial reorganization, which saw five Roman municipalities created, Claudius granted en masse the so-called "Latin rights" (not quite full citizenship, but still privileged status); and he also gave to selected individuals full citizenship. (At the same time, Rome's own military presence within the region shifted from the interior of the country to the Danube.) In the Mauretanian war, we also already noticed, in recognition of help from the men of Volubilis, he granted these auxiliary troops citizenship and right of legal marriage with non-citizen women, so that their sons would be legitimate in Roman law as well.[76] This was the same reward Pompeius Niger received, though he had served not as an auxiliary but a full legionary – presumably with the understanding that he

Fig. 36 Travertine boundary-stone, marking the extended *pomerium* of Claudius, AD 49 (*CIL* 6.31537a). A digamma (one of the three new Claudian letters), which looks like an inverted "F," appears twice in the last line. Antiquarium Comunale di Celio, Rome.

would gain citizenship upon release.[77] That was less typical, even perhaps specific to Egypt, but the papyrus makes it clear that it happened.

But beginning in the reign of Claudius, it seems, for time-served auxiliaries a standard bundle of rewards was created – the emperor's grant of citizenship to the discharged man and his descendants, and the right of a marriage valid in Roman law – and bronze diplomas were issued to the discharged auxiliaries as tangible proof of their rewards.[78] Thanks to their durable material, many of these have been found archeologically, and the first is dated to AD 51; its text is said to have been "copied and certified from the bronze tablet which is attached in Rome on the Capitolium to the Temple of Loyalty of the Roman People on its right side."[79] The location of the original bronze tablet is obviously deeply symbolic. The effort put into issuing the diploma, at the same time, shows the significance that the emperor attached to citizenship.

A rather different document is preserved, again in the form of a bronze tablet (found near Trent, in the Italian Alps), which also demonstrates the emperor's policy, along with other distinctively Claudian features.[80] According to it, Claudius was hoping to settle an old dispute between two communities in northern Italy, already at issue in the time of Tiberius, who started to look into the matter but never resolved it because of his "persistent absence" (on Capri). Claudius sent his "friend and companion" Planta to investigate and, after receiving his written report, decided that Planta should rule on it as he saw fit – an excellent illustration of how the emperor delegated power to a man on the spot. This makes it all the more revealing that Claudius did give his own ruling on a further concern an informant happened to bring to Planta's attention: several Alpine peoples were alleged to have illegally usurped Roman citizenship by having themselves assigned to the community of the Tridentini (which had, indisputably, been granted the franchise). As it would be hard to enforce a separation, Claudius says:

I allow them to remain by my special favor in the status in which they thought they were, and I do this all the more willingly because many from this group of people are said to have served even in my Praetorian Guard, some indeed to have become officers too, and a few are said to have been incorporated into the panels at Rome and to have judged cases.

For their service to Claudius and Rome – even as jurors! – citizenship is a fitting recognition.

As with embassies, documents concerning citizenship survive because they record success – it is no accident that the military diploma and the edict

on the Alpine tribes were both in bronze – but another side of Claudius'
policy is reflected in literary sources which claim he revoked citizenship
from those who held it illegally or without merit. Indeed, he is said even to
have had some usurpers executed on the Esquiline field: the severity of the
punishment suggests they may have been thought slaves.[81] But the sources
emphasize something else even more – that citizenship was almost being
given away under Claudius. Dio says Claudius gave it indiscriminately to
individuals and groups, while Messallina and the freedmen sold it for large
sums of money (one thinks here of Claudius Lysias, the tribune of Acts).[82]
Seneca has one of the Fates in his satire on Claudius' apotheosis facetiously
say that she wanted him to live just a little longer, to give the last few
remaining foreigners citizenship: "He had decided, you know, to see all the
Greeks, Gauls, Spaniards, and Britons in togas."[83]

Obviously Seneca's comment is hyperbolic, but something lies behind
it and Dio's report: this was not a routine charge against the stereotypi-
cally "bad" emperor. In part the allegations may have been related to the
substantial increase in citizens Claudius reported. But contemporary documents such as the edict on the Alpine peoples do suggest that Claudius
in his own name *was* generous with the citizenship, more so than his
immediate predecessors, of set design, and for some good reasons. These
policies offended those who wanted the franchise guarded more jealously –
it was a battle that went far back into Rome's history. They also offended
those who thought they should benefit but did not. At the same time, it
is not unreasonable to suppose that with citizenship being bestowed more
widely, there was more opportunity for obtaining it illicitly – if not from
Claudius himself, or from Messallina and the freedmen, then perhaps a
compromised subordinate, for a bribe: it is this sort of practice that may
lie behind Claudius Lysias in Acts. It even may be that one purpose of the
census was, in keeping with the value Claudius attached to citizenship, to
root out imposters as best as possible across the empire. The paradox would
be that it could instead allow chances for malfeasance. This is a paradox
that bedeviled other features of Claudius' principate.[84]

The census underscored the value of citizenship, and, in a highly traditional manner, it underscored the value of the two highest orders in Roman
society, Senators and equestrians. In fact, the equestrian Suetonius' account
of Claudius' censorship focuses on this aspect of it, and is replete with anecdotes to illustrate his favorite theme of Claudius' inconsistency.[85] But the
basic picture seems right – Claudius staged the traditional inspection of
the knights on horseback and also reviewed and revised the Senatorial
rolls: members deemed unworthy were eliminated. Tacitus adds, in his

account, that Claudius also created new patricians, a practice illustrated by inscriptions.[86] This was the first occasion a censor did this, and so it represents another Claudian innovation that looked to the past. Patricians were an ornament to society, and several priestly roles were still limited to them, so rather than let them lapse, Claudius tried to reinvigorate the tradition by rewarding those who, again, seemed worthy of it. Men selected were those who served Rome – and the emperor – well, including Veranius, Plautius Pulcher (brother of Claudius' first wife, who held several offices in Claudian Rome), and the Salvius Otho who, judged to have saved Claudius from a plot to kill him, also received a statue on the Palatine.[87] This was not, then, all antiquarianism by any means; as with the measures concerning property, here too was a tool Claudius could use to help (or harm) prominent Romans as he liked.

There is now a final episode of Claudius' censorship to consider, the one that most drew Tacitus' attention. In AD 47, as the historian tells it, a discussion arose as to whether to admit to the Senate chieftains of Long-haired Gaul (to be distinguished from the part of Gaul that had been formed into a province almost a hundred years earlier, Narbonensian Gaul).[88] While the rich territories of Narbonensian Gaul, and also Baetica in Spain, had already produced Senators and high-ranking equestrian officials (such as the Corduban Seneca), Long-haired Gaul had not, and the nobles who held sway there could still arouse suspicions, not least because of the rising against Rome led by two of them, Florus and Sacrovir, in AD 21.[89] Tacitus reports objections made to Claudius by certain nameless advisors – as censor Claudius had the power to add new members to the Senate, but to do so would set a precedent of concern to all members of the body.[90] Tacitus then gives Claudius a rather splendid speech before the Senate, recommending admission of the Gauls as another step in the long process by which Rome generously welcomed immigrants and used their talents to grow further: "this (practice) too will become established, and what today we defend by examples will be among the examples."[91] Yet Tacitus can be left aside for the moment, because, remarkably, portions of the speech Claudius gave survive, once again on a bronze tablet, found several hundred years ago in Lyon, France.[92]

The top of the tablet is missing, with the result that the first part of the speech is lost, along with part of its middle; but enough remains to draw some conclusions. Claudius' remarks do show that objections could be expected, that there was a fear that this was a revolutionary measure. Yet he urges the Senators to consider "through how many different forms

of constitution our state has passed, from the very foundation of the City."
A survey of the history of the *res publica* follows, starting, significantly,
with the early kings of Rome, who "did not pass the City onto successors
within their own families." Yet none of it is terribly relevant to Claudius'
immediate goal; much space is taken up with a truly pointless digression, on
King Servius Tullius, which quotes Etruscan authorities – and thus parades
Claudius' own researches; and then the survey ends rather abruptly, with
the emperor ostensibly refusing to boast of "having advanced the empire
beyond Ocean," his most beloved theme.

When the text resumes, Claudius is finally approaching the matter
at hand, claiming that the divine Augustus "my great-uncle" and "my
uncle Tiberius Caesar" admitted to the Senate House "the whole flower of
colonies and municipalities everywhere." (Caligula, naturally, is not mentioned.) But the examples that follow are, to say the least, not entirely
felicitous. Claudius could point out that the old province in Gaul had
been sending Senators to Rome for some time. And indeed, he turns
to the town of Vienne, but from there can only mention an equestrian
(not a Senator), Lucius Vestinus, "whom I esteem most highly," and the
utterly disgraced Valerius Asiaticus and his brother, who also (it seems) was
removed from the Senate: there were better choices available – Domitius
Afer from Nemausus, for instance, or Pompeius Paulinus from Arles.[93]
Claudius then leaves the old Province for Long-haired Gaul and mentions
Lugdunum, his birthplace – but also an old citizen colony, hardly comparable to the other communities of Gallia Comata under discussion. He then
emphasizes the loyalty of the Gauls, mentioning his father Drusus, while
entirely overlooking the rebellion that broke out under Tiberius. Along
the way there is a weak joke about Fabius Persicus' ancestor Allobrogicus –
called such because he *conquered* that Gallic tribe.

However much Claudius believed that provincials should be incorporated into the Senate, however much he aimed to show this as "part of
my censorship," the speech, or at least what remains of it, hardly makes
an effective argument. It was at its worst hectoring – mentioning Asiaticus
vindictively, insisting on pleading "severely" – and otherwise largely beside
the point. It is not, though, let it be said, good evidence for Claudian
weakness, even if the rhetoric itself is feeble. The ideas in it are clearly
Claudius', and the whole initiative was represented as his, and it was not
necessarily bad: good arguments, indeed, could be made for it, as Tacitus
himself shows by rewriting it (with the benefit of hindsight).[94] What the
speech on the tablet of Lyon betrays more than anything else is a lack of

rhetorical training and insensitivity to the feelings of the Senate, or perhaps a nervousness brought on by having to speak before that body. Here one starts to see more clearly the price Claudius paid for lacking the upbringing any other Roman aristocrat would have had, and the coaching for rule other imperial princes received. These may not have been problems for the overwhelming majority of his subjects, including whoever it was who set up the bronze tablet in Lyon, but in the Senate house they were.

The speech certainly must have caused offense in at least some members of the Senate. How, when he talked like this, could Claudius really be called Caesar? How was he fit to rule over them? A more polished presentation – and presenter – might have allayed such criticisms. But for a Senator of conscience there was a deeper problem that not even the smoothest speaker might have solved. How could they all be pretending that the *res publica* was still alive, the Senate and People still meaningful, as busy as they might be kept? And then there was the proposal itself, which would have offended the prejudices of many. Yet the Senate voted to accept the measure, according to Tacitus. Claudius could have carried it out without consulting them, of course, but their vote in principle lent further support.

In the speech preserved on papyrus concerning judicial reforms presumed to be Claudius', the speaker ends by complaining:

Senators, if these proposals meet with your approval, signify straightaway, simply, and with sincerity; but if they do not, find other remedies, here in the temple, or, if perhaps you want to take time to consider the matter at greater leisure, take it, provided that, in wherever place you are convened, you remember to speak your own opinion. For it hardly suits the dignity of this order, Senators, for just one consul designate to speak his opinion drawn word for word from the motion of the consuls and the rest to speak a single word "Agreed" and then, when they have left, "We spoke."[95]

Claudius might have sought to dignify the Senate, but in the end it could seem at least to some that he was only degrading and demoralizing it. In the *Annals* of Tacitus, after rewards are proposed for Suillius and Sosibius to recognize their help in apprehending Valerius Asiaticus, the husband of Poppaea is asked his opinion: "Since I feel the same as everyone about Poppaea's offenses, count me as saying the same as everybody."[96] In such a situation, Tacitus is showing, irony is the only way to retain a shred of dignity.

CHAPTER 8

Practical pyramids

In the year AD 52, Claudius left Rome to celebrate the completion of a massive enterprise he had embarked upon eleven years before.[1] Fifty-three miles east of the City, 2,100 feet above sea level, the Fucine Lake was fed by rain and melting snow from the Apennines but, enjoying no surface outlet, constantly varied in its level, leading to periodic flooding of the surrounding farmland and outbreaks of malaria. The neighboring Marsi, according to Suetonius, had already asked Augustus to look into putting an end to the ongoing problem, but the emperor refused, leaving a challenge for posterity.[2] Claudius, upon his accession, decided to accept it and began excavating a channel that would run three and a half miles through a mountain ridge to carry the waters of the lake to the nearby Liris River.[3] The project would thereby not only create more secure farmland but increase navigability of the river. And so, over those eleven years, gangs of men dug through soil, cleared out stone, and patiently created the canal.

With the tunneling finished, to enhance the magnificence of his under-taking Claudius decided to stage a mock naval battle in the lake imme-diately before the sluices were opened and final drainage began. Augustus had put on such a spectacle in 2 BC, in a pool he excavated by the Tiber River, at which thirty triremes and biremes and a number of smaller vessels joined the fray; in addition to rowers, 3,000 men fought, as he boasted in his *Achievements*.[4] Claudius' show might well have surpassed that: Tac-itus claims that in AD 52, there were quadriremes, as well as triremes, and 19,000 men altogether in competition – all convicts! The much larger Fucine would allow sufficient space to show "the violence of the rowing, the helmsmen's skills, the onslaught of the ships, and the battle routines." To make sure the prisoners put on a good show, rafts were positioned around the periphery of the lake, on which stood squadrons of Praetorians, stationed behind catapults and ballistae. And, to add to the wonder of it all, the signal for battle (Suetonius notes) was to be sounded by a horn on a silver Triton which, through an ingenious mechanical device, could rise up from the middle of the lake.[5]

The banks of the lake, the hills, and the mountain heights around, Tacitus writes, were like a theater, with a crowd drawn from nearby towns, as well as Rome itself. People had come to see the draining of the lake and the battle between the "Rhodians" and the "Sicilians," as the two sides were apparently called.[6] They also had come to see the emperor and his new wife: in a conspicuous position, Claudius presided over the ceremonies in military garb, and Agrippina was nearby in a cloak of spun gold, with her son Nero.[7] As festivities got underway, the convicts at first apparently refused to fight but then finally did so, and bravely; it was then time to open the waterway. With the eager audience looking on, the gates were opened, the lake drained a little . . . and then stopped. The channel, Tacitus says, had not been sunk to a sufficient depth. What should have been a splendid demonstration of the emperor's ability to change the face of the earth was thus turned into a spectacular failure. The Triton was fake, the Sicilians and Rhodians fake, the battle itself – a fake. But perhaps the biggest fake of all, Tacitus suggests, was the man dressed as a general, the miracle-worker who in the end could summon no more than a trickle of water from the lake. Even the convicts who fought to the death might seem more glorious than he.[8]

Could it really have come to this for Claudius?

As with so much else, for answers one has to go back to Augustus. In the days of the Republic, it was the old noble families who had the responsibility of constructing all major buildings within Rome itself, as well as aqueducts that brought water to it, and roads that spread out across Italy.[9] With the responsibility came the chance for prestige. The classic example is Appius Claudius the Blind, the censor of 312 BC, whose fame to a large degree rested on the Appian Way he paved to Capua, the Appian aqueduct he built, and also a temple to the war goddess Bellona vowed during a battle with the Etruscans and the Samnites.[10] While the treasury might have funded a project, the individual in charge – typically a censor, but also sometimes a consul – was able to take credit for his work by inscribing his name on it, even giving his name to it, and in doing so he perpetuated his name for posterity.[11] There was no modesty here. In sharp contrast to the practice of the Greeks, who typically recorded on a monument the names of the architects or artists involved, the Romans were usually only interested in the politician directly responsible – even the restoration of an earlier work could allow a building to be renamed.[12]

And it was not just city magistrates who built: from the spoils of war returning generals paid for, and decorated, a splendid series of temples across the City (like Appius' for Bellona).[13] The bigger such temples were, or the fancier, the better. Temples, too, perpetuated a name and were maintained by subsequent generations of the family as a way of showing dynastic strength. Temples, basilicas, porticoes, arches, and more – in a fiercely competitive city all these monuments jostled for an onlooker's attention, trying to remind posterity of the great exploits of the men who built them.

Yet with Augustus all that changed, in ways that few might have predicted even a generation before. While not unmindful of the glory Roman aristocrats won through building, Augustus looked also to the great cities of the east, to Athens and Pergamum, Alexandria and Antioch, where individual rulers had, through concerted effort, used architecture to articulate a whole political program.[14] As a builder, Augustus could announce his own unique pre-eminence in Rome. He, and his family, would come to control all new construction – new temples, new porticoes, a new Senate house, a new theater, a new forum, a new aqueduct. The temples, such as that of Mars the Avenger, were especially dazzling – a whole forest of white Carrara columns grew up through the center of the City, changing its face forever. Augustus came to monopolize most rebuilding too, whether of roads, bridges, aqueducts, or buildings.[15] In one year, Augustus could boast, he restored no fewer than eighty-two temples.[16] Rather ostentatiously, he boasted too of not assigning his own name to certain such efforts.[17] He could afford to.

Building announced Augustus' pre-eminence in Rome, but it also aimed concurrently to announce Rome's pre-eminence in the world. Whereas before cities such as Athens or Pergamum had been the center for new architectural ideas, and Rome was more typically a receptacle of Greek traditions, now from Rome a new imperial style, featuring a new and full Corinthian order, radiated across the Mediterranean for use in public buildings.[18] The higgledy-piggledy design of most of the City's central spaces, reflecting exactly the chaotic competition of Republican politics, was to be replaced with grandiose, and carefully designed, monumental zones that could overwhelm any visitor. Services also were to be improved; there were new commissioners drawn from the ranks of the Senate for aqueducts, for roads, for public buildings, for the banks of the Tiber (the floods of which could be devastating).[19] Architecturally, Rome became under Augustus a city worthy to be the head of a world empire. It was the main stage on which he and his family would perform for fellow Romans and the world; for this reason, it was where the most spectacular of the buildings funded by Augustus were to be found.

"I found Rome built of brick: I leave it to you in marble": the famous boast attributed by posterity to a dying Augustus shows just how much he was remembered as a builder.[20] Indeed, he wanted to be remembered as a builder, and he made building a key part of what future rulers of Rome should do. Building, for Augustus, instantiated, as well as symbolized, the effort the Leader put into governing; both activities should go beyond self-aggrandizement, and show regard for fellow citizens, and the image of Rome; and he expected his successors to live up to his example. Nowhere is this clearer than the *Achievements* Augustus had inscribed on bronze tablets in front of his gigantic mausoleum which lay near a number of other monuments constructed by him. There, a long section enumerates his new constructions as well as his restorations; "I built the Senate House, and the Chalcidicum next to it, the temple of Apollo on the Palatine with its porticoes" the triumphal catalogue begins.[21] Yet in it, he notes a restoration just reaching completion at the time of writing, that of the Basilica Julia: "I began to rebuild it on an enlarged site, with an inscription in the name of my sons, and I ordered that if I have not completed it in my lifetime, it be completed by my heirs."[22]

Still, as with their use of statues, or wars fought beyond the borders of the empire, it would be left to Augustus' successors to decide how much they would follow his precedents. To be sure, a full-scale renovation of the City such as Augustus himself presided over was beyond anyone's resources – there was no plunder from Egypt to pay for it.[23] When, after the Great Fire of AD 64 such a task was forced on Nero, it helped lead to serious financial troubles.[24] Financing major public works was an extraordinary challenge – an emperor had to think carefully about how he would pay for them. Choices had to be made. Tiberius was famously abstemious, resulting in Suetonius' succinct judgment: "As emperor, he built no magnificent public works and the few things which he made a start on, the Temple of Augustus and the restoration of Pompey's Theater, he left uncompleted after so many years."[25] Tiberius, though, had contributed to Augustus' own building program while Augustus was still alive, being responsible for the last two great temples, of Castor and Concord.[26] His position was secure enough after his accession that, as with military enterprises, he could forgo anything grandiose.

Very different, evidently, was the situation for Caligula. Because of the shortness of his principate – which did not allow for completion of long-term projects – and because of the blackening of his memory, it is difficult to evaluate Caligula's activities as a builder. Certainly one must be suspicious of Suetonius' report that he *intended* to rebuild the palace of the tyrant Polycrates at Samos or dig a canal through the Isthmus of Corinth, in emulation of the Persian King Xerxes.[27] Such tales might only have been invented to suggest his tyranny, and a lack of concern for the needs of Rome. It seems, in fact, that there was, with Caligula, something of a return to the Augustan role of mighty builder – he definitely embarked on a major new aqueduct for Rome and also a new stone amphitheater.[28]

Two detailed verdicts of Claudius' public works survive, one (not surprisingly) in the biography composed by Suetonius who regularly includes such a discussion in his imperial biographies. For Claudius, he begins:

He undertook great public works which were necessary rather than numerous, in particular: an aqueduct begun by Caligula, as well as the canal from the Fucine Lake and the harbor at Ostia, although he knew that Augustus had refused to undertake the canal, despite the frequent requests of the Marsians while the Deified Julius had several times set his mind to the harbor but abandoned it because of the difficulties involved.[29]

By the time Suetonius was writing under Hadrian, it is clear, one criterion for judging an emperor was his building activities – that is, after all, why Suetonius regularly uses this rubric in his lives.[30] Through his buildings, Suetonius believes, as much as through his statues or edicts, an emperor told his subjects, and posterity, who he was. Buildings allowed him to show what his priorities were – and also to make a statement about his relationship with previous emperors. In tackling projects left undone by Caesar and Augustus, Claudius was trying to show that he could not just equal but even surpass his imperial predecessors.

The other account of Claudius' program of building is perhaps of greater interest, for it comes from the pen of one who lived through it, Pliny the Elder. In the course of a survey of Rome's buildings – in which there is a fair deal of criticism as well as praise – the author comes finally to aqueducts, "marvels that are unsurpassed if a proper assessment is made."[31] He then writes:

The cost of all aqueducts has been surpassed by the most recent, the work on which was begun by Caligula and completed by Claudius, inasmuch as the Curtian and Caerulean Springs, as well as the Anio Novus, were made to flow from the 40th milestone at such a height as to supply water to all the hills of the City; disbursed for the work was 350,000,000 sesterces. But if one takes into careful consideration the abundant supplies of water in public buildings, baths, pools, open channels, private houses, gardens, and country estates near the city – the distances traveled by the water, the raising of arches, the channeling of mountains, the evening out of deep valleys – he shall admit that there has never been anything in the whole world more marvelous.

For my part, I would consider among the achievements of the same Claudius worthy of memory, abandoned though it was because of the hostility of his successor, the digging of a channel through a mountain to drain the Fucine Lake. The expense was indescribable, as was the host of workers over so many years, because where earth formed the interior of the mountain, the spoil from the channel had to be brought to the topmost part through winches, and elsewhere the rock itself had to be cut away. All this great effort, which cannot be conceived except by those who saw it nor described with words at all, happened in darkness.

Now I must pass over construction of the harbor at Ostia, and likewise the roads cut through the mountains, the separation of the Tyrrhenian Sea from the Lucrine Lake by moles, and all the bridges built at such great cost.[32]

Discussion of Claudius' two aqueduct lines carries Pliny onto the draining of the Fucine Lake, a second major effort at engineering undertaken by Claudius. And since the harbor at Ostia is known to have been a third Claudian project, it seems clear that the passage as a whole is fixated on this emperor. Hence, the "roads driven through hills" might in particular be those which Claudius is known to have thrown over some of the most mountainous parts of Italy, and perhaps at least some of "all the bridges." (But the moles at the Lucrine Lake remain otherwise unattested.[33])

Pliny especially admires Claudius' projects because they were all intended to be useful. Indeed, for Pliny, those monuments are most praiseworthy which have a clear use: he can famously denounce the pyramids of Egypt as "an absurd and pointless display of the wealth of kings" (even as he is impressed by their dimensions and marvels at their construction), while the great lighthouse at Alexandria is obviously to be admired.[34] While not all Romans shared his view – certainly not the Gaius Cestius who constructed his own tomb in Rome in the form of a pyramid! – Pliny's thinking did tap into a venerable strain of Roman moralizing which held that while private luxury was to be condemned, splendor on behalf of the community was a special Roman virtue.[35]

Certainly Pliny's younger contemporary Frontinus, who served as super-intendent of the City's aqueducts, thought in these terms. In the elaborate work he wrote that gathered up prior information on the subject, pro-moted his own reforms, and commemorated his time in office, *The Water Management of the City of Rome*, he begins with a description of each of the nine aqueducts then in use in Rome, starting with the first, the Aqua Appia of the redoubtable Appius Claudius the Blind and ending with the two completed under Claudius, which in their final approach to the City shared an impressively high arcade, in parts (Frontinus notes) over 100 feet tall.[36] "With these structures, so great in number and indispensable," Frontinus concludes with a flourish, "carrying so much water, would you compare the idle pyramids or other useless, though famous, works of the Greeks?"[37]

If the usefulness of Claudius' monuments is what Pliny admires most, his celebration also strikes two other notes. Three times he mentions their stupendous cost, giving a truly dizzying sum of 350 million sesterces for the aqueducts. And he also shows that, whatever their costs, he believes that building on such a scale is what an emperor should do: Caligula has to get some credit for starting the aqueduct work completed by Claudius; Nero shamelessly neglected the Fucine Lake. Also implicit in Pliny's train of thought is the idea that Claudius showed concern through his building program not just for the City of Rome, but all of Italy. Pliny's whole account suggests, then, how Claudius himself projected his own specific identity, and at the same time contributed to emerging ideas about what an emperor should be, through his buildings.

Claudius' building projects, apparently like those of Caligula, were efforts to strengthen his position – or, more fundamentally, to show his power. The main ones would be few but spectacular: the completion of two new aqueducts, the construction of a harbor for Rome at Ostia, the building of the mountain roads, and the draining of the Fucine Lake. Through them, the emperor would triumph over nature and become akin to a god; that was the effect of a spectacular engineering project, as an ingenious poem by Statius celebrating Domitian's construction of a new road from Rome to Naples shows.[38] Diverting streams and draining lakes, excavating harbors and cutting through mountains, Claudius would try to alter the face of the earth. But the projects were also meant to be useful, and economically viable; with Claudius, there was an emphasis on financial responsibility and creating new posts to maintain the projects once built. The four main projects were, if successful, to advertise his regard for the Roman people in the City and Italy, and the spirit of Claudius' principate; they would be especially conspicuous to those traveling to or from Rome. Though all were embarked on before AD 47, they complemented Claudius' activities as censor, and indeed, in Claudius' mind may even ultimately have had a link to the censorship: like those venerable censors of old, men such as Appius Claudius, he too was building roads and aqueducts that would bear his name, reviving an old and worthy practice for imitation by future generations.[39]

The two new aqueducts were jointly dedicated in AD 52, well over a decade after Caligula embarked on the undertaking, which helps to show its scale.[40] One phase of the enterprise was apparently completed, and another embarked on, in AD 47, when Claudius assumed the censorship, for in that year, Tacitus writes, "Claudius drew off springs of water from the Simbruine Hills and brought them into the City."[41] (It may be that Caligula had only planned initially to build one line, while Claudius decided to add a second.) Of the two aqueducts, one directly commemorated Claudius through its name Aqua Claudia. Its water was taken from springs in the Anio valley about forty miles from Rome, near the source of the Aqua Marcia, which delivered to the City's inhabitants their freshest and purest water. The Claudia followed a similar route as the Marcia, and dramatically emerged above ground near modern Capannelle, where it ran on a long series of 1,000 arches for the final six miles to Rome.

Substantial portions of the arcade survive, and to this day are impressive for their height and the quality of their construction (Fig. 37). Each pier rests on a concrete platform buried underground; a course of peperino tuff projects out at the base; the pier itself is solid stone, laid without any mortar. The piers are capped with a cornice also of peperino, from which the arches spring directly. The base of the Claudian channel rests on the peaks of these arches and is clearly defined by peperino slabs projecting outwards. A cheaper, but quite efficient type of concrete construction might have been employed in place of the more traditional ashlar, suggesting that through this design, the architects had specific messages to impart.[42] The new aqueduct would be able to stand up, visually, to the beauty of the earlier Aqua Marcia, which could be seen nearby. But the ashlar arches also suggested the magnitude of the whole undertaking, and they suggested longevity. Some of the oldest monuments still to be seen in Claudius' Rome, such as the Servian Wall (which, as seen, was possibly incorporated into his *pomerium*), were ashlar (Fig. 38); in using it, Claudius' architects were, in a sense, looking to the past and promoting a fading practice as something worth preserving for the future.[43]

Claudius' other aqueduct (this one perhaps not intended by Caligula) was called New Anio, to distinguish it from a previously existing Anio. Its source was some miles beyond that of the Claudia and it followed an initial course on the other side of the Anio River. But also coming above ground near Capannelle, it was piggy-backed onto the channel of the Claudia

Fig. 37 Part of the arcade of the Aqua Claudia / Aqua Anio Novus, completed AD 52.

for the remainder of the distance to Rome. Faced in concrete, rather than stone, it was thus clearly defined for spectators as a second aqueduct (Fig. 37).

Perhaps not surprisingly, given the complexity of the project, and the piggybacking of the two lines, some subsequent repairs were necessary.[44] But both were able ultimately to support new branch lines within Rome. In Frontinus' day, official figures indicated that together they offered 47.9 percent of water available in the City, and 42.4 percent of water actually delivered.[45] Precise measurements were in fact almost certainly not attainable, but still the scale of these numbers is suggestive. In all likelihood, for capacity they were only approached by the Marcia and Anio Vetus; Frontinus writes that the new lines distributed water to all fourteen wards of the City, with over two hundred basins.[46] Pliny's claim of a

Fig. 38 Part of the so-called Servian Wall of Rome, dating to the fourth century BC.

cost of 350,000,000 sesterces is almost certainly a gross exaggeration (and there might even be a problem with his text), but if so is perhaps all the more revealing of a still tremendous sum involved. These two aqueducts, it has recently and rightly been said, were among the greatest works of engineering carried out in the course of Roman imperial history.[47]

That cannot have been lost on Claudius, and it would not be lost on travelers to Rome who saw the above-ground arcade. An even more explicit celebration, though, was designed, a work of astonishing creativity. Where the two aqueducts came into the City of Rome and crossed over two great roads immediately adjacent to each other, the Via Praenestina and the Via Labicana, it was decided to build a monumental gate, no less than 100 feet high (Figs. 39–40).[48] This sort of spot was ideal for a triumphal arch – such as Drusus' on the Appian Way – which of course suggests that the double gate is itself a kind of triumphal arch too.[49] The tuff of the arcade gives way for a space of three piers to bright travertine; and the gate is constructed in a heavily rusticated style, especially clear in the engaged columns which border the small decorative arches that perforate the piers. The rustication, like the ashlar masonry of the aqueducts, again evokes the past, but there is more to it than that. The whole monument almost seems to be a sort of baroque repudiation of the more austerely classical architecture

Fig. 39 The so-called Porta Maggiore of Rome, completed by AD 52. The top inscription registers Claudius' construction of the Aqua Claudia and Anio Novus; the lower inscriptions were added by Vespasian and his son Titus.

Fig. 40 Detail of scale model of the City of Rome at the time of Constantine, showing the great aqueduct crossing over the Via Praenestina and the Via Labicana constructed by Claudius, later incorporated into the Aurelian Walls. The massive gate, with its large dedicatory inscription on either side, greeted visitors entering the City as well as those departing. Museum of Roman Civilization, Rome.

favored in Augustan Rome – akin to the portraits of Claudius that likewise abandon the earlier cool classicizing.[50] There is energy here and emotion, similar almost to what one finds in Claudian edicts.[51] The idiosyncratic architecture, it is certain, was considered distinctively Claudian, because a similar rusticated style can be seen in surviving portions of the podium built for the Temple of Divine Claudius constructed after the emperor's death and deification by the Senate in AD 54 (Fig. 61).[52] But it is also especially appropriate for this monument, for the way in which the architectural forms seem to break out of the living stone suggests the triumph of man – or god – over nature.

What completes the monumental gate, and makes it even more like a triumphal arch, is the massive inscription that graces both its sides:

Tiberius Claudius Caesar Augustus Germanicus, son of Drusus, pontifex maximus, in his twelfth year of tribunician power, consul 5 times, imperator 27 times, father of his country, at his own expense had brought into the City the Aqua Claudia, from the springs which are called Caeruleus and Curtius, from milestone 45, and also the Aqua Anio Novus, from milestone 62.[53]

The recording of the total mileage, while an innovation in such inscriptions, quantifies the achievement in a typically Roman way and, at the same time, suggests the emperor's interest in such details.[54] Of even greater interest is another novelty in this context: Claudius' claim to have built the aqueducts "at his own expense" – clearly, an effort to show his regard for the people of Rome.[55] Since not all of the new water was for public use (much went to the emperor himself and other high-ranking members of society for their houses and gardens), this furthermore was an assurance that they were not footing a bill for the enjoyments of others.

Although building the two new aqueducts surpassed all else, there was other activity in this field under Claudius. Caligula had torn down a portion of the Aqua Virgo in Rome, apparently to make way for his amphitheater, but Claudius then had it restored.[56] Part of the arcade survives, including one still half-buried arch that spanned an ancient road and was monumentalized in a manner that recalls the great gate for the new aqueducts (Fig. 41). Atop heavily rusticated travertine piers sits a slightly projected attic, on which can be read (on both sides):

Tiberius Claudius Caesar Augustus Germanicus, son of Drusus, pontifex maximus, in his fifth year of tribunician power, imperator 11 times, father of his country, consul designate for the fourth time, rebuilt and restored to their original site the arches of the aqueduct Aqua Virgo razed to the ground by Gaius Caesar [i.e., Caligula].[57]

Fig. 41 Arches built as part of the restored Aqua Virgo in AD 46.

The text itself exemplifies how a contest between emperors past and present in the realm of public works was developing. That the British victory arch was incorporated into the arcade where it crossed the busy Via Flaminia also added to the contrast between Claudius' successes and Caligula's failings, while again advertising most prominently Claudius' concern for the people of Rome.[58] (The positioning of the British arch, incidentally, also enhanced the triumphal character of the great aqueduct gate at the Via Labicana and Via Praenestina.)

Administrative changes were also tied to the new aqueducts and further showed that Claudius was taking greater responsibility for the city's waters. A gang of slaves was organized, numbering 460 men, to complement the body of 240 already set up by Agrippa to maintain the earlier aqueducts:

the new group would no doubt handle Claudius' new lines in particular.[59] Also, Claudius introduced his own freedmen into the procedure by which individuals had to petition the commissioner for the right to draw water for private use.[60] Presumably the goal here was to keep an eye out on the distribution of the precious new water, which had cost the emperor so much to bring in. Unauthorized tapping of the lines was a recurring problem – Senatorial commissioners might even have tolerated it for their own gain, or traded better access for other favors – and would have been especially tempting after AD 52.

If the aqueducts were designed to serve directly the needs of Rome, so too was the new harbor at Ostia. Almost immediately after his accession, it seems clear, Claudius was faced with some kind of grain shortage: coinage issued from AD 41 with the goddess August Ceres suggests the crisis, as well as a resolution of it (Fig. 42).[61] As he would have to during another shortage ten years later, Claudius probably persuaded merchants to sail during winter months by offering to indemnify them.[62] By Claudius' day, Rome, as Tacitus laments in his account of the second shortage, was fed primarily by the transport of grain from overseas, especially Africa and Egypt.[63] The prefect oversaw a complex operation with subordinates in Italy and in the provinces, to insure smooth collection of the grain from its producers and smooth distribution in Rome. But independent shippers and traders were key players too; copious evidence survives, in the form of an archive of financial documents written on wax tablets found at Pompeii, to show how they might try to manipulate the market to drive up prices.[64] As the emperor did not wish to manage that part of the distribution chain himself, his only other means of preventing shortages was to encourage greater supply: Claudius therefore established substantial legal privileges for those who put ships with capacity of seventy tons (or more) into the grain trade and kept them in service for a minimum of six years.[65]

A new harbor at Ostia, at the mouth of the Tiber River, would also help minimize the problem of periodic shortages. In AD 41, Puteoli, just north of the Bay of Naples, was still the main grain port for Rome. After the large transmarine ships arrived there, their cargoes would be off-loaded and eventually transferred to smaller coastal vessels bound for Ostia, where the cargo would again be shifted, this time onto river boats.[66] Ostia was not able to handle the large sea-faring vessels. If it could, inefficiencies would be eliminated; a larger port, too, would offer better protection for ships during storms. Claudius, it seems, traveled early in his principate to Ostia to look into the construction of a harbor there and by AD 42 had

Fig. 42 *Dupondius*, c. AD 41. The obverse shows the head of Claudius; the reverse the figure of "August Ceres" seated on a throne, holding in her right hand two stalks of grain.

made the decision to carry out the plan left unfulfilled by Julius Caesar.[67] Cassius Dio tells the story of the emperor meeting with his architects, who, upon being asked the cost of the project, declared: "You don't want to do it!"[68] The anecdote nicely shows the enormous cost involved, typical of the Claudian public works.

Suetonius, along with Dio, reports the main features of the harbor – so elaborate a project, it would only be inaugurated under Claudius' successor Nero.[69] According to them, a large area was deepened, it was surrounded with moles on the left and right, and an island was placed in the water across from the entrance atop which sat a tall lighthouse, modeled on the famous Pharos of Alexandria. Coinage issued under Nero depicts the new marvel, crowned by a statue perhaps of Claudius himself, along with the harbor, moles, and ships (Fig. 43).[70] Though it was not finished in his lifetime, Claudius found ways to promote the project. In building the artificial island, he first sank the infamous ship on which Caligula had brought an obelisk from Egypt to adorn his own private circus.[71] That suggested a contrast with his predecessor – and was itself simply a visually impressive act. So too was a most unusual spectacle staged by the emperor. A large whale, according to Pliny, tempted into the partially completed harbor by the wreck of a ship filled with hides, soon became stuck; "Caesar gave orders for deep nets to be stretched between the mouths of the harbor and setting out in person with the Praetorian cohorts gave a show for the Roman public; the soldiery showered lances from the vessels making the attacks, one of which we saw sink after it was filled with water from the beast's snorting."[72] This was another attempt to triumph over nature.

Fig. 43 *Sestertius*, c. AD 64. The reverse shows a bird's-eye view of the harbor at Ostia, with moles on either side, including a portico on the left; in the center are several merchantmen, with sails furled; below them are a depiction of Neptune and above the harbor lighthouse along with another merchantman entering the harbor and a trireme on police duty.

Modern excavation has shed further light on Claudius' port, showing in particular just how elaborate the twenty-year project was.[73] An outer harbor basin was created with two moles that have been partially uncovered; there was also an inner harbor basin, where river ships could be kept and transshipment could securely take place. Part of a portico, facing onto the harbor, has been found here which shows the rusticated masonry that is distinctively Claudian, and again appropriately evoking here a triumph over nature (Fig. 44). There were also extensive facilities for the port, including an aqueduct.

Archaeology also reveals that a canal connected the inner harbor to the Tiber, allowing ships to pass through; and a second canal was also built to the north, its primary purpose being drainage of the Tiber River. These were an early phase of the project – both would have come in handy for transporting materials for the project – and are commemorated on an inscription found at Ostia, perhaps originally adorning an arch:

Tiberius Claudius Caesar Augustus Germanicus, son of Drusus, pontifex maximus, in his sixth year of tribunician power, consul designate for the fourth time, imperator 12 times, father of his country, by digging ditches from the Tiber on account of the construction of the port and extending them into the sea, freed the City from the danger of flooding.[74]

Here the emperor poses as triumphant savior of Rome, who ensures the people's security. As with the aqueducts, there is a military inflection to the emperor's building achievement.

Fig. 44 Part of portico from the Port of Claudius at Ostia, constructed c. AD 50. The brick
walls were added in a later adaptation of the structure.

How the canals, considerably downstream from Rome, protected the
City remains a puzzle, but other evidence attests Claudius' concern to
minimize the damage caused by Tiber flooding, which could affect in
particular grain warehouses. On his own authority, he had the Senatorial
commissioners for the river banks set up stones marking the boundary
of public land.[75] (All of the banks were, in principle, public, but were
constantly encroached on, thereby increasing the damage done by floods.)
A new prefect for the banks of the Tiber, directly answerable to Claudius,
was also created, and perhaps a procurator.[76] Related to this were other
administrative reforms, conforming to the pattern now becoming familiar:

Map 5 Claudius' construction projects in Italy

in place of the old Senatorial quaestor of Ostia, a procurator was established to be in charge of the city. The first attested was a freedman of Claudius, Claudius Optatus.[77] Cohorts were stationed at Ostia, and at Puteoli too – which would still handle grain vessels – to help protect the precious crops bound for Rome.[78]

Quite different from the aqueduct and harbor were the great Claudian roads, "driven through hills in cuttings," according to Pliny. Milestones have been found throughout the empire attesting to Claudian reconstruction of roads, for instance on the old Via Domitia in southern France: "Tiberius Claudius Caesar Augustus Germanicus, son of Drusus, pontifex maximus, with tribunician power, consul designate for the second time, imperator twice, repaired this."[79] How much the emperor knew of such repairs is not made explicitly clear (their volume, anyway, suggests that he gave at least some governors instructions to make all needed repairs in their provinces), and they seem not to be what Pliny had in mind. And while there is also some evidence for construction of new roads in the provinces, what Pliny really seems to be referring to is the three major roads Claudius had constructed through mountainous regions in Italy, each of which would bear his name. From these three, milestones have been found with more elaborate texts, suggesting that they were indeed in a special category.

First, in the central Apennines, Claudius finished by AD 47 the Via Claudia Nova, a mountain road that helped to connect previously existing routes in the north and to the south.[80] According to a milestone, it ran from Foruli in the Sabine country to the confluence of the rivers Aternus and Ticinus, "a distance of 47 miles, 192 paces."[81] The precise measurement of distance is, again, a tribute to the emperor's exactness in such matters. Second, in the same region and part of this overall scheme, Claudius extended the old Via Valeria under the name Via Claudia Valeria from the basin of the Fucine Lake to Corfinium and down the valley of the Aternus to the Adriatic coast.[82] An inscription from AD 48 attests that Claudius completed this as "censor" and also that he built in conjunction with it "43 bridges" – perhaps referred to by Pliny in his account of Claudian achievements.[83] While "censor" was part of Claudius' titulature at this time, it hints at the old connection between the holding of this office and the construction of major highways, first embodied by Appius Claudius the Blind.

Finally, and more impressive than the Apennine roads, Claudius constructed a major road from Italy through an Alpine pass to the Danube basin of Raetia.[84] As young men, his father Drusus and uncle Tiberius had secured this mountainous region, strengthening Italy's defenses, improving communications with Germany – and also winning glory for themselves and their stepfather Augustus. As an aging Horace wrote in a splendid ode of celebration: "Nothing there is that Claudian hands will not accomplish."[85] In keeping with his development of the upper Danube – Noricum, next to Raetia, also saw much activity under Claudius – Claudius revived an unfulfilled plan of Drusus to build a road along the route his campaign had followed.[86] Milestones from its two forks in northern Italy explicitly link the son's achievement to his father's, another example of Claudius' attempt to magnify himself through a dynastic claim: "Tiberius Claudius Caesar Augustus Germanicus . . . built the Via Claudia Augusta which Drusus, his father, had marked after opening the Alps by war."[87]

And then, last of all, was the most audacious of the Claudian projects, the draining of the Fucine Lake. That enterprise, we now see, showed all the typically Claudian features. It was to be a dramatic display of the triumph over nature. Yet it was eminently useful. It was costly, too, but costs were apparently to be offset by an investment scheme: individuals, we are told, could subscribe to the project, in exchange for reclaimed land.[88] Further, Claudius may have transferred workers who had dug the underground portions of the aqueduct to this project once aqueduct construction had gone aboveground (the upstream portion of the aqueducts was very close to the Fucine Lake).[89] The tasks were quite similar, though for the Fucine Lake channel, a much deeper excavation was required. A full and finally successful draining of the lake in the nineteenth century, while destroying all of the ancient structures leading to the canal, was able to reveal something of the canal itself and its construction. There are traces of approximately forty shafts, some dozens of yards deep, which allowed workers to shape the tunnel beneath and remove excess material.[90] It was the most ambitious project of its kind in antiquity.

Yet it all ultimately was a fiasco. After the disappointment following the mock naval battle, further work was done, and another celebration held – this time, gladiatorial pairs were placed on bridges over the lake – but again the drainage was apparently unsatisfactory.[91] The more admiring Pliny, rather tellingly, has nothing to say of any of these failures in his *Natural History*, and instead blames Nero for his negligence, but this is only to acknowledge by other means what really did happen; the project simply had to be abandoned. For most who wrote about it, the celebrations of the Fucine Lake became, more than anything else, a spectacular staging of Claudius' own failings.

Perhaps the construction was shoddy, as Tacitus alleges.[92] Perhaps there were more honest technical mistakes too.[93] But probably the most significant point for a historian to recognize is that there were, as every emperor had to discover, limits on what he could spend on public works. Suetonius claims that the construction of the channel required the labor of 30,000 men over eleven years.[94] Assuming a subsistence wage, one can translate this into a cost of 36 million sesterces – quite substantial indeed, if nowhere near the 350 million sesterces Pliny claims for the aqueducts.[95] But the land itself, it has been calculated, probably would only have been worth less than 20 million sesterces. The initial investment could not be paid off – whatever hopes Claudius may have had – and it must have seemed less than fruitful in the long run to continue pouring money into the enterprise (though Trajan and Hadrian would try, also in vain). The land could only produce a small fraction of the wheat the city of Rome needed to feed its inhabitants.

The ancient writers on Claudius naturally do not embark upon such calculations. They mention the shoddy construction, and they also hint darkly of corruption: the emperor's freedman Narcissus, they claim, in charge of the project, spent less than he received, and, according to Dio, to cover his embezzlement arranged for the whole undertaking to fail.[96] It is to charges of corruption – for this is by no means an isolated instance – that we also now must turn. They, too, will point to the paradox of Claudius that is also already revealed by his efforts to achieve spectacular public works. The loftier the goals the emperor set for his administration, the more likely he was to fail, and to open himself to allegations of incompetency, or even corruption. Yet precisely to try to win loyalty and increase his prestige, Claudius had to set loftier goals than those of Tiberius, even those of Caligula. In Claudius' public works is highlighted his dilemma – the heroic struggle for achievement and the failure he was almost bound to suffer. To wrestle with the waters of the Fucine Lake really was to be emperor of Rome.

CHAPTER 9

The burden of government

The Centennial Games, the empire-wide census, the aqueducts and port of Ostia: all these and more projected the energy that Claudius was devoting to ruling the Roman world. But the emperor sometimes expressed in public an even mightier goal for himself: to provide a just as well as efficient administration, one that would give all men their due, citizens *and* provincials. After the negligence of Tiberius, the errors of Caligula, upon both of which Claudius had looked in impotence as he only got older and older, he would now show the requisite firmness, the *constantia* that was the special virtue of his coins. The imperial finances would be recovered and rebuilt; he would break up fraudulent or collusive arrangements by which his patrimony dwindled. Fair treatment was owed not just to men in Rome but the provincials who paid the tribute and taxes on which the empire survived.

The emperor's aspirations are evident even in a fragment of an edict he issued concerning the requisitioning of services by officials in transit.[1] This was a never-ending source of complaint among Rome's subjects. Already in the days of the Republic it was set by law that provincial governors and their staffs could demand free lodging wherever they stopped for the night and, for a fee, the use of vehicles, mules, donkeys, and the like.[2] Under Augustus the privileges were extended, to incorporate (for instance) freedmen of the emperor traveling on his business or those in military service to him. The privileges were clearly abused: officials demanded more than their due, refused to pay required fees, claimed to be on official business when they were not, used forged passes. When a soldier appeared in a small provincial town, he might well be viewed as less an upholder of law and order than a bully and a thief.[3] Hence Claudius could fume: "Although I have often tried to relieve not only the colonies and municipalities of Italy but also those of the provinces, and also the communities of each provinces, from the burdens of providing transport, and although I thought that I had found a sufficient number of remedies, it has nonetheless not been possible because of the iniquity of men." In this characteristic outburst the emperor shows not just his efforts to end the corruption but also the frustration of his "remedies," whatever they might have been.

Not only did Claudius articulate such ideals, so too did men who governed provinces under him. Especially memorable is the preamble to an edict issued by Paulus Fabius Persicus, proconsul of Asia, which tried to rein in the finances of the great Temple of Artemis of Ephesus, where priests and other officials were lavishing excessive salaries on themselves:

> While it is very much my own view . . . that office-holders in charge of provinces must perform the office entrusted to them with all steadiness and good faith, so that they give thought to the lifelong good of the individual, of the whole province and of each city, and not for their own year of office alone, nevertheless, I gladly confess that I have been drawn to this view by the example of the most excellent and most truly just Leader, who has taken the whole race of men into his personal care and has granted among his benefactions, most welcome one and all, this favor in particular: to each person he has restored what is his own. I have therefore taken a decision which is burdensome but also necessary.[4]

Lofty sentiments – and reminiscent of the image of Claudius in Seneca's *To Polybius*, "the universal consolation of all men."[5] And yet, if one is to take Fabius literally, how, it might be asked, could a single mortal man take the whole world "into his personal care?" And if a man could think that he did have care for the whole world, what would be the results?

A further problem presents itself when one sets alongside the official rhetoric the fact that Claudius' principate afterwards was known for remarkable corruption, particularly among members of his court: his freedmen and his wife Messallina. Cassius Dio's account of the first seven years of the reign offers an extraordinary catalogue of acts of venality, even outright criminality. To be sure, Dio sometimes only acknowledges the influence of individuals within the court: when, for instance, Messallina and the freedmen issued dinner invitations on the same day as Claudius, the guests neglected Claudius.[6] But for Dio that influence quickly shades into wrongdoing that could prove deadly.

Dio can claim that Messallina and the freedmen sold the citizenship so often that it was said that it could be bought for a few glass beads; that they also sold military commands, procuratorships, and governorships; that they sold so much there was a scarcity of goods in Rome.[7] He can claim that Messallina, Narcissus, and others made false accusations in the trials following the plot of Scribonianus; that the freedmen worked to eliminate the Senator Umbonius Silio, who offended them; that Messallina forced leading women to commit adultery in the palace, while their husbands looked on; that she eliminated Catonius Justus, Prefect of the Praetorian Guard; that she poisoned Vinicius; that she brought down Valerius Asiaticus.[8] Claudius' wife and freedmen, according to Dio, manipulated him totally, enticing him with drink or sex, seizing on his cowardice.[9] If they desired somebody's death, they would terrify Claudius.[10] Frightful dreams were reported to him, dark rumors whispered into his ear.[11] Messallina tricked Claudius into forcing the actor Mnester to sleep with her, and when Mnester ceased to appear in the theater, and the people protested, Claudius appeared, apologizing, swearing that Mnester was not at his house.[12] Claudius alone failed to realize what was going on in the palace.

How much of this can be taken seriously? Certainly Dio's account is colored by his attitudes to the imperial women and freedmen of his own age: Julia Maesa, for instance, who was thought to have been behind the *coup* that put Elagabalus on the throne, or Cleander, the freedman chamberlain who became prefect of the Guard with the new title "Bearer of the Dagger."[13] Yet there is overlap between Dio and the earlier writings of Tacitus and Suetonius. To Tacitus we will turn more later.[14] Suetonius' less convincing portrait has already been mentioned.[15] Everything was done to suit the wives and freedmen, Suetonius claims at the end of a section of the biography that actually seems to reveal more of Claudius' personality than not; and then Suetonius later adds:

Enslaved to his freedmen and wives, as I said, he acted not as a *princeps* but a servant, conferring magistracies, armies, pardons, and punishments, for the gain of each one of them, or even because of their desires and lusts, while he for the most part remained unaware and ignorant. So that I do not have to include each small episode one by one: gifts were recalled, judgments rescinded, letters granting appointments were substituted or even blatantly altered.[16]

While details differ among the three authors, all share a perception of a Claudius manipulated by members of his court, selling their influence or using it to satisfy their own lusts.

That was the later perception, but contemporaries writing after Claudius' death suggest that at least a kernel of it went back to the reign itself. Pliny the Elder writes of a Thessalian eunuch who "for the sake of power" had himself enrolled among the freedmen of Claudius.[17] The accumulating wealth of the freedmen is noted by Pliny too, and also the power of the wives.[18] Seneca, in his *Apocolocyntosis*, also laments the power of the freedmen, along with corruption in the court (the selling of citizenships, for instance, is mentioned) and the flouting of judicial procedure.[19] According to Tacitus, the speech Seneca wrote for Nero to give to the Senate after Claudius' death outlining the form the new principate would take struck similar notes: Nero promised that he would not be the judge of everything, with accusers and defendants shut into the house; nothing "in his dwelling" would be for sale; house and state would be separate; the Senate would hold onto its ancient responsibilities, though Nero would pay heed to the armies.[20]

Seemingly it is a problem to reconcile Claudius' professed concern for good government (and justice) with the charges of rampant corruption (and injustice). But Nero's speech, as given by Tacitus, helps to suggest a resolution, as does the fragmentary edict on transport too. It may well be that the two go together. In trying to offer a more tightly controlled administration, the emperor took on more responsibilities, and also concentrated more power within his house, but in doing so he ended up opening the door to malfeasance and failure, and certainly brought on criticisms, especially from the Senators in Rome who felt edged out. The argument here is not that Claudius had a concerted "policy of centralization." Claudius could not have thought in terms of "a strong central organization"; his goal could not even have been "to extend and intensify his authority in the provinces" in any profound way.[21] That could only have been achieved (as it was in the late Roman Empire) with a great deal more coercion and decentralization – and, for reasons to be seen, was likely to lead only to greater corruption. But for what can be called his "government," Claudius did have priorities and plans, and these will be elucidated here. In doing so, the role of the freedmen and their notoriety in the later tradition are explained – while Messallina, along with her successor Agrippina, are best saved for later, when the great crisis of AD 48 is discovered.[22]

As Nero's speech in Tacitus suggests, the Roman "government" in the early empire had two chief branches: the old but still functioning *res publica* and the new imperial *domus*.[23] In earlier days executive power was concentrated in the hands of individual Senators, while some judicial power was shared with equestrians; the People passed the necessary laws. Now, the Senate still functioned, passing numerous decrees that came to have the force of law; its men were still sent out to govern most of the provinces, although those areas with a significant concentration of troops had legates appointed directly by the emperor; and Senators served in new posts to help the emperor with the responsibilities he had taken on (superintendency of the water supply, for instance). Yet with Augustus, quite new figures appeared on the scenes, beyond the Leader himself. There were equestrians directly

Table 4 *Major (and a few minor) officials of the early imperial government, c. AD 50*

	Senators	Equestrians	Freedmen and Slaves
Rome	quaestor of state treasury (*quaestor aerarii Saturni*) prefect of grain distribution (*praefectus frumenti dandi*) superintendent of roads (*curator viarum*) superintendent of water supply (*curator aquarum*) prefect of military treasury (*praefectus aerarii militaris*) prefect of the City (*praefectus Urbi*) superintendent of sacred buildings etc. (*curator aedium sacrarum . . .*) superintendent of public records (*curator tabularum publicarum*) superintendent of Tiber banks and bed (*curator riparum et alvei Tiberis*)	Praetorian prefect (*praefectus praetorii*) prefect of the grain supply (*praefectus annonae*) prefect of the watch (*praefectus vigilum*) prefect of Egypt (*praefectus Aegypti*) procurator of banks of the Tiber (?) (*procurator riparum et alvei Tiberis*)	household of Caesar (*familia Caesaris*) –correspondence (*ab epistulis*) –embassies and petitions (*a legationibus* and *a libellis*) –finances (*a rationibus*) –literary affairs (*a studiis*) procurator of water supply (?) (*procurator aquarum*) procurator of port of Ostia (*procurator portus Ostiensis*) prefect of the Misenum fleet (*praefectus classis Miseni*) (*cont.*)

Provinces

proconsuls	legates	procurators	agents (*procuratores*)
			– of imperial provinces
			– of public provinces (managing properties of the emperor)
			– of imperial estates
Sicily	Hispania Tarraconensis	Raetia	
Hispania Baetica	Lusitania	Noricum	
Narbonensis	Aquitania	Thrace	
Macedonia	Lugdunensis	Judea	------>
Achaea	Belgica	Mauretania Tingitana	
Asia	Germania Superior	Mauretania Caesariensis	
Bithynia-Pontus	Germania Inferior	Sardinia	
Cyprus	Britannia	Cappadocia	
Crete-Cyrene	Dalmatia		
Africa	Pannonia		
	Moesia		
	Galatia		
	Lycia-Pamphylia		
	Syria		
	Numidia		

Note: This chart is not exhaustive but rather intended primarily to guide the reader through chapters 8–9 in particular.

in service to him, such as the prefect of Egypt and the prefect of the grain supply. There were also true members of his household, slaves and former slaves, who had important administrative functions such as the management of the finances. Equestrians and freedmen alike could serve as "agents" (*procuratores*) of the emperor, indispensable men, and ever more relied on, in charge of minor provinces, the emperor's properties including mines and quarries, and collection of revenue across the empire (especially in provinces directly controlled by the emperor's legates). Members of his immediate family, including his wife Livia, had influence, and public roles to play as well.

Who the "government" really was under the immediate successors of Augustus is well illustrated by an edict concerning requisitioned transport and lodging issued by a governor in the early part of Tiberius' reign.[24] According to it, the people of the small Galatian village of Sagalassos were required to provide transport to "the excellent Leader's procurator" and for "those in military service," including Senators, equestrians "on duty for the excellent Leader," and centurions; lodging must be given free of charge to the governor's staff, "those on military duty from all provinces," and "the excellent Leader's freedmen." The catalogue reflects the personnel of government one would typically see outside of Rome – and it also reflects the main functions of this government. While the City of Rome and to a lesser extent Italy received special attention, in the provinces Rome primarily aimed to maintain security, enforce a basic system of justice, and, above all, collect taxes and other forms of tribute.

The Senatorial legate's repeated use of the expression "excellent Leader" reflects another important feature of the imperial government. The fundamental requirement for any office-holder, be he Senator or freedman, was loyalty to the emperor; diligence and competency came after that. This had the unsettling effect, for Senators anyway, of diminishing the gap between their high status and the low state of one born a slave. Pliny the Younger, a haughty Senator of the early second century AD – he had gone farther than his uncle and adoptive father, the equestrian Pliny the Elder – reflected on the matter in a pair of letters that casts a flood of light on the Rome of Claudius.[25]

Walking on the road to Tibur, less than a mile outside of Rome (Pliny writes), he came upon the tomb of Claudius' freedman Pallas with the inscription: "For this man in recognition of his loyalty and devotion to his patrons the Senate decreed the insignia of a praetor and 15 million sesterces, but he was satisfied merely with the distinction." Shocked – Pallas, in charge of the imperial finances, had a reputation for nothing so much as arrogance and avarice – Pliny decided (according to the second letter) to look up the Senatorial decree referred to in the inscription and was even more horrified by what he found there. According to the decree, Pallas deserved the rewards voted to him – the insignia of the Senatorial office of praetor and the largesse – for his "unique loyalty and unique diligence."

That was unpalatable enough, but even worse was what the rest of the decree suggested to Pliny: the servility of Claudius, and the servility of the Senate itself. The sum voted to Pallas had been rescinded on the plea of Pallas, which was relayed to the Senate by Claudius; the Senate had no choice but (in its own words) to "obey in this matter the wish of the Leader in this matter, whom it thought it was not right to oppose in any issue." As if to abase themselves further, the Senators also decreed:

since it is expedient that the benevolence of the Leader, which is most prompt in praising and rewarding those who deserve it, should be illuminated everywhere, especially in those places where those in charge of the administration of his affairs could be stirred to imitate him, and the manifest loyalty and integrity of Pallas could by his example incite the enthusiasm to emulate such honorable conduct, those remarks read out by the excellent Leader before our most distinguished order on 23 January last, along with the decrees of the Senate on these matters, should be inscribed on bronze, and this bronze tablet should be affixed to the mailed statue of the deified Julius.

In honoring so publicly Pallas' loyalty to Claudius, the Senate in turn showed theirs.

Pliny could be horrified by the episode; no doubt, to judge by Seneca's later complaints, some Senators were at the time. But to have a role in the government where one man was supreme and beyond the reach of law, you had to express loyalty. It was a black-and-white matter. Either you were for the emperor, or you were against him. Claudius, if he wished to survive, certainly had to think in those terms, and given the circumstances of his early life and accession, the question of loyalty was particularly acute. In trying to achieve an efficient and just government which was also viable he had to have men who were loyal. Whether they came from his *domus* or the *res publica* was a secondary matter. At the same time, if men vied with one another to show ever more loyalty, in order to earn the emperor's favor, there was a good chance that he was shielded from their true views.

Keeping these constraints in mind, as well as the loftier goals Claudius publicly set himself, we can discern four main tendencies in his administrative practice. First, though it is almost a truism, Claudius had to place great reliance on himself to achieve what he wanted. Given the evidence that has inexorably accumulated from papyri, bronze, and stone, it seems hard to disbelieve the later sources that give the impression of a Claudius constantly at work – issuing floods of edicts or assiduously presiding over hearings.[26] Claudius seems genuinely to have liked trying to intervene in, and solve, ongoing problems. One can guess that correspondence also took up a fair amount of his time, as it was said to have for Augustus.[27] Piles of letters had to be read each day, along with reports from officials within Rome. Answers had to be composed, especially for those serving abroad. There were embassies to hear as well.

Certainly, in generating edicts, or writing letters, there was ample help available behind the scenes; and it should also be recognized that part of what Claudius, and probably his staff, were doing was to create precisely a *picture* of the hardworking emperor. The image emerges brilliantly in the edict from AD 46 concerning citizenship of the Alpine Anauni; though issued from the resort town of Baiae, it depicts Claudius hard at work, settling disputes left over from the time of Tiberius, investigating new problems, rebuking that emperor's "persistent absence."[28] Similar depictions are found in the edict on transportation, or the speech to the Senate recommending admission of the Gauls.[29]

Second, there can be no doubt that Claudius relied certainly more openly, probably more deeply, than his predecessors on selected members of his *domus*, including the freedmen: Pallas (for the finances), Narcissus (for the correspondence), Callistus (for embassies), and Polybius (for literary activities of the court and perhaps petitions too).[30] It was not that earlier emperors lacked freedmen or slaves; indeed, as the epitaphs show, Claudius inherited many of his from members of his family, and they were valuable to him precisely because they were well-experienced in the affairs of the August House.[31] The differences seem to have been that their influence and authority had grown while that of Senators and equestrians was diminished, and that Claudius actually was eager for that influence to be recognized. Seneca's *To Polybius*, on one level a plea aimed to bring its writer out of exile, should be enough to show that.[32] The Senate decree concerning Pallas shows it even more, and makes plausible other testimony concerning their role in government (Dio's report, for instance, that freedmen were present at the trials in the Senate following the rebellion of Scribonianus in AD 42.)[33]

In fact, thanks to Pliny's evidence, there is good reason to lend credence to the version of the Pallas episode Tacitus gives, which further underscores the influence of the freedmen. According to Tacitus, the honors for Pallas were voted shortly after another debate in the Senate, concerning the punishment of women who chose to marry slaves.[34] At the meeting, Claudius placed a motion before the Senate recommending that if the woman had done so without the knowledge of the slave's master, she should be held to be in slavery; but that if the master consented, she was to be regarded as a freedwoman; and it was Pallas, Claudius said, who devised the motion. That would reflect Pallas' influence further – while the contents of the decree itself, which became a recognized part of Roman civil law, probably reflected the growing significance of the freedmen as a whole.[35] For the law, it has been suggested, was devised because more and more male slaves with inordinate power and influence were contracting unions with freeborn women; a measure was needed to allow the imperial house to keep certain legal rights over the children of such unions (who otherwise would be illegitimate and fatherless, but freeborn). To lose these rights would not have been in the interest of the emperor's purse – which was guarded, after all, by Pallas.

Third, for positions in the government that did require Senatorial appointees, new men, or descendants of recent new men, were favored over the old, and ever-dwindling, Republican nobility.[36] Whereas in the age of Tiberius 50 percent of the known Senatorial governors of provinces were patrician, the figure drops to 20 percent in Claudius'. For those provinces where Claudius directly named a legate, the figure drops even further – and two of the patricians in this group were granted that status by Claudius himself during the censorship. It was men from families who had risen up under the new empire who tended to do best, men from the towns of Italy, southern France, even Spain. Their lineage was no threat to the emperor (or themselves), and, it must be said, they often were more willing to embark upon a life of service to Caesar in exchange for the recognition they would receive: consulships were typically awarded to them later than patricians and other distinguished nobles, inspiring them to work harder, longer.[37] They were duller than the old nobility, but it is hard not to feel some sympathy for them. Men such as Quintus Veranius, Didius Gallus, Domitius Corbulo, Ummidius Quadratus, Memmius Regulus, and Flavius Sabinus: they epitomized the sort who found especial favor under Claudius – not that this was a policy utterly peculiar to him. It was part of a longer, more inexorable trend.[38]

They could take pride in their achievements, in lives of active service from one Caesar to the next. Parts of Veranius' grandiose epitaph from Rome survives, recounting his successes in the annexation of Lycia, recording his nomination as consul "at the instigation of Tiberius Claudius Augustus Germanicus," celebrating his adlection to patrician status and his award of superintendency of sacred buildings and public works and places by Claudius.[39] Erected during the principate of Nero, it provides a remarkable contrast to Seneca's snarling criticisms of the late emperor.

Bases for statues of Didius Gallus and Ummidius Quadratus, again set up after Claudius' death, rattle off their achievements, in a fashion that became so conventional that modern scholars can reconstruct in detail patterns of "Senatorial careers" in which the old Republican magistracies sit by side with the new imperial posts.[40] Didius was the "the legate of Tiberius Claudius Caesar Augustus Germanicus," Claudius' "companion" in the initial British expedition, who governed Sicily, Asia, Moesia, and finally assumed command of the whole British war; he also served as superintendent of the water supply of Rome.[41] Ummidius, legate of Tiberius in Lusitania, of "divine Claudius" in Illyricum, of Nero in Syria, served as "proconsul of the province of Cyprus, quaestor of the divine Augustus and Tiberius Caesar Augustus, curule aedile, praetor of the treasury, one of the fifteen for the settlement of disputes, superintendent of public records, prefect of grain distribution."[42] Ummidius was still in Lusitania, another inscription reveals, when news of Tiberius' death reached the province, and he immediately enforced an oath of loyalty to the new Leader Caligula.[43] He could be counted on, for loyalty.

Fourth, in all the men sent out to govern provinces, whether his appointees or not, Claudius tried to instill a sense that they should uphold fairness. Even men appointed by the Senate rather than himself, Claudius insisted in an edict, were to leave promptly for their new posting; intermissions were required between an individual's governorships to permit prosecution for extortion; and in the instructions given by the emperor to the governors of the provinces (known as *mandata*), an edict of Domitius Corbulo, proconsul of Asia under Claudius, happens to reveal, there were explicit directions on which disputes should be sent onto the emperor for adjudication and which should rest with the governor himself.[44] This last is the spirit of Claudian government, the hope to give "to each person . . . what is his own." As Fabius Persicus said in his decree on abuses at the Temple of Artemis in Epheus, "I have taken a decision which is burdensome but also necessary."[45]

A strong concern for just dealing is seen in a series of edicts from the Claudian prefects of Egypt, beginning with Aemilius Rectus. After promulgating the letter of Claudius concerning the Alexandrians, several months later he echoed the language of the new emperor – and the law governing requisitioned transport:

Lucius Aemilius Rectus declares:

No one shall be permitted to press into service the people in the country districts or to demand provisions or anything else gratis without a permit from me; anyone holding a permit from me may take sufficient necessities, provided he pay their cost. But if any of the soldiers or police or anyone at all of the aides in public service is reported to have acted contrary to my edict or to have used force against any of the people in the country districts or to have exacted money, from him I shall exact the severest retribution.[46]

Vergilius Capito later had an edict posted throughout the country, threatening once again those who abused the system of requisitioned transport, this time by pretending to travel on state business when they were not; the existence of an "audit department" based in Alexandria is revealed, the head of which was one Basilides, "the freedman of Caesar."[47] In the last year of Claudius' principate, Lusius Geta, responding to the complaints of priests of the god Socnopaeus, who were being forced to work the land in contravention of an earlier ruling: "if anyone is shown to have acted or intended to act so as to put my decisions, once made, in doubt, he will be duly punished either by a fine or corporally."[48]

Expressing lofty ideals, faced with the problem of survival, Claudius aimed for a just, as well as viable, government, and the concern for justice shines through, but as the edicts start to mount they seem to proclaim nothing so much as the actual impotence of the government to effect reform. Of course, given the surviving evidence, there is no way now to measure the overall success of Claudius' administration; evidence, in fact, may point to exceptions rather than the norm. Still, some credit probably should be given in two areas, the handling of finances and the appointment of provincial governors, before we finally expose the problems brought on by some of Claudius' decisions. The successes can be deemed such because there were continuities into the principate of Nero that followed.

Finance was a priority for any emperor, and especially for Claudius.[49] While Augustus already effectively had control of all the government monies, they were subdivided among various treasuries and the emperor's personal account, Claudius blurred the lines further and, from the point of view of future emperors, more effectively. In AD 44 he transferred control of the public treasury from praetors to new officials specially appointed by the emperor who would hold the office for a term of three years.[50] The decree concerning Pallas, at the same time, shows the Senate praising that individual for his careful control of the emperor's wealth, as if it were a matter of public concern.[51]

Pallas probably did work feverishly, with Claudius, to secure the patrimony that could be passed onto successors and help sustain imperial rule. According to the edict issued at Baiae, one Julius Planta was sent by Claudius to investigate whether certain territory in fact belonged to the emperor; he was to confer with the emperor's agents in the area.[52] Such agents, to judge by a difficult passage of Tacitus, whether equestrians or freedmen, were later entrusted by Claudius with greater legal authority over such matters, to allow quicker decisions, even probably in provinces that were not directly under the emperor's control.[53] Acilius Strabo was sent on a special assignment to Cyrene, to reclaim estates left there to Rome over a hundred years earlier which had, apparently, been seized by local proprietors.[54] Such lands would yield rents, and perhaps also grain that could be used directly to feed the city of Rome; the major road-building in Cyrene under Claudius also might have been motivated by a desire for better access to the crops.[55] There was also the Senate decree on freedmen's marriages proposed by Pallas, likely a financial boon for the imperial purse. Whatever scorn he aroused, even if he did feather his own nest, Pallas quite likely did a superb job of managing the emperor's, and the empire's, accounts. He was not dismissed on Nero's accession, at least not immediately, and the succession was well planned for financially, as well as in other respects.[56]

Second, it can be noted that men who served in important positions under Claudius did so under Nero as well. Domitius Corbulo became legate of Cappadocia and was entrusted with command of the war against the Parthians.[57] Didius Gallus, appointed legate of Britain by Claudius, stayed in the post several years into Nero's reign, the most difficult one, militarily speaking, at the time.[58] He was succeeded by Veranius, and Veranius by Suetonius Paulinus, Claudius' commander during the Mauretanian war.[59] Flavius Sabinus was legate of Moesia under Claudius and Nero, and Nero made him urban prefect; his brother, Vespasian, had to be sent by Nero to crush the Jewish rebellion at the end of AD 66.[60] These were strenuous and efficient men, not court intellectuals like Suetonius, and as subsequent developments proved, Claudius showed good judgment in promoting them.

In considering the longevity of the Roman empire, the work such men did should not be forgotten. If the abuse of delegated authority looms large in the extant evidence, that should not blind us to all those other, routine duties that were carried out by imperial officials, which over time did improve the lives of at least some of Rome's subjects. Settling disputes between communities and helping individual communities themselves when they were in trouble, traveling through the province to hear individual petitions and insuring the maintenance of communication networks within the province, enforcing existing legal privileges and finding worthy recipients for new ones, the best governors contributed to a justifiable sense of well-being and inclusion among at least some of Rome's subjects, as well as Roman citizens themselves; these governors, like their emperor, helped unify the Roman world too. At the same time, we also must remember, city councils enjoyed a fair degree of autonomy; local cults were mostly tolerated; living in a peace previously unknown in the Mediterranean, a myriad of peoples enjoyed ever more amenities in their cities. The hard work was theirs, but the peace of Augustus allowed its rewards to be enjoyed more predictably.

If it remains impossible to make a more detailed evaluation of Claudius' achievement, one can at least, on the other hand, point to problems inherent to some of his measures and the emerging principate itself. First, the emperor was, at the end of the day, only one man, and could only achieve so much. His power in the provinces, as seen, was qualified: at times it could be stupendous, affecting the lives of millions, but normally on a day-to-day basis it was limited. It might have helped to have an effective sharer in power, as Augustus, for instance, did in Agrippa, and then Tiberius. But eliminating petty abuses of requisitioned transport was, paradoxically, beyond Claudius' reach. He could try to increase the (tiny) number of officials monitoring the situation on the spot, or give them greater power. Yet that would require more taxes, and the likely outcome, anyway, was only more abuse. As Claudius' own edict on transport suggests, the power and prestige of officials over lowly provincials simply overwhelmed legal pronouncements, even from the emperor himself.[61] Claudius could lament the "the iniquity of men," but there was little he could do about it. And the prestige of government, and the emperor, would only suffer when the gap between stated goals and actual outcome widened. In the eyes of some, anyway, a pedantic – and pointless – interest in rules seems to have been the image Claudius ended up leaving.

Even the emperor's own house, with members in Rome but also busy across the empire, defied his close supervision. Structurally it might have made sense to turn over more authority to the freedmen; Claudius needed to be able to rely on men loyal to him. The weakness, though, was that they were not accountable in ways that senatorial or even equestrian officers would have been, nor was there a clear chain of command. The law's failure to reach them mirrored the inapproachability of the emperor himself. This may well have encouraged the improprieties that are a feature of any government – skimming money off accounts, pulling strings for friends, and the like; it most certainly led to endless suspicions and resentment. Even worse, from the emperor's point of view, the strengthening of his house created (we shall see) a kind of monster potentially strong enough to bring him down.[62] He himself might have to show respect publicly for the freedman, if he wanted to succeed.

This needs to be taken into consideration, when Claudius' practice is compared to that of his predecessors, especially Augustus and Tiberius. It is all too easy simply to assume that Claudius' dependence on the freedmen was entirely a consequence of his weak character; but at least some of his dependence, the argument is here, should be considered rather a sign of his relatively weak position, in AD 41 and following. When Augustus discovered that his freedman secretary Thallus had divulged the contents of a letter for 2,000 sesterces, the emperor (Suetonius writes) had the freedman's legs broken.[63] That sort of behavior, admirable as it no doubt was in the eyes of equestrians (like Suetonius) or Senators, might have been a risky one for Claudius to adopt, should he have found irregularities in his own household. Yet, as Suetonius' report shows, it was a worthwhile course of action for Augustus to take: part of his claim to rule was staked on the moral superiority of himself above all, but also that of the members of his house.[64] To forfeit it was to risk losing authority.

Some Senators and equestrians must have bridled at being likened to slaves and freedmen, or having to seek the favor of slaves and freedmen, rather than that of their own peers, to advance politically and gain the ear of the emperor – even to be released from exile. Seneca cannot have been alone. Vespasian allegedly obtained his command in Britain through Narcissus; the former master of Callistus allegedly was kept waiting at the freedman's door, while others were admitted.[65] Bruised feelings were an undeniable flaw of Claudius' statesmanship, and this alone may be enough to account for much of the hostility found in the later tradition; it may not be necessary to bring in rampant corruption into the indictment too. At the same time, it must be remembered that all the overt criticisms of Claudius recoverable now were made later: surrounded by sycophants and suppliants, it was perfectly possible for the emperor to be insulated from many of the resentments his policies might have raised.

Severe enforcement of thorough and thoughtful rules, promoting full accountability and transparency for all officials of the government, would not have seemed conducive to Claudius' survival, especially in the short term. Moreover, such measures were really beyond the reach of a society so obsessed with distinctions of status (even if there was mobility too). Early imperial Rome was a world where even in government it seemed right to get things done by calling in favors, even pulling strings. For most, the question of good government, in practice, was who would have the clout or connections, who would dispense the favors, and who would benefit from them, not whether there was a viable alternative. It was the position of the freedmen under Claudius that seemed an aberration at the time and afterwards, repellent to those of high status, and it would be cut back by Claudius' successors who found ways to function with less reliance on them. That was made easier by fuller acceptance of the principate among the top orders of society. Loyalty to the emperor had become a more engrained virtue.

By the age of Suetonius, it was equestrians, like Suetonius himself, who were in charge of the emperor's correspondence, finances, literary pursuits. This, indeed, helps explain the disdain Suetonius shows for Claudius in his biography; men of high status, Suetonius feels, should always have been the ones an emperor looked to for real help with administration. An imperial freedman might have had a very different view on the matter. But by Suetonius' day, the battle was largely over. The equestrians had won. It is their side of the story that survives.[66]

The Senator Cassius Dio, in his great history of Rome, imagines a discussion that occurred between Augustus and his closest advisors, Agrippa and Maecenas, in 29 BC, after their final victory in the civil wars.[67] What form should the new government take? Should it be more democratic, or monarchical? While Agrippa takes the former view, the crafty Maecenas takes the latter, offering a long catalogue of specific recommendations. In regard to the freedmen, Dio has his Maecenas say, Augustus should show his respect for them as well as others in his entourage; his security depends on it. But the freedmen "should not enjoy excessive powers, but should all be kept under strict discipline, so that your reputation should never suffer from their actions. For everything they do, whether for good or ill, will be attributed to you, and your own character will be judged in the light of the conduct which you tolerate in them."[68] When one thinks of posterity's judgment of Claudius, the Senator's words ring true.

CHAPTER 10

The judgment of Pallas

It can require a great deal of effort to lodge from one's mind the lurid portrait of Messallina found in accounts written after her death. If Claudius became synonymous with foolishness, his wife became a byword for much worse, the very lowest forms of depravity. Already Pliny the Elder can speak of her staging a showdown with a professional prostitute – in which she won with a score of twenty-five![1] Perhaps even more indelible is the truly pornographic picture drawn by Juvenal in his satire on the misdeeds of Roman wives:

listen to what Claudius endured. When his wife ascertained that her husband was asleep, she would leave, with no more than a single maid in her company. Preferring a mat to her marriage bed on the Palatine, she dared to put on a night-time hood, the August whore. Like that, with a blonde wig hiding her black hair, she entered the warm brothel with its old curtains to an empty cubicle – her own. Then she stood, naked and for sale, with her nipples gilded, under a sign "She-wolf," showing off the belly you came from, noble-born Britannicus.[2]

The woman of high status turned whore was already a figure of fascination in the days of the Republic; in the Empire it could reach new extremes – the wife of the emperor here comports herself as the lowest type of prostitute, one put on display naked for the reader of the poem.[3]

The reality, though, was that throughout his early years as emperor, Claudius' wife Messallina was conspicuously honored in public. As Augustus' wife Livia had before her, she won the right to sit with the Vestal Virgins and the use of a special carriage, on which she rode at the British triumph of AD 44.[4] A prefect of Egypt, C. Julius Postumus, dedicated in the August Forum a statue of sixteen pounds of gold fulfilling a vow made for Claudius, "Valeria Messallina, wife of Augustus, and their children."[5] Her name was inscribed, with that of Claudius, on a city gate of Verona.[6] In Arneae, in Lycia, and Leptis Magna, in Tripolitania (archaeology happens to reveal) statues were set up of her.[7] Her portrait appeared on the coinage

Fig. 45 Silver didrachm of Caesarea in Cappadocia, AD 41–48. The obverse shows a bust of Messallina; the reverse Claudius' three children, Octavia, Britannicus, and Antonia.

of provincial cities: Alexandria and Sinope, Nicomedia and Cnossus, to name a few.[8] A silver coin of Cappadocian Caesarea juxtaposes her bust with a representation of Claudius' three children, Octavia, Britannicus, and Antonia – the first two from her, the last from a previous marriage (Fig. 45).[9]

Whatever stories later circulated of Messallina's scandalous activities behind the scenes, publicly she was of great value to her husband. As the great-granddaughter of Augustus' sister Octavia, she helped to reinforce Claudius' claim to membership in the August House. Indeed, Claudius' marriage to her, in the principate of Caligula, mirrored his own belated entry into public life at that time.[10] (His first wife was Plautia Urgulanilla, daughter of a close personal friend of Livia; his second, Aelia Paetina, a relation of the ambitious Praetorian prefect Sejanus.[11]) Messallina's value only grew after Claudius became emperor and she bore him a male heir, Britannicus, in AD 41.[12] Well could coins of that time feature the new goddess "August Hope" (Fig. 46): Britannicus would ensure the survival of imperial rule, and help secure Claudius' own position.[13] Thus could Messallina be honored explicitly as Livia was before her: in the words of a recently discovered decree of the Senate from AD 20, Augustus' wife had "served the *res publica* superlatively" in giving birth to Tiberius.[14] But the women of the August House also had a more symbolic value, because women, in the Roman imagination, served as personifications of virtues such as Constancy, Faithfulness, Moderation, or, indeed, Hope.[15]

Fig. 46 *Sestertius*, c. AD 41. The obverse shows the head of Claudius in his early portrait style; the reverse the figure of "August Hope" holding a flower and raising her skirt with her left hand. The goddess is depicted in an archaic style.

The emperor's womenfolk could bring to him and his rule a strong sense of morality, and from Augustus onwards a claim to morality was one justification for imperial rule. In the same decree from AD 20, Claudius' mother, Antonia, is praised for "the purity of her character."[16]

Securing the continuity of the imperial house and embodying its moral integrity: these were reasons enough to explain the new roles in public life taken on by the emperor's women. It is not necessary to assume that the role reflected any significant degree of outright power. To be sure, by their position, female members of the August House could exert influence: Livia, in AD 20, used hers to exonerate her friend Plancina when the latter was implicated in charges against her husband, and according to the same Senate decree of that year, Livia "rightly and deservedly should have supreme influence in what she requested from the Senate, but she used that influence most sparingly."[17] Claudius' mother Antonia had her web of connections too.[18]

Some ability, then, to influence her husband, as well as other members of the house, Messallina no doubt had. She also, presumably, had sway over the wives of leading men, women such as Caligula's one-time consort, the fantastically rich Lollia Paulina; Messallina's position here mirrored her husband's, and she helped to set the tone for Senatorial society as a whole.[19] And it is perfectly possible that Messallina dallied with prominent men (if not paying customers), to win further influence for herself. But it is difficult to take at face value, and impossible to verify, such reports, or the claims of Messallina selling political offices or citizenship, condemning personal enemies and acquiring confiscated property for her personal use.[20] For such charges may only have taken shape after her fall, or even years after that.

Certainly, though, in AD 48, something went drastically wrong. Tacitus' is the fullest account, one that, on first glance, might seem little more reliable than that of a satirist (and in fact, Juvenal, in another of his satires, has something to say of Messallina's final days too).[21] According to the historian, while Claudius was busy with his censorship, Messallina became so inflamed with the handsome consul designate, C. Silius, that she compelled him to divorce his wife, commit adultery with her, and host at his own house the empress and her large entourage. But then Silius himself "urged . . . their dissembling be broken off" and sought an open marriage; his own reason for doing so is not really clear, but he enticed Messallina to act by talk of bringing down the emperor. While Claudius was away at Ostia, they celebrated a wedding, complete with a witnessed contract, celebratory supper, and a night spent in "marital license." That the marriage occurred might seem fantastic, Tacitus writes, "yet nothing has been made up to achieve sensationalism; I have only transmitted, and only will, what was heard and written by my elders." The admission underscores a key fact about his narrative: rumors swirl around in it, allegations are made, but what Silius and even Messallina were actually planning to do after their marriage is never clearly explained by the historian. Nor does Tacitus indicate that it was actually well known at the time either.

And so, appropriately, "the Leader's household shuddered." Whatever was afoot, the freedmen, fearing for their own position, give Claudius a report of Messallina's marriage through two concubines. Narcissus is then brought in: "Are you aware of your divorce? Senate, people, and soldiers witnessed the marriage to Silius, and, if you don't act quickly, her husband holds Rome!" Claudius calls in advisors, is enveloped by rival cries, and can only ask repeatedly whether he is still in control of the empire.

As the emperor is brought back to Rome, accompanied by Vitellius, Narcissus, and Claudius' friend Caecina Largus, the freedman refuses Messallina a hearing with her husband and, after a visit to Silius' house, during which some of the imperial heirlooms were found, leads the way to the Praetorian Camp. In a grim echo of Claudius' accession seven years earlier, the cohorts clamor for Silius' condemnation. Silius, along with several Senators and equestrians judged accomplices, quickly met their ends. Messallina, meanwhile, struggling to save herself in the gardens of Lucullus that had been confiscated from Valerius Asiaticus, was dispatched on the orders of Narcissus. Her corpse was granted to her mother, Domitia Lep-ida, Narcissus was awarded quaestorian insignia, and the Senate voted that Messallina's name and images be removed "from private and public places."

Suetonius and Cassius Dio, and Juvenal too, corroborate Tacitus' basic narrative of Messallina's marriage to Silius, and her subsequent execution, without trial.[22] But they also do not disclose what, if any, the imperial wife's ultimate intentions were. As in Tacitus, there are *hints* of political ambition: Suetonius writes that Claudius believed that Silius was aiming for power, Dio that Narcissus frightened Claudius into believing that Messallina was going to kill him and set up Silius as ruler in his stead. But ultimately, in all the accounts, the emphasis is placed on Messallina's prodigality.

There are good reasons to wonder if this is entirely convincing. For one thing, while Tacitus may certify that he is only transmitting what he found in previous accounts, that need not make them true. Evidently some kind of official version was disseminated at the time – with the emphasis likely placed on the immorality of Messallina and her associates, Silius above all. But given that there was no public trial for her, and given the very real condemnation of her memory, it was perfectly possible that details were few and misleading – and also that slander, or surmises, came to fill in for reliable testimony. Interestingly, Pliny's tales of Messallina's sexual enormities find no place in Seneca's *Apocolocyntosis*, where the empress is presented as an innocent victim of Claudius, disgracefully put to death. It could well be that much of the tale of her final days originated in the memoirs later produced by her own replacement, Agrippina – a work Tacitus says that he consulted.

To be sure, according to the same logic by which an emperor's wife could support the imperial house symbolically, she could also undermine him symbolically, and on these grounds adultery could, perhaps had, to be condemned publicly.[23] And so, even if we are inclined to distrust the later tales of Messallina's excesses, there need not have been anything more political about her adulterous affair with Silius than that (assuming that there was an affair). But Tacitus' account of Messallina, like the others, does insist that it was finally Messallina's *marriage* to Silius that brought her down, and that the marriage had a number of witnesses; it was not simply the standard charge of adultery behind closed doors. Marriage, in fact, was no crime, and by private law anyway, Messallina could in principle divorce Claudius and remarry, even without his consent.

Keeping that marriage in view, along with the hints of political intrigue in the sources, modern scholars have not been short of theories suggest-ing what really was going on.[24] Perhaps Silius and Messallina really were together plotting to overthrow Claudius. Perhaps Silius alone was plotting to overthrow Claudius, with Messallina as a pawn in his scheme. Perhaps Silius was just part of a wider Senatorial plot against Claudius. Perhaps Messallina was, by marrying Silius, aiming to establish a more elective principate. Perhaps the freedmen fabricated the whole episode to bring down Messallina. Perhaps Messallina, with the help of Silius, was trying to subvert the power of the freedmen. Perhaps, perhaps: the multiplication of theories shows the futility of the exercise – not that all are equally plausible. And these in fact are not all, for another line of investigation suggests that Messallina turned to Silius only *after* her position was endangered.[25] Claudius had been facing down threats, real or perceived, posed by Senators and equestrians, throughout his years in power, most recently (it would seem) from Valerius Asiaticus. Perhaps Claudius was already looking to a new marriage as a way to bolster *his* position. There was one woman above all who might be able to help, and she was now available to do so.

Julia Agrippina, the eldest daughter of Claudius' brother Germanicus, was born probably in AD 15 in Ara Ubiorum, on the Rhine frontier, during her father's campaigns there.[26] Through her mother, Vipsania Agrippina, herself the daughter of Agrippa and Julia, she was of the blood of Augustus. Tiberius arranged for her marriage as a young teenager to Domitius Ahenobarbus, from a distinguished noble family, and together they had one child, born in AD 37.[27] By this time, her brother Caligula had acceded to the principate, and Agrippina, along with her two sisters Drusilla and Livilla, enjoyed renewed prominence in public life.[28] But after Drusilla's death the following year, Agrippina and Livilla were exiled, in the aftermath of the execution of Drusilla's late husband Aemilius Lepidus.[29] They were only brought back early in Claudius' reign, and it was now that Agrippina showed her mettle.[30]

While Livilla would be back in exile within a year, Agrippina, now husbandless, worked at restoring her own fortunes, and those of her young son. She solicited, it is recorded, the aristocrat Sulpicius Galba in marriage but meeting with no success turned to an older man as wealthy as he was witty, Passienus Crispus, who had formerly been married to Agrippina's sister-in-law, Domitia Lepida, the mother of Messallina.[31] Passienus died before AD 47, murdered by his wife, a later source claims.[32] His death undeniably left her free, and her son rich. But less clear were the future prospects of the ten-year-old, with the blood of Augustus flowing through his veins. Perhaps, then, the real plot of AD 48 was Agrippina's – on her own behalf, and her son's. Again, there can be no certainty whatever with such a hypothesis, even if it has the advantage of pointing to the real benefits

Claudius derived when he did contract a marriage with his own niece Agrippina.

However it was, the tale of Messallina's fall, as recounted by Tacitus, still has other lessons to offer. In these pages of his *Annals*, the historian helps to isolate problems engendered by the rise of an imperial court as part of the establishment of the principate. Already under Augustus there was something very much like a monarch's court. To a large degree it overlapped with the emperor's household, comprising members of his own immediate family and his slaves and freedmen, but it could also include highly trusted friends from the Senatorial and equestrian orders (men such as Vitellius).[33] Individually, members of the court fought for influence with the emperor, to advance their own position or simply secure their survival. The result was a perpetual contest for the emperor's ear, one that, at its worst, could degenerate into a welter of innuendoes and allegations, out of which the emperor would have to try to discern fact from fiction. The court did not just shield itself from public scrutiny; its affairs, Tacitus well dramatizes, could be opaque even to its insiders. The court might even turn on itself.[34]

A single mistake might cost the emperor his life. As the principate grew into more of an institution, the most adroit members of the court, surviving from one ruler to another, could come to see themselves as less dependent on the survival of the current *princeps*, rather than the principate itself. Indeed, they might even try to replace an individual ruler, if they thought it would benefit them, individually or collectively. The court was a source of strength to the emperor, but it also represented, literally, his most immediate source of danger. All monarchs have to fear their court, but the problem was especially acute for Rome's early emperors precisely because Rome was not fully a monarchy. Thanks to lingering Republican sentiment, the court could not be regulated by formal rules that would contain its individual members' powers; even worse, there was no firm law of succession to deter rival claimants to the throne. Ongoing tension between emperors and Senate might enlarge the pool of willing candidates – the events of AD 41 were enough to show that, and had made the whole situation worse. If Messallina conducted an affair with a prominent Senator, much less contracted a marriage, Claudius would have been foolish not to consider the alliance at least a *potential* political threat.[35]

At the same time, because members of the emperor's family in particular were useful to him as "arguments" for imperial rule – they could guarantee a smooth succession of power – if the emperor's household came undone, so too, it could be thought, did the *res publica* itself. That is, in a Rome where the *res publica* was patently not kept separate from the emperor's *domus* – where the Senate could thank Livia for serving the state because she had borne a child – the court was not just a physical threat to the emperor, but through its doings could symbolically undermine his position as well. Whatever doubts one may entertain about Messallina, Tacitus is not at all wrong to invite the reader to think that if, as seems clear, Messallina was attempting to divorce her husband and marry Silius, Claudius' grip on the empire was suddenly made more tenuous. Whatever other intentions she and Silius had, and even if she was responding to the perceived threat of Agrippina, that was enough to condemn her, without a trial. And so her statues were taken down, her name chiseled out of inscriptions – and stories came to circulate that may to a large degree have forever buried the truth about this woman.[36]

Tacitus significantly ends the eleventh book of his *Annals* with the fall of Claudius' wife and opens the twelfth with an echo: "Because of the slaughter of Messallina, the Leader's household was broken apart, and a competition arose among the freedmen as to who would select a wife for Claudius."[37] There were, Tacitus claims, three women in contention, Julia Agrippina, Lollia Paulina, and Claudius' divorced wife Aelia Paetina, and each found a champion in one of the three principal freedmen, Pallas, Callistus, and Narcissus respectively.[38] Claudius, vacillating, finally held a council at which the three former slaves made their cases, with Pallas prevailing. He was helped by Agrippina's own enticement of her uncle; and even as she plotted her own union – a legal prohibition of marriages between paternal uncle and niece being the only obstacle – she also "began to build something greater," a match between her own son, the 10-year-old Domitius, and Claudius' daughter Octavia, who was betrothed to the young noble Lucius Silanus (himself a great-grandson of Augustus too).[39] With the aid of Vitellius, who accused Silanus of incestuous relations with his sister Calvina, Agrippina persuaded Claudius to break the engagement and remove Silanus from political office and even membership in the Senate.[40]

Still, at the start of AD 49, the legal obstacle of marriage between uncle and niece remained; "it was incest, and if that were disregarded, there was fear that it would break out into a disaster for the state."[41] According to Tacitus, it was again Vitellius who would make things happen, "with his own special skills."[42] A consensus had to be formed. Vitellius appeared before the Senate and, as if it were an emergency, interrupted the proceedings to state that Claudius needed a wife to help him with the heavy labor of supporting the globe: Agrippina excelled in her lineage; she was of proven fertility; she was a woman of nobility, sanctity, and honor. It might be said that the

marriage of daughters of brothers was a novelty, but they were solemnized
by other nations, and other matches, once prohibited, had come to be
accepted in Rome; "this also would be among the things that were later in
regular use."[43]

Vitellius' echoes of Claudius' speech on the admission of Gallic nobles
into the Senate could be a Tacitean joke, but there can be no doubt that
a Senate decree was passed legalizing weddings between uncles and their
brothers' daughters: later legal sources record it as a part of Roman civil
law.[44] It should not then be too difficult to accept also Tacitus' report that
crowds were on hand in Rome to entreat Claudius to the marriage – had
they not arisen spontaneously on behalf of Germanicus' daughter, they
could easily have been arranged.[45] Senate and People together would show
their consensus. And so the union took place, and (Tacitus says) on the
very same day, Silanus took his own life, while his sister was banished from
Italy.[46] The consul designate, Mammius Pollio, then made another motion
before the Senate, in which Claudius was begged to betroth Octavia to
Agrippina's young son Domitius.[47]

Throughout his narration of the emperor's new marriage, Tacitus is
once again meditating on the way the imperial court, and the emperor,
operated. With the fall of Messallina, a hole was blown in the court,
and those left standing must surely have tried frantically to reconfigure
arrangements to their own benefit. Intrigues no doubt there were, even if
we need not take entirely at face value Tacitus' account. His council scene
is surely an invention, so obviously does it parody the mythical tale of the
judgment of Paris. Even the domineering role assigned to Agrippina may
only reflect the later blackening of her memory, while the highhandedness
of the freedmen fits into the tradition that grew up surrounding them.
Still, at least something of what happened can be determined. That is,
Tacitus, through his likely more reliable narrative of the Senate and People's
doings, once again can demonstrate something historically authentic, and
of significance: the role that the old organs of the Republican government
played in lending legitimacy to the doings of the imperial house and forging
a new consensus after the crisis of AD 48.

The clue to understanding Claudius' final marriage to Agrippina lies in
the lengths he went to enact it – flouting the taboo on incestuous unions,
and changing the rules of Roman private law to permit it – and the lengths
he went to celebrate it. In principle, any new wife for Claudius of suitable
status would have been welcome and, truly, needed, as a sign of renewal
for the *domus*. Agrippina alone had something more to offer. She herself
had the blood of Augustus, and a son approaching maturity with the blood

of Augustus.[48] But it was not only that: when, with his own blood heirs having failed him, Augustus adopted Tiberius and promoted him as his successor, Augustus had made Tiberius adopt in turn Germanicus.[49] The plan was that Germanicus ultimately would succeed, and, with his wife the elder Agrippina, have produced heirs also of the blood of Augustus. As it happened, Germanicus died prematurely, and it was left to his son Caligula to take over from Tiberius. Now, as young Domitius was approaching puberty, he with this blood could lay a claim to fulfilling the hopes of the founder Augustus in a way that Claudius did not.

Messallina and Britannicus had, also, proven unable to constitute with Claudius a dynasty that could stave off the threats Claudius faced since AD 41; and now, with Messallina dead and disgraced, it might have seemed harder to continue promoting Britannicus. The hope for the new marriage, from the start, must have been that Agrippina and her son Domitius, married to Claudius and his daughter respectively, would be able to succeed here. It was an entirely rational response to Messallina's fall, and even the crises and challenges of the entire first part of the reign (hence the view that Messallina may already have sensed danger when she took up with Silius). Whatever his precise thinking, however it came about, in AD 48 Claudius essentially had to go back to the scheme Augustus had established for a succession long ago. Of course, it was probably not entirely clear from the start that Nero would be the favored successor: he and Britannicus were both still young, and Claudius might cultivate them together, as Augustus had his two grandsons, Gaius and Lucius.[50]

Still, the whole episode was a setback for Claudius – and arguably for the people of Rome and Rome's subjects. It undermined the notion that the principate was an office that could be detached from the charismatic authority of the founder Augustus, with his dynastic aspirations, yet still did not openly acknowledge a principle of hereditary succession. The uneasy compromise would continue. While in AD 41 Claudius set important precedents for successors beyond Nero, in AD 49, a step was taken towards the civil war that erupted after Nero's death, when nobody of Augustus' blood, or family, was left to claim the principate.

And so, just as Messallina's doings were a matter of public concern, and her memory could be condemned by the Senate, so too was the matter of Claudius' new marriage, and also the betrothal of Octavia to Nero. Tacitus may have his fun with Vitellius' speech, but it makes perfect sense that Vitellius should have brought the matter up before the Senate. The Senate and People had been called in before to help buttress the August House in a time of crisis – for instance in the aftermath of the death of Germanicus

and the trial of Germanicus' alleged murderer Piso that followed in AD 20.[51]
Now they were called in again, to help legitimize this newest incarnation
of the August House, in which the novel step of an incestuous union
had been taken. Such close marriages are a familiar, and understandable,
feature of other monarchies: in Ptolemaic Egypt, even full brothers and
sisters on the throne married each other.[52] But they were foreign to the
Republican tradition of Rome, and to give Claudius' union at least a veneer
of credibility, help was needed. The Senate and People provided it.

After the marriage to Agrippina in AD 49, there was a logical next step to
take, and it was taken early in the following year. Tacitus writes:

In the consulship of C. Antistius and M. Suillius, adoption was being hurried
forward for Domitius through the influence of Pallas, who, bound to Agrippina
as the arranger of her marriage and then tied to her through illicit sex, was urging
Claudius to take thought for the interests of the state, to surround the boyhood of Britannicus with mature strength: so in the house of Divine Augustus,
although Augustus had been supported by his grandsons, his stepsons had pros-
pered; Tiberius had taken on Germanicus, in addition to his own stock; Claudius
too should gird to himself a young man who would take on a share of his responsibilities! Overcome by these words, Claudius placed Domitius, the elder by three
years, ahead of his son, delivering before the Senate a speech in the same manner
as he had heard from his freedman.[53]

Applying the lessons learned above, we can put to the side any conversations
Claudius and Pallas shared but still assume that Claudius did speak before
the Senate on the matter of adopting Nero. He did so, because again it was
a way of shoring up his position, and again he wished for the Senate to
lend its authority to a further reconfiguration of the imperial house – one
which would, in due course, entail a brother marrying a sister.

A law was passed, Tacitus goes on to record, by which Domitius was
transferred into the Claudian family and took on the name of "Nero."[54]
Names were thus to work their magic again, for the young man went
from being L. Domitius Ahenobarbus to Nero Claudius Caesar Drusus
Germanicus.[55] Most obviously, the change served to mark Nero as a possible
successor to Claudius; but it also, more subtly, reaffirmed the fitness of the
Claudii, including Claudius himself, to rule in their own name; they had
wrested the bestowal of the name of "Caesar" from the Julii. At just the
same time, Tacitus adds, Julia Agrippina – the key link in all of this –
was honored with the new name "Augusta."[56] She was the first wife of
a ruling emperor to bear it, and so it elevated her over her predecessor
Messallina; but at the same time it patently recalled Livia's acquisition
of the name (through Augustus' will), in AD 14, when her son, Tiberius

Fig. 47 *Denarius*, c. AD 51. The obverse shows the head of Claudius; the reverse the head of "Agrippina Augusta," wearing a crown of wheat leaves.

Fig. 48 *Aureus*, c. AD 51. The obverse shows the head of Claudius; the reverse a bust of Nero in a cloak with the abbreviated legend NERO CLAUDIUS CAESAR DRUSUS GERMANICUS, LEADER OF THE YOUTH.

Caesar, acceded. Precious metal coinage of Rome minted at around this time shows the new names, and a suggestive set of juxtaposed portraits: Claudius with Agrippina, and Claudius with Nero (Figs. 47–48).[57]

Both of these coins have an extraordinary set of messages to impart. To take that with Claudius and Agrippina (Fig. 47): this was another first, the first time on such coins that a ruling emperor was presented with his wife, underscoring the support she lent to him as a member of the August House.[58] She is indeed "Augusta" to his "Augustus," and on the coinage, her features have been assimilated to his: she has a prominent nose, an overbite,

Fig. 49 Portrait of Agrippina, wife of Claudius. Ny Carlsberg Glyptotek, Copenhagen.

and a small but jutting chin. What is more, Agrippina is depicted with a crown of wheat leaves that was a typical attribute of the goddess Ceres. She is the first imperial woman to be so honored on the coinage in her own lifetime. The link to the goddess suggests the virtues of motherhood and fertility, and so the promise that Agrippina would continue the dynasty of Augustus and accordingly bring continued peace and prosperity to the people of Rome.

But the coinage was only a small part of the public honoring of Agrippina and her son: in a sense, it was almost like AD 41 all over again, with old portraits (of Messallina) coming down, and new portraits (of Agrippina and Nero) going up.[59] Images of Agrippina had gone up before, but the great majority of those now preserved likely date to the later years of Claudius' reign.[60] These show a woman with a short broad face, a low forehead, flaring eyebrows, a small mouth with a slightly protruding upper lip, and a small but very pronounced chin.[61] A good example is to be found in Copenhagen (Fig. 49). One notices in particular some resemblance between her facial features and those of her father, Germanicus. The chief difference between this Claudian image of Agrippina and that which came before lies in the coiffure: in the later examples, Agrippina's hair is parted, waved at the parting and in the back, but on the side of the face cut shorter and arranged in a mass of large, corkscrew curls that exploit the sculptor's drill. While the hairstyle looks back to one seen in her mother's portraits – and at the same time may well have corresponded to a coiffure the younger Agrippina adopted in real life – one can also feel that there is a sort of drama to this sculpture that matches the abandonment of Augustan restraint seen elsewhere in Claudian art.

Portraits of Nero, by contrast, cannot have been widespread before the marriage of his mother to Agrippina, but after his adoption by Claudius proliferated.[62] The earliest examples show a young boy with a round fleshy face and even features; he has a full head of hair, brushed in long strands from the crown of his head parted slightly in the center; it also grows long on the nape of the neck (Fig. 50). The facial features, and the coiffure in particular, unmistakably link him to earlier male members of the August House. An especially fine example was found in the basilica of Velleia, in northern Italy, and must have been set up in conjunction with a portrait of Agrippina also found there and one of Claudius re-carved from an earlier statue of Caligula that may for a time have been warehoused.[63] The bust of Nero was inserted into a previously carved body – with a boy's *bulla*, showing that the ensemble should be dated before Nero put on the toga of manhood in AD 51. The ensemble, one can suppose, went up rather hastily as news reached Velleia of the reconfiguration of Claudius' house, authorized by the Senate decrees, which might well have been widely disseminated.

Two more elaborate works register the impact of Agrippina's marriage to Claudius. The first, one of the series of imperial reliefs from Aphrodisias, shows Claudius standing clasping the hand of his new wife and crowned by a togate personification of the Roman Senate or People (Fig. 51).[64] The iconography is an extraordinary, and potent, mixture of Greek and Roman, in keeping with the unique character of this community and its monuments. Claudius is depicted with a heroizing nudity, and Agrippina, wearing Greek garb and holding a bunch of grain ears in her left hand, is assimilated to Demeter – neither would be depicted this way in the city of Rome. Yet the clasping of hands in martial concord is entirely a Roman gesture, as is the crowning of Claudius with a wreath of oak leaves: this is the *corona civica* awarded to a Roman for saving lives. Claudius is shown wearing such a crown in a number of portraits, suggesting that this was

Fig. 50 Portrait of Nero. This statue is very similar to one from the basilica of Velleia (now in Parma), which likewise shows Nero wearing a *bulla* (indicating erection of both statues before the assumption of the *toga virilis* in AD 51 and widespread distribution of Nero's portrait). Louvre, Paris.

Fig. 51 Relief from the Sebasteion at Aphrodisias, depicting Agrippina, Claudius, and a togate figure likely personifying the Senate or People of Rome.

an official type, perhaps to be connected with his accession in AD 41. By yoking together the marital clasp with the award of the civic crown, the designers of the panel are suggesting that the safety and security of Rome's citizens is directly tied to the emperor's marriage to Agrippina.

That seems to be the message of a very different work, a small cameo, depicting double cornucopiae out of which two sets of paired imperial portraits emerge (Fig. 52).[65] There can be no doubt that on the left hand side is Claudius, wearing again the crown of oak leaves, and Agrippina, wearing a mural crown. Claudius is assimilated to Jupiter through the aegis he wears. The identity of the couple on the right has caused debate, but most

Fig. 52 Gemma Claudia, showing Claudius and his wife Agrippina the Younger on the left and (most likely) Germanicus and Agrippina the Elder on the right. Kunsthistorisches Museum, Vienna.

likely it is Agrippina's parents, Germanicus and Agrippina the Elder. With the cornucopia, which points to abundance and prosperity, the bed of arms that it rests on, and the eagle, Jupiter's bird, which looks to Claudius, the cameo, which may have been a private gift for the imperial couple, suggests again the link between the marriage to Agrippina and the re-establishment of Claudius' political position. As on the relief in Aphrodisias, the well-being of the Roman state depends on the imperial marriage.

Works of art such as these sprang from the crisis of AD 48 and its aftermath. Previously Messallina was important to Claudius, as the mother of the potential successor Britannicus who could promise stability, and, in principle, symbolize the virtues the emperor upheld. After her attempt to marry Silius, Claudius' house was in tatters, and in a sense he gave his principate a new start with an incestuous marriage to Agrippina, who helped symbolically knit Claudius into the old August House more firmly than he had been before. She was accorded even greater honors, such as the title "Augusta" – not necessarily a reflection of her power, but certainly of symbolic value. Still, like Livia before her, from whom she must have taken inspiration, she could exert real influence. Posterity certainly saw her, like her predecessor, as a potent force behind the scenes. When Claudius died, in AD 54, and her son, a mere sixteen years old, succeeded, she almost surely was. Before then, it remains less clear.

If Claudius' marriage to Agrippina and his promotion of her (along with the adoption of Nero) made sense, these decisions also carried a risk, and the risk was precisely that more traditional Romans might suspect that increased honors for women did reflect increased power, and of that they disapproved. Haughty Senators or equestrians, in particular, would not care to imagine a woman overruling them – and yet their support was crucial, so much power was delegated to them in commanding armies, managing finances, and governing the provinces. The counterpart to Juvenal's indignation is found in the younger Pliny's panegyric for the emperor Trajan, delivered in AD 102. In it, Pliny devotes several sections to lauding the emperor's wife, and sister, and in doing so, makes clear an ideal in place by this time.[66] Trajan's wife, Plotina, Pliny says, "contributes to your honor and glory. What would be more pure than her, what more honest?" He goes on: "How simple she is in her attire, how sparing in her attendants, how unassuming when she walks around! This is the work of her husband who trained and instructed her to be thus; for a wife, the glory of obedience suffices." Trajan's sister Ulpia Marciana is a pillar of moderation too. There are no rivalries between these two paragons, they subordinate themselves entirely to the emperor; each refused the title Augusta, though this is the title they deserved.

Tacitus' Messallina and Agrippina represent the dark inversion of this virtuous pair. Yet Claudius had a good reason for promoting them – he was trying to secure his weak position in novel ways. He had to, or anyway felt that he had to, in order to survive. The salient point was not that he was under their thumbs, as the later tradition has it. He was, far more, a prisoner of his position. He may have loved the women, but he needed them too; and yet they could hurt him. Even Augustus, by promoting the womenfolk of his family, came to believe that on some level he could be threatened by them, politically: in 8 BC he banished his only child, Julia, on grounds of adultery, and in AD 8 he banished his granddaughter, again on grounds of adultery.[67] The famous refusal of Tiberius, who was married to the elder Julia at the time of her banishment, to support elevated honors for his mother Livia, and his decision never to remarry after Julia's banishment, considered in this light, make sense: Tiberius did not want to be held accountable for what the women around him did, or were thought to be doing.[68] For Pliny was right, when he addressed the emperor Trajan: an emperor was judged, by Senators, on the women around him. As the first Caesar himself had famously pronounced: members of his household must be above suspicion.[69]

CHAPTER II

Signaling retreat?

Some cities of the Roman empire lived on their memories, and perhaps none more so than Ilium. Well-located just off the Hellespont, where Asia meets Europe, it missed no chance to draw attention to its earlier incarnation as Troy – atop the ruins of which it did indeed sit. Local guides were ready to show the tombs of Hector and Achilles, they boasted that a statue of Athena dated back to the Trojan War.[1] A long record of visitors, coming for the relics and to make sacrifices to the goddess, only added to the layers of legend: Xerxes on the eve of his invasion of Greece, Alexander with his copy of the *Iliad*, Germanicus soon before his death. Already by the second century BC, Romans started visiting and conferred special favors on the community in recognition of their shared ancestor Aeneas. Augustus, especially eager to promote the Trojan myth (his Julian family traced its ancestry back to Aeneas' son Iulus), helped rebuild the entire city: his name proudly stood on the architrave of a refurbished temple of Athena, and he probably contributed to a theater and council house.[2] Augustus almost certainly visited the city in 20 BC, and was honored several years later with a statue erected by one Melanippides. A cult was also established, in which Melanippides served as priest. Statues went up too for Agrippa and Agrippa's son Gaius Caesar, for Antonia and Tiberius, celebrating the city's shared kinship with the August House. It was a mutually beneficial relationship.

It is true it had limits: when the Ilians competed in AD 23 with ten other Asian cities to host a new temple for Tiberius, Livia, and the Senate, they lost to Smyrna. As each city made its case, the Ilians, Tacitus observed, had nothing to offer but the glories of their past.[3] Still it was not surprising that Claudius would wish to demonstrate his regard for the people of this storied city. A year before his own death, the Roman Senate voted to exempt Ilium from all tribute in perpetuity.[4] In support, an ancient letter was produced, written from the Senate and People of Rome to King Seleucus, who had once ruled over this part of Asia.[5] It promised friendship to the king, if he were to allow the Ilians, "kin of the Romans," freedom from all burdens. The old letter – a nice touch for the antiquarian emperor – was not the only argument offered. Claudius' adopted son, Nero, delivered a speech, in which, according to Tacitus, "he fluently rehearsed the Romans' descent from Troy, Aeneas as progenitor of the Julian stock, and other old stories not far removed from fiction, so that the Ilians were freed from all official obligation."[6] Suetonius adds that the speech was delivered in Greek.[7]

The whole episode might on first glance seem trivial, a mere footnote in the great Troy legend, but much was actually at stake when Nero, about fifteen years old, stood up to speak. By turning over the floor to him, Claudius was allowing his adoptive son to establish a relationship with this renowned, and well-trafficked, provincial community. Out of loyalty to their new benefactor, the Ilians were sure to honor him publicly. And sure enough, a statue base has been found from the city, initially inscribed with dedications to Claudius' three children Britannicus, Octavia, and Antonia, to which was subsequently added the name of Nero, "kinsman of the city."[8]

But that was not all. In dwelling on Rome's descent from Troy, Nero was showing his appreciation for his own City's cherished foundation story; and in dwelling on the connection between Aeneas and the Julian family, Nero was reminding his listeners of his own descent from Augustus, through his mother Julia Agrippina. Then there was the quality of the speech itself – it showed his culture and, in welcome contrast to Claudius, skill in oratory. (Nero, the Senators must have known, had been studying rhetoric for several years now under Seneca, who finally had been restored from exile after Messallina's death.[9]) Above all, though, the Senators were to remark simply on the spectacle of an adolescent, the adopted son of the ruling Leader, speaking before them. The speech was to show them, and the empire, that he was now the favored successor of his father, not Britannicus.

The speech was just one part of a larger and well-executed plan. After Claudius' adoption of Nero, on February 25, AD 50, the new son was immediately promoted as a successor who could buttress the authority of Claudius' house after Messallina's fall.[10] It was not a new pattern, there were earlier models: Marcellus, then Gaius and Lucius, then Tiberius and Germanicus, and so on. The promotion of these "princes" was a way not just to prepare for their future accessions, but to strengthen imperial rule by promising its stability and even perpetuity.[11] Crucial constituencies – the Senate, the people of the City of Rome, Italian and provincial communities, the armies – would be honored by the princes, and would give back honors in turn, knitting together the Roman world and creating a more unified political culture.

A damaging interruption to the pattern, though, had occurred when Claudius had acceded. He had tried to revive it with Britannicus – holding him up to the soldiers, to the people assembled at games.[12] Then, for awhile, it must have seemed that both Nero and Britannicus were possible successors. Now by AD 53, when Nero gave his speech, the plan obviously was to mark Nero as the clear, if not absolutely explicit, designate. Winning favor for him was akin to what Claudius had to do for himself in AD 41. In essence, a new principate was now taking shape; Claudius' star was starting to fade. A parallel is the final years of Augustus' principate, when focus shifted from the infirm emperor onto Tiberius, and Tiberius' adopted son Germanicus.

Modern discussions of these last years of Claudius' rule, taking their lead from Tacitus, are dominated by the figure of Nero's mother.[13] In Tacitus, and in history books ever since, it is Agrippina who masterminds the displacement of Britannicus and the promotion of her own son, slowly but methodically, with utter ruthlessness.[14] Here there was none of the recklessness of Messallina, Tacitus says; under Agrippina, it was a "strict and, in a manner of speaking, manlike servitude."[15] It began with the destruction of Octavia's fiancé, Silanus, appropriately coinciding with Agrippina's own wedding day.[16] Then others perceived to be in the way were removed from the scenes – Lollia Paulina, a rival to Agrippina in marriage to Claudius, and Domitia Lepida, Agrippina's former sister-in-law and Nero's aunt.[17] The young boy had special affection for aunt Domitia, Tacitus says.[18] (Perhaps more salient, modern scholars add, she was the mother of Messallina, and so the grandmother of young Britannicus.[19])

Agrippina, Tacitus also writes, snatched for herself the vast wealth of Statilius Taurus – it included gardens – when she toppled him with a trumped-up prosecution.[20] Lollia too had been worth a fortune, most of which was confiscated.[21] Building her treasure chest, Agrippina also secured crucial allies; it is she who is said to have brought back Seneca to tutor Nero, and she is also said to have removed the two prefects of the Praetorian Guard and replaced them with her own single appointee, Afranius Burrus.[22] (An inscription helps to suggest that it was a rather remarkable promotion for this provincial from Narbonensian Gaul, likely to keep Burrus loyal to whoever was responsible for it.[23])

It is a compelling picture, for the most part. Certainly, immediately after Claudius' death, when her 16-year-old son acceded, Agrippina must have played a key role in the unfolding of events. And before then, it is hardly implausible that she fought for the advancement of her son: that was the only way, in a world where only men could publicly hold power, for her to secure her own position. Livia had shown the way, while the fate of Agrippina's own mother, who died in exile after brutal treatment by Tiberius, must have weighed on her mind; Agrippina was about eighteen years old at the time. Then there was her own exile, under Caligula. Well might she have vowed never to let *that* happen again, whatever it might take. Still, many of the stories in Tacitus defy verification – as they already did in the historian's own day too. What came to be accepted as fact might only have been fossilized rumors or hypotheses, or later willful distortions. Agrippina herself probably contributed to the mythology, when she released her own memoirs in Nero's reign, promoting herself and all she did for Nero, and likely denigrating Messallina.[24]

In fact, Claudius could have been as much responsible for decisions attributed primarily to her. Silanus was potentially a threat to Nero's position (and so that of Claudius), Domitia Lepida too. Taurus too might have been perceived dangerous, for he was the brother of the Statilius Corvinus implicated in a plot against Claudius in AD 46.[25] In 52, Furius Scribonianus, the son of the Camillus Scribonianus who had led the futile rising against Claudius ten years earlier, was exiled on a charge of consulting Chaldaean astrologers about the emperor's end.[26] Old resentments might have been more important than Agrippina's ambitions.

Tacitus' account of the secret transactions of Agrippina the Younger is therefore more safely appreciated as an often brilliant reconstruction than primary historical evidence. More fruitful is to inquire into the way Nero was publicly promoted as a prince to strengthen Claudius' own position, as well as to prepare for an actual succession of rulers. Of course, public measures were not enough for a new Leader to succeed: Claudius' own accession showed that. Money and arms were the crucial foundations of the emperor's dominance. Though it is harder to make judgments here – the imperial finances were one of the secrets of empire, also screened from view – it is not impossible. Claudius, and the court, it can be argued, smoothed the way for Nero, by avoiding expensive new financial commitments (except those undertaken on Nero's own behalf) and by trying to leave the new emperor free from problems on the borders of his realm. The display of energy that had burst forth at the start of Claudius' principate was winding down. Naturally Claudius did not know in AD 50, when he turned fifty-nine years old, that he would die just a few years later; but to fixate on the matter of succession did raise the possibility of his demise; and there is some evidence, we shall see, that his health was starting to deteriorate.

After Nero's adoption in AD 50, the first notable step in his public promotion as *the* successor of Claudius came early the following year, when, a year before the normal age, he assumed the *toga virilis* that marked the passage of a Roman boy into manhood.[27] Here was another example of how the August House used ritual and costume to send a clear message.[28] To underscore the significance of the ceremony, Claudius held a consulship at the time (his fifth), precisely as Augustus had done at the equivalent moment for his grandsons Gaius and Lucius in 5 and 2 BC.[29] As part of the festivities, Nero headed a parade of the Praetorians.[30] A gift to the soldiers and to the people of Rome was announced in his name – especially welcome, if the ceremony followed a grain shortage at the start of the year for which Claudius was sharply criticized.[31] And games were held, at which Nero wore the costume of the *triumphator* – another potent message, and all the more so because Britannicus still wore only the child's striped toga.[32]

It was at this time, too, that Nero made his first speech before the Senate, expressing his gratitude to his father, while the Senate heaped on the young man honors, duly ratified by the People.[33] He was voted a consulship, which he would assume when he turned twenty; and he was given the title "Leader of the Youth" (*princeps iuuentutis*), which effectively made him symbolic head of the equestrian order.[34] The order included not just lifelong equestrians, but also young men of Senatorial families who had not yet entered the Senate; in the parade of equestrians that appeared before the emperor each year, these youths were prominently featured, and Nero would now be at their head.[35] Exactly these honors had been given to Augustus' grandsons so many years before.[36] To them, in AD 51, the Senate added two more: Nero would henceforward hold proconsular *imperium* outside the City (power that would outlast Claudius' death); and he was awarded a (permanent) membership in all of Rome's major priestly colleges.[37] Precious metal coinage issued at the time advertises some of the honors (Figs. 53–54).[38]

These coins must be seen not just as evidence for the honors but a means by which Nero was presented to the key constituencies of the empire, in order to secure a relationship with them meant to be lasting. The official mint did not issue a regular stream of currency to facilitate monetary exchange as such; rather, coins were minted from bullion in fits and bursts, typically in response to specific, immediate, and sometimes extraordinary needs.[39] During the principate of Claudius there were three major precious metal emissions: in AD 41, in AD 46/47, and now in AD 51.[40] The emission of AD 41 clearly was needed to pay Claudius' large accession donatives; this emission from 51 must have been needed to pay out the donatives and largesse promised by Nero when he put on the toga of manhood. (That of AD 46/47 remains more mysterious, but is perhaps to be connected with an influx of bullion from the British war, used to meet expenses associated

Fig. 53 *Aureus*, c. AD 51. The obverse shows the head of Nero; the reverse priestly
equipment and the abbreviated legend CO-OPTED AS PRIEST SUPERNUMERARY
IN ALL THE COLLEGES BY DECREE OF THE SENATE.

Fig. 54 *Denarius*, c. AD 51. The obverse shows the head of Nero; the reverse a spear
and shield with the legend THE EQUESTRIAN ORDER, TO THE LEADER
OF THE YOUTH.

with the public works and the celebrations for Rome's eight hundredth
year.) While the exact sums involved for AD 51 are not recorded, evidence
from other occasions allows a guess of about 50 millions sesterces paid
out to the people, and to the army perhaps 50 million sesterces.[41] Along
with the games, this might have represented something like a 20 percent
addition to a year's necessary expenses.[42]

Because large issues were so often minted in conjunction with extraordinary events, such as an accession, new coinage was an excellent mechanism
for disseminating, or at least reinforcing, imperial messages.[43] Although

the precise means by which designs were selected remains unknown, the messages themselves speak loud and clear, from across Claudius' whole principate. The coins of AD 41 dwell on Claudius' accession and prominently feature in particular the new relationship between Claudius and the Praetorians.[44] Those of AD 46/47, repeating earlier themes, add an image of a triumphal arch with the legend "Over the Britons."[45] Now, in AD 51, old themes are again repeated, but Agrippina makes her appearance, with Nero, and the honors Nero was voted. As these coins were handed out to a doubtless grateful populace in Rome and to the Praetorians, as they made their way to soldiers farther beyond, and were circulated throughout the empire, the message cannot have been lost on those who handled them. The coins, through their distribution and imagery alike, showed that a new Leader was in the making.

The year AD 53, the year Nero turned sixteen, saw fresh advances for the boy. Not only did he now marry Claudius' daughter Octavia,[46] he gave the speech before the Senate on behalf of the Ilians, along with three other orations. He recommended that freedom be restored to the island of Rhodes, which Claudius had earlier taken away as a reprisal for the murder of Roman citizens; he spoke for the Apameans, securing a five-year tax remission after an earthquake ruined their city; and he secured 10 million sesterces from the Senate for the colony of Bononia in northern Italy, after a devastating fire.[47] Each was an opportunity to secure new relationships, and show oratorical skill; collectively, they exhibited the beneficence a god-like emperor was to show, to provincials and citizens alike. In this year, Nero served as prefect of the city when the Latin festival was held which took all the normal magistrates away from Rome for several days; in this capacity he presided over judicial hearings.[48] He also held a set of games that he had pledged to the gods in exchange for Claudius' recovery from illness.[49]

In all of this, Nero was not only getting the training Claudius never had; he was once more securing relationships with all of those most important elements of the Roman world beyond the imperial court. To summarize thus far: with the Senate his dealings were extensive from AD 51 onwards; for the equestrian order he served as symbolic head; to the urban *plebs* he gave largesse in AD 51 and the votive games of AD 53; the army received donatives in AD 51 also; specific communities throughout the empire received Nero's aid; his image also, as seen, was made available to them for display, along with that of his mother Agrippina. The empire was coming together around the young man, the grandson of Germanicus, great-great-grandson of Augustus.

Fig. 55 Bronze coin of Corinth, c. AD 50. The obverse shows the head of Agrippina the Younger; the reverse Nero and Britannicus standing face to face.

One sign of this is the coinage that provincial cities, especially in the east, issued for local use. While images of Messallina had appeared on these, Agrippina, after her marriage to Claudius, proved even more popular.[50] The young Nero was depicted too, attesting to communities' new awareness of him, from Greece, to Asia, to Syria.[51] To be sure, Britannicus had appeared on coins of most of these same communities (including Ilium).[52] Perhaps even more startlingly, Britannicus and Nero appeared together on coins from citizen colonies such as Corinth and Sinope, even as late as AD 54 (Fig. 55).[53]

This reflects an important fact. While Nero was being given priority in Rome through ritual, costume, and the like, it might not have seemed desirable to give him so unambiguous a title as "*princeps* designate" (for example). That was offensive to Republican sentiment, and the lingering spirit of the Augustan compromise of a principate that lay between monarchy and magistracy. To go so far in promoting Nero might end up hurting him – and Claudius. Also relevant was the fear that Nero could have died before Claudius; unlikely as it might seem, notoriously princes had perished prematurely before, and it was wise for the court to keep Britannicus in reserve. The goal, then, was to suggest that Nero was ready – or would be soon – to be emperor, not to state explicitly that a boy would inherit a throne.

While from hindsight one sees a clear, and brilliant, logic to the way Nero was gradually promoted in Rome and throughout the empire, it must be admitted that plans might have been improvised over time, not developed overnight. In particular, the lavish ceremonies of AD 51 perhaps did owe something to the grain shortage at the start of the year. In this year, too, the Praetorian prefects were replaced by Burrus, and there also was (Tacitus records) a plot to remove Vitellius from the scene – one way, or another, suggesting further troubles for Claudius, either in response to the promotion of Nero, or perhaps additional motives for it.[54] Still, on the whole, the threats Claudius faced from Senators after his marriage to Agrippina and adoption of Nero seem to have been less serious than those before; none of those now appointed to consulships, for instance, turned on him, as men apparently had in the first part of his principate. Those implicated in plots against him had earlier scores to settle.[55]

A further consequence of the manner of Nero's promotion was that it would have been harder for those farther away from the City to be certain of the plans of the August House. Aphrodisias seems to have been atypically, but characteristically, alert, in incorporating a relief in its Sebasteion showing the two boys, but with Nero holding the greater symbols of power (Fig. 56).[56] For most, it would be enough if they had at least some familiarity with Nero, his adoption by Claudius, and his relationship with the Augustus and the August House (through his mother). Even coins with him and Britannicus show that objective met.

There were, at the same time, some potentially far less pleasant corollaries to the policy of promoting Nero as successor. First, the young Britannicus and his adult supporters could be a problem for Nero (and his mother). It is quite plausible, for instance, that not just the Praetorian prefects, but even Britannicus' tutors were replaced, as Tacitus reports; it would have been risky to surround the boy with any but those loyal to Claudius and Agrippina.[57] There surely cannot have been much surprise when Britannicus did die, in AD 55, fourteen years old, just a few months after his father: if it were not from natural causes, it would have happened anyway.[58] In favoring Nero, Claudius sealed the fate of his son – and perhaps his own.[59] Second, while such intriguing within the court, real and important as it no doubt was, is beyond secure recovery now, policies can be detected that were put in place, or intensified, in the last few years of Claudius' principate to ensure that financially, and militarily, the successor would not be vulnerable. He would not, on his accession, wish to face a shortage of coin, or serious trouble on the edges of the empire that could open up the possibility of rebellion.

First, finances. Here, owing to a lack of good evidence, less can be said than one would like.[60] While, as seen, strictly speaking there still existed the old Republican treasury, and a treasury to fund military discharges, in

Fig. 56 Relief from the Sebasteion at Aphrodisias, depicting two princes, identified as Nero (left, holding a globe and aplustre, symbols of conquest and victory) and Britannicus (right).

addition to the emperor's own "personal" accounts, the reality was that the emperor and his staff controlled the budget overall. If the Senate is said to have bequeathed 10 million sesterces to Bononia after its conflagration, while Claudius boasted of building new aqueducts "at his own expense," that was chiefly for the sake of appearance. The emperor, at the end of the day, had to reconcile a stream of outgoing expenses with an incoming flow of revenues, both personal and public at once. On the expenses side of the ledger were the costs of the army, civilian employees, the emperor's household, handouts to the people of Rome and the armies, public works, and occasional subsidies (for instance, relief after an earthquake), as well as the costs of maintaining the imperial properties. As intake there were taxes both direct and indirect; rents and revenues from agricultural land, urban properties, and mines, including actual bullion that could be minted into coins; gifts and legacies; property confiscated from the condemned or that had otherwise fallen ownerless; plunder from war; and gold crowns bequeathed by provincials.

As large-scale long-term "public" debt was not an option – though privately the emperor and his agents might borrow – and money could not really be printed (a coin was supposed to be worth exactly its metal content), essentially the two flows of intake and out-take had to match. If the emperor wanted to spend more, he could only do so by increasing revenues. Aside from winning plunder in war from Rome's enemies, there was no popular or easy way to do this; even Augustus had to introduce a new series of taxes in Rome and Italy very carefully. Claudius seems in general to have refrained from such techniques as instating new taxes or confiscating estates for the sake of their value alone. Nonetheless, estates of Senators and equestrians were confiscated, while attention also was paid to recovering properties Claudius believed to be part of his patrimony, the British war probably brought in plunder in its very early stages, and new annexations such as Lycia in principle increased tribute received.

A likelier alternative to increasing spending overall was to rebalance the budget. Choices, in other words, had to be made, and a good emperor and his staff would try to make those choices responsibly. The emperor was thus constrained, but it hardly made him totally "passive": different emperors made very different choices. Some might spend on lavish improvements to the Palace, others on grand buildings for Rome, for instance – but only on both with great difficulty. Claudius' most significant extraordinary expenses would have been, in addition to the ongoing cost of two extra legions for the British war and associated items, the donatives and largesse he paid out in AD 41 and 45, and the massive public works projects undertaken at the start of his reign. Then, in AD 51, he was faced with the costs of funding Nero's own gifts.

But it was not only that. A *reserve* of money most likely was also being created: Nero promised the Praetorians a donative upon his accession, one said to have been equivalent to that of Claudius, and there is no sign that he had trouble paying it.[61] That such a reserve could exist for use after an emperor's death is explicitly attested for by Augustus. According to the terms of his will, 40 million sesterces were left to the Roman people, to the tribes of the people 3.5 million sesterces, to the Praetorian Guard 1,000 sesterces a man, to the city cohorts 500, and to the legionaries 300; altogether, this would have amounted to around 100 million sesterces.[62] The sum, he ordered, was to be paid at once, for he had it to hand and ready. Claudius might have established such a fund for distribution of legacies in his own name. Oddly, no will of his was ever made public, and it may be that Nero and his advisors decided to take such a fund and use it to pay for donatives in Nero's name. One way, or another, some surplus evidently existed on Nero's accession – and that represented another significant expense for Claudius.

And so, while much necessarily remains mysterious, it seems clear that Claudius elected not to spend his monies on any major new projects in his own name in the last few years of his principate; even basic road-building, the milestones show, came to a virtual standstill.[63] While he did complete the massive works previously embarked upon, he chose instead to focus his remaining uncommitted resources on the donatives for Nero in AD 51 and then a surplus which Nero was able to use after Claudius' death.

Hand in hand with careful fiscal planning went an extreme reluctance to get the empire entangled in new wars with its neighbors. The wave of annexations that marked the first half of the principate was over, leaving Britain as the only major theater of war. Though opportunities, both fresh and long-standing, presented themselves, Claudius assiduously avoided them – perhaps finally to a fault. For while Nero could truthfully say in his eulogy for Claudius that "nothing dreadful during Claudius' rule had befallen the state at the hands of foreign peoples" (not perhaps without irony), Claudius did end up leaving his successor an unresolved problem in Armenia.[64] In the very long run, different arrangements would be necessary for Rome in the far east, with more troops, more widely spread out along the Euphrates. Still, Claudius deserves credit here too, for thinking that might fairly be characterized as strategic.

Even in Britain, in the latter part of his principate, to judge by the imperfect evidence of Tacitus, Claudius retrenched rather than risk overstretching himself and his forces.[65] After Plautius left, much remained available for conquest, including Wales and Scotland; a good deal of England, though, was controlled by Rome or her clients, the tribes of the Atrebates, the Iceni, and the Brigantes, and consolidation of that initial conquest, along with some expansion inland, appears to have been at least the short-term goal, with establishment of a colony at Camulodonum, where a cult was established for Claudius and ultimately a great temple would be built.[66] But relations with the clients, as events would show, were fragile. When Ostorius Scapula arrived in 47 as successor to Plautius, he found the client kingdoms under threat from their Welsh neighbors, who likely had been encouraged by the wily Caratacus. The Iceni then took the chance to rebel – perhaps in response to the tightening of Rome's grip – and were only put down with some difficulty. After an onward assault by the Romans against the Decangi, which took them to the Irish Sea, it was the turn of the Brigantes to give trouble, and Ostorius had to turn back. Further trouble with Caratacus ensued, but Scapula then prevailed, and sent Caratacus to Rome after he was betrayed by Cartimandua, queen of the Brigantes. (His display in Rome afforded Claudius and Agrippina an excellent opportunity for publicity.[67]) Worn out, Tacitus claims, "by weariness of his responsibilities," Scapula soon expired in AD 52, a very grudging acknowledgment of the challenges he had faced.[68]

It was now Didius Gallus' turn to take command, and a more defensive strategy began in earnest. Gallus, a thoroughly trusted and experienced man, also had the advantage of already having won great military glory from his activities in the war in Thrace.[69] Tacitus blames him for inactivity, but it is far likelier that he was under orders to focus on consolidating what Rome had already won, and he was willing to obey them.[70] When he arrived, Britons on the fringe of the Roman zone of occupation tried to intimidate him, but he stood them down. He then turned to helping Queen Cartimandua, whose former husband was trying to overthrow her. Britain was effectively kept quiet, and Gallus remained on in service for several more years under Nero.

Trouble was to be avoided in Germany too, along the Rhine and the Danube.[71] This, essentially, had been Claudius' policy all along. At the start of his principate, to be sure, he inherited some problems from Caligula, which were successfully handled by Galba in the north and Gabinius Secundus in the south.[72] Further trouble erupted in Lower Germany, when the Chauci invaded the Roman province and tried to disrupt shipping there.[73] The capable Domitius Corbulo pushed back the enemy and was set to work fortifying Rome's control of the region; when he tried to carry his operations further and more aggressively, a letter reached him from Claudius ordering him to desist. He was to devote his time to fatigue work, digging a canal between the Mosa and Rhine rivers. Around the same time, Claudius refused to lend military support to Italicus, the Roman nominee to rule the kingdom of the Cherusci.[74] Raised in Rome, but a native of this tribe, he encountered fierce resistance when he arrived to take control, and finally had to secure help from the neighboring Langobardi.

Then, in AD 50, there was trouble from the Chatti in Upper Germany.[75] Pomponius Secundus, Pliny's patron, sent auxiliary troops from the left bank of the Rhine to envelop and crush the troublemakers, and the Chatti were compelled to send hostages to Rome. The situation was thus defused without escalation, or the shedding of any Roman blood. Right around this time a military colony was founded among the Ubii – and named Colonia Agrippinensis in honor of Claudius' wife, who was born here – another example of entrenchment rather than commitment to new and potentially costly endeavors.[76] When, during the same period, Rome's client king Vannius was expelled by the Suebi over whom he ruled, Claudius, though asked, would not interpose arms in the quarrel, and wrote to Palpellius Hister, the governor of Pannonia, to use his troops only as a deterrent force to prevent the quarrel from escalating; the plan was successful.[77]

It was just around this time that Claudius also successfully avoided a major entanglement in the Black Sea.[78] Several years before, his appointee to the throne of the kingdom of Bosporus, Mithridates, had apparently tried to plot against Rome and was betrayed by his brother Cotys to Claudius, who in turn gave control of the kingdom to Cotys; while its grain was vital to Roman interests, Rome had no interest in ruling it directly.[79] Didius Gallus, then serving in Thrace, was sent to install the new king.[80] After successfully doing so, Gallus left behind a few cohorts to support the new appointee, while Mithridates began plotting revenge and seized the neighboring kingdom of the Dandaridae as a base. Cotys and the Roman cohorts, under attack, scrambled for help, especially from King Eunones of the Aorsi. Together, the forces under Cotys successfully pursued Mithridates, and Mithridates finally sought asylum with Eunones. Eunones offered to turn the king over to Claudius, and Claudius accepted. It was better to avoid a major war over the matter. Mithridates came to Rome and, though displayed as a sort of captive, was allowed to spend his final days there under house arrest.[81]

The same caution only failed Claudius, and Rome when it came to another client kingdom, Armenia, also coincidentally ruled by a man named Mithridates.[82] A source of unending friction between Rome and the neighboring empire of the Parthians, Armenia apparently was a part of the last major negotiations that took place between the two larger powers probably at the start of Caligula's principate.[83] At this time (or so it would appear), the aggressive Parthian king, Artabanus, decided to patch up relations with Rome and make peace with the new emperor, through the alert governor of Syria then on duty, none other than Vitellius. A meeting was held in a luxury pavilion in the middle of the Euphrates, at which (according to Roman sources) Artabanus made a gesture of compliance – homage to the Roman eagles and standards and statues of Augustus and Caligula.[84] Artabanus' price for cooperation may have been a cooling of relations between Armenia and Rome, for soon afterwards Caligula removed Mithridates from the throne of Armenia.[85]

Shortly before Claudius' reign, Parthia was thrown into new turmoil when Artabanus fell at the hands of his brother Gotarzes, who then was challenged in turn by his own brother Vardanes. Claudius, upon gaining power, took the chance to restore Mithridates to Armenia, who would receive the support of Mithridates' own brother Pharasmanes, king of Iberia, and some Roman troops. This drove the Parthian brothers back into each other's arms, and they turned their attention to Armenia; a possible invasion was thwarted by another capable Syrian governor, Vibius Marsus. The Parthian brothers broke out into hostility again, and Vardanes was soon killed while hunting. Secret appeals were then made to Rome in AD 47 to install a new monarch, Meherdates, son of old King Phraates, who had been raised in Rome as a hostage. Claudius assented. Meherdates was escorted by Cassius Longinus, governor of Syria, and Cassius tried to bolster up the appointee with what power he could, showing some force, but only on the Roman side of the Euphrates. Claudius clearly was not going to let himself get embroiled in a Parthian war.

It was not enough. Meherdates failed in his quest, but then Gotarzes perished shortly afterwards, leaving control of the Parthian kingdom to Vonones and then Vologaeses in quick succession. The names matter little. For what happened next, according to Tacitus, was the result of an intrigue rather by Radamistus, the son of Pharasmanes, to bring down their relation on the Armenian throne.[86] Mithridates was finally driven into the stronghold of Gorneae, in charge of which were the prefect Caelius Pollio and the centurion Casperius. Radamistus, Tacitus claims, bought off Pollio, while the honorable centurion was sent on a futile mission to try to make a truce with Pharasmanes.[87] Suborning the garrison further, Radamistus finished off Mithridates and had him killed.

It fell primarily to the governor of Syria, Ummidius Quadratus, to decide what to do. Tacitus claims that a council was held, at which some clamored for vengeance of Rome's honor, and immediate restoration of Armenia; others thought it wiser to let Radamistus keep his spoils. Meanwhile, though, Julius Paelignus, the procurator of Cappadocia – an old friend of Claudius who also had, Tacitus says, a "derided physique" – assembled auxiliaries on the grounds that he would recover Armenia, but actually only went on a plundering raid and formed an alliance with the traitorous Radamistus. A proper legion was finally sent by Quadratus, but was then ordered to return to Syria lest a war break out – with Parthia. For by this time, the Parthians were well on their way to capturing Armenia. Radamistus soon paid for his treachery with his life.

Tacitus sneers at the whole incident, and modern scholars have also been critical: "in the east," one says, "opportunities were lost and Rome's reputation smirched by incompetence."[88] Still, a clear and entirely comprehensible policy is discerned even in Tacitus' jaundiced narrative: war was to be avoided at all costs with Parthia, and immediate, unsupported intervention in Armenia might lead exactly to that.[89] With a war on in Britain, Claudius, and his commanders in the east, could not instantly adopt a more aggressive approach without great danger. The paramount goal was the protection of Roman territory, and in that Claudius succeeded: on his death, Quadratus lay in wait on the Euphrates, ready for a Parthian invasion of Roman territory should it come.

Certainly, Roman prestige did take a blow as a consequence of Claudius' policy in the east, and it would be left to Nero to repair that. He had ample time, though, to prepare for a campaign of vengeance. The situation did not have to be handled instantly. But even in the end, Nero left a Parthian prince on the throne of Armenia, on condition that he was acknowledged as Rome's vassal too.[90] That was an acceptable compromise. Whereas, immediately after his accession, Claudius faced trouble on the Rhine, renewed rebellion in Mauretania, riots in Alexandria (the bottleneck of Egypt's vital grain supply), seething hostility in Judea, and unrest in Britain, Claudius left Nero better off. Work remained in Britain but a capable and cautious man was on the spot; and Armenia would, in due course, have to be sorted out. At the same time Nero may not have been left with a huge surplus, but enough, evidently, to see him through his first months in power: the troops got their donative, and had already received one in Nero's name in 51.

The smooth succession, without even a threat of civil war, should have proved to be one of Claudius' most substantial achievements. It was the smoothest yet on record, even surpassing that of Tiberius, which had proved awkward for the Senate and had also led to rebellions among the armies of Germany and Pannonia. And yet, because of who Nero finally

showed himself to be, it ultimately cast a terrible shadow on Claudius'
principate. Claudius accepted marriage to Agrippina and the succession of
Nero because it must have seemed to him his best prospect for survival. A
smooth succession was in Rome's best interest too. But that a still unproven
adolescent could be considered the best choice for a position whose powers
were not well-defined showed the limitations of the emerging principate.
It was a fitting legacy of Augustus, himself just eighteen years old when he
launched his own takeover of the Roman world.

CHAPTER 12

The golden predicament

On the thirteenth of October AD 54 an announcement was made that Claudius was dead, after an illness.[1] Comic actors had been brought in, to try to lift the emperor's spirits; and the Senate made vows for his recovery, as they had done the year before.[2] But it was all to no avail. It seems to have been an unhealthy year, with plague in the City.[3] And so, on the thirteenth of October, around noontime, the doors of the palace were flung open, and Nero emerged with the prefect Burrus at his side. The 16-year-old was hailed by the guardsmen assembled there, placed on a litter, and taken to the Praetorian Camp.[4]

Later historians, not surprisingly, had a more sinister story to tell of the final days of Claudius.[5] Numerous portents, they say, were observed at the time, leading to panic everywhere: the birth of two-headed babies, a lightning strike on the tomb of Claudius' father Drusus, the appearance of a comet in the western sky.[6] Comets, by popular belief, foretold the death of kings, and there is good evidence that a comet was in fact visible this year.[7] But it was Agrippina who was especially worried, and for more mundane reasons. Claudius, she believed, was having second thoughts about his marriage to her, even about his adoption of Nero.[8]

The emperor, writes Suetonius, on encountering Britannicus, embraced his son and promised him that on growing up, he would receive an account of all that his father had done; and then Claudius said to him in Greek: "The one who delivered the wound will heal it."[9] Tacitus, in contrast, envisions Claudius as dull to the end: it was the canny freedman Narcissus who grew suspicious of Agrippina, and it was he who embraced Britannicus, with a prayer that the boy grow up, drive off his father's enemies, and avenge his mother's killers.[10] Falling ill afterwards, Narcissus left for Sinuessa with its healing waters. Agrippina saw her opportunity. She would poison her husband.

"That Claudius was killed by poison is generally agreed, but when and by whom it was given are disputed," Suetonius would later write.[11] And the truth was, nobody, at least outside the palace, could be sure. According to the biographer, some claimed that it was given by Claudius' taster, the eunuch Halotus, while the emperor was banqueting on the Capitoline with other priests; others said it was at a family dinner, at which Agrippina herself drugged a mushroom, a food of which Claudius was very fond. Some reported that he died the very next morning, others that he vomited up the contents of his stomach and had to be administered a second dose of the poison.[12] Cassius Dio prefers the tale of Agrippina's fatal mushroom, with the toxin supplied by Locusta, a famous dealer in poisons – on consuming it, Dio says, Claudius was carried off to bed, as if drunk, but then passed away.[13]

Tacitus has the most elaborate story of all, which tries to bring the different traditions together: Locusta used her arts to prepare a fatal concoction which was then administered by Halotus, once again in a dish of mushrooms.[14] But it proved ineffective, Agrippina had to call in Claudius' own physician, Xenophon, and "Xenophon is believed to have inserted into the man's throat, as if to aid his efforts at vomiting, a feather dipped in a quick-acting poison." The desired effect was immediate, but Agrippina needed time to make the necessary arrangements, and so she had the Senate make its vows, she then announced that Claudius was getting better, she draped his body with coverings, and she kept Britannicus safely in a bedroom. It is a thrilling narrative, replete with deceptions – the taster who offers unsafe food, the delicious mushroom that is deadly, the doctor who kills his patient, the Senate that prays for a corpse to recover, the body kept warm as if it is alive, and Agrippina herself acting "as if overcome by grief and seeking comforting." The whole tale suggests the trickery at the very core of the principate, symbolized above all by that delicious, deadly mushroom.

Of course, an emperor did have to be careful about every bite he ate. As epitaphs show, there were tasters in the palace to make sure his food was safe.[15] Poison was an all too real fear. A book of medical recipes, written during the principate of Claudius by Scribonius Largus, contains an extraordinary prescription for a comprehensive antidote devised by the physician Marcianus for Augustus.[16] It contained several dozen ingredients, including cinnamon, saffron, incense, white pepper, myrrh, rose petals, Celtic nard, valerian, dittany, asafetida, parsley, fennel seed, Ethiopian cumin, dried blood of a sea tortoise, and Attic honey. Scribonius boasts that he, too, has made this preparation – perhaps for Claudius. He had close ties to the emperor, accompanying him to Britain, serving Messallina, and dedicating his book of recipes to the freedman Callistus.[17] And the concoction would have been fantastically expensive, suggesting the lengths an emperor would go to preserve himself, and the depth of fear into which he might easily fall.

An emperor had to be wary even of the doctors themselves: their skills might be needed, but, it is clear, they could abuse the trust placed in them. As an adult, Tiberius, blessed with a strong constitution, avoided all physicians, it is said – if so, another sign of his canniness – but Claudius almost certainly could not.[18] So, instead, he tried to instill the greatest loyalty in his doctors, as his relations with Xenophon show. Hailing from the island of Cos, where a school of medicine had existed for centuries, this enterprising Greek probably first came to Rome in AD 23.[19] That year, as an envoy, he successfully confirmed the asylum rights of the Temple of Asclepius, on Cos, and also won Roman citizenship from Stertinius Maximus, who was then consul.[20] By the reign of Claudius, Stertinius Xenophon, as he was now called, had achieved equestrian status – his practice in Rome, according to Pliny, was fantastically lucrative – and he served the emperor's medical needs during the trip to and from Britain, for which he was rewarded with decorations and a promotion to officer in charge of Greek embassies to Rome.[21] He enjoyed the old Hellenistic title of "High Doctor"; his relatives won citizenship from Claudius; he was even given access to waters from the new Aqua Claudia![22] But the real coup came in AD 53, when the Senate made Cos immune to taxation, on Claudius' recommendation.[23] In his speech on the matter, the emperor praised Xenophon for his medical knowledge, while on Cos itself the celebration of the doctor who secured the precious privilege was lavish.[24]

Could this man, just a year later, have really inserted a poisoned feather down his patron's throat? Was Claudius killed at all, or did the 63-year-old die of natural causes? What did Tacitus actually know? The tale of Agrippina's poisoned mushroom goes back at least to Pliny the Elder, who sharply comments:

Among the things which are eaten recklessly, I would include mushrooms, a very choice food, to be sure, but indicted in a case of enormous proportions, when poison was given by this means to Tiberius Claudius the Leader by his wife Agrippina, in doing which she bestowed another poison upon the earth, and upon herself in particular – Nero, her son.[25]

Pliny, in his encyclopedia, mentions some of the portents too, suggesting that his version of Claudius' death was influential, perhaps even the original source for the tale of the poisoned mushroom.[26] But there might be reasons to doubt it.[27] For one thing, it seems almost too coincidental that it should be a *mushroom* that was smeared with poison; perhaps Claudius ingested, purely by accident, a naturally toxic specimen, his death then catching everyone off guard.[28] Another problem is that it seems unlikely that Pliny could have had much evidence that Claudius was turning on Agrippina and Britannicus; certainly there was not the least sign of it officially. And how, if Pliny's version is so obviously correct, does one explain the doubts of Suetonius, who knew other stories? The refrain is becoming familiar: there can be no certainty now of what happened behind the closed doors of the Palatium. Perhaps Agrippina did kill her husband, by some means. Full reconstructions could be given in historical writings only after Nero's death; rumors may have cropped up at the time of Claudius' death, but the facts could not be securely ascertained.[29]

Speculation and rumors were likely to arise, for the simple reason that even Nero's succession might not have seemed entirely proper. Certainly, in the eyes of many, it would have had more basis than that of Claudius. In the manner of Augustus, Claudius had adopted Nero, and married Nero to his own daughter; he also had powers bestowed on Nero, including *imperium* outside of Rome.[30] Like earlier "princes," and unlike Claudius, by his accession, Nero had already developed significant relationships with all the key elements of Roman society.[31] And, even if one were inclined to disregard Claudius' own wishes, in Nero's veins flowed the blood of Augustus, and his accession ultimately was in accord with the plans of the dynastic founder. But still there were questions anyone might ask. What of Britannicus – should his claim be utterly disregarded? Even more worrisome was the thought of a sixteen-year-old becoming ruler of the whole Roman world. Caligula had been twenty-four on his accession, and that, many would have thought, had led to troubles enough.

Thus, for all the promotion that Nero had enjoyed, the reality was that his accession ended up looking more than a little like that of Claudius.[32] Claudius' accession, it now became clear, had set some key precedents. Exiting the Palace on the thirteenth of October, Nero was, as his "father" had been, taken straight to the Praetorian Camp. There he addressed the guardsmen, promised donatives, and was proclaimed *imperator*, the title that now, effectively, meant "emperor."[33] Only then was he taken to the Senate, where a meeting was held until nightfall.[34] The fathers (along, in due course, with the People) granted him the powers they had previously voted Claudius, and the honors; also Nero, already called "Caesar" thanks to his adoption, would now be "Augustus" too.[35] He did, though, refuse the title "Father of the Fatherland" – it might seem inappropriate for one of his age, and a new emperor, after all, was supposed to refuse something.[36]

Fig. 57 *Denarius*, c. AD 54. The obverse shows confronting busts of Nero and Agrippina, with the abbreviated legend AGRIPPINA AUGUSTA, WIFE OF DIVINE CLAUDIUS, MOTHER OF NERO CAESAR. The reverse shows a garland of oak leaves encircling the abbreviated words BY DECREE OF THE SENATE. Around the garland is the abbreviated legend: TO NERO CLAUDIUS CAESAR AUGUSTUS GERMANICUS, SON OF A GOD, *IMPERATOR*, WITH TRIBUNICIAN POWER.

"Nor," Tacitus asserts, "was there any hesitation in the provinces."[37] The armies would stay loyal as news reached them: Claudius had left Nero in a secure position here. Communities also began their celebrations – and sent the familiar embassies to Rome. Given Nero's subsequent disgrace, it is not surprising that far less documentation survives for the burst of activity, and chiefly in the form of papyrus scraps.[38] In response to a delegation from Egypt, it has only recently been revealed, Nero wrote that he would decline the honor of a temple and send back their gold crown, "not wishing at the beginning of my principate to burden you." But naturally he confirmed their privileges.[39]

New statues went up in Rome of course and across the empire, in all their variety, though again unlike Claudius on his accession, Nero already enjoyed a wide distribution of his portraits.[40] The official precious metal coinage helps to reveal some subtle changes to the image being projected in Rome itself. On issues from fall of AD 54 – used, no doubt, to help pay the donatives Nero promised – the young emperor is depicted much as he was before, with the same coiffure, although the more developed features suggest a slightly older person (Fig. 57).[41] What is more remarkable is that on these his portrait only appears with his mother's, and it is her name alone which appears on the obverse: "Agrippina Augusta, wife of the Divine Claudius, mother of Nero Caesar." Nero's name only appears on

Fig. 58 *Denarius*, dated AD 55. The obverse shows paired busts of Nero and Agrippina with the name of Nero; the reverse a carriage drawn by elephants bearing figures of Divine Claudius and Augustus, with the name of Agrippina.

the reverse, enclosed in an oak wreath, which signals the civic crown the Senate awarded him at the start of his principate. Yet over the following year, the format of the coins changed: Nero's portrait is given precedence over hers, and also shows a more truly individual set of facial traits – fleshy cheeks, a prominent under-chin, and bulging neck (Fig. 58).[42] After AD 55, Agrippina's image was removed from the coinage altogether.

Through their imagery, these distinctive coins from AD 54 and early 55 show how Nero could try to overcome objections to his accession. If one thought, for instance, that Britannicus' claim should take precedence, the response was that Nero too was the son of Claudius, while his own mother, Agrippina Augusta, linked him back to Augustus. This is sufficient to account for her prominence on the coins, which is mirrored by other honors she received at the time, for instance the award of two lictors, the attendants who traditionally accompanied magistrates.[43] A further reflection is a relief from Aphrodisias, depicting Nero, dressed in military garb, being crowned by his mother Agrippina (Fig. 59).[44]

At the same time, the coins did not disguise another potential vulnerability, Nero's youthfulness. To the contrary: it was advertised because Nero, or his advisors, realized that it could actually be used to suggest the dawning of a new Golden Age. Decades earlier, in the midst of the civil war that followed the assassination of Julius Caesar, Vergil had written his mysterious Fourth Eclogue, prophesying that a young boy, as he grew to manhood, would bring peace to the whole Roman world.[45] To describe the

Fig. 59 Relief from the Sebasteion at Aphrodisias, depicting Nero and Agrippina.

peace, Vergil used features of the Golden Age from Greek mythology, and
also probably borrowed from Jewish apocalyptic literature. It was a bold
step, the first time in Roman culture that such imagery was applied to a
contemporary political situation. It would be redeployed throughout the
principate of Augustus, but Nero, just on the cusp of full manhood, could
tap into it perhaps even more effectively.[46]

So it was that Seneca, in his *Apocolocyntosis*, could imagine the Fates cutting off the thread of Claudius' life and spinning a Golden Age under Nero. As they busily work, Apollo sings to them of the new ruler:

For the weary he will bring an era of prosperity and break the silence of the laws... like the shining Sun, as soon as rosy Dawn has dispelled the shadows and brought in the day, as he gazes on the world and begins to race his chariot from the starting-barrier: such a Caesar is here, such a Nero will Rome now gaze upon. His bright face shines with gentle brilliance and his handsome neck with flowing hair.[47]

Implicit in Apollo's verses – and the coin imagery too – is the contrast between the old and ill Claudius and the youthful Nero. Similar language is found in the court poet Calpurnius Siculus, who (it is often believed) was writing around this time pastoral poetry that looked back to Vergil's verses.[48] Stories were spread too, of Nero's miraculous birth, "just as the sun was rising, so that he was practically touched by its rays before he could be laid on the ground."[49] It was all an effective way of turning Nero's greatest liability into an advantage.

Still, as always with an emperor, and especially with this sixteen-year-old, much was surely taking place behind the scenes that was less than idyllic. "The first death in the new principate, that of Junius Silanus, proconsul of Asia, was contrived with Nero unaware through the cunning of Agrippina." So Tacitus begins the thirteenth book of his *Annals*, in which Nero is helped into power by his mother, along with his tutor Seneca, and the Praetorian prefect Burrus. Agrippina, Tacitus writes, made the Senate meet on the Palatine, so that she might attend, separated from the fathers by a curtain; she presided with her son at the hearing of embassies, or tried to anyway; letters were sent by her to provincial governors, client kings, foreign rulers, Dio adds.[50] That she did exercise some power at this critical time must be true; an inscription has been discovered, in Corinth, honoring some time after the death of Claudius an agent of "Caesar and Agrippina Augusta," that is, Agrippina and her son Nero.[51] But one may guess that the influence of Burrus and Seneca was also very potent: Burrus would have made the crucial arrangements with the Praetorians, and Seneca with leading members of the Senate and equestrians. It was surely to a large degree because of their efforts that everything went so smoothly on October 13, and directly afterwards.

The palace staff was also on hand to make the necessary financial arrangements. Donatives needed to be paid, and Pallas would have seen to it.

The court, overall, needed less reconfiguration than it had on Claudius'
accession, for in a sense Nero's principate was underway even before AD 54,
with Agrippina providing a crucial link. Britannicus' own slaves likely had
been removed – and also his influential grandmother, Messallina's mother,
the formidable Domitia Lepida.[52] Britannicus himself would die the following year.[53] The notable casualty of AD 54 in fact was Narcissus, who had
handled Claudius' correspondence. Tacitus reports that he was taken into
custody and driven to suicide.[54] Perhaps his loyalty was open to question,
perhaps he was to be made a scapegoat for crimes perpetrated by others,
including Agrippina herself.

And what of M. Junius Silanus, the consul of AD 46? His own brother,
once betrothed to Claudius' daughter Octavia, had been expelled from the
Senate and apparently took his life in AD 49; his sister Calvina was expelled
from Italy at the same time.[55] That might be enough to arouse suspicions;
but perhaps even more salient, in AD 54, was his descent from Augustus,
through his mother Aemilia Lepida; there was "frequent talk among the
common people," Tacitus claims, "that ahead of Nero, who had scarcely yet
left boyhood and had acquired the empire through crime, should be a man
of settled years, blameless, noble, and – something which was considered at
that time – among the posterity of the Caesars: for Silanus too was a great-
great-grandson of Divine Augustus. That was the cause of his death."[56]
Agrippina, Tacitus further claims, arranged for poison to be administered
by imperial agents in Asia, where Silanus was serving as proconsul. Dio also
implicates Agrippina, alleging that she sent to Asia some of the same toxin
by which Claudius was killed, while Pliny, on the other hand, maintains
that it was Nero himself who was responsible for the murder.[57] Perhaps it
matters less (for the historian at least) whether there was any truth to the
tale; the motive for the crime certainly is not implausible, for Claudius'
own accession had now shown that even an inconspicuous member of
Augustus' family, not marked for succession, could become emperor; but
at the same time, the deceased's brother, Decimus, did live on for some
years.[58] What really counts, especially for Tacitus, is that the imperial system
of government could allow such crimes to go unprosecuted, unpunished.[59]
The accession of Nero made no difference to that.

That is an important insight because just at this time Nero was making
rather different assurances in public. At the Senate meeting of October 13
honors were voted not just for Nero and Agrippina but also for Claudius –
a funeral and a decree conferring cult honors for the deceased emperor.[60]
This was the first time, since Augustus, that a deceased emperor was so
honored, and the funeral, which would have taken place several days later,

Fig. 60 *Aureus*, c. AD 54. The obverse shows the head of Claudius, with the legend DIVINE CLAUDIUS; the reverse an empty horse-drawn triumphal chariot, symbolizing the departure of the new god from earth.

likely was patterned on that of the first emperor.[61] There would be a eulogy in the Forum, delivered by Nero, followed by a procession to the Field of Mars where cremation would occur – with the pyre likely lit by Nero – and then interment of the ashes, probably in the Mausoleum of Augustus. The cremation completed the consecration of Claudius; released from his service on earth, he was henceforward to be Divus Claudius, Claudius the God (Fig. 60).[62] And with the new name went priests and a temple. The priests who kept the cult of Augustus would maintain Claudius' too – and Agrippina was also given a position as priestess – but Claudius would enjoy his own massive temple, on the Caelian Hill (Figs. 61–62).[63] In its final form, it paid tribute to the idiosyncratic style favored in Claudius' own public works, and appropriately enough an extension of the Aqua Claudia abutted it. It was also probably at this time that plans were made for the great temple of Divus Claudius at Camulodunum, in Britain, marking the emperor's other mightiest achievement.[64]

In the eulogy he delivered for Claudius, Nero would have praised the achievements of the late emperor. Tacitus suggests that he dwelt on Claudius' ancestry, his attainments as a scholar, and perhaps also his expansion of the empire, and this is likely enough.[65] Yet he also suggests that the speech, though elegant (Seneca was said to have written it), fell flat in places.[66] Real doubts, in truth, could be voiced about Claudius' record, as much as about Nero. Even an ordinary member of the crowd of onlookers might wonder: what of the trials of AD 42? the death of Valerius Asiaticus? or Messallina herself? There had been quite a few casualties over the years.

Fig. 61 Arcade of the west side of the terrace for the Temple of Divine Claudius, Rome.

Afterwards, Tacitus continues, Nero would deliver another speech, to the Senate, which again was thought to have been Seneca's work.[67] Now Nero needed to start distancing himself from his predecessor: unlike Claudius, he had not come to power in a way that seemed illicit, and so there were no wrongs or hatreds to avenge; his principate would see a repudiation of those practices which had of late caused so much resentment. "He would not," he said, implicitly rebuking Claudius, "be the judge of all legal proceedings, so that, with prosecutors and defendants shut together within a single house, the powerfulness of a few might act without restraint; nothing at

Fig. 62 Detail of scale model of the City of Rome at the time of Constantine, showing in the foreground the Temple of the Divine Claudius on its massive rectangular terrace (Fig. 61) high on the Caelian Hill. The model helps convey the monument's scale, and also shows the extension of the Aqua Claudia to the Palatine Hill. Museum of Roman Civilization, Rome.

his dwelling would be for sale or open to intrigue; house and state were separate. The Senate would hold onto its ancient functions."[68]

That Seneca contributed to such a speech is also likely enough, because its ideas overlap with those he articulated about Claudius in the short pamphlet he wrote just around this time, *Apocolocyntosis*.[69] In this wicked, and very clever, satire – the title, a nonce word formed on analogy with "apotheosis," seems literally to mean "Pumpkinification" but its exact connotation remains obscure – the reader is treated to an account of Claudius' arrival, on the thirteenth of October, in Olympus, where the gods have their own debate about whether to accept his apotheosis.[70] Thoroughly dissuaded by Augustus, who for the first time since his own earlier arrival addresses his divine peers, they send Claudius back to earth, just in time to witness his own very elaborate funeral, and then to the place where all mortals ultimately must go, the Underworld. There, fittingly, Claudius is immediately put on trial – an adjournment is denied – and, before his side is heard, he is condemned to serve, for infinity, a freedman of his, Menander.

Claudius truly belongs in the Underworld, though, because that is the place of monsters, and even more than a man, Claudius is in this satire a monster.[71] Hercules, who is the first to spot Claudius in the heavens, is said to have been badly shaken by the experience: "When he saw the shape of unprecedented kind, the unusual gait, and the voice that belonged to no land creature but such as usually belongs to large creatures of the sea, hoarse and inarticulate, he thought his thirteenth labor had arrived."[72] Even as the Senate officially declared Claudius a god, Seneca through his "apocolocyntosis," reclassifies Claudius as a beast, hard to understand, of difficult gait, frightening in appearance, and, ultimately, bloodthirsty.[73]

All of the faults imputed to Claudius in Nero's speech to the Senate are brought out here, and more. Claudius is pedantic, yet stupid; he takes fright easily; he is a slave to the freedmen; he is excessively generous with the citizenship; there was rampant injustice under him; worst of all, he persecuted his fellow citizens – the final indictment, appropriate for the one-time censor, runs to 30 Senators and 321 Roman knights – and even killed members of his own family.[74]

Especially damning is the speech of Augustus, the only other deified emperor on Olympus.[75] While one of the other gods, who has done well for himself in the false citizenship racket, can try to argue that Claudius "is related by blood to both the Divine Augustus and no less to the Divine Augusta, his grandmother," Seneca's Augustus sets the record straight – with an eloquence that underscores Claudius' own deficiencies as an orator.[76]

"I can no longer dissemble, or hold back the pain, which my sense of shame aggravates," Augustus proclaims in horror at the monster he has unwittingly unleashed on the world. "Was it for this that I brought peace to land and sea? Was it for this that I put an end to civil war? Was this why I laid a foundation of laws for Rome, beautified her with public works?" Turning to Claudius, Augustus accuses his successor of hiding "under my name," only to kill Augustus' own relatives, including Lucius Silanus, and even Messallina. "Tell me, Divine Claudius: why did you condemn anyone of the men and women you killed, before examining the case, before hearing the evidence? Where is this the usual practice? It doesn't happen in heaven!"

For Seneca, Claudius' principate was one long Saturnalia, full of inversions that culminated in the emperor being made a god. And yet, again by means of the "apocolocyntosis" of Claudius, Seneca can suggest that some sense of normalcy is returning. Claudius may at one point be called a "Saturnalian *princeps*," but as one of the wraithlike jurists, barely alive, says at Claudius' funeral, when he sees a group of advocates bewailing the loss of the man who gave them so much work: "I told you it won't always be the Saturnalia!"[77] Now, with Nero, there could be hope for something else – a more godlike ruler, godlike not least because he would dispense justice. The new *saeculum* was only starting now; that of AD 47 was an illusion.

The more serious counterpart to Seneca's *Apocolocyntosis* was his essay *On Clemency* which he probably released the following year.[78] Ostensibly an exhortation to Nero, the work actually serves to advertise the new emperor's virtues, in ways not entirely reconcilable with Nero's accession speech. For here, the rule of the emperor is more clearly that of a king. And when, Seneca suggests, such a ruler can show mercy to those who would try to bring him down, and when this can be recognized as a virtue for which the ruler deserves recognition – and not (say) a humiliation, as it might have been for Roman Senators and equestrians – then a way might be seen out of the trap in which rulers like Claudius found themselves ensnared. Claudius, in trying to stave off threats, only created more of them.

In the earlier *Apocolocyntosis*, Seneca also was issuing a warning along these lines. But, even more, he was also specifically attacking Claudius, for he was eager to undercut his own earlier performance in the essay *To Polybius*, which must have seemed mortifying now.[79] He also, undeniably, was providing entertainment for courtiers in Rome. And really, so large is the gap between this performance and what Seneca purportedly wrote in the funeral speech for Claudius (to say nothing of the consecration of Claudius itself), it has been suggested that Seneca wrote his hilarious screed for performance at the Saturnalia of December, AD 54.[80] Certainly, for all that Claudius' own reign is represented as Saturnalian (and hope of something else is attached to Nero), this piece itself is an inversion of Seneca's own normal canons. At the end of this outrageous travesty, a reader almost has to feel, it is time to turn back to realities – and the make-believe reality was that Claudius was a god, and would remain a god (and that Nero was all too mortal).

And so posterity was left with two contrasting images of Claudius – a god in heaven, or a monster in hell. There is an official version, and an unreliable satire. The man himself remains harder to find. What judgment, then, is posterity to make? We, too, could try to whitewash Claudius, or to blacken him unduly, on the basis of imperfect evidence. Or, perhaps more responsibly, one can try to recognize his significance historically.

For all of the criticisms Divus Augustus makes in *Apocolocyntosis*, Claudius actually in many ways helped to strengthen the nascent institution of the principate. Through his accession and maintenance of power for almost fourteen years, he showed that one not designated emperor before his accession – and one who suffered from a physical disability at that – could still rule, and rule with some success. Faced with limited resources, he made hard decisions about what his priorities would be, and he carried out much of his chosen strategy effectively: after the disaster of Caligula, the earlier absence of Tiberius, Romans were given a sense of renewal that extended into the principate of Nero. Claudius left his imprint across the empire, in Britain and Judea, to be sure, but everywhere else too, including Italy and Rome – through roads, temples, statues, decrees, speeches, diplomas, and so on. He tried to acknowledge the needs of provincials, as well as citizens, in an empire where the two were becoming more and more alike. For many of his subjects, provided they accepted imperial rule, his image would have been largely positive. Indeed, as has been recognized throughout this book, they themselves helped to make that image (or, better, images).

Achieving that image was a triumph, as was the smooth transmission of power in AD 54. Long after his death, statues of Claudius were still standing, and his edicts still cited, far more than those of Caligula, Nero, or even Tiberius; it was Claudius, Augustus, and (to a lesser extent) Tiberius who were cited as the precedents in the law concerning Vespasian's powers. For Romans, Claudius proved to be the crucial link not just within the Julio-Claudian dynasty but from Augustus to the Flavians, who engaged in projects similar to those of Claudius – massive and utilitarian public works, expansion of the citizenship, census-taking, celebration of military triumphs, and extension of the *pomerium*, to name just a few.

Yet however smooth Nero's succession was, it points to the very real weaknesses of the emerging principate that Claudius helped, very dramatically, to show, and even to some extent caused. At times Claudius did not realistically assess the limits of his capabilities – he could not stamp out all corruption, as he promised, or single-handedly dispense justice rapidly and fairly. In relying on his household, and in trying to fashion a new dynasty, he offended some key elements of Roman society. His gravest problems were in Rome, with his fellow Senators and equestrians. Claudius tried a policy of clemency in AD 41, and it failed; but he probably veered too far in the other direction subsequently. While, to be sure, it is unlikely that Senators acted blamelessly, a real lack of transparency allowed the darkest suspicions to arise about the emperor and members of his court, including the freedmen, already despised. Full and fair trials of his opponents, even Messallina herself, were she at fault, might have brought him down, and destroyed his children too, but a riskier approach might have helped defuse some of the problem of his perceived illegitimacy. Instead, above all in AD 42, he intensified the ill-will for the long run, and this came to distort the record overall. So, finally, did the discredit Nero brought on himself and the principate as well, at least in the eyes of many Senators and equestrians. But by the start of AD 49, with his house in tatters, and with it the *res publica*, Claudius had little choice but to co-opt Nero (and Agrippina). His disability had prevented him from achieving true *gloria*, as the Romans called it, at least among fellow Senators; an acceptable basis for rule could still seem lacking. Even as he made a start at suggesting how somebody not designated for succession could be made emperor, finally the blood of Augustus re-asserted its strange and magical power.

The real significance of the principate of Claudius, historically speaking, is not what it reveals of Claudius the man, but what it shows about the emerging institution of the principate. As envisioned by Augustus, after the civil wars, Rome's leaders would effectively be monarchs in the power they wielded, but they would not be called monarchs. The idea, instead, was that the *princeps* would be like a citizen – especially in Rome, in public – and that the legal basis of his power would rest with the old organs of the republic, the Senate and the People. Emperors could prepare for successions, even hereditary successions – there was an August House – but there was no legal basis for a hereditary succession as such.

The consequence, as Claudius' own accession first dramatically showed, was that when there was no clear designate, soldiers would step in to choose

the *imperator* they wanted – and they could do so, because they had force
on their side. The Senate and People had largely lost control of the armies.
Rome's was, in reality, a military monarchy, but that reality sat alongside
the ideology of the "civil leader." This was a tension all of Augustus'
successors inherited. That is, the dissonance between the survival of the
res publica and the realities of where power now lay was profound, and
the successors' inevitably imperfect ways of dealing with the dissonance
were bound to create very damaging opposition to them in the Senate,
and hostility beyond the grave. It did not help that as a consequence of
the emperor's monopolization of military campaigning, the chief source of
new and rapid wealth for Senators in the Republic was gone. Something
more like a zero-sum struggle for resources among members of the top
echelons of society had set in, as they struggled to outdo each other in
displays of wealth.

Because of the failure to define the emperor's position and principles of
succession constitutionally, because of the power of the armies, because of
the resentment shown by fellow Senators, the reality was that all emperors,
if they wanted to survive in power and yet rule effectively, had to work
frantically to promote their accomplishments. *All* emperors, in a sense,
had the problem of Claudius. Claudius just suffered from it to an extreme
degree. Conscientious as some of them might have been, they all needed to
justify their existence to the Senate and People of Rome, to the communities
of Italy and the provinces, and to the armies, through laws, through public
works, through statues and buildings, through donatives and largesse,
through games, through gladiatorial shows and wild beast hunts, through
religion, through rituals, through marriages and adoption of heirs, and
through so much more. Some would be more successful than others, and
sometimes for reasons beyond their control; they all could find a range
of willing helpers. Still, especially in the decades immediately following
Augustus, it was a tough job for anyone to do well. Tiberius finally to
a large degree simply walked away from the position; Caligula, and then
Nero, tried to refashion the emperor's role more radically, and both paid
the price for it. Claudius tried to return to the example of Augustus and,
one must say, be a conscientious ruler of Rome. His failings were not the
product of an inner struggle of his mind; nor was he fundamentally the
prisoner of his entourage, although his entourage could harm him. He
was the prisoner of his position. Claudius was caught between forces that
would protect Rome from civil war and those that, for the sake of some
men's "liberty," would plunge it into chaos.

The principate would prove to be a strong institution, strong enough to overpower the old republican constitution because it did address the needs of more, and commanded more assent, but it was also flawed, because of the peculiar circumstances in which it arose, the transition from a republican government to autocracy, through military usurpation. The legacy of the republican past threatened to undermine it, as Momigliano so clearly saw, and hindered the emergence of a new and explicit constitution. The lack of a constitution, Roman imperial history demonstrates, is perilous for a civil society. Just fourteen years after Claudius' death, when the line of Augustus finally was extinct with the fall of Nero, a terrible civil war swept across the empire, as rival contenders, all with armies behind them, stepped forward. A similar catastrophe was only very narrowly avoided after the assassination of Domitian, in AD 96. It would happen just a century after that. There were other tremors along the way.

A strong constitution, alone, cannot guarantee the success of a society, even if it is essential to it. The constitution has to be respected, by citizens and government alike. And when a government becomes willing to enforce its own beliefs by any and all means necessary, Roman imperial history also shows, the crushing of a sense of liberty can lead to demoralization, and ultimately the potential for total amorality among the victims of such policies, while apathy afflicts the rest. Perhaps the largest lesson of empire is this: when a society is held together by no values beyond knee-jerk loyalty to the government, there is no reason to fight for the government when it comes under serious threat. And when the imperial government falls, there may be no clear reason in the eyes of its former subjects to stay together. The old and faithful servants will be weeping, but who else will there be to mourn the fallen ruler?

Notes

PROLOGUE: THE ROMAN EMPIRE IN AD 41

Brief bibliographic essay. Good general accounts of the Roman empire can be found in Millar (1967), Garnsey and Saller (1987), Wells (1992), and Goodman (1997). Goodman (2007), primarily concerned with the Jewish people of the empire, also gives a good portrait of the empire as a whole. Especially vivid (though not documented) is Danziger and Purcell (2005), focused on the age of Hadrian, but of wider relevance. *CAH* (second edn) vols. 10 and 11 offer more finely grained discussions of specific subjects, while Scheidel *et al.* (2007), covering economic history, is a mine of useful information. The collected papers of Brunt (1990) and Millar (2004) present two influential scholars' views on the theory and practice of government.

A more recent development in the field is greater effort to compare Rome with other pre-industrial states, often using social scientific methods. The comparisons made here with Han China are owed to various papers in Scheidel (2009a), especially those of Scheidel himself and Bang; further bibliography can be retrieved there. Note in addition Morris and Scheidel (2009), including the contribution by Keith Hopkins, a pioneer in this field. There are also a number of collections employing a case-study approach, e.g., Hekster and Fowler (2005) and Alcock *et al.* (2001).

The two standard studies of Tiberius in English, both written in the 1970s, have been reissued with some of the authors' second thoughts: Seager (2005) and Levick (1999a). Neither is strictly biographical: Seager hews more closely to issues raised by Tacitus' account in the *Annals*, while Levick is especially good on problems of constitutional development. (For some biographical reflections, see the remarkable papers of Syme on "History or biography: the case of Tiberius Caesar" [*RP* 3.937–52] and "Diet on Capri" [*RP* 6.409–20]). Since the 1970s, there have been major epigraphic discoveries in Spain: (1) the so-called *Tabula Siarensis* records honors voted to the deceased Germanicus (Tiberius' adopted son) by the Senate; (2) the *Senatus consultum de Cn. Pisone patre* gives a record of the Senate's findings in the trial of Cn. Piso, Germanicus' accused murderer. Text and translation of the former can be found at Crawford (1996) nos. 37–38, and also an English translation in Sherk (1988); for the latter see Eck *et al.* (1996), and for one English translation Griffin (1997). These epigraphic texts have shifted scholars' attention onto Augustus' articulation of dynastic rule, and the fate of that vision under Tiberius: Rowe (2002) is an especially useful study, and see also Severy (2003) esp. 187–251, the former (rightly, in my view) envisioning Augustus' vision of dynasty taking shape earlier. This focus on the public articulation of power harmonizes with a more critical approach to the later accounts of Suetonius, Tacitus, and Dio (on which see brief bibliographic essay for the Introduction, below). At the same time, the *senatus consultum* has confirmed Tacitus' value as a source for Senatorial affairs under Tiberius: see below, p. 296.

With very little surviving documentation aside from later accounts, and Tacitus' account no longer extant, the principate of Caligula is especially difficult to assess: Barrett (1990) – a meticulously researched work, conveniently summarized in Barrett (2008b) – revised the more exculpatory portrait of Balsdon (1934), while the study of Winterling (2003), now translated into English (Winterling [2009]), attempts to show that Caligula was consciously repudiating Augustan traditions in favor of a more Greek-style monarchy. But given the evidence, much remains uncertain here.

1 Scheidel (2007) 45–49 presents the relevant data. Romans' conceptions of their empire are discussed further below, pp. 107–15.
2 Scheidel (2009b) 11.
3 Again, see Scheidel (2007) 45–49.
4 Goodman (2007) 115–52 gives a good overview of the local cultures of the empire, and the very imperfect evidence for studying them.
5 MacMullen (1966) and Millar (2004) 249–64 ("Local cultures in the Roman Empire: Libyan, Punic, and Latin in Roman Africa") are two classic studies.
6 Number of Jews: Hopkins (1998) 212–13. Goodman (2007) is an accessible introduction.
7 Crook (1967) 36–67 gives an excellent overview of the Roman law of status.
8 Census of AD 14: Aug. *RG* 8.4 with Scheidel (2007) 45.
9 Talbert, *CAH* 10 (second edn) 324–43 ("The Senate and Senatorial and equestrian posts") provides details on Senators and equestrians. On patricians, nobles, and new men, see also below, p. 283 n. 25.
10 Further details on provincial administration, including a list of provinces, can be found in Bowman, *CAH* 10 (second edn) 344–70 ("Provincial administration and taxation").
11 In addition to Bowman, *CAH* 10 (second edn) 344–70, see also Ando (2006) for an excellent brief overview.
12 Scheidel (2009c) 19.
13 Data on the number and size of cities: Scheidel (2007) 74–80.
14 Keppie, *CAH* 10 (second edn) 371–96 ("The army and the navy") provides details on the armed forces. Note, in particular, the tally given by Tacitus for AD 23 (*Ann.* 4.5).
15 See below, p. 87.
16 See below, p. 33.

17 Parthian invasion: see, e.g., Osgood (2006a) 184–87 and 225–31. Africa: see n. 37 below.
18 Dio 60.8.7.
19 See, e.g., Bowman, *CAH* 10 (second edn) 687.
20 Tac. *Ann.* 4.5.1, with Syme (1970) 19–29.
21 See, e.g., Millar (1993) 27–56 for a discussion.
22 See, in addition to Bowman, *CAH* 10 (second edn) 344–70, Galsterer, *CAH* 10 (second edn) 397–413 ("The administration of justice").
23 Suet. *Aug.* 33.1.
24 A splendid introduction to the city of Rome can be found in Edwards and Woolf (2003); also highly recommended is the brilliant essay by Purcell, *CAH* 10 (second edn) 782–811 ("Rome and its development under Augustus and his successors"). Coulston and Dodge (2000) and Potter and Mattingly (1999) are very useful collections on a range of relevant topics.
25 See, e.g., Dodge (2000), and further below, pp. 302–3 n. 40.
26 See, e.g., Aldrete and Mattingly (1999) or (2000), and further below, p. 301.
27 Beacham (1999) is a full-scale study.
28 Aug. *RG* 22.3.
29 Discussions are numerous: two especially good overviews are given by Brunt (1990) 324–46 and Lo Cascio (2000) 177–219.
30 Luke 2.1–3, with the classic discussion of Schürer (1973–87) 1.399–427. See the useful table of references to the provincial census at Brunt (1990) 345–46.
31 This comparison between Rome and China is made by Bang (2009).
32 Posting system: Suet. *Aug.* 49.3 and the inscription published by Mitchell (1976), whence *AE* 1976.653, discussed below, p. 196. On speeds of travel see the classic article by Ramsay (1925).
33 A good overview of the finances is given by Rathbone, *CAH* 10 (second edn) 309–23 ("The imperial finances"); for further details, see below, pp. 312–13.
34 See, e.g., Osgood (2006a) 88–92 and 370–71.
35 See especially the narration of Tac. *Ann.* 1.16–51, with full discussions by Seager (2005) 48–61 and Levick (1999a) 71–75.
36 See again Tac. *Ann.* 3.40–47, with discussions by Seager (2005) 140–42 and Levick (1999a) 132–35.
37 See Tac. *Ann.* 2.52; 3.20–21, 32, 73–74; 4.13, 23–26, with discussions by Seager (2005) 142–43 and Levick (1999a) 131–32.
38 The chief accounts are Phil. *Leg.* 184–338; Joseph. *AJ* 18.261–309, *BJ* 2.184–203; see discussions by Barrett (1990) 182–91 and Winterling (2003) 147–50; also further below, p. 274 n. 4.
39 On Han China, see Scheidel (2009c) 17.
40 On the translation of the term, see further below, p. 265 n. 12.
41 See especially the (very spare) accounts of Dio 59.22.5–23.2 and Suet. *Calig.* 24.3, 29.1, 39.1; *Claud.* 9.1. Modern scholars offer various reconstructions: Barrett (1990) 91–113 gives a clear guide, while Winterling (2003) 103–15 is more speculative.

INTRODUCTION: THE PROBLEM OF CLAUDIUS

Brief bibliographic essay. Many valuable resources for the study of Claudius exist, and have been relied on throughout this book. The three principal monographs, discussed further in the main text of this Introduction, are Momigliano (1934), Scramuzza (1940), and Levick (1990), the last particularly valuable for data it collects and the cautious assessment of that data. There are also useful contributions in proceedings of two conferences on Claudius: Strocka (1994) and Burnand *et al.* (1998). The former is especially important for archeological topics, while the latter is strong on provincial affairs. Smallwood (1967) is an invaluable collection of "documents" (i.e., inscriptions, papyri, coin legends, and a few other non-literary texts) in the original languages, translations of most of which can be found in Braund (1985), a work of great help to me in producing translations for this book; for more recently discovered documents, see pp. 74–75, 90–91, and 115–17. Coinage is best studied in the standard catalogues, *RIC* I (second edn) and *RPC* I; and see also von Kaenel (1986). Also to be commended here is the very full study of the consuls under Claudius by Tortoriello (2004). Fasolini (2006) is a monograph-length annotated bibliography with helpful reviews of topics of major importance.

There also exists a vast array of resources to help with the three major ancient literary sources for Claudius discussed in this Introduction: Suetonius, Tacitus, and Dio. The best English translation available of Suetonius is the Loeb edition of Rolfe, as revised by Hurley (Rolfe [1998]); of Tacitus' *Annales*, Woodman (2004); and of Dio, the Loeb edition of Cary (1914–27); here I acknowledge my debt to Woodman (2004) in particular, whose work is now an indispensable resource for the study of Tacitus, and often provides a basis for my translations throughout. The Loeb editions may also be used for the Latin and Greek text of Suetonius and Dio, while for Tacitus' *Annales* the Teubner of Koestermann (1971) is better consulted. The commentary on Suetonius' life of Claudius by Hurley (2001) is invaluable, and much relied on here; Edmondson (1992) is strong on the selections of Dio that he covers and also has a very useful introduction; for the Claudian books of Tacitus' *Annales* a new commentary would be welcome, but see Furneaux (1896–1907) and Koestermann (1963–68). In general, there are two major problems in accepting uncritically what these authors report. First, they all wrote significantly after the events in question and in trying to determine what took place "behind the scenes" would have had to rely primarily on earlier historical accounts (or documents) which may well have failed to achieve objectivity and accuracy (cf. the famous admissions of Tacitus at *Ann.* 1.1.2–3 and also 13.20.2; and Dio at 53.19). Second, in reconstructing the past, ancient writers sometimes relied on techniques of rhetoric – including the use of stereotypes – which may have distorted their narratives; some essential reading on this point is Saller (1980), Woodman (1988), and Edwards (1993). See also Kraus and Woodman (1997) for an overview of historical writing in Latin.

This increased skepticism has helped contribute to some provocative new ways of studying Roman emperors. For reflections on the practical problems of a narrowly biographical approach, see, e.g., Syme *RP* 3.937–52 ("History or biography: the case of Tiberius Caesar"), Lendon (1998), Griffin (2005), and Hopkins (2005) – this last provocatively resorting to fictionalizing, a subject also considered in Griffin's essay. (The more philosophical objections raised above all by Millar [1977] are discussed here in the Introduction.) One fruitful, and still underexploited, strategy has been to look at representations of the emperor in literary texts, not infrequently alongside representations in other media; some good examples here are the essays on Nero in Elsner and Masters (1994), the analysis of theatricality in Bartsch (1994), and the exploration of erotics in Vout (2007). Another, sometimes overlapping approach, and one I use more in this book, is to shift focus onto the often symbolic role of emperors within the political culture of the empire as a whole – looking at what emperors signified as opposed to what they actually did: see further n. 50 below. Finally, it should be noted that the older tradition of *Kaisergeschichte* ("Emperor-history"), i.e., of using an individual emperor's years in power as a window onto the state of the empire itself and the strength of its institutions, still flourishes (and helps inform this study). Many seemingly biographical studies are closer to this form (including Levick [1990] on Claudius, as well as, e.g., Griffin [1984] on Nero); and note the recent studies of Valens by Lenski (2002) and Theodosius II by Millar (2006) himself.

1 These arrangements are widely discussed, recently by Hurlet (1997b) 139–62 and Severy (2003) esp. 187–93. Of course, they took on further significance after Tiberius successfully gained the principate in AD 14 (so Severy) – and then Caligula in AD 37. Augustus himself did not publicly speak of a "succession policy" (see the succinct reminder in Gruen [2005]), but he surely did wish that what he achieved be perpetuated.

2 For one discussion: Levick (1999a) 148–79. In the deliberations of the Senate that followed the trial of Germanicus' alleged murderer, Piso, it was at first forgotten to commend Claudius along with the other members of the August House (Tac. *Ann.* 3.18.3–4, now confirmed by the odd position of Claudius' name in the *Senatusconsultum de Pisone patre* (Eck *et al.* [1996], line 148). Tacitus almost certainly found this out through the record of the Senate proceedings (*acta senatus*): see p. 296 below.

3 Dystonia: Valente *et al.* (2002). Review of earlier views on Claudius' physical problems: Levick (1990) 13–14 and Fasolini (2006) 41–44.

4 Suet. *Claud.* 3.2.

5 Quoted at Suet. *Claud.* 4.2. Suetonius consulted letters of Augustus firsthand and quotes from them on over a dozen occasions, sometimes at length, suggesting that they might not have been widely available previously.

6 Suet. *Claud.* 2–6 is the fullest account of the early life of Claudius.

7 Note especially Suetonius' quotations from the letters of Augustus (*Claud.* 4, above, n. 5).

8 Tutor: Suet. *Claud.* 2.2 (citing a *libellus* written by Claudius himself!).

9 Drinking and dicing: Suet. *Claud.* 5. Scholarly endeavors: again, Suetonius (*Claud.* 41–42) is the main account; Pliny quotes from the histories at *HN* 5.63, 6.27, 6.31, 6.128, 7.35, and 12.78. Recent discussions are given by Schmidt (1994) and Malitz (1994). The classic treatment is Momigliano (1934) 1–19.

10 See esp. Suet. *Claud.* 7–9.

11 Suet. *Claud.* 30.

12 I base this translation on the rendering of *princeps* in Greek translations of Augustus' *Res gestae* as *hêgemôn* (*RG* 13, 30.1, 32.3). See further Cooley (2009) 160–61, who also translates *princeps* as "leader."

13 Hurlet (1997a) is right to emphasize that Claudius did have a (gradually more significant) place within the August House, but that is not to show that he would easily be accepted, or thought of, as a successor; cf. especially n. 1 above. While Claudius was certainly a name worth having – and one Augustus may have wished preserved (cf. Suet. *Claud.* 2.1, which I interpret to mean that Claudius in AD 4 took on the *cognomen* of Nero when Tiberius and Germanicus became Julii) – Julius was far more potent.

14 The circumstances of Caligula's assassination are more fully addressed below, pp. 29–30.

15 Wiseman (1982) 61–62 more fully surveys the field of candidates. See further below, pp. 42–46.

16 Gibbon's view: Wormersely (1994) 1.33; Mommsen (1992) 157–58.

17 Mommsen (1992) 160.

18 Ibid. 159.

19 The entry, composed by Leonhard Schmitz, is found in Smith (1849) 1.775–77.

20 Ruth (1924).

21 There are numerous discussions of the historiographical tradition concerning Claudius; see the three main studies of the emperor Momigliano (1934) 74–79, Scramuzza (1940) 5–34, and Levick (1990) 187–97; and also a number of the papers in the two conference proceedings: Strocka (1994) and Burnand *et al.* (1998). Fasolini (2006) 9–20 surveys more specialized publications; add to them Aveline (2006). Especially valuable are a series of papers by Griffin (1982), (1990), and (1994). More generally, on Suetonius see Wallace-Hadrill (1983); on Tacitus, Syme (1958); and on Dio, Millar (1964). For further guidance, see the brief bibliographic essay above.

22 See the fuller discussion below, pp. 254–56.

23 On this, and the other lost works – of Cluvius and Pliny – and their relation to the later tradition, there has been much discussion; in addition to those studies noted above (n. 21), guidance can be sought especially in the following works: Wilkes 1972 gives a good basic overview; Wiseman (1991) 111–18 and Wardle (1992a) review the various theories concerning the intriguing Cluvius Rufus; Syme *RP* 2.742–73 ("Pliny the procurator") and Baldwin (1995) present the more abundant evidence on Pliny. Though focused on the Neronian period, the discussion of Champlin (2003a) 36–52 is relevant here – and in my view most judicious. Two historians who wrote important accounts of the principate of Tiberius, Aufidius Bassus and Servilius Nonianus, both died in the principate of Nero (Servilius in AD 59, Tac. *Ann.* 14.19) and almost certainly therefore did not produce significant accounts of most of Claudius' principate, given how sensitive the subject still would have been: to judge by a passage of Pliny the Younger (*Ep.* 1.13.3). Servilius was giving recitations of his work already under Claudius, for whom less than flattering views of Tiberius and Caligula

would not have been entirely unwelcome (cf. Claudius' reference to Tiberius' "persistent absence" in Smallwood [1967] no. 368).

24 Tac. *Ann.* 14.2; 13.20.2.

25 See, again, Baldwin (1995).

26 Plin. *HN* 36.60. Messallina's contest: Plin. *HN* 10.172.

27 Momigliano (1934) 78.

28 Suet. *Claud.* 25.5.

29 Bell (1924) 1–2 gives a partial account of the discovery and purchase of the papyri. See further Hanson (1979) 60–62. In an extraordinary series of papers, Hanson has done much to put the archive back together; it is discussed further below, pp. 135–37.

30 Identification of the hand: Hanson (1984) 1108–9. On the letter, see further below, pp. 65–67, 78, and 80.

31 Bell (1924) 10.

32 Radin (1925) 369.

33 See Bell's own summaries of these publications in Bell (1925) 94–95, Bell *et al.* (1927) 98–99 and 106–7, and Milne *et al.* (1928) 143.

34 Bell (1924) 22.

35 The account of Momigliano's early career here depends on the informative and insightful essay of Brown (1988).

36 Momigliano (1934) xiii.

37 Brown (1988) 409.

38 Momigliano in *CAH* 10 (first edn) 316–39 ("Herod of Judaea").

39 Momigliano (1934) xv.

40 Ibid. 73.

41 Ibid. 74.

42 A helpful account of the genesis of Graves' novels: Seymour-Smith (1995) 227–33. One discussion of the famous television adaptation: Joshel (2001).

43 Graves (1934a) 13.

44 Graves (1934b) 10.

45 Ibid. 113.

46 See especially Levick (1990) 81–90 and her earlier study Levick (1978), as well as Demougin (1994) for more plausible views on where in the past Claudius found his real inspiration.

47 Momigliano (1934) xv.

48 Again, see the important pages of Levick (1990) 81–91, on the problems with the term and the concept. Also well worth reading are several articles by Burton (1998), (2002), and (2004), and see further below, p. 305.

49 As claimed by Momigliano (1934) 41–42.

50 An excellent recent study of the emerging political culture of the early principate, Rowe (2002), ends in AD 41; on one level, this book is a supplement to Rowe. Other recent important interpretations of imperial political culture, sometimes more synchronic, include Flaig (1992) on the rituals of the emperor as a basis for his rule; Lendon (1997) and (2006) on the importance of prestige; Hurlet (1997b) on the interplay between Republican forms and dynastic

realities; Ando (2000) on provincial perceptions of the emperor; Roller (2001) on the development of ideology among Senators; and Flower (2006) on the imperial construction and control of memory. Veyne (2005) 15–78 is a remarkable synthesis, pointing to the "double and uncertain nature" of the principate, which could make holding onto power difficult. These studies make clear earlier work of importance, e.g., Béranger (1953) and Alföldi (1970). Path-breaking articles by Wallace-Hadrill, e.g., Wallace-Hadrill (1986) and (1990), are also essential reading.

51 See especially Flaig (1992) and Rowe (2002), and also, on the different messages addressed to different audiences, Ando (2000) 131–74.

52 For relevant bibliography, see further below, pp. 268–69.

53 The concept was applied to study of the Roman empire in a pioneering article of Hopkins (1965) and subsequently used to powerful effect by Meeks (1983) in his re-assessment of the first Christian communities that took root precisely in the early Roman empire.

54 A classic example is Petronius' portrait of the freedman Trimalchio in his novel *Satyricon*, probably written soon after Claudius' death; for a possible link between Trimalchio and Claudius: Focardi (1999). See also p. 318 n. 21.

55 See the brief bibliographic essay above.

56 See, e.g., discussions below of the death of C. Appius Silanus (p. 43), the fall of Valerius Asiaticus (pp. 147–49), the fall of Messallina (pp. 206–13), and the death of Claudius (pp. 209–13).

57 Important passages are Tac. *Ann.* 1.1, 3.19.2, 4.11, 13.20.2; and Dio 53.19.

58 A few examples of this format: Levick (1999a) on Tiberius, Griffin (1984) on Nero, Jones (1992) on Domitian, Barrett (1990) on Caligula. Notably different are a series of biographical studies by Birley which employ a prosopographical approach, e.g., Birley (1997) on Hadrian.

59 Scramuzza (1940) and Levick (1990).

60 Millar (1977) xi.

61 Note the comments in Millar (1966); but also note that Millar himself went on to produce in Millar (2006) a focused study of the rule of Theodosius II, arguing that it could illumine larger themes.

62 Some noted with calculated provocation in the review of Hopkins (1978a); note here Millar's afterword to a reprint of his book, Millar (1992) 636–52, reviewing some objections, acknowledging other developments, but ultimately affirming his model of 'petition-and-response.'

63 The work of two German art historians has been especially influential in showing other historians the vital importance of the imperial image: see, conveniently, Zanker (1988) and Hölscher (2003). There are now powerful art historical investigations into the construction of imperial rule as dynasty in Rose (1997) and Boschung (2002), and material evidence plays an important role too in such studies as Hurlet (1997b), Ando (2000), and Flower (2006); on the material aspects of the rise of the principate see also now the brilliant synthesis in Wallace-Hadrill (2008). On imperial cult the revolutionary study was Price (1984). Note here Millar (1992) 638.

64 Extremely minimalist views of the Roman government are now coming into question as the evidence for the government's activity is reexamined: see, e.g., the comments in Burton (1998) and (2002) and Ando (2006); and further below, p. 305. Cf. also the concessions at Millar (1992) 641–45.

65 Champlin (2003a) on Nero; Hekster (2002) on Commodus. On Nero, note too the edited collection Elsner and Masters (1994).

1 CLAUDIUS CAESAR

Brief bibliographic essay. A fundamental feature of the early principate – and one highlighted in this chapter, because it was made so apparent in AD 41 – was that there was no law of succession as such, and yet the post of *princeps* was not elective either. Rather astonishingly, the manner in which emperors gained power was not treated in Millar's landmark study, Millar (1977); it is (rightly) put front and center in the remarkable essay of Veyne (2005) 15–78 (on the subject "What was a Roman emperor?"), building on his earlier work in Veyne (1976). Timpe (1962) highlighted the problem for the early imperial period, focusing on constitutional issues (and see also Parsi [1963]), and these (rightly) continue to be an important focus: see, for instance, Brunt (1977), Scheid (1992), and, on the significance of tribunician power, Rowe (2002) 41–54. More regularly considered now, as part of imperial "political culture," are largely extra-constitutional relations between the emperor and the people and the army as well as provincial subjects, and also the (circumscribed) way in which dynastic rule was constructed (see above, pp. 266–67 n. 50). Charlesworth (1939) and Béranger (1953) 137–69 drew attention to a distinctive pattern of behavior on the accession of new emperors – namely that of refusing various honors or powers – and this is explored further in Wallace-Hadrill (1982) on the ideology of the "citizen-emperor" and the advantages offered by such an ideology. Refusals masked the reality that emperors were, as Veyne puts it, "adventurers." On the significance of the year AD 41 itself, several works of Wiseman are crucial, in particular Wiseman (1982) and (1991).

One offshoot of the greater attention devoted to extra-constitutional features of the principate has been the rediscovery of the (very dangerous) imperial court, present from the start but more conspicuous under Caligula, Claudius, and Nero, as monarchical features of the principate grew more pronounced: this is observed in a remarkable chapter in Syme (1986) 168–87 ("Princesses and court ladies"), where of the twelve women of the court discussed, it is observed that "only one . . . was spared either banishment or violent end" (185); Paterson (2007) is excellent on contextualizing the problems engendered by studying the court and reviews earlier literature, including the classic pages of Friedländer (1908–13) 1.30–97. Millar (1977) 59–131 ("Entourage, assistants, and advisers") looked at some members of the court, while further description can be found in Turcan (1987), Winterling (1999), Belayche (2001), and Pani (2003). Wallace-Hadrill in *CAH* 10 (second edn) 309–23 ("The imperial court") draws attention to the strengthening of the court in the early imperial period; see also his brilliant study, Wallace-Hadrill (1983), of Suetonius, whose *Lives of the Caesars* is a key source for, as well as artifact of, court life.

On the emperor's relationship with the army, omitted in Millar (1977) except for discussion of military guards at 61–66, Campbell (1984) is now the basic study. On the army itself Webster (1998) and Le Bohec (1994) offer general overviews; more succinct, for this period, is Keppie, *CAH* 10 (second edn) 371–96 ("The army and the navy"). The papers in Sabin *et al.* (2007) are of great help too. A full guide to the legions can be found in Le Bohec (2000–3), helpfully reviewed by Wilkes (2002). On the Praetorian Guard, see, in addition to Campbell (1984) 109–20, the classic study of Durry (1938), as well as Keppie (1996) for its early history; on the separate German Bodyguard, and its place in the longer history of imperial "horse guards," see Speidel (1994).

1 Briefer accounts of the events of January 24–25, AD 41, and the whole plot against Caligula, are given by Suet. *Calig.* 56–60 and *Claud.* 10; and Dio 59.29–60.2.1. A much more elaborate version, imperfectly blending more than one tradition, is to be found in Joseph. *AJ* 19.1–273, for which the indispensable guide is Wiseman (1991). Note also Sen. *Constant.* 18 for remarks from a contemporary.

2 Suet. *Claud.* 10.

3 Dio 60.1.3a.

4 Joseph. *AJ* 19.164; this version is not easily reconciled with Josephus' own later account at *AJ* 19.212–22 (which is closer to Suetonius and Dio).

5 See, e.g., already Joseph. *AJ* 19.17–69 for the complicity of the Praetorian prefect Arrecinus Clemens and the Senator Annius Vinicianus (mistakenly called Minucianus), as well as the freedman Callistus (cf. Suet. *Calig.* 56.1 and Dio 59.29.1, the latter also implicating Callistus by name and one prefect of the Guard); but this could be later guesswork. Modern discussions include Timpe (1960) and (1962) 77–93; Swan (1970); Jung (1972); Ritter (1972); Levick (1990) 33–39; Barrett (1990) 154–71; Winterling (2003) 161–74; and Cogitore (2002) 63–78. Some, e.g., Timpe, are inclined to see Vinicianus as the real force behind the conspiracy; Winterling attaches more significance to Callistus; on the possibility of Claudius' involvement see especially Jung and Levick.

6 In Republican times, only an army could grant the title, while the Senate could choose to accept, or reject, it; see Linderski (2007) 115–17. To judge by the fragmentary record of the Arval Brethren (Scheid [1998] no. 13), the Senate accepted (rather than granted) the title for Caligula on March 18, before it later discussed Caligula's powers. See Barrett (1990) 55–71, though note that it is technically imprecise to say that the Senate had "the traditional right to acclaim a victorious commander as *imperator*"; cf. also Timpe (1962) 68–69.

7 Dio 60.1.4. Dio, a Senator himself, throughout his history most carefully observes the Senate's doings; the partially extant law outlining Vespasian's powers (Crawford [1996] no. 39) attests powers also held by Claudius and is strong evidence that in AD 41 the Senate's decrees concerning Claudius' powers were passed into law by the People (cf. Tac. *Hist.* 4.3.3); on this document, see

especially the classic article of Brunt (1977) with earlier discussions cited there. And, from the Record of the Arval Brethren for AD 69 (Scheid [1998] no. 40), it can be deduced that after the Senate voted the new emperors Otho and Vitellius tribunician power and membership in the priestly colleges and the like, magistrates convoked the assemblies to enact formally the Senate's wishes: see Scheid (1992) and more briefly Ando (2000) 155–56. Note, too, how the Senate arranged for ratification by the People of the honors it decreed for the dead Germanicus: *Tabula Siarensis* frag. (b) col. II lines 27–31 (at Crawford [1996] nos. 37–38).

8 Caligula: see, e.g., Barrett (1990) 50–71; Tiberius: see Levick (1999a) 68–81.

9 On all these measures, and the amnesty: Dio 60.3.5–4.6 and Suet. *Claud.* 11.1; on statues, also see below, pp. 50–51.

10 Suet. *Claud.* 21.1 and Dio 60.6.8–9; on the politics of dedicatory inscriptions, also see below, pp. 169–71.

11 Suet. *Claud.* 21.1 and Dio 60.6.8–9 (it is only Dio who reports that Claudius wore triumphal dress, a privilege that in this period was technically voted by the Senate, hence Dio's interest in the matter).

12 See, e.g., Wallace-Hadrill (1983) 127–28; for emperors and games more generally: Veyne (1976) 701–30 and Beacham (1999), along with the classic Friedländer (1908–13) 2.1–19.

13 See further below, p. 153.

14 See Table 2 and the works mentioned in the brief bibliographic essay above.

15 Phil. *Leg.* 259.

16 See especially Joseph. *AJ* 19.247; cf. Suet. *Claud.* 10.4 and Dio 60.12.4.

17 Von Kaenel (1994) 54–55 and Burgers (2001) 106–8; the coins are *RIC* I (second edn) Claudius nos. 2–18. von Kaenel (1986) is a full study of the Claudian coinage, relied on throughout this book for matters of chronology and iconography in particular; Sutherland (1951) 123–47 and (1987) 74–87 makes some keen observations.

18 Dominance: note that not illustrated here is *RIC* I (second edn) Claudius nos. 17–18, depicting on the obverse the "Victory of Augustus."

19 Constancy (and other virtues on Claudius' accession coinage): Fears (1981) 893–95.

20 Suet. *Claud.* 10.4; for the details that follow see especially Campbell (1984) 166–68.

21 See especially Tac. *Ann.* 1.8.1–2; Suet. *Tib.* 76 and *Calig.* 16.3; and Dio 59.2.1.

22 See further below, pp. 229–30.

23 See Table 3 for an estimate of the annual expenses of an emperor, taken to be roughly equivalent to annual revenue, with, e.g., Campbell (1984) 161–65 and Duncan-Jones (1994) 33–46.

24 In considering the imperial finances I have drawn especially on recent work by Duncan-Jones (1994) 3–63; Hopkins (1995/96); Rathbone in *CAH* 10 (second edn) 309–23 ("The imperial finances"); M. A. Speidel (2000); and Lo Cascio (2000) and (2007) as well as the studies listed below, pp. 312–13. But there is

a long and controversial literature on the subject; see also the fuller discussion below, pp. 229–30 and 233–36. Scheidel (1996) is essential reading on numerical references in literary sources.

25 Suet. *Aug.* 101.4, Tac. *Ann.* 1.11.3–4, and Dio 56.33.2. Note also Suet. *Aug.* 28.1.

26 See Dio 55.12.5.

27 Noted especially clearly by Ehrhardt (1978) 52 and Weaver (2004) 201. Here I would disagree with Ando (2000) 27 esp. n. 36.

28 Key studies of the emperor's slaves and freedmen are Chantraine (1967); Boulvert (1970) and (1974); and Weaver (1972). For the court as a whole, see the brief bibliographic essay above.

29 Ti. Iulius Secundus: *CIL* 6.37752; Ti. Claudius Alcibiades: *ILS* 1734; Ti. Claudius Quadratus: *ILS* 1750; Amoenus: *ILS* 1781; Paezusa: *ILS* 1786.

30 See, e.g., Sen. *Ira* 2.33.2 and *Tranq.* 6.2.

31 Note especially *ILS* 1765, an epitaph for Ti. Claudius [Di]pterus, a freedman of Divus Claudius and "clothes-maker of Caesar in charge of theatrical costume."

32 *ILS* 1671 (*scrinarius ab epistulis*).

33 Cf. *ILS* 1675 and *CIL* 15.7444; and Phil. *Leg.* 181.

34 Note especially *ILS* 1682, an epitaph for Ti. Claudius Lemnius, a freedman of the Divine Claudius, *a studiis*.

35 See further below, pp. 203–5.

36 Hermeros: *ILS* 3481; and Eutrapelus: *CIL* 6.10090.

37 Plin. *HN* 33.145.

38 *ILS* 1655.

39 Tiberius' surplus: Suet. *Calig.* 37.3 and see especially Burgers (2001) 103–5. Note, too, the surplus Augustus always had, set aside, to pay off the generous legacies in his will: Suet. *Aug.* 101.2. On mines and the money supply: Wilson (2007).

40 *RG* 21.3; cf. Dio 51.21.4. See Duncan-Jones (1994) 7 and further below, p. 101.

41 For one discussion with some examples: Millar (1977) 69–83.

42 Dio 60.4.5 (and cf. 59.26.1–2); Claudius is also said to have executed Gaius' freedman Helicon: Phil. *Leg.* 206.

43 Joseph. *AJ* 19.64–69.

44 See Suet. *Claud.* 28 and Dio 60.30.6[b], with fuller discussion below, pp. 190–205. Note also Polybius 143.

45 The career of Pallas is discussed by Oost (1958); for his fortune note especially a papyrus showing that Pallas held land in Egypt (*P London* 195) and the record of the *horti Pallantiani* in Rome (e.g., Frontin. *Aq.* 19, 20, 69).

46 A very full discussion is now given by Kokkinos (2002); see especially 6–33.

47 See esp. Joseph. *AJ* 19.236–45 and 265–66, *BJ* 2.206–10; and cf. Dio 60.8.2–3. Josephus' account in *AJ* might be overdrawn, but Agrippa seems, at a minimum, to have served as an intermediary between Claudius and the Senate: see further below, pp. 76–77.

48 *IGRom.* 1.1295 and 1109; Sen. *Brev. Vit.* 20.3; and Tac. *Ann.* 1.7.2 and 11.31.1. The origin in Spain rests on the assumption that he is the writer interested in agronomy mentioned by Plin. *HN* 3.3, 9.11, and 18.75.

49 Tac. *Ann.* 11.33–4.1 with Tortoriello (2004) 470–73. House of Caecina Largus: Asc. p. 27 Clark and Plin. *HN* 17.5.

50 Accounts of the banishment of Julia Livilla are Suet. *Claud.* 29.1 and Dio 60.8.5 (cf. 60.18.4 and 60.27.4).

51 Seneca was himself later accused of committing adultery with Julia Livilla, but the allegation in AD 41 might only have been that he was an accomplice to the crime; contrast the wording of Dio 60.8.5 and schol. ad Juv. 5.109 with that found in Tac. *Ann.* 13.42.2–3 and Dio 61.10.1.

52 Accounts of the Silanus affair are Suet. *Claud.* 37.2 (and cf. 29.1) and Dio 60.14.2–15.1; note also Sen. *Apocol.* 11.5 and Tac. *Ann.* 11.29.1.

53 See Suet. *Claud.* 37.1 and Tac. *Ann.* 11.4.2 with the discussion of Harris (2003) 30.

54 A few discussions: McAlindon (1956) 117–18, Ehrhardt (1978) 61–62, and Levick (1990) 57–59. A further possibility is that marriage with Lepida was a trap to bring Silanus back to Rome.

55 Sen. *Apocol.* 11.5. For this whole problem, see also the discussion below, p. 257.

56 Dio 60.15–16; the two other main sources are Suet. *Claud.* 13.2 and 35.2; and Plin. *Ep.* 3.16; see also Tac. *Ann.* 12.52.2 and 13.43.2; *Hist.* 1.89.2 and 2.75; and Oros. *Hist.* 7.6.6–8. The best modern discussions are Wiseman (1982) and Galimberti (1999), although some aspects of Wiseman's analysis of the "civil war" in the poet Calpurnius Siculus have been doubted, e.g., Griffin (1984) 259 n. 81.

57 Dio 60.15.2.

58 Plin. *Ep.* 3.16.8.

59 In addition to the literary sources see especially *ILS* 5950 (dating Scribonianus' arrival in Dalmatia to before the accession of Claudius).

60 Had plans only been formulated in response to news of Silanus' death, it seems likely that Scribonianus would have waited until the start of the campaigning season of AD 43 to unleash his plot, to allow time to communicate with other generals and Senators in Rome.

61 Plin. *Ep.* 3.16.6.

62 See Joseph. *AJ* 19.160 and 263–64 and *BJ* 2.205; and Dio 60.1.4. For his activity under Caligula: Swan (1976).

63 The granting of the title to the legions is confirmed by epigraphic evidence, e.g., *ILS* 2702.

64 Quint. *Inst.* 8.5.15–16 with Rogers (1945). Erasure of names: *ILS* 157 (erasure of L. Arruntius Camillus Scribonianus, significantly, from a dedicatory inscription to *Securitas Augusta* celebrating the fall of Sejanus); *CIL* 6.2015 = 14.2241 (erasure of Q. Pomponius Secundus).

2 A STATUE IN SILVER

Brief bibliographic essay. Statues, a key part of the dialogue between ruler and ruled in Hellenistic and Roman society, are receiving more and more attention from ancient historians; a great stimulus has been the wide-ranging work of Zanker, most famously Zanker (1988); and historians also are greatly indebted to major improvements in the collection, publication, and interpretation of data by archeologists; for the Julio-Claudian period in particular there has been an explosion of research, detailed below. The fundamental work contextualizing statues of the emperor, drawn on extensively here, is Pekáry (1985), part of the very important *Herrscherbild* series on imperial portraiture; it is helpfully reviewed by Gergel (1987). Højte (2005) supplements it with a study of statue bases from Augustus to Hadrian (see my review, Osgood [2006b]). On statues in imperial society see also the important studies of Lahusen (1983) and (1984) on honorific commissions, and Gregory (1994) and Stewart (2003) for the larger backdrop. Ando (2000) 206–73 is especially relevant to my theme, examining how images of the emperor symbolized power relations and thereby perpetuated imperial rule.

On the statues of Claudius himself, the best starting place is the article of Massner (1994); other works are detailed in the notes below. Massner is preparing a full study of Claudius' portraits for the *Herrscherbild* series, and also contributed a valuable earlier volume to that series, Massner (1982), which studies the adaptation of Augustus' image in portraits of other members of his dynasty. Examination of this visual language is now prominent in studies of the important phenomenon of dynastic group portraits: see, in particular, Rose (1997) and Boschung (2002), much relied on in this study. Rose (1997) indeed is probably the best single book to read for an introduction to the whole subject of Julio-Claudian portraiture; also strongly recommended for understanding methodology are Smith (1996) on portraits of Augustus and Bartman (1999) on portraits of Livia. Other monographs are valuable for examining the significance of iconographical features of portraits, e.g., Brilliant (1963) on gesture, Hallett (2005) on nudity, Bergmann (1998) on the radiate crown of the ruler's head (the last helpfully reviewed by Smith [2000]).

More broadly on the relation between imperial art and power – a truly vast topic – one might consult the often cursory remarks in the general book by Hannestad (1986) as well MacCormack (1981) and the early chapters of Elsner (1998), examining the later empire; and also more focused works such as those by Price (1984) on imperial cult; Rogers (1991) on the procession of images in Ephesus; Davies (2000) on imperial funerary monuments in Rome; Varner (2004) on destruction of images; Dillon and Welch (2006) on images of warfare. Kleiner (1992) is a useful work of reference, with rich bibliographies. Also to be noted here are a series of well-researched, but speculative, articles on the Claudian period in particular by La Rocca, especially (1992a), (1992b), and (1994). Works on the imperial women that exploit archeological evidence are discussed below, p. 309.

1 Chaeremon: van der Horst (1984). A few discussions of Alexandria: Fraser (1972), Harris and Ruffini (2004), McKenzie (2008).

2 Apion: Jacobson (2001) and Dillery (2003) are recent discussions, while Schürer (1973–87) 3.604–7 gives basic information.

3 Philo: Alston (1997), van der Horst (2003), and Taylor (2003) are a few recent discussions, while Schürer (1973–87) 3.809–90 gives a valuable survey. Note also the editions of Box (1939) and Smallwood (1961). See also bibliography below, p. 279 n. 24.

4 The unrest of AD 38 has been extensively discussed, not least because the chief account, penned by Philo himself, while rich in incidental details may be misleading on the precise cause of the troubles; see also Joseph. *BJ* 2.184–203 and *AJ* 18.257–309. In addition to the works above, p. 262 n. 38, for a sample of varying reconstructions see discussions in Kasher (1985), Gruen (2002), Gambetti (2003), and Ritter (2003).

5 Not mentioned by Philo himself in any extant work, but Josephus: *AJ* 19.276.

6 See above, pp. 41–42.

7 On the problematic testimony for the work and its sub-divisions Schürer (1973–87) 3.859–64 presents the evidence.

8 A second extant work, concerning the prefect of Egypt at the time, Avillius Flaccus, may not be part of *On Virtues* but is obviously connected in subject matter.

9 Philo's explanation: e.g., *Leg.* 210–12 and 290. Claim of Apion: Joseph. *Ap.* 2.80 (and repeated elsewhere, e.g., Tac. *Hist.* 5.4.2).

10 First fruits: e.g., *Leg.* 156. Sacrifices in outer courts: e.g., *Leg.* 157. Philo's visit: *Prov.* 2.64.

11 *Leg.* 191.

12 See esp. *Leg.* 143–61, 298–305, and 310–18.

13 Phil. *Leg.* 148.

14 Ibid. 151 and note the reference to it in Claudius' letter to the Alexandrians (Smallwood [1967] no. 370).

15 Phil. *Leg.* 151.

16 Ibid. 134–36.

17 See the works cited in the brief bibliographic essay above.

18 Some helpful discussions of the portraits of Augustus: Vierneisel and Zanker (1979), Zanker (1988), Boschung (1993b), and Smith (1996).

19 This crucial point, emphasized in an essential article by Wallace-Hadrill (1990), is now confirmed by the catalogue of statue bases for Augustus assembled by Højte (2005) 229–63.

20 Two early studies of importance were Swift (1923) and Stuart (1939); a recent discussion is Ando (2000) 228–32. On reconstructing the "models" for the early imperial period, in addition to the works above, p. 273, two very good overviews are offered by Boschung (1993a) and Rose (1997) 57–72; and note Boschung (2002) 181–92. One discussion of the significance of the head: Stewart (2003) 47–59.

21 Aug. *RG* 24.2.

22 Stewart (2003) 20–28 discusses the Latin terminology for statues.

23 Ando (2000) 206–73, esp. 209–15, emphasizes the connection between the replication of images and imperial stability.

24 Dio 60.5.4–5; see further Pekáry (1985) 72–76. On the record(s) of Senate proceedings, see below, p. 296.

25 Price of statues (deriving chiefly from second-century AD evidence): Duncan-Jones (1982) 78–79, Pekáry (1985), 13–21, and Højte (2005) 52–56.

26 *ILS* 103.

27 Dio 60.25.2–3; see further Stewart (2003) 133–34.

28 *CIL* 6.40307; full study by Morizio (1996).

29 There is evidence for three or four statues. Claudius was included among the members of the imperial family depicted in association with the arch voted posthumously to Germanicus by the Senate (*Tabula Siarensis* frag. (a) lines 9–21 at Crawford [1996] nos. 37–38); in the principate of Caligula statues went up in Pola (*ILS* 198) and Alexandria Troas (*CIL* 3.381). On *ILS* 107 see now Rose (1990). For the known statues of Claudius, see Stuart (1938); and Højte (2003) and (2005).

30 Massner (1994) is the best starting place. See also Fittschen (1977) 55–58, Massner (1982) 126–39, Menichetti (1983/84), Fittschen and Zanker (1985) 16–17, von Kaenel (1986), Boschung (1993a) 70–71, and Rose (1997) 70–71. Varner (2004) 25–30 discusses portraits of Caligula re-carved as Claudius. Fuller bibliography on individual works can be traced through this literature.

31 The argument rests in large part on numismatic evidence: see especially von Kaenel (1986) 262–76 and Massner (1994) 166–73.

32 Fuller lists can be found, e.g., at Fittschen (1977) 55–58 and Menichetti (1983/84) 202–7.

33 Varner (2004) 27.

34 *RIC* I (second edn) Claudius nos. 2, 13–14, 31–32, etc. See above, pp. 34–36.

35 Dio 60.4.6 (and cf. Suet. *Claud*. 11.3), on which see Flower (2006) 148–59. For archeological evidence see especially the detailed discussion of Varner (2004) 21–44.

36 Rose (1997) and Boschung (2002) are now the leading discussions of the phenomenon; see in particular Rose (1997) 39–46 and Boschung (2002) 153; note also Cogitore (1992) and Fasolini (2006) 129–35. For the larger context: Pekáry (1985) 90–96.

37 See above, p. 9.

38 Claudius' honors: Suet. *Claud*. 11.2 and Dio 60.5.1. Antonia as priestess of Augustus: Suet. *Calig*. 15.2 and Dio 59.3.4. For a fuller discussion: Kokkinos (2002) *passim*. On her portraiture: Wood (1999) 142–76.

39 *RIC* I (second edn) Claudius nos. 65–68 and 92. On the coins see further Trillmich (1978).

40 Suet. *Claud*. 11.2 and Dio 60.5.2 with the evidence of the records of the Arval Brethren for January 17, AD 44 (Scheid [1998] no. 17). Full discussion in Barrett (2002), esp. 222–23.

41 The evidence is the record of the Arval Brethren for January 17, AD 44 (Scheid [1998] no. 17): the priests of this group dedicated on this day a cow to Diva Augusta (and a bull to Divus Augustus); present at this ceremony were some of

the most important men of Claudian Rome including L. Vitellius, Claudius' prospective son-in-law L. Silanus (and Silanus' brother Marcus), and Claudius' son-in-law Pompeius Magnus. On these individuals, see the Index. For the new statue of Livia the primary piece of evidence is the bronze coin issue *RIC* I (second edn) Claudius no. 101. See further on the portraits of Livia Winkes (1995), Wood (1999) 75–141, and Bartman (1999), also briefer comments by Boschung (1993a) 45–47 and Rose (1997) 60–61 and 112–13.

42 See previous note for the evidence for the date.

43 These sculptures, the so-called "Reliefs of the Vicomagistri," have been thoroughly reanalyzed by Gradel (2002) 165–86, whose views are presented here. Earlier discussions: Ryberg (1955) 75–80, M. Anderson (1984), and Kleiner (1992) 147–48.

44 "Father of the Fatherland": Dio 60.3.2 with the records of the Arval Brethren for January 12, AD 44 (Scheid [1998] no. 17). See especially Gradel (2002) 178–88.

45 See above, n. 41.

46 Suet. *Claud.* 11.2; and cf. Dio 60.6.1–2. Note also the appearance of Germanicus on Claudian coinage: *RIC* I (second edn) Claudius nos. 105–6.

47 Games for Drusus: Suet. *Claud.* 11.2. Coins: *RIC* I (second edn) Claudius nos. 3–4, 35, 69–74, 93, 98, 109, and 114. Claudius' name "Germanicus": Suet. *Claud.* 1.3 and 2.1; and Dio 55.2.3.

48 Dio 60.8.7.

49 *CIL* 6.40420–26; full study by De Caprariis (1993).

50 See primarily Tac. *Ann.* 3.56–57.

51 The inscriptional evidence is the record of a dedication to Pietas Augusta (*ILS* 202), voted by the Senate in AD 22 and dedicated by Claudius in AD 42/3. The dates here match those recovered from the Via dell' Impresa fragments.

52 See especially Rose (1997) 116–18 and Boschung (2002) 69–76. Linderski (2007) 428–31 shows the earlier identification of the building as an Augusteum maintained by local Augustales is likely mistaken.

53 On this portrait see also Varner (2004) 28–29 and 230–31.

54 See especially Rose (1997) 100–2, whose views are followed here; the reliefs are widely discussed, e.g., by Kleiner (1992) 145–47 and Bartman (1999) 135–36.

55 So Rose (1997) 100–2. But other identifications have been suggested; see, e.g., Boschung (2002) 195 and Hallett (2005) 121.

56 On this problem see further below, pp. 140–45, and in general Hallett (2005) 159–222.

57 La Rocca (1992a) relates the altar at Ravenna to a presumed visit of Claudius there in AD 44 (see Plin. *HN* 3.119), on which see below, p. 91. Cf. also Cavalieri Manasse (1992).

58 See especially Højte (2005) 634 with 165–68.

59 Council of Sestinum: *CIL* 11.5999. Lanuvium: *ILS* 6194. *Negotiatores* from Moguntiacum: *ILS* 7076. Citizens in Asia: *AE* 1924.69 = *IK* 17.1.3019. Full list of statue bases in Højte (2005) with comments by Osgood (2006b). See also below, pp. 218 and 246.

60 The main sources are Joseph. *AJ* 19.278–79 and Claudius' letter to the Alexandrians (Smallwood [1967] no. 370); further discussion below, pp. 76–80.

61 Smallwood (1967) no. 370. Tcherikover and Fuchs (1957–64) no. 153 give a good text with clear and useful commentary. On the letter, see also above, pp. 16–17. Harker (2008) 25–26 suggests that in the form in which it is preserved, it omits a few portions of Claudius' original communication (e.g., dating formula, names of the Jewish ambassadors).

62 Rose (1997) 185–88 rightly gives a full discussion of this evidence.

63 Images of Claudius and his family: on the basis of numismatic evidence (*RPC* 1.5113–30), Rose (1997) 185–88 suggests that statues went up for Claudius, Antonia, Messallina, and Claudius' three children.

64 On this refusal and the whole topic of ruler cult, see further below, pp. 137–46.

65 On the identity of the man, see below, p. 279 n. 9.

66 In his sketch of Philo's life and writings, Eusebius (*Hist.* 2.18.8) states that Philo read before the Senate his work on the "impiety of Gaius," called *On Virtues*. See also below, p. 78.

3 IMPERIAL FAVORS

Brief bibliographic essay. Embassies, which made possible dialogue between citizens and provincial subjects of Rome, on the one hand, and the emperor, on the other, played an important role in the early Roman empire and have become far better understood as epigraphic evidence accumulates, and the data is re-interpreted. An excellent discussion, focusing on the problems of the data, is given by Eck (2009), part of a useful collection of papers looking at diplomacy in both the Republican and imperial periods, Eilers (2009); on the Republican period see also the wonderful pages of Linderski (2007) 40–60. In his important book, Millar (1977) 375–84 looked at the administrative implications of the embassies, and also (410–20) at my main subject here, embassies concerning the retention of privileges; in a later, far-ranging essay, Millar (2002) 292–313 ("State and subject: the impact of monarchy"), he located the origins of the practice in the pregnant moment after the battle of Actium, when a new relationship between provincial communities and a Rome now ruled by one man crystallized. Other valuable discussions include Souris (1992), focusing on the size of embassies; Habicht (2001/2), on the eastern epigraphic evidence and the political life of the Greek cities; and Rowe (2002) 124–53, on embassies and a culture of loyalty in the early empire. The monograph of Ziethen (1994) presents much data but is less helpful as an overall guide to the subject. Of major importance, and not mentioned anywhere in Eilers (2009), is the recent publication of a long (though incomplete) inscription from Samothrace, containing a decree of the Thracian city of Maroneia which records not only a successful embassy under Claudius but also establishment of procedures for sending embassies in the future: Clinton (2003) and (2004), and Wörrle (2004), whence *AE* 2003.1959 and *SEG* 53.659.

Also of relevance to this chapter (as well as Chapter 5) is the burgeoning (and largely non-Anglophone) scholarship exploring how official pronouncements were disseminated from Rome to the provinces and made known there (and the related question of the nature of imperial as well as local archives containing the sometimes precious communications). Ando (2000) esp. 73–130, in an adventurous discussion, examines not just the evidence for such pronouncements, but suggests how written documents, ambitiously promulgated and distributed by the imperial government, contributed to a sense of shared civic life across the empire. Documents, he points out, play an increasing role in literary productions of the imperial era; Philo, Josephus, and (much later) Eusebius are obvious examples, and also to be noted here is the so-called *Acta Alexandrinorum*, a series of (semi-)fictional "documents" illustrating the relations between Alexandrians and the Roman emperor (including Claudius): an excellent study is now offered by Harker (2008), situating the origins of this genre in the aftermath of the Alexandrian riots of AD 38 and the ensuing embassies. One might further note the letter of the tribune Claudius Lysias included in Acts of the Apostles (discussed further below, p. 130). Further on the distribution of documents and their display in ephemeral as well as permanent forms, see several essays in Capdetrey and Nelis-Clément (2006), the collected papers of Corbier (2006), and also now the contributions in Haensch (2009), as well as Meyer (2004) on the distinctive Roman form of wooden tablets. On the archives at the disposal of the emperor, as well as the record kept by each emperor, see Millar (1977) 252–72, Haensch (1992), and also various papers published under the auspices of the French research initiative devoted to Roman archives (*La mémoire perdue*), Nicolet *et al.* (1994), Moatti *et al.* (1998), and (2000). And for local archives see in addition: Haensch (1994), Pucci ben Zeev (1998) 381–408, Gagos and Potter (2006), and Harker (2008), esp. 99–119.

1 Discussions of the Artists include Pickard-Cambridge (1968) 279–305, Millar (1977) 458–62, Le Guen (2001), and Lightfoot (2002). See also now three recently discovered letters of Hadrian to the Artists dating to AD 133/34: Petzl and Schwertheim (2006), with Jones (2007).

2 Plut. *Ant.* 56.5.

3 Ibid. 57.1.

4 On imperial cult and related activities, see further below, pp. 137–46.

5 Three papyri from Oxyrhynchus, submitted to the town council by individual performers, contain a series of (earlier) pronouncements by emperors guaranteeing privileges (*P Oxy.* 2610, *BGU* 1074 = *SB* 5225; *P Oxy.* 2476). The first is a letter from Claudius dating to January AD 43 (= Smallwood [1967] no. 373a) in which he writes, "I preserve the rights and privileges granted by the Divine Augustus." Note also Smallwood (1967) 373b, discussed below, pp. 79–80.

6 See the works cited in the brief bibliographic essay, especially Millar (1977) 375–84 and Habicht (2001/2).

7 Phil. *Leg.* 180–86 and 349–67; cf. also Joseph. *AJ* 18.257–60.

8 Phil. *Leg.* 171–72.

9 Cf. Smallwood (1967) no. 370 (Claudius' letter to the Alexandrians) with Smallwood (1967) no. 261, a damaged inscription from Ephesus, and also Smallwood (1967) no. 418 (with Tac. *Ann.* 13.22.1, Plin. *HN* 19.3, and Sen. *Q Nat.* 4.2.13).

10 On the importance of documents, see the brief bibliographic essay above, p. 278.

11 The source for what follows is *IGRom.* 4.1608 (= Smallwood [1967] no. 372, but Smallwood omits some portions of this fragmentary inscription; see further below, p. 138). Friesen (2001) 104–13, esp. 105–6, gives a helpful discussion.

12 On this cult see, conveniently, Friesen (2001) 25–32. See also below, p. 138.

13 Smallwood (1967) no. 380.

14 "August Gods" is a restoration, but likely; see further below, pp. 138–39.

15 The source for what follows is Smallwood (1967) no. 371. Dunant and Pouilloux (1958), esp. 66–69 give detailed guidance.

16 Suet. *Tit.* 8.1.

17 So Hammond (1959) 339–45 concludes. Certainly, if an emperor granted citizenship and related privileges to an individual and his family – which could be deemed *beneficia* – the understanding was that this was permanent; see Ando (2000) 35, discussing the evidence of the so-called *Tabula Banasitana* for an ongoing record kept in Rome of those granted citizenship from Augustus onwards.

18 Phil. *In Flacc.* 97.

19 Ibid. 101.

20 Ibid. 103; cf. *Leg.* 178–79.

21 League of Greek cities: Smallwood (1967) no. 361. Assos: Smallwood (1967) no. 33. Maroneia: Clinton (2003) and (2004), and Wörrle (2004).

22 See below, p. 83.

23 Suet. *Tit.* 8.1; and Dio 66.19.3 and 67.2.1 (the latter passage referring to Domitian). See further Millar (1977) 414.

24 The sources for what follows are Joseph. *AJ* 19.274–92 and (far less relevant) *BJ* 2.214–17; and Smallwood (1967) no. 370 (the letter to the Alexandrians). Hard to reconcile completely, and also difficult to correlate exactly to the controversial happenings of AD 38 in Alexandria, they have generated an enormous literature, for which Fasolini (2006) 59–69 offers some guidance. Schwartz (1990) 90–106 is an especially cogent discussion, which I follow here; Harker (2008) 8–31 also gives a judicious overview. Note also the recent treatment of Gruen (2002) 54–83, as well as the rather different conclusions still in Ritter (2003) and Gambetti (2003). See also above, pp. 47–49 and below, p. 80.

25 Joseph. *AJ* 19.236–45 and 265–66, *BJ* 2.206–10; and Dio 60.8.2–3. See above, p. 42.

26 Four papyrus fragments (Tcherikover and Fuchs [1957–64] no. 156) remain of a record of a hearing held by Claudius for two Alexandrian leaders, Isidorus and Lampon, at which Agrippa was present to weigh in: these papyri are part of the so-called *Acta Alexandrinorum*, on which see now Harker (2008).

27 For this hugely controversial episode, every detail of which is disputed, Schwartz (1990) 94–96 is followed here. The evidence is Suet. *Claud.* 25.4, Dio 60.6.6, and Oros. *Hist.* 7.6.15, as well as Acts 18.2. Other major recent discussions include Botermann (1996), Slingerland (1997), and Gruen (2002) 36–41. Agrippa as persecutor: Acts 12.1–19.

28 Dio 60.8.2–3.

29 Joseph. *AJ* 19.287–91. But the edict may be lightly edited, to accommodate a second document included by Josephus, on which see immediately below, pp. 78–79. For Josephus' documents: Pucci ben Zeev (1998), with this edict discussed at 328–42.

30 See above, p. 65.

31 Smallwood (1967) no. 370.

32 Joseph. *AJ* 19.280–85. Very full discussion in Pucci ben Zeev (1998) 294–328; and see also 328–44.

33 E.g., Kasher (1985) 263–74.

34 See especially Schwartz (1990) 99–106 for the view taken here. Cf. also now Harker (2008) 26–28.

35 On Philo's *On Virtues*, see above, p. 48.

36 Tac. *Ann.* 3.60–63. Under Trajan, a freedman *a commentariis beneficiorum* is attested (*ILS* 1792).

37 Two statues: *FD* III.4 469 and *FD* III.1 531; witnessing: *SEG* 51.606. See Rigsby (2004) for discussion.

38 Smallwood (1967) no. 376 (translation includes some supplements to this lacunose inscription).

39 Ibid. no. 373b is the source for what follows.

40 Ibid. no. 370.

41 Claudius' reference to the "two embassies" is puzzling, and perhaps best explained by assuming that two different groups representing the Jewish community arrived in Rome who, in Claudius' view, should have joined together first. Alternatively, it is possible that the Jewish delegation had not sought the permission of the prefect to travel to the emperor in Rome (for that procedure, cf. Phil. *In Flacc.* 97, discussed above, p. 74).

42 Useful general accounts include Raven (1993); Mattingly (1995); Mattingly and Hitchner (1995); Whitaker in *CAH* 10 (second edn) 586–618 ("Roman Africa: Augustus to Vespasian"); and Cherry (1998).

43 See below, pp. 110–15.

44 Plut. *Caes.* 55.1.

45 Suet. *Galb.* 7, Aur. Vict. *Caes.* 4.2, *Epit. de Caes.* 4.4, and Dio 60.9.6; the governor was Ser. Galba, appointed by the Senate and emperor (instead of the more typical use of the lot for this province), and evidently given some kind of military command: see the informative article of Konrad (1994). The disturbances may be related to the annexation of neighboring Mauretania, discussed below, pp. 110–15.

46 His activity in Africa is attested solely by inscriptions, described below. Note that his tenure in the proconsulship was two years, suggesting his command was extended by Claudius (cf. Syme, *RP* 4.348 and also n. 45 above).

47 Mela 1.41–42.
48 See below, pp. 112–13.
49 Højte (2005) 594.
50 Ibid. 601–2.
51 Two discussions: Hurlet (2000) and Rives (2001).
52 Statue base from Zian: *CIL* 8.11002. Arch dedication from Lepcis: *AE* 1987.989. For further archeological evidence from Zian and Lepcis for statue groups of the August House, see Rose (1997) 182–85 and Boschung (2002) 8–24 and 55–57.
53 *AE* 1951.85.
54 Smallwood (1967) no. 405.
55 Cirta: *CIL* 8.19492. Thugga: *CIL* 8.26519.
56 In other instances, epigraphic evidence suggests unusual zeal on the part of a governor. Just two examples: (1) it may be to the legate Sex. Sotidius Strabo Libuscidianus that we owe the text of the *Res gestae* of Augustus, as all three copies of the text were found from monuments in Galatia likely commissioned during his tenure (see Osgood [2007b]); (2) the survival of multiple copies (on bronze) of the *Senatus consultum de Cn. Pisone patre* (above, p. 260) all from Baetica is likely owed to the ambitions of the governor there, Vibius Serenus: see Eck *et al.* (1996) 279–87.
57 See *AE* 1951.85.
58 For a general suggestion along these lines, see Eck (2009) 198–202.
59 Colonies: Crawford (1996) no. 25 (*lex Coloniae Genetivae*), sec. 92. Presence of ambassadors in Rome in AD 19/20: see the *Tabula Siarensis*, frag. (b) col. II lines 24–25 (at Crawford [1996] nos. 37–38), with the discussion of Eck (2009) 202, noting also the sending of embassies to Augustus by the colony of Pisa on the deaths of Lucius and Gaius Caesar in AD 2 and 4 respectively (*ILS* 139–40).

4 SUBDUING THE OCEAN

Brief bibliographic essay. The publication of Luttwak (1976) provoked a vigorous (and salutary) debate among ancient historians not only as to whether the Roman Empire could be said to have had a "grand strategy" but how all decisions surrounding what we would call "foreign policy" were made. Lendon (2002) helps to contextualize the debate: while some scholarship tried to stress an intellectual incapacity on the part of Romans to formulate strategy (e.g., Isaac [1990] esp. 372–418, criticized especially by Wheeler [1993] and see also Kennedy [1996]), much work has emphasized, more persuasively, cultural and institutional reasons for limited, but comprehensible, "strategic" goals (see, e.g., Millar [2004] 160–94 ["Emperors, frontiers, and foreign relations, 31 BC to AD 378"]; Whittaker [1994]; and Mattern [1999], emphasizing honor as the paramount goal of Rome's foreign relations, consistent enough to count as "strategy"). Kagan (2006), in my view, is right to emphasize further the necessity of careful allocation of all resources, across the empire, to meet those objectives, in what might fairly be called "grand strategy" (even if the objectives set were not those identified by Luttwak, and borders must not be viewed monolithically – or anachronistically, as clear lines on maps); this chapter, in exploring Claudius' decision to annex Britain, tries to buttress Kagan's analysis, while also conceding the validity of Mattern's insistence on honor and prestige as chief Roman goals – primary goals, it need hardly be pointed out, of many modern regimes too, for much foreign policy is really domestic policy by other means. Mattern's discussion perhaps underplays the security of Roman citizens, as such, as another conscious strategic objective, which will be addressed in Chapter 5 below. See also the works listed in n. 16 below.

The actual invasion of Britain in AD 43 has generated a surfeit of scholarship, in part because of ongoing interest in the British Isles at this pivotal historical moment, in part because the main source scholars must rely on (Dio 60.19.1–22.2, 23) leaves many questions answered (only a few other details are added by Suet. *Claud.* 17 and *Vesp.* 4.1; Tac. *Agr.* 14.1; Oros. *Hist.* 7.6.9–11; and Eutr. 7.13). For guidance to this enormous scholarly literature see, in addition to Momigliano (1934) 54–57, Scramuzza (1940) 200–13, and Levick (1990) 137–48, the surveys of Hurley (2001), 133–34, Todd (2004a), Mattingly (2006), 87–127, and Fasolini (2006) 86–98. (Also note an invaluable work of reference, Birley [2005]). One recent – and fascinating, if perhaps not very fruitful – debate has focused on the strategy employed in the (very difficult) maritime crossing (see, e.g., Frere and Fulford [2001]). More productive has been the attention to Rome's relations with (dependent) British kings such as Cunobelin, for, it has been observed, the death of such dependent kings in other areas (e.g., Cappadocia) facilitated a quick takeover by Rome: see especially the works of Braund (1996) 67–117 and the more speculative, but stimulating, Creighton (2000) and (2006), followed largely by Mattingly (2006) 68–80 and here. But overall the discussion in this chapter is focused less on the actualities of the invasion than its significance for Claudius' image, for which extraordinary new evidence has emerged in the last few decades, as detailed in notes 42, 45, and 92 below.

1 My account of the Forum draws on *LTUR* s.v. *Forum Augustum*, J. Anderson (1984) 65–100, Zanker (1988) 192–215, Ganzert (1996), Galinsky (1996) 197–213, Spannagel (1999), Meneghini and Valenzani (2007), and Geiger (2008). Important ancient sources are: *RG* 21.1–2, 29.2, and 35.1; Ov. *Fast.* 5.545–98; Vell. Pat. 2.100.2; Suet. *Aug.* 29.1–2, 31.5, and 56.2; and Dio 55.10.1–9.

2 "On private land I built the Temple of Mars the Avenger and the August Forum from the spoils of war" (*RG* 21.1).

3 Alluded to by Vell. Pat. 2.39.2.

4 *ILS* 57 (from Arretium), translation reflecting some supplements.

5 *CIL* 6.40330.

6 Suet. *Claud.* 1.2.

7 Livy, *Per.* 142.

8 Cf. Livy, *Per.* 142.

9 See especially Tac. *Ann.* 1.11.3–4; the account of Dio 56.33.3–6 is open to some objections, recently discussed by Swan (2004) 314–19. See also above, p. 38.

10 For the *lex templi* see Dio 55.10.2–5; Suet. *Aug.* 29.2 also mentions these three provisions.
11 See especially Rose (2005) 45–50.
12 Suet. *Aug.* 31.5, translation reflecting a proposed emendation to this corrupt passage.
13 *RG* 26.4, 27.2, 29.2, and 31–33.
14 Ibid. 12.2–13, 25.1, and 26.2–3.
15 Ibid. 26.1, 27.1, and 30.1.
16 Just a few discussions of important facets of this fascinating problem in the early empire: Griffin (1984) 221–34; Brunt (1990) 96–109, 288–323, and 433–80; Gruen in *CAH* (second edn) 147–97 ("The expansion of the empire under Augustus"); and Ando (2000) 277–335. Cornell (1993) is an especially clear guide to the whole issue. For broader perspectives on strategy, see the brief bibliographic essay above.
17 *RG* 30.1; cf. 27.2.
18 Two discussions: Seager (2005) 61–74, 147–50 and 218–19; and Levick (1999a) 141–47.
19 Caligula's activities in northern Europe are notoriously difficult to piece together from the two chief sources: Suet. *Calig.* 43–48 and Dio 59.25.1–5. It is sometimes doubted that he even was contemplating a British war: for one discussion see Barrett (1990) 125–39.
20 Visit to Gaul and Germany: frequently mentioned in the sources, e.g., Suet. *Calig.* 20 and *Claud.* 9.1. Two legions (Legiones XV and XXII Primigeniae): the key piece of evidence is Smallwood (1967) no. 278; see conveniently Barrett (1990) 125–26. Caligula's purpose in traveling to the Channel coast is widely discussed, recently by Woods (2000) and Malloch (2001).
21 See the brief bibliographic essay above for the sources and scholarship in Claudius' invasion of Britain.
22 On these developments in Britain: Dio 60.19.1 and 20.1. Dio's Bericus is assumed to be the Verica portrayed on coinage of the Atrebates; on the British coinage of the period, see Creighton (2000).
23 Dio 60.21.2. It is thanks to the researches of Suetonius that we have much information on this man and his family: Suet. *Vit.* 1–6. Other references to his early career include Plin. *HN* 15.83; Joseph. *AJ* 15.405, 18.88–126 *passim*, and 18.261; Tac. *Ann.* 6.32.3–4, 36–37, 41.1 and 11.3; and Dio 59.27.2–6.
24 Suet. *Vit.* 2.5.
25 Sex. Palpellius Hister (at least forty-five years old) and L. Pedanius Secundus (likely at least forty): see Tortoriello (2004) 416–18 and 536–40. Morris (1964) demonstrates that after Tiberius new men (and other plebeians) typically held the consulship about ten years later than patricians and other very distinguished nobles, allowing more opportunity to the former group to display their loyalty in military posts held after the praetorship (while the latter group had the distinction of earlier consulships); see also Morris (1965).
26 Plin. *HN* 10.35.
27 Dio 60.8.7; cf. Suet. *Claud.* 24.3.

28 II Augusta: *ILS* 2696, Tac. *Hist.* 3.44, and Suet. *Vesp.* 4.1; IX Hispana: *CIL* 5.7165; XX: *AE* 1924.78; and XIV Gemina: *RIB* 292–94.

29 For the larger context here: Kagan (2006).

30 Full sketch of the man and his career: Birley (2005) 17–25. Relationship with Vitellius: Tac. *Ann.* 3.49, *CIL* 6.6866, and *SEG* 14.646.

31 Revealed by a milestone, Smallwood (1967) no. 332.

32 Flavius Sabinus: Dio 60.20.3. Flavius Vespasianus: Joseph. *BJ* 3.4–5; Tac. *Agr.* 13.3 and *Hist.* 3.44, 66.3; and Suet. *Vesp.* 4.1–2. Hosidius Geta: *ILS* 971 and Dio 60.20.4, with Birley (2005) 234–35.

33 Eutr. 7.13; Camodeca (1999) nos. 13, 14, and 27.

34 See especially Joseph. *AJ* 19.160–85 and *BJ* 2.205 for initial opposition; but he remained in office with his colleague through June: Tortoriello (2004) 414–16.

35 Cf. Dio 60.23.2–4. See the list of known participants in Birley (2005) 214–23, and see further below, p. 90.

36 Dio 60.18.4; perhaps the father of the future emperor Otho was involved (Suet. *Oth.* 1.3). Cf. also Suet. *Claud.* 13.1 and 36.

37 Sen. *Apocol.* 10.4 and 13.5; Ps.-Sen. *Oct.* 944–46; Tac. *Ann.* 13.32.3 and 43; Suet. *Claud.* 29.1; and Dio 60.18.4.

38 Dio 60.19.2.

39 See, e.g., Barrett (1980) 31–35 for problems with Dio's account.

40 Again, see Barrett (1980).

41 Senators: Smallwood (1967) no. 234, *ILS* 971, Suet. *Galb.* 7.1, etc.; see Birley (2005) 214–23. Praetorians: Smallwood (1967) no. 283 (and perhaps no. 282) and Dio 60.23.2. Stertinius Xenophon: Smallwood (1967) no. 262. L. Silanus: *ILS* 957; Tac. *Ann.* 12.3.2; Suet. *Claud.* 24.3; and Dio 61.21.5 and 31.7. Pompeius Magnus: Dio 60.21.5.

42 Vicirius Proculus: *AE* 1980.457. Caecilia Secunda: *CIL* 12.4334. Evidence for other vows: *CIL* 6.3571 and 6.917; and Bérard *et al.* (1998), whence *AE* 1998.944. See also the discussion of Standing (2003).

43 See below, pp. 95–96.

44 A good account of the site at Mitchell and Waelkens (1998).

45 Christol *et al.* (2001), whence *AE* 2001.1918. For Caristanius see also *ILS* 9502–3.

46 Dio 60.21.2–5; cf. Suet. *Claud.* 17.2.

47 Surrender of kings: Dio 60.21.4 and cf. *CIL* 6.40416, from the Arch of Claudius in Rome, discussed below, pp. 93–94. Orkneys: Eutr. 7.13 with Stevens (1951); cf. Galimberti (1996). Imperatorial acclamation: Dio 60.21.4 and note that by the end of AD 43 or the very start of 44 Claudius had eight acclamations (see, e.g., *CIL* 2.6324 and 2.4929), at the start of 43 only three (e.g., *ILS* 202, *CIL* 9.5426).

48 Dio 60.21.5 and 23.1.

49 Plin. *HN* 3.119.

50 Levick (1990) 143 and Thomas (2004) 439.

51 Dio 60.22.1–2 is the main source for what follows.

52 Livia's privileges: Tac. *Ann.* 4.16.4 and *RIC* I (second edn) Tiberius nos. 50–51.

53 See especially Suet. *Claud.* 17.2–3 and Dio 60.22–23 for the details that follow.

54 According to Plin. *HN* 33.54; Smallwood (1967) no. 374 records the gift of a gold crown from the guild of Traveling Athletes. See further below, p. 101.

55 Note too Sen. *Polyb.* 13.2.

56 Suet. *Claud.* 21.6 describes the mock-battle but does not date it; for further discussion of the whole phenomenon see Coleman (1990) and (1993).

57 Dio 60.25.7–8 with Duncan-Jones (1994) 248–50. These evidently are not the games voted by the Senate.

58 Tac. *Ann.* 13.32.2 and Suet. *Claud.* 24.3.

59 *Ann.* 12.36.2–3. The full account is *Ann.* 12.36–38.

60 See above, pp. 55–62.

61 See above, pp. 32 and 61–62.

62 Suet. *Claud.* 17.3.

63 Camodeca (1999) nos. 13, 14, and 27.

64 Dio 60.22.1 alone observes the arch, but there is significant, if problematic, archeological data, as discussed immediately below. For discussions of monuments celebrating the British war see Richard (1998) and Fasolini (2006) 135–54. More generally see, e.g., Melmoux (1990) and Braund (1996) 96–108.

65 A few valuable works: Kleiner (1985), De Maria (1988), Kleiner (1989), and Wallace-Hadrill (1990), this last of wider significance.

66 *Tabula Siarensis* frag. (a) lines 9–21, at Crawford (1996) nos. 37–38; cf. Tac. *Ann.* 2.83.2. On the statue group of the "August House," see Flory (1996).

67 Discussions include Laubscher (1976); Koeppel (1983a) and Koeppel (1983b) 78–80 and 119–23; Kleiner (1985) 59–62; De Maria (1988) 280–82; and Barrett (1991).

68 Suet. *Claud.* 1.3; cf. *RIC* (second edn) Claudius nos. 2, 35, 69–72, and 98.

69 So Wiseman (2008).

70 Claudius' repairs on Aqua Virgo: Smallwood (1967) no. 308 (b) and see further below, pp. 180–81. Coinage: *RIC* (second edn) Claudius nos. 30, 33–34, and 44–5.

71 Revised text in *CIL* 6.40416.

72 This is the attractive proposal of Flower (2006) 187–88. Several inscribed stones, excavated in the vicinity of the arch, record dedications to Germanicus, Antonia, Agrippina, Nero, Britannicus, and Octavia dating to AD 51–54, and were long associated with the arch but, as Rose (1997) 113–15 argues, are hard to work into its (final) design. Still, there seems to be some sort of link between Claudius' military achievements and the imperial house (albeit reconfigured after Messallina's disgrace). A comparison might be made with the statues of the August House in the vicinity of the posthumous arch for Germanicus (above, pp. 93–94). See also further below, p. 213.

73 There is a huge literature on these reliefs, long identified as belonging to the Ara Pietatis Augustae, a building that may never have existed: see Koeppel (1982) but cf. above, pp. 61–62. Torelli (1982) 63–88 proposed that they belonged to the Ara Gentis Iuliae known from epigraphic sources but the suggestion rests on a doubtful identification of one of the temples shown. The proposal set out here, while not definitive either, is that of La Rocca (1992b) and (1994). A

few other discussions: Ryberg (1955) 65–75; Koeppel (1983b) 72–80 and 98–116; Cordischi (1985); Kleiner (1992) 141–45.

74 On the incorporation of the cult of the *genius* of Claudius into the state religion, see above, p. 58.

75 Kleiner (1971).

76 Ehrhardt (1978) is an especially astute discussion of Claudius' shaping of a new house.

77 The clear implication of *RG* 21.3 is that provincial communities were expected to offer the crowns, in recognition of military events, and that they were accepted. Crowns were also expected on the accession of a new emperor: see above, p. 41. Ando (2000) 175–90 offers a discussion; see also Millar (1977) 140–42.

78 Plin. *HN* 33.54. Laubscher (1976) argued that these were shown on the Britannic victory arch.

79 Gold crowns could be a significant stream of revenue for the emperor: see Duncan-Jones (1994) 7. Emission of AD 46: von Kaenel (1994) 55 and Burgers (2001) 108–9.

80 Mela 3.49.

81 Sen. *Polyb.* 13.2.

82 The poems are preserved, along with other epigrams purporting to be by Seneca, under the heading *Laus Caesaris* in the manuscript Latinus Vossianus Q86 in Leiden: see discussions by Tandoi (1962) and Barrett (2000). Holzberg (2004) argues that they are part of an "impersonation" by a later poet of Seneca in exile; if so, they still may give some sense of the impact of the conquest of Britain on the Roman imagination.

83 *Apocol.* 12.3.13–18.

84 Ibid. 12.3.21–22.

85 *Claud.* 17.1.

86 Smallwood (1967) no. 281.

87 Ibid. no. 282; and Tac. *Ann.* 15.50.3, 60.4–61, and 71.2 with Keppie (1971).

88 Smallwood (1967) no. 283.

89 Ibid. no. 45 gives the text of the partially extant dedicatory inscription.

90 Kent (1965) no. 75.

91 *RPC* 1.3625.

92 Full description and discussion at Smith (1987) 115–17.

93 An attractive introduction is offered by Erim (1986) but work has continued on the site; for the results of recent excavations see Ratté and Smith (2008) and other work cited there.

94 See Smith (1987) 87–98 and see also Smith (1988); note also Ando (2000) 311–12, an interpretation partly overlapping with mine here.

5 LISTS OF PEOPLES AND PLACES

Brief bibliographic essay. Roman geographical conceptions, along with the significance of these conceptions for imperial decision making, have benefited from much recent analysis that informs this chapter. On the lack of maps, as we know them today, and the alternatives to them, see especially the major works by Janni (1984) and Brodersen (1995), as well as the appealing article by Syme *RP* 6.372–97 ("Military geography at Rome") and also the recent review article of Brodersen (2004), which discusses the extraordinary *Barrington Atlas of the Greek and Roman World*, an indispensable tool for research. Rawson (1985) 250–66 traces intellectual developments in the Republican era, while Nicolet (1991) focuses especially on the Augustan period, looking at administrative developments as well as intellectual: on the latter work note the important review article by Purcell (1990b) of the (earlier) French edition. Mattern (1999) 24–80 situates geographic knowledge within the context of imperial aspirations; cf. much more briefly Millar (2004) 160–94 ("Emperors, frontiers, and foreign relations, 31 BC to AD 378"). On the (related) literary tradition of ethnography, see also the works of Thomas (1982), Shaw (1982/83), Evans (1999), and Murphy (2004). Romm (1992) explores the peculiar status assigned to the perceived edges of the earth in Graeco-Roman thought.

Also directly relevant to the theme of this chapter is the reconstruction of the processes, both conceptual and concrete, by which Romans turned newly annexed territories into provinces of their empire. A now classic discussion, focused on landscape of Cisalpine Gaul in the Republican period, is given in the essay of Purcell (1990a). Also valuable are discussions by Mitchell (1993) 61–79 on Galatia (made a province in 25 BC) and Bowersock (1983) 76–109 on Arabia (made a province in AD 106). More general background is provided by Lintott (1993) esp. 22–42, and see also again Nicolet (1991) for administrative practices, as well as Moatti (1993) and Nicolet (1996); and also on the provincial *formulae* (lists of communities with their financial obligations) Shaw (1981) and Christol (1994) and on territorial disputes Burton (2000).

Lying between the provinces and the world beyond the empire were the so-called "client kingdoms," ruled by monarchs recognized by the Senate (and, later, the emperor) not actually as clients, but "friends and allies" expected to fulfill certain military demands in particular. Braund (1984) is the standard study of these rulers; and note also Millar (2004) 229–45 ("Emperors, kings, and subjects: the politics of two-level sovereignty"), with a focus on the extraordinary Bosporan kingdom. I am inclined to agree with Braund that there was no firm notion that the status of client kingdom was one consciously intended to prepare for full and imminent annexation, even if in practice a number of the kingdoms did later become provinces. Specifically on client rulers under Caligula and Claudius see the articles by Wardle (1992b) and Dmitriev (2003), with further bibliography there.

1 See the brief bibliographic essay above for the scholarship drawn on here.

2 On ethnography and the edges of the earth, again see the brief bibliographic essay above.

3 See especially Caes. *B Gall.* 5.12–14 and 6.11–28; and Sall. *Iug.* 17–19. For the digressions in Sallust's *Histories*, see, e.g., Syme (1964) 192–95.

4 Seneca's works: Serv. on *Aen.* 6.154 and 9.30; and Plin. *HN* 6.60. On *Germania* see now Rives (1999).
5 Mela 1.1.
6 Plin. *HN* 3–6. In addition to Murphy (2004) there are studies of particular passages, e.g., Shaw (1981), Hoyos (1979), and Christol (1994). Note also Evans (2005).
7 Plin. *HN* 5.2–7.
8 Batty (2000). For more general introductions to Mela: Silberman (1988) and Romer (1998).
9 Mela 2.9, 3.62.
10 Ibid. 1.1.
11 Flora: e.g., Plin. *HN* 12.20 and 111 (ebony and balsam at triumph of Pompey). Aediles and animals: e.g., Plin. *HN* 8.96 (hippopotamus and five crocodiles at games of the aedile Scaurus).
12 Map of Italy: Varro, *Rust.* 1.2.1. Agrippa's map: Plin. *HN* 3.17; and cf. *HN* 3.8, 3.16, 3.86, etc.
13 Caesar and Britain: Caes. *B Gall.* 5.12–14; Catull. 11, 29, 45; etc. Gaius and Arabia: Plin. *HN* 6.141, 12.56, and 32.10.
14 In addition to the following references, note that Claudius is cited in the index of sources for books 5, 6, 12, and 13 of the *Natural History*.
15 Plin. *HN* 5.63, 6.27, and 6.31.
16 Ibid. 6.128.
17 Ibid. 7.35 and 12.78.
18 Ibid. 7.35.
19 Ibid. 7.74.
20 Ibid. 8.22 and 8.54.
21 Ibid. 8.65.
22 Ibid. 10.5.
23 See above, pp. 91–92.
24 Mela 3.49.
25 Sen. *Med.* 365, 368–71.
26 Plin. *HN* 6.84–91, recently discussed by Murphy (2004) 105–13.
27 Suet. *Calig.* 35.1; Dio 59.25.1; and Sen. *Tranq.* 11.12. See the discussion of Malloch (2004) for the chronology adopted here.
28 The main sources for Claudius' involvement in Mauretania are Dio 60.8.6 and 60.9; and Plin. *HN* 5.2–21 *passim*. Further evidence is provided by inscriptions, especially Smallwood (1967) no. 407 (a) and (b), discussed below. Valuable modern studies include Fishwick (1971), Gascou (1981), and Rebuffat (1998).
29 Plin. *HN* 5.14–15. Paulinus is also mentioned in the index of sources for book 5.
30 Hdt. 4.184.
31 Plin. *HN* 5.14.
32 Tortoriello (2004) 567–69.
33 Triumphal decorations: Dio 60.8.6 (slightly inaccurate on chronology). Imperatorial acclamations: Claudius was hailed *imperator* altogether twenty-seven

times (see, e.g., Smallwood [1967] no. 309). Boasts: Smallwood (1967) nos. 44
and 369, discussed below, pp. 159–61 and 166.

34 E.g., *RG* 12.2–13, 25.1, and 26.2–3; Hor. *Carm. saec.* and *Carm.* 4.5; and Verg.
Aen. 1.257–96.

35 Cf. Plut. *Mor.* 207.8.

36 See the brilliant analysis of Pliny's African geography by Shaw (1981), arguing
that one key source for it was a survey drawn up by Caesar enumerating all
administrative units and their revenue obligations.

37 See, e.g., Mitchell (1993) 1.63 on the Via Sebaste of Galatia and, more broadly
on "provincial landscape," Purcell (1990a).

38 See the analysis of Shaw (2006).

39 Details at Gascou (1981); see also Fasolini (2006) 69–86.

40 Smallwood (1967) no. 407 (b); and see no. 407 (a).

41 Mackie (1983) discusses the Mauretanian colonies of Augustus.

42 So, e.g., Magie (1950) 529 and 547–48; cf. Momigliano (1934) 53–61, Scramuzza
(1940) 179–213, and Levick (1990) 149–61. On developments in Noricum,
sometimes treated in this context, see below, p. 161.

43 For the grants to Agrippa and his brother Herod, see above, pp. 76–77. Claudius
entrusted Commagene, on the all-important Euphrates boundary, to Anti-
ochus, who had regained the kingdom from Caligula in AD 38 (Dio 60.8.1;
Joseph. *AJ* 19.276 and 338; Smallwood [1967] no. 374). Caligula's appointment to Armenia, Mithridates, who had been temporarily removed, was also
continued (Dio 60.8.1, Sen. *Tranq.* 11.12, and Tac. *Ann.* 11.8–9). In the Black
Sea basin, Claudius confirmed Mithridates of Bosporus, made king in AD 38
(Dio 60.8.2 and 28.7, with Dmitriev [2003]; Tac. *Ann.* 12.15–20); and Claudius
kept the extraordinary trio of brothers, Polemo, Cotys, and Rhoemetalces in
Pontus, Lesser Armenia, and Thrace respectively: sons of the late Cotys, king
of Thrace under Augustus and Tiberius who was murdered in AD 18, they
were taken to Rome by their mother Antonia Tryphaena and educated in the
household of Antonia. After his accession, Caligula granted the three their
new Black Sea territories and held a lavish celebration of it in the Forum.
Tryphaena had settled sometime before on the well-trafficked city of Cyzicus,
on the Sea of Marmara, and an inscription reveals her staging games there in
honor of Caligula's sister Drusilla, to which came Rhoemetalces and Polemo,
"the bodyguards of empire" (Joseph. *AJ* 19.338; Tac. *Ann.* 11.9.2; Smallwood
[1967] nos. 374 and 401). Client kings in the regions of the Upper Danube and
Rhine are discussed below, p. 313. And see also the general works cited above
in the brief bibliographic essay for this chapter.

44 Smallwood (1967) no. 370.

45 Festival: Wörrle (1988) with Mitchell (1990). Epicurean philosophy: see, e.g.,
Gordon (1996).

46 Syme (1995) 270–85, a splendid discussion drawn on throughout this paragraph.

47 Letter: Plin. *HN* 13.88. On his *Mirabilia* see recently Williamson (2005) and
Ash (2007).

48 Retreat to Asia: Tac. *Hist.* 1.10.1. Oysters: Plin. *HN* 32.62. Wine: Plin. *HN* 14.54.
49 Plin. *HN* 12.9. Note also Mucianus on saffron of Lycia: Plin. *HN* 21.33.
50 Statue: Plin. *HN* 36.131. Oracular fish: Plin. *HN* 32.17.
51 Discussion of Veranius and his career: Gordon (1952) and Birley (2005) 37–43. On Onasander consult Le Bohec (1998).
52 Epitaph: *CIL* 6.41075, preferable to the text printed at Smallwood (1967) no. 231 (c).
53 Statue bases: Smallwood (1967) no. 231 (a); Balland (1981) nos. 37–40; and cf. also Smallwood (1967) no. 231 (b). Stele with decree: Wörrle (1975), whence *AE* 1976.673. Pillar from Patara: Işik *et al.* (2001), whence *SEG* 51.1832, and Jones (2001), whence *AE* 2001.1931; and see Şahin and Adak (2004). Altar: Marksteiner and Wörrle (2002), whence *AE* 2002.1472. In addition to these works note the discussions of Thornton (2001), Kolb (2002), Kokkinia (2003) and Thornton (2004).
54 Statue: French (1999/2000) 174–77, whence *SEG* 50.1350. Temple inscription: *IGRom.* 3.577.
55 Suet. *Claud.* 25.3 and Dio 60.17.3–4.
56 For the earlier view, see, e.g., Magie (1950) 529.
57 I translate from the text printed at *SEG* 51.1832.
58 Coins: see especially *RPC* 1.3334–52.
59 I translate from *SEG* 50.1350 (text restored).
60 I translate from the text offered by Wörrle (1975).
61 Both are mentioned in the inscription on the Pataran pillar.
62 Smallwood (1967) no. 231 (b), an honorary decree for Veranius from Cibyra.
63 *CIL* 6.41075, with the discussion of Gordon (1952) 251–54.
64 The embassies are mentioned in an honorary decree for Q. Veranius Philagrus, Smallwood (1967) no. 408.
65 See Gordon (1952) 246–51; cf. Tac. *Ann.* 6.41.1 and 12.55.
66 Governorship of Britain: Tac. *Agr.* 14.2 and *Ann.* 14.29.1.
67 Millar (1993) 27–79 explicates the relation between geography and Roman power in the region. For a more detailed administrative history of Judea under Roman rule see Schürer (1973–87) 1.330–41; more briefly Goodman in *CAH* 10 (second edn) 737–81 ("Judaea"), as well as Goodman (2007), esp. 379–423.
68 See above, p. 6.
69 See above, pp. 76–77.
70 Joseph. *BJ* 2.218–20 and *AJ* 19.292–359, on which see the detailed commentary of Schwartz (1990) 107–44.
71 Joseph. *AJ* 19.338–42, with the analysis of Schwartz (1990) 137–40, not entirely followed here.
72 Joseph. *AJ* 19.355.
73 Ibid. 19.300–11.
74 Ibid. 19.304–5.
75 The suspicious document is the edict of Claudius (Joseph. *AJ* 19.287–91), discussed above, pp. 78–79.

76 Joseph. *BJ* 2.220 and *AJ* 19.360–62.
77 Joseph. *AJ* 19.363–20.14 and 20.97–99; cf. *BJ* 2.220.
78 See further below.
79 Joseph. *BJ* 2.220 and *AJ* 20.100–3.
80 On the family, see above, pp. 47–48.
81 *RPC* 1.4749–50; Smallwood (1967) no. 350; and Plin. *HN* 5.75.
82 Kolendo (1998) now gives a full discussion; for the history of the Danubian and Balkan provinces in this period see Wilkes in *CAH* (second edn) 545–85 ("The Danubian and Balkan provinces") as well as the illuminating account of Syme in the predecessor volume *CAH* (first edn) 340–81, 781–90 and 803–7; note too Syme (1971) and (1999) 129–220.
83 On the rulers of Thrace see, e.g., Sullivan (1979).
84 *Ann.* 4.46–51.
85 See above, n. 43.
86 Suet. *Claud.* 25.3 and Dio 60.24.1.
87 Legio VIII Augusta: inferred from *AE* 1914.93.
88 These sources are Syncellus and several chronicles, including that of Eusebius: see Kolendo (1998) 322.
89 Didius Gallus: Tac. *Ann.* 12.15.1 with Smallwood (1967) no. 226 and see below, p. 238. Intensity of campaign: Tac. *Ann.* 12.63.3. Legions: inferred from Smallwood (1967) no. 285.
90 Maroneia: see above, pp. 74–75. Black Sea cities: Smallwood (1967) no. 384.
91 Apri: *ILS* 2718 and Plin. *HN* 4.47. Roads: Smallwood (1967) no. 351 and *AE* 1912.193.
92 Tac. *Hist.* 2.83–84, 3.46, and 4.4.
93 As argued by Syme *RP* 3.998–1013 ("The march of Mucianus").

6 CAESAR-LOVERS

Brief bibliographic essay. Provincial perceptions of the emperor, along with other high-ranking Roman officials in the age of Claudius, are the main subject of this chapter. The topic as a whole, essentially ignored in Millar (1977), has received much attention – it is a running thread in Ando (2000), though the account there, in keeping with the author's theme, privileges expressions of loyalty. Other recent accounts of political culture provide different perspectives, for instance Lendon (1997), esp. 107–236, on the "honor" rulers and ruled showed one another as a way of achieving consensus but also masking less pleasant realities; and Rowe (2002) esp. 124–53 on the culture of loyalty in Greek cities. The research network "Impact of Empire" has put out a number of volumes relevant to the topic and worth studying: see especially de Blois (2001), de Blois and Rich (2002), de Ligt *et al.* (2004), and de Blois *et al.* (2006). Millar himself subsequently offered an extraordinary contribution to the subject in his paper on Apuleius' second-century novel, the *Metamorphoses*, as a source for the social history of the provinces (Millar [2004] 313–35 ["The world of the *Golden Ass*"]); in it, the emperor appears as a very distant, but still powerful, figure, the model largely followed here (cf. also my own extension of Millar's analysis in Osgood [2006c]).

The (related) topic of emperor worship, and other cult activities on behalf of the emperor, has also been widely discussed. The single most revelatory study, focused on Asia Minor, remains Price (1984); and note the earlier path-breaking paper of Hopkins (1978b) 197–242. This chapter also draws on major works by Fishwick (1987–2004), Small (1996), Clauss (1999), Friesen (2001), Gradel (2002), and Cancik and Hitzl (2003). Some of the works mentioned in the previous paragraph also discuss emperor worship (e.g., Lendon [1997] 160–72). See also the overviews in Beard *et al.* (1998) esp. 1.313–64 and Price, *CAH* 10 (second edn) 812–47 ("The place of religion: Rome in the early Empire").

1 Phil. *Leg.* 11–12.
2 Smallwood (1967) no. 33.
3 As famously, and persuasively, argued in the landmark study of Millar (1977). See above, p. 25. For some further qualifications, see also below, pp. 202–3.
4 Only a few examples, all involving Claudius, are given here. Earthquake relief: Smallwood (1967) no. 316 and Tac. *Ann.* 12.58.2. Judgment: Smallwood (1967) no. 368; and Joseph. *AJ* 20.118–36 and *BJ* 2.232–46 (discussed below). Tax obligations: Tac. *Ann.* 12.58.2 and 63.3. Walls and buildings: Smallwood (1967) nos. 231b, 315, and 318. Religious practices: Suet. *Claud.* 25.5 and *Acts* 18.2 (discussed above, p. 77).
5 E.g., for Claudius, Smallwood (1967) no. 136 and *SEG* 49.1863.
6 See the works cited in the brief bibliographic essay above.
7 As Curran (2005) suggests, one can rely with some confidence on the "structural features" of Roman power revealed by Josephus, even if his narrative of events is not free of bias. Other works to consult: Schürer (1973–87) 1.357–82, Smallwood (1976), Millar (1993) 56–69, Goodman in *CAH* 10 (second edn) 737–81 ("Judaea"), McLaren (1998), and Goodman (2007) 379–423.
8 Joseph. *AJ* 20.97–99. See also Acts 5.36.
9 Joseph. *AJ* 20.102.
10 Joseph. *AJ* 20.105–12 and *BJ* 2.223–27.
11 Joseph. *AJ* 20.113–17 and *BJ* 2.228–31.
12 Joseph. *AJ* 15.405 and 18.90–95.
13 On what follows: Joseph. *AJ* 20.6–14; this and the following episode are recently discussed by McKechnie (2005).
14 Joseph. *AJ* 20.12.
15 The version here is *AJ* 20.118–36; *BJ* 2.232–46 varies in some details, while Tac. *Ann.* 12.54 is tellingly different. See McKechnie (2005) 345–49.
16 The scholarly literature is virtually without bounds but much of it not essential to the goal here, exploration of the author's *perception* of Roman power. A few good starting places: Haenchen (1971), Hemer (1989), Bruce (1990), Gill and Gempf (1994), and Bauckham (1995). Two classic studies: Knox (1950) and Cadbury (1955).
17 The narrative commences in Acts 21.26.
18 Ibid. 22.25. Translations are those of the New Revised Standard Version.

19 Ibid. 22.28.
20 Cf. Joseph. *BJ* 6.125–26 with Schürer (1973–87) 1.378 n. 115.
21 Ibid. 23.11.
22 Ibid. 23.23–30.
23 Ibid. 25.9.
24 Ibid. 25.12.
25 On the complex problem of appeals to the emperor, see the summary of Millar (1977) 507–16; Paul's "appeal" to Festus seems not to be an instance of *provocatio* (as argued by Jones [1953]), nor is it an appeal after trial (on such *appellationes* see, e.g., Suet. *Aug.* 33.3), but rather simply a petition to have his case heard before a different court, granted in this instance at least in part because of his privileged status: so Garnsey (1966).
26 Sergius Paulus: *Acts* 13.4–12 with Mitchell (1993) 2.3–10. Junius Gallio: Acts 18.12–17.
27 Acts 11.28.
28 Ibid. 11.29.
29 See immediately below, n. 30 and n. 56.
30 The source for what follows is Joseph. *AJ* 20.51–53 and 101; cf. *AJ* 3.320–21. Discussions include Gapp (1935), Hobson (1984), Montevecchi (1982/3), and Hanson (1986).
31 Rom. 15.26.
32 1 Cor. 16.1–3.
33 2 Cor. 9.7.
34 See below, n. 56.
35 See above, pp. 74–75.
36 Further information can be found in Lewis (1983), Bowman (1986), Bowman in *CAH* 10 (second edn) 676–702 ("Egypt"), Thomas (2001), Bagnall and Rathbone (2004), and Gagos and Potter (2006).
37 The full publication is Biscottini (1966), abbreviated as *P Tryphon*. Recent discussions include Whitehorne (1984), Gagos *et al.* (1992), Piccolo (2003), and Alston (2005). Translation of some documents: Rowlandson (1998).
38 See now the splendid account of Parsons (2007).
39 Declaration: *P Tryphon* 1.
40 *P Tryphon* 19.
41 Ibid. 10.
42 New contract: *P Tryphon* 12.
43 *P Tryphon* 17.
44 Some sense of the costs involved is gained from records of the writing office in the village of Tebtunis, mainly dating to the principate of Claudius; *PMich.* vols. II and V are the chief publications. On the working of the office: Husselman (1970).
45 *P Tryphon* 21.
46 Ibid. 23.
47 Ibid. 24.
48 Ibid. 27.

49 Two certificates: *P Tryphon* 28–29.

50 Smallwood (1967) no. 47.

51 The archive has gradually been pieced together above all in a series of brilliant and fascinating articles by Hanson: Hanson (1979), (1981), (1984), (1988), (1989), (1990), (1992), (1994), (2001), (2002), and (2007), all of which I depend on here.

52 See especially Hanson (1984) 1108–9.

53 Embassy: *P Oxy.* 2435. Edicts of Germanicus: Ehrenberg and Jones (1955) no. 320. (Note too the *recto* of *P Oxy.* 2435 contains a record of Germanicus' reception in Alexandria, with the words of Alexandria's spokesman and Germanicus, as well as the acclamations of the crowd reported.)

54 See in particular the sketch presented in Hanson (1989).

55 The papyrus was published in Youtie (1977), whence *SB* 14.12143. Further details were uncovered by Hanson (1989) 429–30.

56 Plin. *HN* 5.58. See especially Hanson (1986) on what follows.

57 Smallwood (1967) no. 439. On Balbillus, see above, p. 66.

58 See bibliography above, p. 292.

59 See further Price (1984) and Friesen (2001) in particular for Asia. Kantiréa (2001) covers developments in Achaea through Nero.

60 Dio 51.20.6–9. For further details on developments discussed in this paragraph see Friesen (2001) 25–55.

61 Tac. *Ann.* 4.15.3, 37–38, and 55–56.

62 Dio 59.28.1, with Smallwood (1967) no. 127 for important information on the foundation of this cult.

63 See Smallwood (1967) no. 127 for the first securely dated attestation (AD 40), with Friesen (2001) 41–42.

64 *IGRom.* 4.1608. See above, pp. 72–73.

65 Maiuri (1925) no. 680.

66 On this title see now Lozano (2007).

67 Coin of Hierapolis: *RPC* 1.2973. Temple in Sidyma: *IGRom.* 3.577. Sebasteion in Aphrodisias: Reynolds (1986). For parallel developments in Achaea see Kantiréa (2001).

68 Priest for Claudius: e.g., Smallwood (1967) no. 133.

69 Festival for Claudius: e.g., Smallwood (1967) no. 134.

70 Arneae statue base: Smallwood (1967) no. 136. Acmonia statue base: Smallwood (1967) no. 138.

71 Ibid. no. 135.

72 Ibid. no. 134.

73 Ibid. no. 371. See also above, p. 73, and note Smallwood (1967) no. 133, recording a priest for Claudius.

74 Caligula's divine pretensions are part of the later tradition concerning him but remain difficult to pin down: see the recent remarks of Gradel (2002) 140–61.

75 See above, p. 58.

76 See above, p. 56–60.

77 The apotheosis of Augustus is much discussed, recently by Gradel (2002) 261–71 and Swan (2004) 350–59; note also the important papers of Bickerman (1973) on *consecratio* and Price (1987), and see further below, pp. 250–51.

78 Sen. *Apocol.* 1.2–3; Suet. *Calig.* 24.2; and Dio 59.11.1–4. Her divine status is regularly noted in the *Acta Fratrum Arvalium* (Scheid [1998]).

79 See for further details Rose (1997) 92 and Boschung (2002) 119–25. The dedicatory inscription is *CIL* 10.1416.

80 This would hold true even if the statue of Augustus was actually set up not at the behest of the soldier but as part of the group of L. Mammius Maximus, which included the deified Livia and Antonia, "mother of . . . Claudius" (*CIL* 10.1413, 1417), for the works of art were clearly displayed together.

81 Hallett (2005) 159–222 is now the starting place for exploration of this phenomenon; see also the more specialized study of the radiate crown of the ruler by Bergmann (1998), with Smith (2000).

82 Hallett (2005) 169–70.

83 An inscription from Lanuvium (*ILS* 6194) displayed with the statue in the Vatican Museum may not belong with the statue, but a very similar sculpture from Olympia (see Rose [1997] 147–49 and Boschung [2002] 100–5), strongly suggesting a common archetype, is to be dated to Claudius' own lifetime.

84 Sen. *Polyb.* 6.5. For more detailed analysis of the panegyric; Döpp (1994).

85 According to Suetonius (*Claud.* 28), Polybius served as *a studiis*, i.e., he dealt with the court's literary pursuits, on which see especially Wallace-Hadrill (1983) 83–86. The petitions Seneca describes here may be envisioned as related to that task, or else (more likely) his duties were broader than Suetonius indicates.

86 Sen. *Polyb.* 7.1–2.

87 Ibid. 7.2.

88 Ibid. 12.3.

89 Ibid. 12.5.

90 Ibid. 13.1–2.

91 Caligula's inconstancy: Sen. *Polyb.* 17.3–6.

92 Good collection of evidence in Levinskaya (1996). One discussion of the appeal of Christianity: Meeks (1983).

7 THE EIGHT-HUNDREDTH YEAR OF ROME

Brief bibliographic essay. The Roman emperor's special relationship with the City of Rome, in matters administrative, religious, architectural, artistic, and intellectual, grew in part out of pragmatic needs, in part out of Augustus' deliberate efforts to shift authority away from the old nobility who dominated the Republic onto himself. A very helpful account of the latter process, with significant explanatory power for actions of Claudius recounted in this chapter, is given in an essay by Wallace-Hadrill (2005), a recast version of Wallace-Hadrill (1997); see also now the book-length treatment, Wallace-Hadrill (2008), including coverage of the material evidence from across Italy for a "cultural revolution" under Augustus. Also of great value is the synthetic account of Augustan culture in Galinsky (1996) and the brilliant sketch of the city of Rome by Purcell, *CAH* 10 (second edn) 782–811 ("Rome and its development under Augustus and his successors"); and for the (related) process by which Rome made itself intellectual center of the world and capital, see the studies of Rawson (1985), Nicolet (1991), and Moatti (1997). Claudius' revisiting of Augustan culture has significant parallels, not explored here, with various actions of Vespasian (and his sons) that also looked back to Claudius as an intermediary: Griffin, *CAH* 11 (second edn) 11–25 gives a succinct account.

On a separate note: underpinning this and subsequent chapters is the view that Tacitus' *Annals*, in particular, provides reliable information on enactments of the Senate (often made on the urging of the emperor), as recorded in the *acta senatus*. Syme (1958) 271–86 argued, somewhat controversially, that in the composition of *Ann.* 1–6 in particular, Tacitus, discovering the unsatisfactory nature of literary sources, made frequent, direct use of the *acta senatus*; see also Syme's subsequent discussions in *RP* 3.1014–42 ("How Tacitus wrote *Annals* 1–III") and 4.199–222 ("Tacitus: some sources of his information"). On sometimes more speculative grounds, he argued for Tacitus' use of the *acta senatus* in *Ann.* 11–12 at Syme (1958) 295 and 703–10; but in this period, as compared to the early years of Tiberius, Syme suggested (295), "the importance of senatorial debates waned," making the *acta* less revealing. While Syme's views were challenged in particular by Momigliano (see, e.g., Momigliano [1990] 110–12), the discovery above all of the *Senatusconsultum de Pisone patre* (Eck *et al.* [1996]), when compared with Tac. *Ann.* 3.12–19, shows that here, for all Tacitus' creativity in disposing his material, his narrative rests on a solid base of research, likely his own: see, e.g., Barnes (1998) and Griffin (1997) for discussions; cf. also the *Tabula Siarensis* (Crawford [1996] nos. 37–38) with *Ann.* 2.83 on honors for the dead Germanicus. Talbert (1984) 308–37 is a helpful guide to what is known of the *acta senatus*, and at 326–34 he accepts the view that Tacitus himself used the *acta*. Incidentally, as Barnes (1998) 140 observes, it most likely was in the *acta senatus* that Tacitus learned (*Ann.* 3.18.3–4) of Claudius' neglect by the Senate when it commended individual members of the August House in AD 20 after the trial following Germanicus' death (above, p. 264 n. 2).

1 The following account derives from Tac. *Ann.* 11.1–3.
2 Purcell (2007) is a typically evocative discussion of the *horti*, on which a vast literature now exists, e.g., the papers in Cima and La Rocca (1998). On the two new aqueducts, see below, pp. 175–80. Broise and Jolivet (1998) argue for a link between their construction and Asiaticus' improvements to his property.
3 Dio 60.29.4–6a.
4 A few discussions: Scramuzza (1940) 93–97, Levick (1990) 61–64, Tagliafico (1996), and Cogitore (2002) 205–11.
5 Papyri: Sijpesteijn (1989).
6 Consulship: Tortoriello (2004) 580–83. Marriage to Lollia Saturnina: deduced from the nomenclature of M. Lollius Paullinus D. Valerius Asiaticus Saturninus (*cos.* AD 94).

7 Joseph. *AJ* 19.159 and 252; and Dio 59.30.2.
8 See above, p. 43.
9 See brief bibliographic essay above.
10 See below, pp. 165–67.
11 Tac. *Ann.* 11.5.1.
12 See above, pp. 42–46. For more general treatments of the whole theme: McAlindon (1956), Swan (1970), Rutledge (2001), and Cogitore (2002).
13 Vinicius: Joseph. *AJ* 19.251 and Dio 60.27.4; also Tortoriello (2004) 588–91. Julia Livilla: see above, pp. 42–43.
14 Asinius Gallus (and Statilius Corvinus): Suet. *Claud.* 13.2 and Dio 60.27.5. Consulship of Statilius: Tortoriello (2004) 563–65.
15 Sen. *Apocol.* 11.2 and 11.5; Suet. *Claud.* 27.2 and 29.1–2; Tac. *Hist.* 1.48.1; and Dio 60.29.6ᵃ. For evidence for the burial of members of the family, including Pompeius and his father Licinius Crassus, see especially Kragelund *et al.* (2003). Antonia's marriage to Faustus Sulla: Suet. *Claud.* 27.2 and Dio 60.30.6ᵃ.
16 Possible threat: e.g., Syme (1986) 183.
17 Tac. *Ann.* 11.5–7.
18 Effort of Augustus: Dio 54.18.2.
19 A few general discussions focused on Claudius: Bauman (1982) 105–11, Levick (1990) 120–26, Wolf (1994), and Hurley (2001) 117–18 and 160. The larger backdrop is set out by Millar (1977) 516–37 and Galsterer in *CAH* 10 (second edn) 397–413 ("The administration of justice").
20 Suet. *Claud.* 15.2 and Dio 60.28.6.
21 Suet. *Claud.* 29.1 and 38.2; cf. Sen. *Apocol.* 12.3.19–22 and 14.2–3. See Griffin (1990) 500–1.
22 Suet. *Claud.* 14 and 23.1; cf. Sen. *Apocol.* 7.4 and 12.3.22–23. Note also Dio 60.4.3–4.
23 Smallwood (1967) no. 367. Stroux (1929) is the essential edition and for a vindication of his identification of the speaker see Griffin (1990) 494–99.
24 Explicitly acknowledged as such by Plin. *HN* 10.5 and Tac. *Ann.* 11.11.1; cf. Aur. Vict. *Caes.* 4.14.
25 Suet. *Claud.* 24.3 and Dio 60.30.2–3; cf. Tac. *Ann.* 13.32.2.
26 See above, pp. 84–85 and 92.
27 On Augustus' games see the sources set out in Pighi (1965) and Schnegg-Köhler (2002), with further discussion at Galinsky (1996) 100–6, Beard *et al.* (1998) 201–6, and Feeney (1998) 28–38.
28 The *saeculum* (centennial) was redefined as lasting 110 years: see especially Cens. 17.9.
29 The oracle is preserved in Phlegon. *Macrob.* 37.5.2–4 and Zos. 2.6.
30 See the revised text of the inscription in Schnegg-Köhler (2002).
31 Dio 54.18.1. Augustus' motives in adopting Gaius and Lucius, and his plans for a "succession" at this date, are contested: for two different perspectives see Syme (1939) 419–39 and Gruen (2005).
32 Suet. *Claud.* 21.2; cf. Momigliano (1934) 89–90.

33 Suet. *Claud.* 21.2; cf. *Vit.* 2.5. Representations of the herald: *RIC* I (second edn.) Augustus nos. 339–42.

34 Plin. *HN* 7.159.

35 Ibid. 10.5; cf. Aur. Vict. *Caes.* 4.14.

36 Race: Plin. *HN* 8.160. Improvements: Suet. *Claud.* 21.3 and Dio 60.7.3–4.

37 Thessalian horsemen, panthers, etc.: Suet. *Claud.* 21.3 and Dio 60.7.3–4.

38 Beacham (1999) is a detailed study. See also above, p. 32.

39 Treggiari (1991) 60–80 and 277–98 discusses the laws in details. Galinsky (1996) 128–40 is a broader contextualization.

40 *RG* 8.5.

41 Claudius (with Vitellius) as censor: see especially Tac. *Ann.* 11.11–15 and 22–25; Suet. *Claud.* 16; and Dio 60.29. Other sources are mentioned in the discussion below. Censors of 22 BC: *ILS* 886, Vell. Pat. 2.95.3, Suet. *Claud.* 16.1, and Dio 54.2. Subsequent censuses of 8 BC and AD 14: *RG* 8.3–4; Suet. *Aug.* 97.1 and *Tib.* 21.1; and Dio 54.35.1. Discussions of Claudius as censor include Momigliano (1934) 44, Levick (1990) 98–101 and 120, Ryan (1993), Demougin (1994), and Hurley (2001) 127–28.

42 See Tortoriello (2004) 598–600. Vitellius' sons Aulus and Lucius (the former the future emperor) were consuls in the following year as well: Tortoriello (2004) 421–22, 595–97, and 602–3.

43 Lintott (1999) 115–20 gives a brief overview. See also Mommsen (1871–88) 2.1.331–464 and Suolahti (1963) 20–79.

44 Suet. *Claud.* 22.

45 See Wallace-Hadrill (2005) for the argument on Augustus' yoking of knowledge to power.

46 Smallwood (1967) no. 365. For the correct date: Tortoriello (2004) 420–21.

47 See, e.g., Garnsey (1976).

48 Smallwood (1967) no. 311. The names of Claudius and Vitellius are restored, but with confidence because of the appearance of a distinctive Claudian letter, on which see below, pp. 156–58. *CIL* 6.40887 (see following note) helps improve the restoration of the text in Smallwood.

49 *CIL* 6.40887. It is possible that this work was related to a simultaneous redrawing of the customs boundary for Rome, as seems to have happened during the censorship of Vespasian and Titus, on which see Palmer (1980).

50 On this census see especially Wallace-Hadrill (2008) 301–12, who suggests periodic updating, though not under Claudius.

51 Tac. *Ann.* 11.13.1.

52 Ibid. 11.13.2.

53 Ibid. 11.15.1.

54 Cf. Syme (1958) 704 and Griffin (1990) 482–84; and see the brief bibliographic essay above, p. 296.

55 Discussions include Torelli (1985), Rose (1997) 83–86, and Boschung (2002) 85–89.

56 The relationship between Claudius' scholarship and his conception of the principate probably has been discussed to excess but there are some important

links, as here. See above, p. 264 n. 9 and also Fasolini (2006) 155–71 for a fuller survey of the question.

57 Suet. *Claud.* 42.2; for the Claudium in Alexandria see also Ath. *Deip.* 6.240b.

58 Tac. *Ann.* 11.13.2–14.

59 Suet. *Claud.* 41.3. See also the testimony cited by Schmidt (1994) 126.

60 A few examples: Smallwood (1967) nos. 14, 44, 99, 100, 186, 311, and 330.

61 *RG* 8.4.

62 See, briefly, Crook (1967) 46–48.

63 Smallwood (1967) no. 369. See further below, pp. 165–67.

64 Tac. *Ann.* 11.25.5.

65 Ibid. 2.60.3.

66 Boast: Smallwood (1967) no. 369. Papyrus: *PSI* 10.1183 with the essential discussion of Rathbone (2001), followed here. Note also Plin. *HN* 7.159 for a reference to the procedure of the Claudian census.

67 See, e.g., Mommsen (1887–88) 2.1.412–13 and Ogilvie (1961) for discussions.

68 Discussions include Ryberg (1955) 106–9, Koeppel (1983b) 80–81 and 124–29, and Kleiner (1992) 141.

69 Tac. *Ann.* 12.23.1 with Wissowa (1912) 525–26.

70 Extension of the *pomerium*: Sen. *Brev.* 13.8–9, Tac. *Ann.* 12.23.2–4, and Gell. *NA* 13.14; further evidence is mentioned in the following discussion and a more complete dossier is found in *LTUR* s.v. *pomerium*; note also now *CIL* 6.40852. Fasolini (2006) 52–58 surveys the detailed scholarship on the matter, e.g., Boatwright (1984) and Poe (1984), and see also Lyasse (2005).

71 Power: included in the partially extant law outlining Vespasian's powers (Crawford [1996] no. 39). Vespasian and Titus' exercise of this power: Levick (1999b) 130.

72 Smallwood (1967) no. 44 gives the standard text. See *LTUR* s.v. *pomerium* for full details of the evidence, adding *CIL* 6.40852.

73 Cf. Plin. *HN* 3.67.

74 General accounts drawn on in the following discussion include Momigliano (1934) 63–67, Scramuzza (1940) 99–144, Sherwin-White (1973) 221–50, and Levick (1990) 93–103 and 163–86. Fasolini (2006) 45–51 also surveys some more specialized research.

75 Alföldy (1974) 78–105 sets out the evidence. It may well be that Claudius appointed the first equestrian procurator for the province (cf. Smallwood [1967] no. 258), in line with developments elsewhere (see above, p. 113), even if Noricum did not at this time lose (even nominal) sovereignty.

76 Smallwood (1967) no. 407. See above, p. 113.

77 See above, pp. 158–59.

78 Discussions include Dušanic (1982) and (1986); Valvo (2001); and Thomas (2004) 436–38.

79 Smallwood (1967) no. 295.

80 Smallwood (1967) no. 368 with Frézouls (1981) for a full discussion of the question of citizenship.

81 Suet. *Claud.* 25.3. Cf., e.g., Suet. *Claud.* 16.2 and Dio 60.17.4.

82 Dio 60.17.5; and *Acts* 22.28 (on which, see above, p. 130).
83 *Apocol.* 3.3.
84 See below, pp. 190–205.
85 Suet. *Claud.* 16. Cf. Suetonius' unique account of Claudius' short-lived reform of the equestrian military service (*Claud.* 25.1), on which see, e.g., Demougin (1994).
86 Tac. *Ann.* 11.25.2. Inscriptions: see, e.g., *ILS* 964 and 975 and also below, p. 200.
87 Veranius: *CIL* 6.41075; Plautius Pulcher: *ILS* 964; and Salvius Otho: Suet. *Oth.* 1.3. Further details in Tortoriello (2001).
88 Tac. *Ann.* 11.23–25.1. Above all because of the survival of Claudius' speech on the so-called "Lyon Tablet" (on which see below, p. 167), this episode has been frequently discussed from a variety of perspectives, e.g., the technique of Tacitus, the policy of Claudius, his activities as a scholar, and the spread of Roman citizenship. Fabia (1929) is a full edition of Claudius' speech, while other studies of note include Momigliano (1934) 10–16, Wellesley (1954), Syme (1958) 317–19, De Vivo (1980), and Griffin (1982). Syme (1999) is the posthumous publication of an early and unfinished work, focused on this episode, which in a sense is also the linchpin of Syme (1958).
89 On senators from Narbonensis and Baetica, see the valuable material collected in Syme (1999) 26–38 and 119–26. Revolt: Tac. *Ann.* 3.40–46.
90 On rules governing admission to the Senate see Talbert (1984) 1–16.
91 *Ann.* 11.24.7.
92 Smallwood (1967) no. 369. See above, n. 88.
93 See above, pp. 147–51.
94 Griffin (1982). Note also the amusing attempt of Syme (1999) 103–4 to rewrite it in English.
95 Smallwood (1967) no. 367 (translation reflects some fairly secure supplements).
96 Tac. *Ann.* 11.4.3, brilliantly discussed by Griffin (1990) 498.

8 PRACTICAL PYRAMIDS

Brief bibliographic essay. This chapter analyzes Claudius' building program in Rome and Italy, where once again precedents set by Augustus were fundamental. A full overview of Augustus' transformation of Rome is given by Favro (1996), and see more briefly Favro (2005). Haselberger (2002) maps Augustan Rome and provides full documentation on relevant structures, while Haselberger (2007) provides a complementary narrative account (with a useful list of Augustan buildings at 256–65). Zanker (1988) intermittently discusses the Augustan transformation, while Gros (1976) focuses on the very important temples. On Rome in this period see also the surveys of Patterson (1992) and Purcell in *CAH* 10 (second edn) 782–811 ("Rome and its development under Augustus and his successors"). On the vast subject of emperors and building more generally a few pertinent discussions are Veyne (1976) 539–730 *passim*, Kolb (1993), Zanker (1997), Belayche (2001), and Hortser (2001). Important studies focused on specific periods include Elsner (1994) on Nero; Jones (1992)

79–98 and Noreña (2003) on the Flavian period; Boatwright (1987) on Hadrian; Thomas (2007) on the Antonine age. For the history of individual structures in Rome *LTUR* is now indispensable; see also Claridge (1998) and Coarelli (2007).

Recent scholarship has done much to reconstruct the remarkable story of how Roman emperors helped to feed the megalopolis of Rome, another concern of this chapter. A convenient, and vivid, overview can be found in Aldrete and Mattingly (1999) or (2000), looking at the grain supply as well as olive oil and wine, the other staples of the city-dweller's diet. On the grain supply in general see Rickman (1980), Garnsey (1983) and (1988). Works on the administration of the food supply include the comprehensive study on the *praefectus annonae* by Pavis D'Escurac (1976); Sirks (1991) on the legal structures involved, especially in the later empire; and Virlouvet (1995) on the distributions of grain (at the Porticus Minucia Frumentaria, where recipients lined up, each presenting a *tessera frumentaria*, a wooden tablet with the individual's name). Virlouvet argues that in the realm of distribution, the principate of Claudius marked far less of a change than used to be thought. Mrozek (1987) studies distributions of grain and coin in imperial Italy. Wider geographical and chronological explorations are found in the essays in Marin and Virlouvet (2004). On the relationship between political power and distribution of food see, in addition to the classic study of Veyne (1976), the review essay by Shaw (1989) considering what he suggestively calls "food power."

1 Tac. *Ann.* 12.56–57 is the principal ancient account for the episode that follows. See also the other sources noted below.
2 Marsi: Suet. *Claud.* 20.1. Cf. also Suet. *Iul.* 44.2.
3 Plin. *HN* 36.124, Suet. *Claud.* 20.2 and Dio 60.11.5 describe the channel and its construction in some detail.
4 *RG* 23 for the *navalis proeli spectaculum*; see also Vell. Pat. 2.100.2, Suet. *Aug.* 43.1, and Dio 55.10.7. Coleman (1993) offers a rich and informed discussion.
5 Triton: Suet. *Claud.* 21.6.
6 Rhodians and Sicilians: Suet. *Claud.* 21.6 and also Dio 60.33.3–4.
7 Claudius, Agrippina, and Nero: see in addition to Tac. *Ann.* 12.56.3, Plin. *HN* 33.63 and Dio 60.33.3. Pliny's account might be that of an eyewitness, and also the original source for the later accounts, which overlap in many details.
8 This is a likely explanation for Tacitus' omission of the tale of reluctant combatants found in Suet. *Claud.* 21.6 and Dio 60.33.4.
9 Coarelli (1977) provides a rich catalogue of evidence for the period down through Sulla.
10 Appian Way and aqueduct: see, e.g., Cic. *Cael.* 34–35; Livy, 9.29.7; *CIL* 6.40943. Temple: see, e.g., Livy 10.19.17 and *CIL* 6.40943.
11 See for a general discussion Eck (1984) and note also Tatum (2008) 80–98.
12 E.g., Lutatius Catulus (*cos.* 78 BC) was able to put his name on the rebuilt Capitol, though the Senate subsequently voted Caesar's name should replace that of Catulus on the grounds that it was Caesar who really completed it: Dio 43.14.6 (cf. Cic. *2 Verr.* 4.69). Cf. Wiseman (2007) 421–22.

13 See Ziolkowski (1992) for one discussion.

14 See brief bibliographic essay above.

15 This emerges clearly from the catalogue of buildings in Haselberger (2007) 256–65. See also, e.g., Eck (1984).

16 *RG* 20.4.

17 *RG* 19.1 and 20.1.

18 See Osgood (2006a) 400 with further references.

19 See especially Suet. *Aug.* 37.

20 Boast: Suet. *Aug.* 28.3 and Dio 56.30.3. Note that Suetonius quotes in the same chapter an edict of Augustus which employs an analogy with building to describe Augustus' own political legacy.

21 *RG* 19–21 is the catalogue. Two discussions: Sablayrolles (1981) and Elsner (1996).

22 *RG* 20.3; cf. Suet. *Aug.* 29.4 and Dio 56.27.5.

23 Cf. Osgood (2006a) 395–96.

24 See Griffin (1984) 125–42 and 197–207 for a balanced discussion.

25 Suet. *Tib.* 47; with this passage cf. Tac. *Ann.* 6.45.1.

26 Concord: Dio 55.8.2 (noting that Tiberius wished to assign Drusus' name to the temple as well as his own) and 56.25.1; Castor: 55.27.4 (again noting the name of Drusus). See also Suet. *Tib.* 20.

27 Suet. *Calig.* 21.

28 Aqueduct: Plin. *HN* 36.122, Frontin. *Aq.* 13, and Suet. *Calig.* 21; amphitheater: Suet. *Calig.* 21 and Dio 59.10.5 with Smallwood (1967) no. 308 (b) and Frontin. *Aq.* 22. On Caligula as a builder see Barrett (1990) 192–212.

29 Suet. *Claud.* 20.1.

30 See especially, in addition to *Claud.* 21, *Aug.* 29–30, *Tib.* 47, *Calig.* 21, *Ner.* 16.1, *Ves.* 9.1, and *Dom.* 5, along with Pliny's attention to Trajan's buildings at *Pan.* 51.

31 Survey: Plin. *HN* 36.101–25 (quotation at 36.121).

32 Plin. *HN* 36.122–25.

33 Perhaps the reference is to Agrippa's construction of the Portus Iulius at Avernus: Osgood (2006a) 299.

34 Pyramids: Plin. *HN* 36.75–82 (with quotation at 36.75). Lighthouse: Plin. *HN* 36.83.

35 Edwards (1993) 137–72 is a good general discussion; for a specific application to Nero: Elsner (1994).

36 *Aq.* 4–15.

37 Ibid. 16.

38 Stat. *Silv.* 4.3.

39 Suet. *Claud.* 24.1 represents Claudius defending a measure of his censorship with an appeal to the precedent of Appius Claudius. Note that the focus here is on the major building projects; other activities of Claudius in this realm are summarized by Fasolini (2006) 101–12.

40 The year of dedication is given by the inscription on the so-called Porta Maggiore (Smallwood [1967] no. 309, on which see below) and also Frontin.

Aq. 13, who adds the date: August 1, the birthday of Claudius. Accounts of the aqueducts and water supply of Rome I have drawn on include: Ashby (1935), Bruun (1991), Hodge (1992), Evans (1994), Aicher (1995), Dodge (2000), and Rodgers (2004).

41 Tac. *Ann.* 11.13.2.

42 See, e.g., the comment of Rodgers (2004) 183 and also below, pp. 177–80 for distinctive stylistic features of Claudian public works.

43 Servian Wall: see above, p. 161.

44 But note that the Flavian inscription on the Porta Maggiore (*ILS* 218), long taken to refer to serious deterioration to the Aqua Claudia, is likely only alluding to the branch line built off the Claudia by Nero: so Coates-Stephens (2004) 65–67.

45 These figures, along with Frontinus' own, are given in *Aq.* 65–73; see the summary chart in Rodgers (2004) 354.

46 Frontin. *Aq.* 86.

47 Coates-Stephens (2004) 35.

48 Coates-Stephens (2004) is now the essential study; and see von Hesberg (1994) for a larger context.

49 See above, p. 94. Claudius' gate can be compared specifically with the far less grandiose and more austerely designed crossing for the Aqua Marcia / Tepula / Julia built on the Via Tiburtina under Augustus.

50 For some suggestions along these lines concerning other Claudian monuments see Torelli (1994).

51 See above, pp. 155–56 and 163.

52 Coates-Stephens (2004) 43–46 is now the best discussion. On the temple, see below, p. 251.

53 Smallwood (1967) no. 309.

54 Coates-Stephens (2004) 40. The spelling of CAESAR as CAISAR in the inscription is a further well-attested idiosyncrasy of Claudian epigraphy.

55 See especially the discussion of Panciera (1998).

56 See above, p. 94.

57 Smallwood (1967) no. 308 (b); and also note the markers Smallwood (1967) no. 308 (a) and *CIL* 6.40880.

58 See above, pp. 93–95.

59 Frontin. *Aq.* 116–18. On this and the following (more controversial) matter, see especially Bruun (1991).

60 Frontin. *Aq.* 105.

61 Specifically attested in an overdrawn passage of Seneca (*Brev.* 18.5–6); the "severe famine" mentioned by Dio 60.11.1 should probably be dated to AD 41 as well (cf. Aur. Vict. *Caes.* 4.3). August Ceres: *RIC* I (second edn) Claudius nos. 94 and 110.

62 Shortage of AD 51: Tac. *Ann.* 12.43 and Suet. *Claud.* 18–19.

63 Tac. *Ann.* 12.43.2. On the supplying of grain to Rome, see the studies cited in the brief bibliographic essay above.

64 For these so-called Murecine tablets, see especially the discussion in Jones (2006); Camodeca (1999) is the full publication of the tablets.

65 Suet. *Claud.* 18–19, Gai. *Inst.* 1.32c, and Ulp. *Frag.* 3.6. See also below, p. 202, on the possible relevance here of activity in the grain-rich Cyrene under Claudius.

66 See the works cited above, p. 301.

67 Suet. *Claud.* 12.3 places Claudius on a trip to Ostia early in his principate; Claudius also departed from Ostia for Britain in AD 43 (Suet. *Claud.* 17.2). And note Suet. *Claud.* 38.1 and 40.3 for further Ostian connections.

68 Dio 60.11.1–4.

69 Suet. *Claud.* 20 and Dio 60.11.4–5. Cf. also Plin. *HN* 16.201–2 and 36.70.

70 *RIC* I (second edn) Nero nos. 440–41, 513–14, and 586–89.

71 Plin. *HN* 16.201–2 and 36.70; and Suet. *Claud.* 20.3.

72 Plin. *HN* 9.14–15.

73 The survey of Keay *et al.* (2005) is the source for what follows.

74 Smallwood (1967) no. 312 (b). Aldrete (2007) 184 offers a discussion.

75 Smallwood (1967) no. 307 (b). See Le Gall (1953) 157. Le Gall (1953) and Aldrete (2007) are key studies.

76 Prefect: Smallwood (1967) no. 257. Procurator: Smallwood (1967) no. 265. See Le Gall (1953) 182 and 261–63.

77 Claudius Optatus, *procurator* of the Ostian port: Smallwood (1967) no. 173. On the reform note also Suet. *Claud.* 24.2.

78 Suet. *Claud.* 25.2.

79 Smallwood (1967) no. 335. Smallwood (1967) nos. 328–48 is a useful collection of epigraphic evidence, while Walser (1980) presents a fuller catalogue with discussion. See also Scramuzza (1940) 157–78 and Levick (1990) 167–77.

80 Gardner (1913) gives a discussion.

81 Smallwood (1967) no. 329.

82 Gardner (1920) and van Essen (1957) provide discussions.

83 Smallwood (1967) no. 330 (with use of distinctive Claudian spelling and a new Claudian letter).

84 Gardner (1941) and Rosada (2001) provide discussions.

85 Hor. *Carm.* 4.4.73. On the campaign see Vell. Pat. 2.95.1–2; Suet. *Tib.* 9.2 and *Claud.* 1.2; and Dio 54.22.3–5.

86 On Noricum see above, p. 161.

87 Smallwood (1967) no. 328 and *ILS* 208.

88 Suet. *Claud.* 20.2.

89 This is proposed in the study of the project by Thornton and Thornton (1985).

90 See the information presented in various contributions in Campanelli (2001) and also the earlier account in Blake (1959) 84–85.

91 Tac. *Ann.* 12.57 and Suet. *Claud.* 32.

92 Tac. *Ann.* 12.57.

93 Cf. Blake (1959) 85.

94 Suet. *Claud.* 20.2.

95 Saller (2005) 234–35 is the source for this and the following calculation.

96 Dio 60.33.5.

9 THE BURDEN OF GOVERNMENT

Brief bibliographic essay. The literature on the Roman imperial government is enormous and full of controversy, largely owing to the very imperfect nature of the evidence. The best attempt to give an overview of its structure is now provided in a series of chapters by Eck in *CAH* 11 (second edn) 195–292; these draw on Eck's many earlier important publications, with Eck (1994) specifically focused on Claudius. See further the chapters by Talbert and Bowman in *CAH* 10 (second edn) 324–70 ("The Senate and Senatorial and equestrian posts" and "Provincial administration and taxation" respectively); Lintott (1993) is also a helpful guide, underscoring continuities between the Republican and imperial periods, as does Ando in a brief but very useful survey article (2006). A long series of more specialized studies very productively helped to strip away a number of anachronistic analogies between Rome and modern bureaucratic states, including Crook (1955) on the emperor's council; Weaver (1972) on the imperial slaves and freedmen; Saller (1982) on patronage and appointments; Lendon (1997) on the ethos of the ruling class; and also various investigations gathered together in Brunt (1990), such as Brunt's analysis of the prefects of Egypt. In his highly influential study of the emperor (Millar [1977]), as well as in various papers (Millar [2004]), Millar put forward a model of a fairly minimal imperial government, in which emperors did not really have policies, but instead reacted to situations as they arose (see above, pp. 25–26); note also, for a review of subsequent literature, Millar (1992) 636–52. Especially to be noted, then, are a series of articles by Burton, including more recently Burton (1998), (2000), (2002), and (2004), which collect and reinterpret evidence, in an effort to show that some aspects of this minimalist view probably need modification: the extant evidence, Burton (2002) 251 argues, has led to a reconstruction that "privileges the reactive and adjudicatory roles of emperors and governors and underplays the regulatory and extractive functions of the imperial state." For corruption in the Roman government, a particular interest of this chapter, note the important study of MacMullen (1988), with especially relevant discussion at 124–37. On status dissonance, another interest of this chapter, see above, p. 24.

One theme less showcased here, but important in considering the early imperial government, is the growing tension between public and imperial officials over financial affairs, especially in the provinces; in particular, there has been much discussion concerning the process by which agents of the emperor (procurators) came ever more to control the finances of all provinces, both those governed by imperial legates and those by Senate appointees. Much debate has centered on Tacitus' account of Claudius' extension of jurisdiction to procurators (*Ann.* 12.60; cf. Suet. *Claud.* 12.1), the best discussion of which is Brunt (1990) 163–87, who proposes that (1) by this measure all procurators, freedmen or equestrians, who managed the emperor's personal holdings in the provinces and the finances of provinces in the emperor's domain were confirmed in extended, though probably not exclusive, jurisdiction over fiscal affairs; and (2) this was just one part of a process whereby gradually procurators came to have greater control of imperial finances overall and government functions more generally; Brunt cites earlier studies of Tacitus' account; see also more briefly Brunt (1983) 52–55 and, for a wider perspective, Burton (1993). On procurators of equestrian status, Pflaum (1950) is the classic study, on which see Millar (2004) 151–59 ("The equestrian career under the Empire"). Also recommended is Syme's study of Pliny the Elder at *RP* 2.742–73 ("Pliny the procurator"); cf. also Syme (1958) 60–62, where Syme comments, "The energy, the tenacity, and the devotion of equestrian officials go far to explain the success of the imperial system."

On equestrians and the offices they filled in the early principate as a whole (in what may loosely be called "career" patterns), see, in addition to the general works above, the massive study of Demougin (1988), with the companion prosopography (1992). Note also Saller (1980), Brunt (1983), Birley (2005) 298–301, and the papers in Demougin *et al.* (1999) and (2006), the latter revisiting the work of Pflaum. On the career patterns of Senators, more properly analyzed as such because legal rules were involved (on which see especially Morris [1964] and [1965]), see the overviews in Birley (2005) 3–10 and (1981) 3–35; also the major study of the imperial Senate by Talbert (1984) as well as the collected papers of Chastagnol (1992).

1 Smallwood (1967) no. 375 (quoted below).
2 Linderski (2007) 307–18 gives an excellent discussion for the Republican period; Mitchell (1976) publishes an important new early imperial inscription (whence *AE* 1976.653), on which see below, p. 196, and collects other evidence; A. Kolb (2000) is a full study.
3 Note especially the vignette in Apuleius' novel (*Met.* 9.39–40), as discussed by Millar (2004) 321–23.
4 Smallwood (1967) no. 380; copies in Greek and Latin (the latter very fragmentary) were found in the theater and lower market of Ephesus. Dörner (1935) is the fundamental edition, while Dignas (2002) esp. 141–56 provides an elucidation within the context of temple finances.
5 Sen. *Polyb.* 14.1; see discussion above, pp. 143–45. On the ideology of the emperor's *cura*, see Béranger (1953) 169–217.
6 Dio 60.2.7.
7 Ibid. 60.17.5–6 and 60.17.8.
8 Accusations: Dio 60.15.5; Umbonius Silio: 60.24.5; adultery in palace: Dio 60.18.1–2; Catonius Justus: Dio 60.18.3; Vinicius: Dio 60.27.4; Asiaticus: Dio 60.29.6.
9 Dio 60.2.5–6; cf. Dio 60.18.3.
10 Ibid. 60.14.2.
11 Ibid. 60.14.3–4.
12 Ibid. 60.28.3–5.
13 Maesa: Dio 79.30.2–4; Cleander: Dio 73.10.2 and 78.12–13.
14 See below, pp. 206–24.
15 See above, pp. 14–17.

16 Suet. *Claud.* 29.1, with *Claud.* 25.5.

17 Plin. *HN* 12.12.

18 The relevant passages are Plin. *HN* 22.92, 33.134, 33.145, 35.201, and 36.60.

19 Griffin (1976) 130 lists the relevant passages: freedmen: *Apocol.* 6.2 and 15.2; venality of court: 9.4; and neglect of judicial procedure: 7.5; 12.3.19–28; 10.4, 14.2.

20 Tac. *Ann.* 13.4, again with the discussion of Griffin (1976) 130.

21 This was the argument of Momigliano (1934), with the quotations from 41–42. Levick (1990) 81–91 offers a sensitive critique. See also above, pp. 18–21.

22 See below, pp. 206–13.

23 For the scholarly literature on the Roman imperial "government" see the brief bibliographic essay above.

24 Published by Mitchell (1976), whence *AE* 1976.653.

25 Plin. *Ep.* 7.29 and 8.6, source of the following quotations.

26 See especially Suet. *Claud.* 12.2, 14, 16.4, and 23; and Dio 60.4.3–4, 60.10.3, and 60.11.6

27 Note in particular a series of references in Suetonius to letters of Augustus, e.g., Suet. *Iul.* 56.7; *Aug.* 50 and 64.2; *Tib.* 21; and *Claud.* 4. An especially good discussion of the whole topic is Millar (1977) 213–28. Just some examples of letters written in Claudius' name: Smallwood (1967) no. 370 (to the Alexandrians, above, pp. 65–67); Smallwood (1967) no. 371 (to Thasos, above, p. 73); Smallwood (1967) no. 372 (to the hymnodists of Asia, above, pp. 72–73); Smallwood (1967) no. 373 (to the Dionysiac artists, above, pp. 69–72); Joseph. *AJ* 19.327 (to Agrippa I of Judea); and Joseph. *AJ* 20.10–14 (to the Jews). Some evidence for letters received by Claudius: Smallwood (1967) no. 368 (from Julius Planta, sent to investigate territorial disputes in northern Italy); Smallwood (1967) no. 376 (from Junius Gallio, proconsul of Achaea); Joseph. *AJ* 19.326 (from Vibius Marsus, legate of Syria).

28 Smallwood (1967) no. 368.

29 Ibid. no. 375 (above, pp. 190–91); and Ibid. no. 369 (above, pp. 165–67).

30 Pallas and finances: e.g., Suet. *Claud.* 28; Narcissus and letters: Suet. *Claud.* 28 and Dio 60.30.6^b as well as *ILS* 1666 (identified as *ab epistulis* on a pipe); Callistus and embassies: Dio 60.30.6^b; and Polybius and literary activities: *Polyb.* 6.5 and Suet. *Claud.* 28. See also above, p. 41.

31 See above, pp. 38–41.

32 See above, pp. 143–45.

33 Freedmen in the Senate, along with the Praetorian prefects: Dio 60.16.3.

34 Tac. *Ann.* 12.53.

35 See especially Gai. *Inst.*1.84. For the interpretation that follows: Weaver (1972) 162–69.

36 The following analysis derives from Tortoriello (2004) 399–410.

37 See above, p. 283 n. 25.

38 This is a pervasive theme of works by Syme, e.g., Syme (1939) 490–508 and (1958) 585–624; Syme (1986) tells the story in the fullest detail.

39 *CIL* 6.41075, preferable to the text printed at Smallwood (1967) no. 231 (c). See above, p. 115.
40 See the works cited in the brief bibliographic essay above.
41 Smallwood (1967) no. 226. Water supply: Smallwood (1967) no. 310 and Frontin. *Aq.* 102.
42 Smallwood (1967) no. 229.
43 Ibid. no. 32.
44 Departures: Dio 60.17.3. Intermissions: Dio 60.25.4–6 (with an antiquarian justification perhaps deriving from a speech of Claudius preserved in the *acta senatus*). Edict of Corbulo and *mandata*: see Burton (1976).
45 Smallwood (1967) no. 375.
46 Ibid. no. 381.
47 Smallwood (1967) no. 382. Lewis (1954) offers a good discussion.
48 Smallwood (1967) no. 383.
49 See also the discussions at pp. 135–41 and 233–36.
50 Dio 60.24.1–3 and Suet. *Claud.* 24.2. An inscription, Smallwood (1967) no. 233, records one of the men first to hold the post.
51 See above, p. 42.
52 Smallwood (1967) no. 368; see discussion above, p. 163.
53 Tac. *Ann.* 12.60 (cf. Suet. *Claud.* 12.1), with the literature cited in the brief bibliographic essay above. Griffin (1990) 489–93 offers a possible reconstruction of Claudius' speech on the occasion, which Tacitus will have reworked.
54 Tac. *Ann.* 14.18.2–3 with the record of his activity there at Smallwood (1967) no. 386. Note also the additional epigraphic evidence presented by Reynolds (1971).
55 As suggested by Reynolds, *CAH* 10 (second edn), 639; on the road-building, see Goodchild (1950).
56 See below, pp. 233–36.
57 Corbulo's activities are principally to be traced through Tacitus: *Ann.* 13.8–9, 13.34–41, 14.23–26, etc.
58 See below, p. 237.
59 Veranius: Tac. *Agr.* 14.3 and *Ann.* 14.29.1. Suetonius Paulinus: Tac. *Agr.* 5 and 14.3; and *Ann.* 14.29.2–3.
60 Flavius Sabinus: Smallwood (1967) no. 384. Vespasian: e.g., Suet. *Vesp.* 4.5–6.
61 Judge (1985) 17–19 makes this point forcefully.
62 See below, pp. 212–13.
63 Suet. *Aug.* 67.2.
64 For the relationship between moral superiority and authority see especially Wallace-Hadrill (2005).
65 Vespasian: Suet. *Vesp.* 4.1. Master of Callistus: Sen. *Ep.* 47.9.
66 But note the study by Millar (2004) 105–19 ("Epictetus and the imperial court") of the views on court life offered by Epictetus, slave of Nero's freedman Ephaphroditus, *a libellis*.
67 Dio 52.1–41.
68 Ibid. 52.37.5–6.

10 THE JUDGMENT OF PALLAS

Brief bibliographic essay. Older discussions of Claudius' wives, the main subject of this chapter, tended to accept the literary portrait of them, above all in Tacitus, or try to rationalize it. But for reasons to be discussed, there are serious difficulties with this approach, and an historical study will proceed more effectively from the more "primary" evidence of inscriptions, statues, coins, and the like. The study of Agrippina by Ginsburg (2006) is in this regard exemplary. For a detailed art historical approach to Messallina and Agrippina see Wood (1999) 249–314, with discussion of the difficulties of securely identifying portraits of Messallina – on which see also Boschung (1993a) 71–73. For criticism of the literary sources, see, e.g., Questa (1995), Joshel (1997), and the more comprehensive works on Tacitus including Seif (1973), Mehl (1974), and Aveline (2006); see also p. 263. Ehrhardt (1978), Meise (1969) 123–69, and Fagan (2002) make important contributions. Valuable suggestions are also made in the (more or less) biographical studies such as Griffin (1984) 18–33, Levick (1990) 53–80, Eck (1993), and Barrett (1996), the last especially useful for the full catalogue of evidence concerning Agrippina – although newer methodology might make one occasionally skeptical of these authors' use of the literary evidence. Moltesen and Nielsen (2007) is an attractively illustrated collection of essays on Agrippina the Younger. A few other relevant works for imperial women (often art historical in approach): Purcell (1986), Hahn (1994), Bartman (1999), Kokkinos (2002), Kunst and Riemer (2000), Temporini-Gräfin Vitzthum (2002), Alexandridis (2004), and Flower (2006) 160–96.

Study of the imperial women is part of the larger, and extraordinary, revolution in the study of women in the Roman world, in which there has been a tension between an understandable effort to recover real women's lives, and a countervailing insistence that male-authored sources, written in a pre-feminist world, are very inadequate for recovering female experience and attitudes. An admirably frank introduction to the whole problem, with review of previous scholarship, is Dixon (2001), who argues, in connection with the depictions of imperial women in various media, that neither "the fertile exemplar nor the frivolous wanton represented any real woman so much as a collection of qualities assembled for the particular purpose" (150). Also strongly recommended are Hallett (1989), Henderson (1989), and Gold (1993), as well as the collected papers in Wyke (2002). In the second half of her volume, Wyke, building on her uncovering of ancient representations of women, turns to the reception of Cleopatra and Messallina in more modern times; such reception studies are now flourishing, while another approach, in the face of the difficulties in recovering female experience, is to explore the relationship between gender and power: see Milnor (2005) for a study in this vein on the Augustan period.

1 Plin. *HN* 10.172.
2 Juv. 6.115–24.
3 Cicero's treatment of Clodia in his speech *For Caelius* is the classic example.

4 Vestals: Dio 60.22.2; carriage: Suet. *Claud.* 17.3 and Dio 60.22.2. See above, p. 91.

5 Smallwood (1967) no. 99 (a).

6 *AE* 1992.739b with the full discussion by Cavalieri Manasse (1992).

7 Arneae: Smallwood (1967) no. 136. Leptis Magna: Reynolds and Ward Perkins (1952) no. 340, on which see also Rose (1997) 184–85.

8 Alexandria: *RPC* 1.5113–16, 5131–32, 5145–46, 5162–65; Sinope: *RPC* 1.2130; Nicomedia: *RPC* 1.2074; and Cnossus: *RPC* 1.1001–2.

9 *RPC* 1.3627.

10 Marriage to Claudius: Suet. *Claud.* 26.2. Relationship to Augustus: noted explicitly at Sen. *Apocol.* 11.1.

11 See especially Suet. *Claud.* 26.2.

12 Suet. *Claud.* 27.1–2 and Dio 60.12.5 (both, curiously, in error on the date; cf. Tac. *Ann.* 12.25.1 and 13.15.1); on his acquisition of the name Britannicus, see above, p. 91.

13 *RIC* I (second edn) Claudius nos. 99 and 115.

14 *Senatusconsultum de Pisone patre* (Eck *et al.* [1996]), line 115. Good English translations and discussions of the text are given in Griffin (1997), Meyer (1998), Potter (1998), and Damon and Takács (1999).

15 See Kampen (1991) for an especially good discussion.

16 *Senatusconsultum de Pisone patre* (Eck *et al.* [1996]) line 141.

17 Ibid. lines 117–18.

18 See above, p. 42.

19 Lollia Paulina's jewels: Plin. *HN* 9.117.

20 See especially Dio 60.8.4–5, 60.14, 60.15.5, 60.17.5–18.4, 60.22.3–5, 60.27.4, 60.28.2–5, 60.29.6–6a; cf. Suet. *Claud.* 29.

21 Tac. *Ann.* 11.26–38 (with background at 11.12); the quotations that follow derive from these passages; and Juv. 10.329–45.

22 Suet. *Claud.* 26.2, 29.3, 36, and 39.1; Dio 60.31.1–5; and Juv. 10.329–45.

23 This is to modify slightly the central insight of Fagan (2002), especially 575–79.

24 My summary here is owed to the convenient (and fuller) résumé of Fagan (2002) 573 n. 32.

25 So, e.g., Meise (1969) 166–69, Griffin (1984) 29, and Barrett (1996) 90–94.

26 Place of birth: Tac. *Ann.* 12.27.1. Year: inferred from Suet. *Calig.* 7 and Tac. *Ann.* 2.54.1.

27 See especially Suet. *Ner.* 5–6 and Tac. *Ann.* 4.75.

28 Suet. *Calig.* 15.3; Dio 59.22.9; and cf. *RIC* I (second edn) Gaius no. 33.

29 Suet. *Calig.* 24 and 29.2 and *Ner.* 6.3; and Dio 59.22.5–9.

30 Suet. *Ner.* 6.4 and Dio 60.4.1. See above, p. 32.

31 Galba: Suet. *Galb.* 5.1. Passienus Crispus: Plin. *HN* 16.242 and Suet. *Ner.* 6.3.

32 Schol. ad Juv. 4.81.

33 See above, p. 88.

34 Mehl (1974) gives a thorough analysis of Tacitus' creation of a drama around this theme in the Claudian books of the *Annales*, with Claudius depicted less

a stock tyrant than a victim, in contrast with the portrayals of Suetonius and Dio.

35 Cf. Meise (1969) 217–21.

36 Varner (2004) 95–97 and 257–58 and Flower (2006) 182–89 provide thorough discussions.

37 Tac. *Ann.* 12.1.1.

38 Ibid. 12.1–2.

39 Ibid. 12.3.2; cf. Suet. *Claud.* 27.1, and Dio 60.5.7 and 60.31.8. See above, p. 96.

40 Tac. *Ann.* 12.4; cf. Suet. *Claud.* 29.2 and Dio 60.31.8.

41 Tac. *Ann.* 12.5.1.

42 Ibid. 12.5.2.

43 Ibid. 12.6.3.

44 See especially Gai. *Inst.* 1.62 (and cf. *Cod. Theod.* 3.12.1). Note that Dio 60.31.8 also refers to Vitellius' speech to the Senate; and cf. Suet. *Claud.* 26.3.

45 Tac. *Ann.* 12.7.

46 Ibid. 12.8.1; cf. Suet. *Claud.* 29.2. And see Sen. *Apocol.* 8.2, 10.4, and 11.5; and Dio 60.31.8.

47 Tac. *Ann.* 12.9.

48 Wiseman (2004) 252–62 is especially cogent on this and what follows, "the blood of Augustus."

49 See above, p. 9.

50 On Augustus' adoption of Gaius and Lucius, see above, p. 152.

51 Note the full text of the *Senatusconsultum de Pisone patre* (Eck *et al.* [1996]), and the references within it to the "devotion to the *princeps*" shown by the people and the equestrian order (lines 155–56); crowds evidently were on hand to express suitable outrage at Piso (lines 156–58). Rowe (2002) 41–66 and 85–101 offers an especially good discussion.

52 Cf. Smith (1963).

53 Tac. *Ann.* 12.25. See also Suet. *Claud.* 27.2, 39.2, and 43; and *Ner.* 7.1; and Dio 60.33.2². The date of adoption is known through the records of the Arval Brethren; see especially that for February 25, 59 AD (Scheid [1998] no. 27).

54 Tac. *Ann.* 12.26.1.

55 So *RIC* I (second edn) Claudius nos. 76–77 and 82–83. Some issues feature the alternative title Nero Claudius Drusus Germanicus (nos. 78–79 and 108). He is Nero Claudius Caesar Drusus Germanicus on a dynastic monument from Rome (Smallwood [1967] no. 100) and also seems to have a similar titulature in the records of the Arval Brethren (Scheid [1998] no. 22, though he is also called simply Nero Caesar, no. 20).

56 Tac. *Ann.* 12.26.1; cf. Dio 60.33.2ᵃ.

57 *RIC* I (second edn) Claudius nos. 80–83. von Kaenel (1986) 18–19 argues convincingly that the type *RIC* I (second edn) Claudius no. 75, juxtaposing on obverse and reverse portraits of Agrippina and Nero, is inauthentic.

58 *RIC* I (second edn) Claudius nos. 80–81. Wood (1999) 289–95 and Ginsburg (2006) 57–74, esp. 69–72 offer thorough discussions.

59 Portraits of Messallina: see above, n. 7. Even Claudius himself, it has been surmised, received a new portrait type around this time, named after an example in Turin, which differs from the main type mainly by the more cubic structure of the head and a squarer face. See, e.g., Boschung (1993a) 70–71 and Massner (1994) 171–73.

60 Discussions of the portraiture of Agrippina include Fittschen and Zanker (1983) 6–7, Kleiner (1992) 139–41, Boschung (1993a) 73–75, Rose (1997) 69–70, Wood (1999) 295–304, and Ginsburg (2006) 79–91.

61 These are the so-called Ancona and Milan types, discussed in the literature cited above, p. 309.

62 Discussions of the portraiture of Nero include Hiesinger (1975), Fittschen and Zanker (1985) 17–19, Kleiner (1992) 135–39, Boschung (1993a) 76–77, Rose (1997) 71–72, and Varner (2004) 46–83.

63 See Rose (1997) 121–26 and Boschung (2002) 25–35 for discussion and further references.

64 Full description and discussion in Smith (1987) 106–10. See also Rose (1997) 164–69, Wood (1999) 301, and Ginsburg (2006) 87–88.

65 Full description and discussion in Megow (1987) 200–1. See also Kleiner (1992) 151–52, Wood (1999) 306–8, and Ginsburg (2006) 91–92.

66 Plin. *Pan.* 83–84.

67 Recent discussion in Severy (2003) 180–84 (Julia the Elder) and 197–98 (Julia the Younger), rejecting in each instance theories of some grander conspiracy than the sources indicates, and arguing that adultery itself was a political crime, all the greater when carried out by a member of the August House.

68 Tiberius' refusals: Tac. *Ann.* 1.14.1–2, 5.1–3; Suet. *Tib.* 50.3, 51.2; Dio 58.2.1–6.

69 Suet. *Iul.* 74.2.

11 SIGNALING RETREAT?

Brief bibliographic essay. An excellent introduction to all aspects of the imperial finances in the early empire is given by Rathbone, *CAH* 10 (second edn) 309–23 ("The imperial finances"); see also Lo Cascio (2007) with a broader economic focus. Also recommended are the more technical studies of Lo Cascio (2000) and Duncan-Jones (1994), the latter much concerned with money supply. On taxation in particular Brunt (1990) 324–46 is a good starting place and see Hopkins (1995/96); and also see now the publication of the customs law for Asia recovered from an inscription of Ephesus, Cottier *et al.* (2009). On the sources of the emperor's wealth in particular Millar (1977) 133–201 gives a focused treatment. On expenditure and the issuing of coin (in unprecedented quantities for Mediterranean history), see Crawford (1970) and the important response in Howgego (1990). The exact organization of the various treasuries has been much disputed (see especially Brunt [1990] 134–62 and 347–53 and Millar [2004] 47–72 ["The fiscus in the first two centuries"]), but it seems clear that basically in the early empire the old treasury (*aerarium*) still functioned, but from Augustus onwards was effectively in the hands of the emperor, with the lines between his private wealth and public funds growing ever more blurred. (See further above, pp. 305–6, on the problem of fiscal jurisdiction by the emperor's own agents.) Note also the useful discussions of Nero and Vespasian by Griffin (1984) and Levick (1999b) 95–106 respectively; and for Claudius in particular see the works of Green (1930), von Kaenel (1994), and Burgers (2001), drawn on here.

Rome's relations with neighboring peoples in the Rhineland and along the Danube – a number of whom were treated essentially as "client kingdoms" – are, though patchily documented, explored by Will (1987) and Pitts (1989) respectively. The essential Augustan and Tiberian background to German conquest is discussed in Wells (1972), Gruen, *CAH* 10 (second edn) 178–88, and Wells (1998), among others; more general works, exploiting archeological evidence, include Schönberger (1969), Mócsy (1974), Alföldy (1974), King (1990), Creighton and Wilson (1999), and Todd (2004b). Tacitus' *Germania*, and the pervasive influence of the historian's views on Germany, can be accessed through Rives (1999).

Rome's relations with the neighboring empire of Parthia and the client kingdom of Armenia (where again Tacitus' perceptions have been influential) form the subject of two recent papers, Campbell (1993) and Kennedy (1996b), the latter focused on the Republican period; see also the fuller studies of Kahrstedt (1950), Ziegler (1964) with the review of Gray (1965), and Chaumont (1976). Once more, crucial to understanding Claudius' decisions is the Augustan background, including the sending of four sons (as well as grandsons) by the Parthian King Phraates (IV) to live in Rome, one of whom, Vonones, was installed on the Parthian throne with Augustus' support around AD 6 (see esp. Aug. *RG* 32–33); Vonones was expelled in AD 12, when Artabanus took the throne. On Rome's use of such *pignora* ("pledges"), *obsides* (imperfectly translated as "hostages"), and related figures see the full study of Allen (2006), where Tacitus' views are specifically discussed (224–44); and on Tacitus see Gowing (1990).

1 On Ilium's use of its past see the well-documented study of Erskine (2001).
2 Relations between Augustus, his house, and Troy: Erskine (2001) 251–52.
3 Tac. *Ann.* 4.55–6 (and note Suet. *Tib.* 52.2). On the temple see above, p. 138.
4 Tac. *Ann.* 12.58.1. See also the evidence noted below, and the comment of Callistratus preserved at *Dig.* 27.1.17.1.
5 Suet. *Claud.* 25.3.
6 Tac. *Ann.* 12.58.1.
7 Suet. *Ner.* 7.2.
8 Smallwood (1967) no. 101. For details see Rose (1997) 178–79; and cf. Boschung (2002) 112.
9 Tac. *Ann.* 12.8.2; Suet. *Ner.* 7.1 and 52; and Dio 60.32.3.
10 On Nero's adoption and its date see above, p. 311 n. 53.
11 See especially the crucial study of Rowe (2002), and also Hurlet (1997b) 79–224. On the controversy surrounding Augustus' plans for a "succession" before Tiberius, see also above, p. 264 n. 1.

12 See above, p. 91. For Claudius' display of his son: Suet. *Claud.* 27.2. Dio 60.17.9 notes public celebrations of the young Britannicus' birthday.

13 E.g., Griffin (1984) 67 writes: "By the year 51, Agrippina was putting the finishing touches to the scheme whereby her son would succeed the ageing Claudius." More nuanced is Levick (1990) 69–79, who still attributes a great deal of power to Agrippina though. See also Aveline (2004) 458–64.

14 See especially Tac. *Ann.* 12.3, 7–8, 25, 41–42 (especially important), and 65–69.

15 Tac. *Ann.* 12.7.2. But Tacitus does assign her "womanly" motives at *Ann.* 12.64.2, and note too her "gaping for gardens" at *Ann.* 12.59.1, quite reminiscent of Messallina.

16 See above, p. 214.

17 Lollia Paulina: Tac. *Ann.* 12.22; cf. Dio 60.32.4. Domitia Lepida: Tac. *Ann.* 12.64.2–5.1; cf. Suet. *Ner.* 7.1.

18 Tac. *Ann.* 12.64.3.

19 E.g., Levick (1990) 76.

20 Tac. *Ann.* 12.59.

21 Ibid. 12.22.2. See also above, p. 208. Epigraphic evidence shows the transfer of her gardens on the Esquiline into imperial hands: *CIL* 6.31284–85.

22 Seneca: Tac. *Ann.* 12.8.2. Afranius Burrus: Tac. *Ann.* 12.42.1.

23 Smallwood (1967) no. 259.

24 These memoirs are explicitly mentioned by Tac. *Ann.* 4.53.2 and almost surely referred to by Plin. *HN* 7.46; the latter passage, in conjunction with Suet. *Ner.* 6.1 and 4 and Tac. *Ann.* 11.11.2–3, suggests the possibility of denigration of Messallina. Barrett (1996) 198–99 gives a full discussion, including the (likely) date.

25 See above, 149.

26 Tac. *Ann.* 12.52.1–2. See above, pp. 43–46.

27 Tac. *Ann.* 12.41; cf. Suet. *Ner.* 7.2.

28 Cf. above, p. 32.

29 Augustus: Suet. *Aug.* 26.2 and Dio 55.9.9–10.

30 Suet. *Ner.* 7.2.

31 Gifts: Tac. *Ann.* 12.41.1 and Suet. *Ner.* 7.2. Shortage: Tac. *Ann.* 12.43 and Suet. *Claud.* 18–19. Gifts recorded from 5 and 2 BC appear to have served a similar function with Augustus' grandsons: *RG* 15.2 and 4.

32 Tac. *Ann.* 12.41.2.

33 Nero's speech: Suet. *Ner.* 7.2.

34 Consulship: Tac. *Ann.* 12.41.1 and see the record of the Arval Brethren for March 4, AD 59 (Scheid [1998] no. 27), which refers to *comitia*, indicating that the People voted for the consulship, as well as Smallwood (1967) no. 100; "Leader of the Youth": Tac. *Ann.* 12.41.1 and *RIC* I (second edn) Claudius nos. 76–79, 82–83, etc.

35 Rowe (2002) 67–84 discusses the role of the equestrian order in early imperial political culture.

36 See especially *RG* 14; and Dio 55.9.2–4 and 9–10.

37 Proconsular command: Tac. *Ann.* 12.41.1; priestly colleges: *RIC* I (second edn) Claudius nos. 76–77 and 107; and note Smallwood (1967) nos. 100 and 132.

38 *RIC* I (second edn) Claudius nos. 76–79; and cf. *RIC* I (second edn) Claudius nos. 82–83.

39 Two important discussions are Crawford (1970) and Howgego (1990) and for further perspectives see Burgers (2001) 102–3 with the other literature cited there.

40 See von Kaenel (1994) and Burgers (2001), on which the following depends.

41 Claudius is reported to have paid 300 sesterces to the *plebs frumentaria* in AD 45 (Dio 60.25.7, above, p. 92), a sum comparable to those mentioned by Augustus at *RG* 15 *inter alia*; 150,000 is an estimate of the number of recipients. See further Duncan-Jones (1994) 39–41, 78–82, and 248–50. A payment of 50 million sesterces to the army would be equivalent to what Augustus left in his will (see below, n. 62) and what Tiberius on his accession is said to have promised in his own name (Suet. *Tib.* 48.2).

42 On the imperial budget, see above, p. 37. Cost of games: Green (1930).

43 Just a few discussions of a controversial topic: Wallace-Hadrill (1986), Howgego (1995) 70–77, Ando (2000) 215–28, and Meadows and Williams (2001).

44 See above, pp. 34–36.

45 See above, p. 94.

46 Tac. *Ann.* 12.58.1, Suet. *Ner.* 7.2, and Dio 60.33.11

47 Tac. *Ann.* 12.58 and Suet. *Ner.* 7.2 (misdated); cf. Suet. *Claud.* 25.3. On Rhodes note also Dio 60.24.4, Smallwood (1967) no. 412, and an epigram of Antiphilus, likening Nero to the Sun (*Anth. Pal.* 9.178).

48 Suet. *Ner.* 7.2.

49 Ibid. and Dio 60.33.9–11.

50 Messallina: see list at *RPC* I p. 776; Agrippina: see *RPC* I p. 775.

51 Nero: see list at *RPC* I p. 777.

52 Britannicus: see list at *RPC* I p. 777 (with *RPC* 1.2314 from Ilium).

53 Corinth: *RPC* 1.1182–83. Sinope: *RPC* 1.2135.

54 Burrus: See above, p. 227. Vitellius: Tac. *Ann.* 12.42.3.

55 See above, p. 228.

56 Full description and discussion in Smith (1987) 123–25. For the identity of the figures shown: Rose (1997) 71–72.

57 Tac. *Ann.* 12.41.3.

58 See especially Tac. *Ann.* 13.15–17; Suet. *Ner.* 33.2–3 and *Tit.* 2.1; and Dio 61.7.4.

59 See below, pp. 242–45.

60 For a guide to the scholarly literature on the imperial finances, drawn on here, see brief bibliographic essay above.

61 Tac. *Ann.* 12.69.2 and Dio 61.3.1; cf. Suet. *Ner.* 10.1.

62 The legacies are listed by Suet. *Aug.* 101.2 and Tac. *Ann.* 1.8.1–2 (very slightly discrepant). A rough calculation would assume 6,000 Praetorians, 1,500 in the city cohorts, and 25 legions each with a strength of 5,500; cf. Campbell (1984) 162–63.

63 Walser (1980).

64 This is Tacitus' phrasing: *Ann.* 13.3.1. The following analysis is mostly in agreement with Levick (1990) 149–61, but see p. 240 below.

65 The following account derives chiefly from Tac. *Ann.* 12.31–40. As with the invasion of Britain (above, p. 282), scholarship is abundant, e.g., Frere (1987) 60–77 and Mattingly (2006) 101–4; Todd (2004a) and Manning (2004) together furnish a survey.

66 On the cult and temple at Camulodunum (Sen. *Apocol.* 8.3 and Tac. *Ann.* 14.31.3–4) see especially Fishwick (1991), citing earlier literature. Fasolini (2006) 180–86 summarizes the scholarly controversy surrounding the chronology, a result of scarce evidence.

67 See above, pp. 92–93.

68 Tac. *Ann.* 12.39.3.

69 See above, p. 124.

70 Tac. *Ann.* 12.40. See, e.g., Frere (1987) 66.

71 For discussions of Rome's relations with her neighbors across the Rhine and Danube see the brief bibliographic essay above.

72 Suet. *Claud.* 24.3 and *Galb.* 6.2–7.1; and Dio 60.8.7.

73 The following account derives from Tac. *Ann.* 11.18–20 and Dio 60.30.4–6. Mehl (1979) explores the relationship between the two passages. Pliny the Elder's service in Germany at this time appears to be reflected in a passage describing the Chauci (*HN* 16.1–6), discussed by Sallmann (1987). He is not likely the source here, but Corbulo himself might have been: see below, n. 89.

74 Tac. *Ann.* 11.16–17.

75 Ibid. 12.27–28 is the main account.

76 Tac. *Ann.* 12.27.1 and *Germ.* 28.5.

77 Tac. *Ann.* 12.29–30.

78 Ibid. 12.15–21 is the main account.

79 This background is set out by Dio 60.8.2 and 60.28.7 (where Mithridates of Iberia is confused for Mithridates of Bosporus). On the significance of the region's grain note Plin. *HN* 18.66.

80 Didius Gallus: in addition to Tac. *Ann.* 12.15.1, see Smallwood (1967) no. 226; also above, p. 124.

81 Perhaps sharing his geographic knowledge to win favor from the emperor among others: Plin. *HN* 6.17 includes a report he made concerning the tribe of the Thali.

82 Tac. *Ann.* 11.8–10, 12.10–14, and 12.44–51 is the main account for affairs in Parthia and Armenia, as follows. More generally on Rome's relations with Parthia, and Tacitus' treatment of them, see the brief bibliographic essay above.

83 The chief sources for this episode (Joseph. *AJ* 18.101–5; Suet. *Calig.* 14.3 and *Vit.* 2.4; and Dio 59.27.3) conflict in important details, but (1) Josephus' earlier dating of the episode may reflect hostility to Caligula while (2) Dio's epitomator seems to have compressed a series of events.

84 See especially Suet. *Calig.* 14.3.

85 In addition to Tac. *Ann.* 11.8.1, see Dio 60.8.1 and Sen. *Tranq.* 11.12.

86 Tac. *Ann.* 12.44–45.
87 Ibid. 12.45.3–4.
88 Levick (1990) 160–61.
89 See the perceptive comments on Tacitus' account in Potter (1996) and Wheeler (1996), the latter raising the possibility that the (tendentious) memoirs of Domitius Corbulo, mentioned at *Ann.* 15.16, have tinged Tacitus' own account. Note, in particular, that the honorable centurion Casperius Aelianus is later to be seen serving under Corbulo: *Ann.* 15.5.2. For Corbulo's work see also Plin. *HN* 2.180, 5.83, 6.23.
90 See, e.g., Griffin (1984) 226–27 for a discussion.

12 THE GOLDEN PREDICAMENT

Brief bibliographic essay. Like that of Caligula, the principate of Nero remains difficult to assess, because of the later manipulation of his memory (see especially Flower [2006] 197–233). Griffin (1984) provides the most coherent interpretation, using the ancient sources to chart the deterioration of Nero's rule, and then the fact of his ultimate failure to investigate "difficulties inherent in the political system of the Principate, difficulties which this vain and insecure Princeps tried but eventually failed to surmount" (185); her views are also summarized in an attractive essay, Griffin (2008). More recently, Champlin (2003a) offers an important restatement of the problems with the literary sources for Nero and tries to recover, from the sources, a penchant in Nero for pageantry which tied in firmly with Rome's culture of performance and could serve as a form of self-justification. The earlier collection of essays by Elsner and Masters (1994) also aims to deconstruct much in the later literary accounts. Rudich (1993), on the other hand, more conservatively, and chillingly, follows Tacitus in an attempt to reconstruct the psychological climate of Neronian Rome; his book is full of interesting speculation, for instance that the sluggish behavior of the alleged victim of AD 54, M. Junius Silanus, grew out of the "multiple tragedies his family suffered at the emperor's hands," which had come to affect his whole personality (3). In marked contrast, Rutledge (2001) has subsequently tried to rehabilitate informers under Nero and his predecessors, an effort that does not sufficiently acknowledge the problems with the system of trials in the Senate, in the presence of the emperor. Momigliano, it might finally be noted, in *CAH* 10 (first edn) 702–42 ("Nero") saw in Nero's principate the rise of a new, almost mystical absolutism, present from the start of the rule, and a key reason for Nero's final failure, insomuch as it cost him the respect of his commanders and soldiers; certainly, if such absolutism was Nero's answer for the problems inherent in the Augustan principate, it was not a satisfactory one. But, it must be remembered, much of this emperor's image, like any other's, was constructed in dialogue with his subjects.

1 The "official" version of Claudius' death is inferred from Tac. *Ann.* 12.69.1, Suet. *Claud.* 45 and *Ner.* 8, and Dio 60.34.3; and even more Sen. *Apocol.* 1.1,

2.2, and 6.1 (where it is implied that Claudius died of fever). See especially Pack (1943).

2 Actors: Sen. *Apocol.* 4.2 and Suet. *Claud.* 45; vows of AD 54: Tac. *Ann.* 12.68.1 and Suet. *Claud.* 45; earlier vows: see above, p. 231.

3 Plague: in addition to Sen. *Apocol.* 6, it is suggested by the death of magistrates reported at Tac. *Ann.*12.64.1, Suet. *Claud.* 46, and Dio 60.35.1.

4 Joseph. *AJ* 20.152, Tac. *Ann.* 12.69, Suet. *Ner.* 8, and Dio 61.3.1.

5 Aveline (2004) is a recent and full discussion; briefer comments in, e.g., Levick (1990) 76–78 and Hurley (2001) 236.

6 For the prodigies, see especially Tac. *Ann.* 12.64.1, Suet. *Claud.* 46, Dio 60.35.1; also below, n. 26.

7 See Plin. *HN* 2.92; and Sen. *Q Nat.* 7.17.2, 7.21.3, and 7.29.3, with discussions by Rogers (1953) and Ramsey (2006) 136–40.

8 So in particular Tac. *Ann.* 12.64.2 and Dio 60.34.1–2.

9 Suet. *Claud.* 43.

10 Tac. *Ann.* 12.65.

11 Suet. *Claud.* 44.2. But note that Joseph. *AJ* 20.148 expresses some doubt.

12 Suet. *Claud.* 44.2–3.

13 Dio 60.34.2–3.

14 Tac. *Ann.* 12.66–68 is the source for the following account.

15 Note, e.g., the epitaphs for tasters (*praegustatores*): *ILS* 1567 (taster for Claudius or Nero), 1734 (taster and chamberlain for Nero), *ILS* 1795 (taster for Augustus, later promoted to managing the Sallustian gardens), *ILS* 1796 (manager of tasters for Claudius or Nero), and *ILS* 9504 (taster for Claudius or Nero).

16 Scrib. *Comp.* 177.

17 This information is all derived from the *Compositiones* (*Ep.* 1; 60; and 163). Baldwin (1992) gives a discussion.

18 Suet. *Tib.* 58.4.

19 Buraselis (2000) 66–110 offers an extended discussion, with information on unpublished epigraphic material.

20 This is inferred from Xenophon's nomenclature, in conjunction with Tac. *Ann.* 4.14.1–2.

21 Plin. *HN* 29.7–8 and Smallwood (1967) no. 262. On the basis of the Pliny passage, Wolters (1999) argues for a veiled reference to Xenophon in Petronius' Trimalchio.

22 Smallwood (1967) nos. 262 and 289; and *CIL* 15.7544.

23 Tac. *Ann.* 12.61.

24 Tac. *Ann.* 12.61 and Smallwood (1967) no. 262.

25 Plin. *HN* 22.92.

26 Plin. *HN* 2.92 and 11.189. For other early references to the death of Claudius, note also Ps.-Sen. *Oct.* 164–65 and Mart. 1.20.

27 Aveline (2004) marshals a range of arguments in this vein, going beyond those presented here.

28 Note especially the ingenious suggestion of Grimm-Samuel (1991).

29 Hence the agnosticism of Champlin (2003a) 44–46 ("we simply do not know") is preferable to the firm conclusion of Aveline (2004) 473–74, namely that Claudius ate at dinner on October 12, AD 54 a mushroom, *amanita muscarea*, which contains a toxin, muscarine, not normally fatal but potentially so for one who suffered from dystonia (on which see above, p. 264 n. 3).

30 There was a departure from Augustan precedent in that Claudius' will was not read out, perhaps because it was being disrespected, or perhaps because the slighting of his own son Britannicus in it might have aroused negative comment (Tac. *Ann.* 12.69.3 makes the latter suggestion, Suet. *Claud.* 44.1 may imply the former). Indeed, despite the use Augustus made of wills, they were to have barely any role in the future in authorizing a successor, and the emperor's estate seems simply to have passed to the successor *de facto*, as Caligula's had to Claudius, p. 38.

31 See above, pp. 228–33.

32 Cf. Timpe (1962) 94–105.

33 Joseph. *AJ* 20.152, Tac. *Ann.* 12.69, Suet. *Ner.* 8, and Dio 61.3.1.

34 Tac. *Ann.* 12.69.2, Suet. *Ner.* 8, and Dio 61.3.1.

35 See above, p. 216. The records for the Arval Brethren for December 4, AD 57 (Scheid [1998] no. 25) show that *tribunicia potestas* must have been granted in assembly some weeks after the Senate meeting; the reason for the delay is not entirely clear.

36 Suet. *Ner.* 8. On the formula of refusal: p. 268 above.

37 Tac. *Ann.* 12.69.2.

38 Preparations for celebrations in Oxyrhynchus: Smallwood (1967) no. 47 (above, p. 135). Smallwood (1967) no. 412 (b), containing part of a letter from Nero to Rhodes from (late) AD 54, does not seem to refer to an accession embassy as such, but rather a group of envoys who had likely set out before they knew of Claudius' death but who were then instructed by the Rhodian council to sacrifice for Nero and his house to Jupiter Capitolinus.

39 Montevecchi (1970).

40 See above, p. 219, and also for the epigraphic evidence Højte (2005) 127.

41 *RIC* I (second edn) Nero nos. 1–5. On the portraiture of Nero, see above, p. 219.

42 *RIC* I (second edn) Nero nos. 6–10.

43 Tac. *Ann.* 13.2.3.

44 Smith (1987) 127–32 gives a full description and discussion.

45 See Osgood (2006a) 193–200, with further references there.

46 See, e.g., Griffin (1984) 37–38 and also now Braund (2009) 11–16.

47 Sen. *Apocol.* 4.1.23–24 and 26–32. Champlin (2003b) suggests that Apollo's song was interpolated into the *Apocolocyntosis* in the 60s, after key innovations in Nero's imperial image (including public performance). Tac. *Ann.* 13.3.3 and Suet. *Ner.* 20.1 do state that Nero had by his accession shown some interest in song.

48 Calp. Sic. 1.33–88. Defenses of a Neronian date include Townend (1980), Mayer (1980), and Wiseman (1982).

49 Suet. *Ner.* 6.1; cf. Dio 61.2.1.

50 Tac. *Ann.* 13.5 and Dio 61.3.2; and see also Suet. *Ner.* 9,

51 *AE* 1927.2. For different assessments of Agrippina's power at this time see Griffin (1984) 37–49 and Barrett (1996) 143–59.

52 See above, p. 227.

53 See above, p. 233.

54 Tac. *Ann.* 13.1.3–2; see also Dio 60.34.4–6.

55 See above, p. 214.

56 Tac. *Ann.* 13.1.

57 Dio 61.6.4–5; Plin. *HN* 7.58. Barrett (1996) 153–55 gives a full discussion.

58 See Tac. *Ann.* 15.35.

59 Hence his deliberate echo of *Ann.* 1.6 (the murder of Agrippa Postumus).

60 See especially Tac. *Ann.* 12.69.3 (implying this date) and 13.2.3. Sen. *Apocol.* 1.1 and 5.1 together also imply this date. (Relevant testimony also at Suet. *Claud.* 45 and *Ner.* 9, and Dio 60.35.2.) The procedure evidently differed from that following the deaths of Augustus and Drusilla (above, p. 140), in that no witness was required to give testimony before deification: see below, n. 62.

61 Tacitus explicitly says (*Ann.* 12.69.3) that the funeral protocol followed that of Augustus, on which see Suet. *Aug.* 100.2–4; Tac. *Ann.* 1.8; and Dio 56.34 and 42.

62 For the procedure used for the *consecratio* of Claudius see especially Fishwick (2002) and Gradel (2002) 299–304, reaching similar conclusions apparently independently of each other on the new procedure involved.

63 Agrippina's priesthood: Tac. *Ann.* 13.2.3; temple: *LTUR* s.v. *Claudius, divus, templum.* A remarkable statue of Agrippina depicted as a priestess, fashioned from the very choice material of green graywacke, whose pieces were found in the vicinity and only very recently joined, likely graced some part of the complex: see the collection of papers by Moltesen and Nielsen (2007) for the remarkable story of the statue's recovery and its possible significance; also Pavolini (2007).

64 See above, p. 237.

65 Tac. *Ann.* 13.3.1. Other references to the funeral: Suet. *Claud.* 45 and *Ner.* 9, Dio 60.35.2, and also Sen. *Apocol.* 12.1.

66 Tac. *Ann.* 13.3.1–2.

67 Ibid. 13.4 and Dio 61.3.1.

68 Tac. *Ann.* 13.4.2.

69 The overlap is noted by Griffin (1976) 130. Senecan authorship of this text has in the past been disputed, but for no compelling reason; the manuscripts attribute it to Seneca, and Dio 60.35.3 refers to a work by Seneca, called *Apocolocyntosis*, on analogy with *athanatisis* ("deification"). A very full bibliographic survey for *Apocolocyntosis* through 2000 is now available: Roncali (2008). Some more recent contributions include Gradel (2002) 325–30, Robinson (2005), O'Gorman (2005), and Osgood (2007a); Eden (1984) is an especially helpful edition.

70 This ludic title, only indicated by Dio 60.35.3, is much discussed, as it likely was at the time too; Roncali (2008) 319–22 cites and discusses some recent views.

71 See further Osgood (2007a) 345.

72 Sen. *Apocol.* 5.3.

73 Osgood (2007a).

74 Indictment: Sen. *Apocol.* 14.1 (with the numbers emended on the basis of Suet. *Claud.* 29.2).

75 *Apocol.* 10.1–11.5.

76 Claim of Claudius' blood relationship to Augustus: Sen. *Apocol.* 9.5.

77 Saturnalian *princeps*: *Apocol.* 8.2 (Seneca here is playing on the "Saturnalian king," chosen during the festival to give ludicrous orders to others as part of a game); jurist: 12.2. For one discussion of the festival and its Neronian context see Champlin (2003a) 145–77.

78 The full edition of Braund (2009) is now the starting-point for exploration of *De clementia*. Griffin (1976) 133–81 gives an essential discussion, supplemented by Griffin (2002), while Leach (1989) reads the work alongside *Apocolocyntosis*. For some other more recent considerations of Seneca's possible contributions to political ideology see, e.g., Roller (2001), various essays in De Vivo and Lo Cascio (2003), and Dowling (2006) 169–218. On Stoicism and the principate see also the classic paper by Brunt (1975).

79 For this work, see above, pp. 143–45. Its relation to *Apocolocyntosis* is fully discussed by Rudich (1987).

80 Two discussions: Nauta (1987) and Versnel (1993). Note the account in Tac. *Ann.* 13.15.2 of the Saturnalia of AD 54, according to which Nero was chosen *rex*; and cf. Dio 60.35.2–4.

Bibliography

Aicher, P. (1995) *Guide to the Aqueducts of Ancient Rome*. Wauconda, IL.

Alcock, S., D'Altroy, T., Morrison, K., and Sinopoli, C. (2001). *Empires: Perspectives from Archaeology and History*. Cambridge and New York.

Aldrete, G. (2007) *Floods of the Tiber in Ancient Rome*. Baltimore.

Aldrete, G. and Mattingly, D. (1999) "Feeding the city: the organization, operation and scale of the supply system for Rome." In *Life, Death, and Entertainment in the Roman Empire*, ed. D. Potter and D. Mattingly. Ann Arbor: 171–204.

(2000) "The feeding of imperial Rome: the mechanics of the food supply system." In *Ancient Rome: The Archaeology of the Eternal City*, ed. J. Coulston and H. Dodge. Oxford: 142–65.

Alexandridis, A. (2004) *Die Frauen des römischen Kaiserhauses: eine Untersuchung ihrer bildlichen Darstellung von Livia bis Iulia Domna*. Mainz am Rhein.

Alföldi, A. (1970) *Die Monarchische Repräsentation im römischen Kaiserreiche*. Darmstadt.

Alföldy, G. (1974) *Noricum*. Trans. A. Birley. London and Boston.

Allen, J. (2006) *Hostages and Hostage-Taking in the Roman Empire*. Cambridge and New York.

Alston, R. (1997) "Philo's *In Flaccum*: ethnicity and social space in Roman Alexandria," *G&R* 44: 165–75.

(2005) "Searching for the Romano-Egyptian family." In *The Roman Family in the Empire*, ed. M. George. Oxford and New York: 129–57.

Anderson, J. (1984) *Historical Topography of the Imperial Fora*. Brussels.

Anderson, M. (1984) "A proposal for a new reconstruction of the Altar of the Vicomagistri," *Bollettino dei musei e gallerie pontificie* 5: 33–54.

Ando, C. (2000) *Imperial Ideology and Provincial Loyalty in the Roman Empire*. Berkeley.

(2006) "The administration of the provinces." In *A Companion to the Roman Empire*, ed. D. Potter. Malden, MA and Oxford: 177–92.

Ash, R. (2007) "The wonderful world of Mucianus." In *Vita vigilia est: Essays in Honour of Barbara Levick*, ed. E. Bispham, G. Rowe, and E. Matthews. London: 1–17.

Ashby, T. (1935) *The Aqueducts of Ancient Rome*. Oxford.

Aveline, J. (2004) "The death of Claudius," *Historia* 53: 453–75.

(2006) *Tacitus' Portrayal of Claudius*. Ph.D. dissertation, University of Calgary.

Bagnall, R. and Rathbone, D. (2004) *Egypt from Alexander to the Early Christians: An Archaeological and Historical Guide*. Los Angeles.

Baldwin, B. (1992) "The career and works of Scribonius Largus," *RhM* 135: 74–82.

(1995) "Roman emperors in the elder Pliny," *Scholia* 4: 56–78.

Balland, A. (1981) *Inscriptions d'époque impériale du Létôon*. (Fouilles de Xanthos, vol. VII). Paris.

Balsdon, J. (1934) *The Emperor Gaius (Caligula)*. Oxford.

Bang, P. (2009) "Commanding and consuming the world: empire, tribute, and trade in Roman and Chinese history." In *Rome and China: Comparative Perspectives on Ancient World Empires*, ed. W. Scheidel. Oxford and New York: 100–20.

Barnes, T. (1998) "Tacitus and the *Senatus consultum de Cn. Pisone patre*," *Phoenix* 52: 125–48.

Barrett, A. (1980) "Chronological errors in Dio's account of the Claudian invasion," *Britannia* 11: 31–5.

(1990) *Caligula: The Corruption of Power*. New Haven.

(1991) "Claudius' victory arch in Rome," *Britannia* 22: 1–19.

(1996) *Agrippina: Sex, Power, and Politics in the Early Empire*. New Haven.

(2000) "The *Laus Caesaris*: its history and its place in Latin literature," *Latomus* 59: 596–606.

(2002) *Livia: First Lady of Imperial Rome*. New Haven.

(2008) "Caligula." In *Lives of the Caesars*, ed. A. Barrett. Malden, MA and Oxford: 61–83.

Bartman, E. (1999) *Portraits of Livia: Imaging the Imperial Woman in Augustan Rome*. Cambridge and New York.

Bartsch, S. (1994) *Actors in the Audience: Theatricality and Doublespeak from Nero to Hadrian*. Cambridge, MA.

Batty, R. (2000) "Mela's Phoenician geography," *JRS* 90: 70–94.

Bauckham, R. (1995) *The Book of Acts in Its Palestinian Setting*. Grand Rapids.

Bauman, R. (1982) "The résumé of legislation in Suetonius," *ZRG* 99: 81–127.

Beacham, R. (1999) *Spectacle Entertainments of Early Imperial Rome*. New Haven.

Beard, M., North, J., and Price, S. (1998) *Religions of Rome*. Cambridge.

Belayche, N. (2001) *Rome, les Césars et la ville aux deux premiers siècles de notre ère*. Rennes.

Bell, H. (1924) *Jews and Christians in Egypt*. London.

(1925) "Bibliography: Graeco-Roman Egypt. A. Paypri (1923–1924)," *JEA* 11: 84–106.

Bell, H., Nock, A., and Milne, H. (1927) "Bibliography: Graeco-Roman Egypt. A. Papyri (1924–1926)," *JEA* 13: 84–121.

Béranger, J. (1953) *Recherches sur l'aspect idéologique du principat*. Basel.

Bérard, F. *et al.* (1998) "Une nouvelle inscription claudienne à Lyon." In *Claude de Lyon, empereur romain: actes du colloque Paris-Nancy-Lyon, novembre 1992*, ed. Y. Burnand, Y. Le Bohec, and J.-P. Martin. Paris: 373–89.

Bergmann, M. (1998) *Die Strahlen der Herrscher: theomorphes Herrscherbild und politische Symbolik im Hellenismus und in der römischen Kaiserzeit*. Mainz.

Bickerman, E. (1973) "Consecratio." In *Le culte des souverains dans l'empire romain*, ed. W. den Boer. Vandoeuvres-Genève: 1–37.

Birley, A. (1981) *The Fasti of Roman Britain*. Oxford and New York.

(1997) *Hadrian: The Restless Emperor*. London and New York.

(2005) *The Roman Government of Britain*. Oxford and New York.

Biscottini, M. (1966) "L'archivio di Tryphon, tessitore di Oxyrhynchos," *Aegyptus* 46: 60–90 and 186–292.

Blake, M. (1959) *Roman Construction in Italy from Tiberius through the Flavians*. Washington, DC.

Boatwright, M. (1984) "Tacitus on Claudius and the pomerium, Annals 12.23.2–24," *CJ* 80: 36–44.

(1987) *Hadrian and the City of Rome*. Princeton.

Boschung, D. (1993a) "Die Bildnistypen der iulisch-claudischen Kaiserfamilie," *JRA* 6: 39–79.

(1993b) *Die Bildnisse des Augustus*. Berlin.

(2002) *Gens Augusta: Untersuchungen zu Aufstellung, Wirkung und Bedeutung der Statuengruppen des julisch-claudischen Kaiserhauses*. Mainz am Rhein.

Botermann, H. (1996) *Das Judenedikt des Kaisers Claudius: römischer Staat und Christiani im 1. Jahrhundert*. Stuttgart.

Boulvert, G. (1970) *Esclaves et affranchis impériaux sous Haut-Empire: rôle politique et administrative*. Naples.

(1974) *Domestique et fonctionnaire sous le Haut-Empire romain: la condition de l'affranchi et de l'esclave du prince*. Paris.

Bowersock, G. (1983) *Roman Arabia*. Cambridge, MA.

Bowman, A. (1986) *Egypt after the Pharaohs 332 BC–AD 642: From Alexander to the Arab Conquest*. London.

Box, H. (1939) *Philonis Alexandrini In Flaccum*. London and New York.

Braund, D. (1984) *Rome and the Friendly King: The Character of the Client Kingship*. London and New York.

(1985) *Augustus to Nero: A Sourcebook on Roman History, 31 BC–AD 68*. Totowa, NJ.

(1996) *Rulers of Roman Britain: Kings, Queens, Governors and Emperors from Julius Caesar to Agricola*. London and New York.

Braund, S. (2009) *Seneca: De Clementia*. Oxford and New York.

Brilliant, R. (1963) *Gesture and Rank in Roman Art: The Use of Gestures to Denote Status in Roman Sculpture and Coinage*. New Haven.

Brodersen, K. (1995) *Terra cognita: Studien zur römischen Raumerfassung*. Hildesheim and New York.

(2004) "Mapping (in) the ancient world," *JRS* 94: 183–90.

Broise, H. and Jolivet, V. (1998) "Il giardino e l'acqua: l'esempio degli *horti Luculliani*." In *Horti romani: atti del convegno internazionale: Roma, 4–6 maggio 1995*. Rome: 189–202.

Brown, P. (1988) "Arnaldo Dante Momigliano, 1908–1987," *PBA* 74: 405–42.

Bruce, F. (1990) *Acts of the Apostles: The Greek Text with Introduction and Commentary*. Grand Rapids.

Brunt, P. (1975) "Stoicism and the principate," *PBSR* 43: 6–35.
  (1977) "Lex de Imperio Vespasiani," *JRS* 67: 95–116.
  (1983) "Princeps and equites," *JRS* 73: 42–75.
  (1990) *Roman Imperial Themes*. Oxford and New York.
Bruun, C. (1991) *The Water Supply of Ancient Rome: A Study of Roman Imperial Administration*. Helsinki.
Buraselis, K. (2000) *Kos between Hellenism and Rome: Studies on the Political, Institutional, and Social History of Kos from ca. the Middle Second Century* BC *until Late Antiquity*. Philadelphia.
Burgers, P. (2001) "Coinage and state expenditure: the reign of Claudius AD 41–54," *Historia* 50: 96–114.
Burnand, Y. *et al.* (1998) *Claude de Lyon, empereur romain: actes du colloque Paris-Nancy-Lyon, novembre 1992*. Paris.
Burton, G. (1976) "The issuing of mandata to proconsuls and a new inscription from Cos." *ZPE* 21: 63–8.
  (1993) "Provincial procurators and the public provinces," *Chiron* 23: 13–28.
  (1998) "Was there a long-term trend to centralisation of authority in the Roman empire?" *RPh* 72: 7–24.
  (2000) "The resolution of territorial disputes in the provinces of the Roman empire," *Chiron* 30: 195–215.
  (2002) "The Roman imperial state (AD 14–235): evidence and reality," *Chiron* 32: 249–80.
  (2004) "The Roman imperial state, provincial governors and the public finances of provincial cities," *Historia* 53: 311–42.
Cadbury, H. (1955) *The Book of Acts in History*. New York.
Camodeca, G. (1999) *Tabulae pompeianae Sulpiciorum (TPSulp.): edizione critica dell'archivio puteolano dei Sulpicii*. Rome.
Campanelli, A. (2001) *Il tesoro del lago: l'archeologia del Fucino e la collezione Torlonia*. Pescara.
Campbell, J. (1984) *The Emperor and the Roman Army, 31 BC–AD 235*. Oxford and New York.
  (1993) "War and diplomacy: Rome and Parthia, 31 BC–AD 235." In *War and Society in the Roman World*, ed. J. Rich and G. Shipley. London and New York: 213–40.
Cancik, H. and Hitzl, K. (2003) *Die Praxis der Herrscherverehrung in Rom und seinen Provinzen*. Tübingen.
Capdetrey, L. and Nélis-Clement, J. (2006) *La circulation de l'information dans les états antiques*. Pessac.
Cary, E. (1914–27) *Dio's Roman History* (Loeb Classical Library). Cambridge, MA and London.
Cavalieri Manasse, G. (1992) "L'imperatore Claudio a Verona," *Epigraphica* 54: 9–41.
Champlin, E. (2003a) *Nero*. Cambridge, MA.
  (2003b) "Nero, Apollo, and the poets," *Phoenix* 57: 276–83.

Chantraine, H. (1967) *Freigelassene und Sklaven im Dienst der römischen Kaiser. Studien zu ihrer Nomenklatur.* Wiesbaden.

Charlesworth, M. (1939) "The refusal of divine honours: an Augustan formula," *PBSR* 15: 1–10.

Chastagnol, A. (1992) *Le Sénat romain à l'époque impériale: recherches sur la composition de l'Assemblée et le statut de ses membres.* Paris.

Chaumont, M.-L. (1976) "L'Arménie entre Rome et l'Iran. I. De l'avènement d'Auguste à l'avènement de Dioclétien," *ANRW* 2.9.1: 71–194.

Cherry, D. (1998). *Frontier and Society in Roman North Africa.* Oxford and New York.

Christol, M. (1994) "Pline l'Ancien et la *formula* de la province narbonnaise." In *La mémoire perdue: à la recherche des archives oubliées, publiques et privées, de la Rome antique.* Paris: 45–63.

Christol, M., Drew-Bear, T., and Taslialan, M. (2001) "L'empereur Claude, le chevalier C. Caristanius Fronto Caesianus Iullus et le culte impérial à Antioche de Pisidie," *Tyche* 16: 1–20.

Cima, M. and La Rocca, E. (1998) *Horti romani: atti del convegno internazionale: Roma, 4–6 maggio 1995.* Rome.

Claridge, A. (1998) *Rome: An Oxford Archaeological Guide.* Oxford and New York.

Clauss, M. (1999) *Kaiser und Gott: Herrscherkult im römischen Reich.* Stuttgart.

Clinton, K. (2003) "Maroneia and Rome," *Chiron* 33: 379–417.

(2004) "Two decrees of Maroneia from Samothrace," *Chiron* 34: 145–48.

Coarelli, F. (1977) "Public building in Rome between the second Punic war and Sulla," *PBSR* 45: 1–23.

(2007) *Rome and Environs: An Archaeological Guide.* Trans. J. Clauss and D. Harmon. Berkeley and London.

Coates-Stephens, R. (2004) *Porta Maggiore: Monument and Landscape: Archaeology and Topography of the Southern Esquiline from the Late Republican Period to the Present.* Rome.

Cogitore, I. (1992) "Séries de dédicaces italiennes à la dynastie julio-claudienne," *MEFRA* 104: 817–70.

(2002) *La légitimité dynastique d'Auguste à Néron à l'épreuve des conspirations.* Rome.

Coleman, K. (1990) "Fatal charades: Roman executions staged as mythological enactments," *JRS* 80: 44–73.

(1993) "Launching into history: aquatic displays in the early empire," *JRS* 83: 48–74.

Cooley, A. (2009) *Res Gestae Divi Augusti: Text, Translation, and Commentary.* Cambridge and New York.

Corbier, M. (2006) *Donner à voir, donner à lire: mémoire et communication dans la Rome ancienne.* Paris.

Cordischi, L. (1985) "Sul problema dell'Ara pietatis Augustae e dei rilievi ad essa attribuiti." *ArchClass* 37: 238–65.

Cornell, T. (1993) "The end of Roman imperial expansion." In *War and Society in the Roman World*, ed. J. Rich and G. Shipley. London and New York: 139–70.

Cottier, M., Crawford, M., Crowther, C., Ferrary, J.-L., Levick, B., Salomies, O., and Wörrle, M. (2009) *The Customs Law of Asia*. Oxford and New York.

Coulston, J. and Dodge, H. (eds.) (2000) *Ancient Rome: The Archaeology of the Eternal City*. Oxford.

Crawford, M. (1970) "Money and exchange in the Roman world," *JRS* 60: 40–48.

(1996) *Roman Statutes*. London.

Creighton, J. (2000) *Coins and Power in Late Iron Age Britain*. Cambridge and New York.

(2006) *Britannia: The Creation of a Roman Province*. London and New York.

Creighton, J. and Wilson, R. (1999) *Roman Germany: Studies in Cultural Interaction*. Portsmouth, RI.

Crook, J. (1955) *Consilium Principis: Imperial Councils and Counsellors from Augustus to Diocletian*. Cambridge.

(1967) *The Law and Life of Rome*. Ithaca, NY.

Curran, J. (2005) "'The long hesitation': some reflections on the Romans in Judaea," *G&R* 52: 70–98.

Damon, C. and Takács, S. (1999) "The Senatus Consultum de Cn. Pisone patre: text, translation, discussion," *AJPh* 120.

Danziger, D. and Purcell, N. (2005) *Hadrian's Empire: When Rome Ruled the World*. London.

Darwall-Smith, R. (1996) *Emperors and Architecture: A Study of Flavian Rome*. Brussels.

Davies, P. (2000) *Death and the Emperor: Roman Imperial Funerary Monuments, from Augustus to Marcus Aurelius*. Cambridge and New York.

de Blois, L. (2001) *Administration, Prosopography and Appointment Policies in the Roman Empire*. Amsterdam.

de Blois, L., Funke, P., and Hahn, J. (eds.) (2006) *The Impact of Imperial Rome on Religions, Ritual, and Religious Life in the Roman Empire*. Leiden and Boston.

de Blois, L. and Rich, J. (2002) *The Transformation of Economic Life under the Roman Empire*. Amsterdam.

De Caprariis, F. (1993) "Un monumento dinastico tiberiano nel Campo Marzio settentrionale," *BCAR* 95: 93–114.

de Ligt, L., Hemelrijk, E., and Singor, H. (eds.) (2004) *Roman Rule and Civic Life: Local and Regional Perspectives*. Amsterdam.

De Maria, S. (1988) *Gli archi onorari di Roma e dell'Italia romana*. Rome.

De Vivo, A. (1980) *Tacito e Claudio: storia e codificazione letteraria*. Naples.

De Vivo, A. and Lo Cascio, E. (2003) *Seneca, uomo politico, e l'età di Claudio e di Nerone: atti del convegno internazionale, Capri, 25–27 marzo 1999*. Bari.

Demougin, S. (1988) *L'ordre équestre sous les Julio-Claudiens*. Rome.

(1992) *Prosographie des chevaliers romains julio-claudiens (43 av. J.-C.–70 ap. J.-C.)*. Rome.

(1994) "Claude et la société de son temps." In *Die Regierungszeit des Kaisers Claudius (41–54 n. Chr.): Umbruch oder Episode?* ed. V. Strocka. Mainz: 11–22.

Demougin, S., Devijver, H., and Raepsaet-Charlier, M.-Th. (eds.) (1999) *L'ordre équestre: histoire d'une aristocratie: IIe siècle av. J.-C.–IIIe siècle ap. J.-C.: actes du colloque international (Bruxelles-Leuven, 5–7 octobre 1995).* Rome.

Demougin, S., Loriot, X., Cosme, P., and Lefebvre, S. (eds.) (2006) *H.-G. Pflaum, un historien du XXe siècle: actes du colloque international, Paris les 21, 22 et 23 octobre 2004.* Geneva.

Dignas, B. (2002) *Economy of the Sacred in Hellenistic and Roman Asia Minor.* Oxford and New York.

Dillery, J. (2003) "Putting him back together again: Apion historian, Apion grammatikos," *CPh* 98: 383–90.

Dillon, S. and Welch, K. (2006) *Representations of War in Ancient Rome.* Cambridge and New York.

Dixon, S. (2001) *Reading Roman Women: Sources, Genres, and Real Life.* London.

Dmitriev, S. (2003) "Claudius' grant of Cilicia to Polemo," *CQ* 53: 286–91.

Dodge, H. (2000) "'Greater than the Pyramids': the water supply of ancient Rome." In *Ancient Rome: The Archaeology of the Eternal City,* ed. J. Coulston and H. Dodge. Oxford: 166–209.

Döpp, S. (1994) "Claudius in Senecas Trostschrift an Polybius." In *Die Regierungszeit des Kaisers Claudius (41–54 n. Chr.): Umbruch oder Episode?,* ed. V. Strocka. Mainz: 295–306.

Dörner, F. (1935) *Der Erlass des Statthalters von Asia, Paullus Fabius Persicus.* Greifswald.

Dowling, M. (2006) *Clemency and Cruelty in the Roman World.* Ann Arbor.

Dunant, C. and Pouilloux, J. (1958) *Recherches sur l'histoire et les cultes de Thasos, II. De 196 avant J.-C. jusqu'à la fin de l'antiquité.* Paris.

Duncan-Jones, R. (1982) *The Economy of the Roman Empire: Quantitative Studies.* Second edn. Cambridge and New York.

(1994) *Money and Government in the Roman Empire.* Cambridge and New York.

Durry, M. (1938) *Les cohortes prétoriennes.* Paris.

Dušanic, S. (1982). "The issue of military diplomata under Claudius and Nero," *ZPE* 47: 149–71.

(1986) "Pre-Severan diplomata and the problem of 'special grants.'" In *Heer und Integrationspolitik. Die römischen Militärdiplome als historische Quelle,* ed. W. Eck and H. Wolff. Cologne: 190–240.

Eck, W. (1984) "Senatorial self-representation: developments in the Augustan period." In *Caesar Augustus: Seven Aspects,* ed. F. Millar and E. Segal. Oxford and New York: 129–67.

(1993) *Agrippina, die Stadtgründerin Kölns: eine Frau in der frühkaiserzeitlichen Politik.* Cologne.

(1994) "Die Bedeutung der claudischen Regierungszeit für die administrative Entwicklung des römischen Reiches." In *Die Regierungszeit des Kaisers*

Claudius (41–54 n. Chr.): Umbruch oder Episode? ed. V. Strocka. Mainz: 23–34.

(2009) "Diplomacy as part of the administrative process in the Roman empire." In *Diplomats and Diplomacy in the Roman World*, ed. C. Eilers. Leiden and Boston: 193–207.

Eck, W., Caballos, A., and Fernández, F. (1996) *Das Senatus consultum de Cn. Pisone patre*. Munich.

Eden, P. (1984) *Seneca: Apocolocyntosis*. Cambridge and New York.

Edmondson, J. (1992) *Dio: The Julio-Claudians: Selections from Books 58–63 of the Roman History of Cassius Dio*. London.

Edwards, C. (1993) *Politics of Immorality in Ancient Rome*. Cambridge and New York.

Edwards, C. and Woolf, G. (2003) *Rome the Cosmopolis*. Cambridge and New York.

Ehrenberg, V. and Jones, A. (1955) *Documents Illustrating the Reigns of Augustus and Tiberius*. Second edn. Oxford.

Ehrhardt, C. (1978) "Messalina and the succession to Claudius," *Antichthon* 12: 51–78.

Eilers, C. (2009) *Diplomats and Diplomacy in the Roman World*. Leiden and Boston.

Elsner, J. (1994) "Constructing decadence: the representation of Nero as imperial builder." In *Reflections of Nero: Culture, History, and Representation*, ed. J. Elsner and J. Masters. Cambridge: 112–27.

(1996) "Inventing imperium: texts and the propaganda of monuments in Augustan Rome." In *Art and Text in Roman Culture*, ed. J. Elsner. Cambridge: 32–53.

(1998) *Imperial Rome and Christian Triumph: The Art of the Roman Empire AD 100–450*. Oxford and New York.

Elsner, J. and Masters, J. (1994) *Reflections of Nero: Culture, History, and Representation*. London.

Erim, K. (1986) *Aphrodisias: City of Venus Aphrodite*. London.

Erskine, A. (2001) *Troy between Greece and Rome: Local Tradition and Imperial Power*. Oxford and New York.

Evans, H. (1994) *Water Distribution in Ancient Rome: The Evidence of Frontinus*. Ann Arbor.

Evans, R. (1999) "Ethnography's freak show: the grotesques at the edges of the Roman earth," *Ramus* 28: 54–73.

(2005) "Geography without people: mapping in Pliny Historia naturalis Books 3–6," *Ramus* 34: 47–74.

Fabia, P. (1929) *La table claudienne de Lyon*. Lyon.

Fagan, G. (2002) "Messalina's folly," *CQ* 52: 566–79.

Fasolini, D. (2006) *Aggiornamento bibliografico ed epigrafico ragionato sull'imperatore Claudio*. Milan.

Favro, D. (1996) *The Urban Image of Augustan Rome*. New York.

(2005) "Making Rome a world city." In *The Cambridge Companion to the Age of Augustus*, ed. K. Galinsky. Cambridge and New York: 234–63.

Fears, J. (1981) "The cult of virtues and Roman imperial ideology," *ANRW* 2.17.2: 827–948.

Feeney, D. (1998) *Literature and Religion at Rome: Cultures, Contexts, and Beliefs.* Cambridge.

Fishwick, D. (1971) "The annexation of Mauretania," *Historia* 20: 467–87.

(1987–2004) *The Imperial Cult in the Latin West: Studies in the Ruler Cult of the Western Provinces of the Roman Empire.* Leiden and New York.

(1991) "Seneca and the Temple of Divus Claudius," *Britannia* 22: 137–41.

(2002) "The deification of Claudius," *CQ* 52: 341–49.

Fittschen, K. (1977) *Katalog der antiken Skulpturen in Schloss Erbach.* Berlin.

Fittschen, K. and Zanker, P. (1983) *Katalog der römischen Porträts in den Capitolinischen Museen und den anderen kommunalen Sammlungen der Stadt Rom. Bd. 3. Kaiserinnen- und Prinzessinnenbildnisse Frauenporträts.* Mainz am Rhein.

(1985) *Katalog der römischen Porträts in den Capitolinischen Museen und den anderen kommunalen Sammlungen der Stadt Rom. Bd. 1. Kaiser- und Prinzenbildnisse.* Mainz am Rhein.

Flaig, E. (1992) *Den Kaiser herausfordern: die Usurpation im Römischen Reich.* Frankfurt and New York.

Flory, M. (1996) "Dynastic ideology, the domus Augusta, and imperial women: a lost statuary group in the Circus Flaminius," *TAPhA* 126: 287–306.

Flower, H. (2006) *The Art of Forgetting: Disgrace and Oblivion in Roman Political Culture.* Chapel Hill.

Focardi, G. (1999) "Claudio e Trimalchione: due personaggi a confronto?" *InvLuc* 21: 149–66.

Frank, T. (1933–40) *An Economic Survey of Ancient Rome.* Baltimore.

Fraser, P. (1972) *Ptolemaic Alexandria.* Oxford.

French, D. (1999/2000) "Inscriptions of southern Lycia," *Adalya* 4: 173–80.

Frere, S. (1987) *Britannia: A History of Roman Britain.* London and New York.

Frere, S. and Fulford, M. (2001) "The Roman invasion of AD 43," *Britannia* 32: 45–55.

Frézouls, E. (1981) "A propos de la tabula Clesiana," *Ktèma* 6: 239–52.

Friedländer, L. (1908–13) *Roman Life and Manners under the Early Empire.* London and New York.

Friesen, S. (2001) *Imperial Cults and the Apocalypse of John: Reading Revelation in the Ruins.* Oxford and New York.

Furneaux, H. (1896–1907) *The Annals of Tacitus.* Second edn. Oxford.

Gagos, T., Koenen, L., and McNellen, B. (1992) "A first century archive from Oxyrhynchos: Oxyrhynchite loan contracts and Egyptian marriage." In *Life in a Multi-cultural Society: Egypt from Kambyses to Constantine and Beyond,* ed. J. Johnson. Chicago: 181–205.

Gagos, T. and Potter, D. (2006) "Documents." In *A Companion to the Roman Empire.* Malden, MA and Oxford.

Galimberti, A. (1996) "La spedizione in Britannia del 43 d. C. e il problema delle Orcadi," *Aevum* 70: 69–74.

(1999) "La rivolta del 42 e l'opposizione senatoria sotto Claudio." In *Fazioni e congiure nel mondo antico*, ed. M. Sordi. Milan: 205–15.

Galinsky, K. (1996) *Augustan Culture: An Interpretive Introduction*. Princeton.

Gambetti, S. (2003) *The Alexandrian Riots of 38 CE and the Persecution of the Jews: A Historical Assessment*. Ph.D. dissertation, University of California, Berkeley.

Ganzert, J. (1996) *Der Mars-Ultor-Tempel auf dem Augustusforum in Rom*. Mainz am Rhein.

Gapp, K. (1935) "The universal famine under Claudius," *HThR* 28: 258–65.

Gardner, R. (1913) "The Via Claudia Nova," *JRS* 3: 205–32.

(1920) "The Via Claudia Valeria," *PBSR* 9: 75–106.

(1941) Review of *La Via Claudia Augusta Altinate*. In *JRS* 31: 209–13.

Garnsey, P. (1966) "The *Lex Iulia* and appeal under the empire," *JRS* 56: 167–89.

(1976) "Urban property investment." In *Studies in Roman Property*, ed. M. Finley. Cambridge.

(1983) "Grain for Rome." In *Trade and Famine in Classical Antiquity*, ed. P. Garnsey and C. Whittaker. Cambridge: 118–30.

(1988) *Famine and Food Supply in the Graeco-Roman World: Responses to Risk and Crisis*. Cambridge and New York.

Garnsey, P. and Saller, R. (1987) *The Roman Empire: Economy, Society and Culture*. London.

Gascou, J. (1981) "Tendances de la politique municipale de Claude en Maurétanie," *Ktèma* 6: 227–38.

Geiger, J. (2008) *The First Hall of Fame: A Study of the Statues in the Forum Augustum*. Leiden and Boston.

Gergel, R. (1987) Review of T. Pekáry, *Das römische Kaiserbildnis in Staat, Kult und Gesellschaft*. *AJA* 91: 344–46.

Gill, D. and Gempf, C. (1994) *The Book of Acts in Its Graeco-Roman Setting*. Grand Rapids.

Ginsburg, J. (2006) *Representing Agrippina: Constructions of Female Power in the Early Roman Empire*. Oxford and New York.

Gold, B. (1993) "'But Ariadne was never there in the first place': finding the female in Roman poetry." In *Feminist Theory and the Classics*, ed. N. Rabinowitz and A. Richlin. London: 75–101.

Goodchild, R. (1950) "Roman milestones in Cyrenaica," *PBSR* 18: 83–91.

Goodman, M. (1997). *The Roman World: 44 BC–AD 180*. London and New York.

(2007). *Rome and Jerusalem: The Clash of Ancient Civilizations*. New York.

Gordon, A. (1952) *Quintus Veranius, Consul AD 49: A Study Based upon His Recently Identified Sepulchral Inscription*. Berkeley.

Gordon, P. (1996) *Epicurus in Lycia: The Second-century World of Diogenes of Oenoanda*. Ann Arbor.

Gowing, A. (1990) "Tacitus and the client kings," *TAPhA* 120: 315–31.

Gradel, I. (2002) *Emperor Worship and Roman Religion*. Oxford.

Graves, R. (1934a) *I, Claudius*. London.

(1934b) *Claudius the God and His Wife Messalina*. London.

Gray, E. (1965) Review of K.-H. Ziegler, *Die Beziehungen Zwischen rom und dem Partherreich: Ein Beitrag zur Geschichte des Völkerrechts*, *JRS* 55: 269–71.

Green, W. (1930) "Appropriations for the Games at Rome in 51 AD," *AJPh* 51: 249–50.

Gregory, A. (1994) "'Powerful images': responses to portraits and the political uses of images in Rome," *JRA* 7: 80–99.

Griffin, M. (1976) *Seneca: A Philosopher in Politics*. Oxford and New York.

(1982) "The Lyons tablet and Tacitean hindsight," *CQ* 32: 404–18.

(1984) *Nero: The End of a Dynasty*. London and New Haven.

(1990) "Claudius in Tacitus," *CQ* 40: 482–501.

(1994) "Claudius in the judgment of the next half-century." In *Die Regierungszeit des Kaisers Claudius (41–54 n. Chr.): Umbruch oder Episode?* ed. V. Strocka. Mainz: 307–16.

(1997) "The Senate's story," *JRS* 87: 249–63.

(2002) "Political thought in the age of Nero." In *Neronia VI: Rome à l'époque néronienne*, ed. J.-M. Croisille and Y. Perrin. Brussels: 325–37.

(2005) "'Lifting the mask': Syme on fictional history." In *History and Fiction: Six Essays Celebrating the Centenary of Sir Ronald Syme (1903–89)*, ed. R. Tomlin. London: 16–39.

(2008) "Nero." In *Lives of the Caesars*, ed. A. Barrett. Malden, MA and Oxford: 107–30.

Grimm-Samuel, V. (1991) "On the mushroom that deified the emperor Claudius," *CQ* 41: 178–82.

Gros, P. (1976) *Aurea templa: recherches sur l'architecture religieuse de Rome à l'époque d'Auguste*. Rome.

Gruen, E. (2002) *Diaspora: Jews amidst Greeks and Romans*. Cambridge, MA.

(2005) "Augustus and the making of the principate." In *The Cambridge Companion to the Age of Augustus*, ed. K. Galinsky. Cambridge and New York: 33–51.

Habicht, C. (2001/2) "Zum Gesandtschaftsverkehr griechischer Gemeinden mit römischen Instanzen während der Kaiserzeit," *Archaiognosia* 11: 11–28.

Haenchen, E. (1971) *The Acts of the Apostles: A Commentary*. Oxford.

Haensch, R. (1992) "Das Statthalterarchiv," *ZRG* 109: 209–317.

(1994) "Die Bearbeitungsweisen von Petitionen in der Provinz Aegyptus," *ZPE* 100: 487–546.

(2009) *Selbstdarstellung und Kommunikation: die Veröffentlichung staatlicher Urkunden auf Stein und Bronze in der römischen Welt*. Munich.

Hahn, U. (1994) *Die Frauen des römischen Kaiserhauses und ihre Ehrungen im griechischen Osten anhand epigraphischer und numismatischer Zeugnisse von Livia bis Sabina*. Saarbrücken.

Hallett, C. (2005) *The Roman Nude: Heroic Portrait Statuary 200 BC–AD 300*. Oxford and New York.

Hallett, J. (1989) "Women as *same* and *other* in classical Roman elite," *Helios* 16: 59–78.

Hammond, M. (1959) *The Antonine Monarchy*. Rome.

Hannestad, N. (1986) *Roman Art and Imperial Policy*. Højbjerg and Århus.

Hanson, A. (1979) "Documents from Philadelphia drawn from the census register." In *Actes du xv congrès international de papyrologie*, ed. J. Bingen and G. Nachtergael. Brussels: 2.60–74.

(1981) "Evidence for a reduction in laographia at Philadelphia in Gaius' second year." In *Proceedings of the XVIth International Congress of Papyrology*, ed. R. Bagnall *et al.* Chico: 345–55.

(1984) "Caligulan month-names at Philadelphia and related matters." In *Atti del xvii congresso internazionale di papirologia (Napoli, 19–26 maggio 1983)*. Naples: 1107–18.

(1988) "The keeping of records at Philadelphia in the Julio-Claudian period and the 'economic crisis under Nero.'" In *Proceedings of the XVIIIth International Congress of Papyrology, Athens 25–31 May 1986*, Athens: 2.261–77.

(1989) "Village officials at Philadelphia: a model of Romanization in the Julio-Claudian period." In *Egitto e storia antica dall'ellenismo all'età araba: bilancio di un confronto*. Bologna: 429–40.

(1990) "*P.Princeton* I 13: text and context revisited." In *Miscellanea papyrologica in occasione del bicentenario dell'edizione della Charta Borgiana I*, ed. M. Capasso *et al.* Florence: 259–83.

(1992) "Egyptians, Greeks, Romans, *Arabes*, and *Ioudaioi* in the first century A.D. tax archive from Philadelphia: P.Mich. inv. 880 recto and *P.Princ.* III 152 revisited." In *Life in a Multi-cultural Society: Egypt from Kambyses to Constantine and Beyond*, ed. J. Johnson. Chicago: 133–45.

(1994) "Topographical arrangement of tax documents in the Philadelphia tax archive." In *Proceedings of the 20th International Congress of Papyrologists: Copenhagen, 23–29 August, 1992*. Copenhagen: 210–18.

(2001) "Sworn declaration to agents from the centurion Cattius Catullus: *P.Col.* inv. 90." In *Essays and Texts in Honor of J. David Thomas*, ed. T. Gagos and R. Bagnall. Oakville, CT: 91–97.

(2002) "Papyrology: a discipline in flux." In *Disciplining Classics*, ed. G. Most. Göttingen, 2002.

(2007) "Sworn declarations of removal from Herakleides Division, Arsinoite Nome." In *Akten des 23. Internationalen Papyrologenkongresses Wien, 22.-28. Juli 2001*, ed. B. Palme. Vienna: 267–71.

Harker, A. (2008) *Loyalty and Dissidence in Roman Egypt: The Case of the Acta Alexandrinorum*. Cambridge and New York.

Harris, W. (2003) "Roman opinions about the truthfulness of dreams," *JRS* 93: 18–34.

Harris, W. and Ruffini, G. (2004) *Ancient Alexandria between Egypt and Greece*. Leiden and Boston.

Haselberger, L. (2002) *Mapping Augustan Rome*. Portsmouth, RI.

(2007) *Urbem adornare: die Stadt Rom und ihre Gestaltumwandlung unter Augustus = Rome's Urban Metamorphosis under Augustus*. Portsmouth, RI.

Hekster, O. (2002) *Commodus: An Emperor at the Crossroads*. Amsterdam.

Hekster, O. and Fowler, R. (2005) *Imaginary Kings: Royal Images in the Ancient Near East, Greece and Rome*. Stuttgart.

Hemer, C. (1989) *The Book of Acts in the Setting of Hellenistic History*. Tübingen.

Henderson, J. (1989) "Satire writes 'Woman': *Gendersong*," *PCPhS* 35: 50–80.

Hiesinger, U. (1975) "The portraits of Nero," *AJA* 79: 113–24.

Hobson, D. (1984) "The role of women in the economic life of Roman Egypt: a case study from 1st c. Tebtunis," *EMC* 28: 373–90.

Hodge, A. (1992) *Roman Aqueducts and Water Supply*. London.

Højte, J. (2003) "The statue bases of Claudius: a reassessment of *The Portraiture of Claudius* by Meriwether Stuart." In *The Cauldron of Ariantas: Studies Presented to A. N. Sceglov on the Occasion of His 70th Birthday*, ed. P. Bilde. Århus: 365–88.

(2005) *Roman Imperial Statue Bases: From Augustus to Commodus*. Århus.

Hölscher, T. (2003) *Language of Images in Roman Art: Art as a Semantic System in the Roman World*. Cambridge and New York.

Holzberg, N. (2004) "Impersonating the banished philosopher: Pseudo-Seneca's 'Liber epigrammaton'," *HSPh* 102: 423–44.

Hopkins, K. (1965) "Elite mobility in the Roman Empire," *P&P* 32: 12–26.

(1978a) "Rules of evidence," *JRS* 68: 178–86.

(1978b) *Conquerors and Slaves*. Cambridge and New York.

(1995/96) "Rome, taxes, rents and trade," *Kodai* 6/7: 41–75.

(1998) "Christian number and its implications," *JECS* 6: 185–226.

(2005) "How to be a Roman emperor: an autobiography." In *History and Fiction: Six Essays Celebrating the Centenary of Sir Ronald Syme (1903–89)*, ed. R. Tomlin. London: 72–85.

Horster, M. (2001) *Bauinschriften römischer Kaiser: Untersuchungen zu Inschriftenpraxis und Bautätigkeit in Städten des westlichen Imperium Romanum in der Zeit des Prinzipats*. Stuttgart.

Howgego, C. (1990) "The supply and use of money in the Roman world 200 BC to AD 300," *JRS* 82: 1–31.

(1995) *Ancient History from Coins*. London and New York.

Hoyos, D. (1979) "Pliny the elder's title Baetican towns: obscurities, errors and origins," *Historia* 28: 439–71.

Hurlet, F. (1997a) "La *Domus Augusta* et Claude à son avènement: la place du prince claudien dans l'image urbaine et les stratégies matrimoniales," *REA* 99: 535–59.

(1997b) *Les collègues du prince sous Auguste et Tibère: de la légalité républicaine à la légitimité dynastique*. Rome.

(2000) "Pouvoir des images, images du pouvoir impérial: la province d'Afrique aux deux premiers siècles de notre ère," *MEFRA* 112: 297–364.

Hurley, D. (2001) *Suetonius: Divus Claudius*. Cambridge and New York.

Husselman, E. (1970) "Procedures of the record office of Tebtunis in the first century AD." In *Proceedings of the Twelfth International Congress of Papyrology*, ed. D. Samuel. Toronto and Amsterdam: 223–38.

Isaac, B. (1990) *The Limits of Empire: The Roman Army in the East.* Oxford and New York.

Işik, F., Işkan, H., and Çevik, N. (2001) *Miliarium Lyciae: Das Wegweisermonument von Patara.* Lykia 4.

Jacobson, H. (2001) "Apion, the Jews, and human sacrifice," *CQ* 51: 318–19.

Janni, P. (1984) *La mappa e il periplo. Cartografia antica e spazio odologico.* Rome.

Jones, A. (1953) "I appeal unto Caesar." In *Studies Presented to D. M. Robinson on his Seventieth Birthday,* II, ed. G. Mylonas and D. Raymond. St. Louis, MO: 918–30.

Jones, B. (1992) *The Emperor Domitian.* London and New York.

Jones, C. (2001) "The Claudian monument at Patara," *ZPE* 137: 161–68.

(2007) "Three new letters of the emperor Hadrian," *ZPE* 161: 145–56.

Jones, D. (2006) *The Bankers of Puteoli: Finance, Trade and Industry in the Roman World.* Stroud.

Joshel, S. (1997) "Female desire and the discourse of empire: Tacitus' Messalina." In *Roman Sexualities,* ed. J. Hallett and M. Skinner. Princeton: 221–54.

(2001) "*I, Claudius*: projection and imperial soap opera." In *Imperial Projections: Ancient Rome in Modern Popular Culture,* ed. S. Joshel, M. Malamud, and D.T. McGuire, Baltimore: 119–61.

Judge, E. (1985) *On Judging the Merits of Augustus.* Berkeley.

Jung, H. (1972) "Die Thronerhebung des Claudius," *Chiron* 2: 367–86.

Kagan, K. (2006) "Redefining Roman grand strategy," *The Journal of Military History* 70: 333–62.

Kahrstedt, U. (1950) *Artabanos III. und seine Erben.* Bern.

Kampen, N. (1991) "Between public and private: women as historical subjects in Roman art." In *Women's History and Ancient History,* ed. S. Pomeroy. Chapel Hill: 218–48.

Kantiréa, M. (2001) "Remarques sur le culte de la *domus Augusta* en Achaïe de la mort d'Auguste à Néron." In *The Greek East in the Roman Context: Proceedings of a Colloquium Organised by the Finnish Institute at Athens, May 21 and 22, 1999,* ed O. Salomies. Helskini: 51–60.

Kasher, A. (1985) *The Jews in Hellenistic and Roman Egypt: The Struggle for Equal Rights.* Tübingen.

Keay, S., Millett, M., Pavoli, L. and Strutt, K. (2005) *Portus: An Archaeological Survey of the Port of Imperial Rome.* London.

Kennedy, D. (1996a) *The Roman Army in the East.* Ann Arbor.

(1996b) "Parthia and Rome: eastern perspectives." In *The Roman Army in the East,* ed. D. Kennedy. Ann Arbor: 67–90.

Kent, J. (1965) *Corinth: Inscriptions, 1926–50.* Princeton.

Keppie, L. (1971) "Legio VIII Augusta and the Claudian invasion," *Britannia* 2: 149–55.

(1996) "The praetorian guard before Sejanus," *Athenaeum* 84: 101–24.

King, A. (1990) *Roman Gaul and Germany.* London.

Kleiner, D. (1992) *Roman Sculpture.* New Haven.

Kleiner, F. (1971) "The flamen of the Ara Pietatis," *AJA* 75: 391–94.

(1985) *The Arch of Nero in Rome: A Study of the Roman Honorary Arch before and under Nero*. Rome.

(1989) "The study of Roman triumphal and honorary arches 50 years after Kähler," *JRA* 2: 195–206.

Knox, J. (1950) *Chapters in a Life of Paul*. New York.

Koeppel, G. (1982) "Die Ara Pietatis Augustae: ein Geisterbau," *MDAI(R)* 89: 453–55.

(1983a) "Two reliefs from the arch of Claudius in Rome," *MDAI(R)* 90: 103–9.

(1983b) "Die historischen Reliefs der römischen Kaiserzeit," *BJ* 183: 61–144.

Koestermann, E. (1963–68) *Cornelius Tacitus: Annalen*. Heidelberg.

(1971) *Cornelius Tacitus: Libri qui supersunt*. Third edn. (Bibliotheca scriptorium Graecorum et Romanorum Teubneriana). Leipzig.

Kokkinia, C. (2003) "Ruling, inducing, arguing: how to govern (and survive) a Greek province." In *Roman Rule and Civic Life: Local and Regional Perspectives*, ed. L. de Ligt *et al*. Amsterdam: 39–58.

Kokkinos, N. (2002) *Antonia Augusta: Portrait of a Great Roman Lady*. London and New York.

Kolb, A. (1993) *Die kaiserliche Bauverwaltung in der Stadt Rom: Geschichte und Aufbau der cura operum publicorum unter dem Prinzipat*. Stuttgart.

(2000) *Transport und Nachrichtentransfer im römischen Reich*. Berlin.

Kolb, F. (2002) "Lykiens Weg in die römische Provinzordnung." In *Widerstand – Anpassung – Integration: die griechische Staatenwelt und Rom: Festschrift für Jürgen Deininger zum 65. Geburtstag*, ed. N. Ehrhardt and L.-M. Günther. Stuttgart: 207–21.

Kolendo, J. (1998) "Claude et l'annexion de la Thrace." In *Claude de Lyon, empereur romain: actes du colloque Paris-Nancy-Lyon, novembre 1992*, ed. Y. Burnand *et al*. Paris: 321–32.

Konrad, C. (1994) "Proconsuls of Africa, the future Emperor Galba and the togatus in the Villa Massimo," *JRA* 7: 151–62.

Kragelund, P., Moltesen, M., and Ostergaard, J. (2003) *The Licinian Tomb: Fact or Fiction?* Copenhagen, 2003.

Kraus, C. and Woodman, A. (1997) *Latin Historians*. Oxford and New York.

Kunst, C. and Riemer, U. (2000) *Die Grenzen der Macht: zur Rolle der römischen Kaiserfrauen*. Stuttgart.

La Rocca, E. (1992a). "Claudio a Ravenna," *PP* 47: 265–314.

(1992b). "Ara reditus Claudii: linguaggio figurativo e simbologia nell'età di Claudio." In *La storia, la letteratura e l'arte a Roma: da Tiberio a Domiziano: atti del convegno: (Mantova, Teatro Accademico, 4–5-6–7 ottobre 1990)*. Mantua: 61–120.

(1994) "Arcus et arae Claudii." In *Die Regierungszeit des Kaisers Claudius (41–54 n. Chr.): Umbruch oder Episode?*, ed. V. Strocka. Mainz: 267–93.

Lahusen, G. (1983) *Untersuchungen zur Ehrenstatue in Rom: literarische und epigraphische Zeugnisse*. Munich.

(1984) *Schriftquellen zum römischen Bildnis, 1. Von den Anfängen bis zum 3. Jahrhundert n.Chr*. Bremen.

Laubscher, H. (1976) *Arcus Novus und Arcus Claudii, zwei Triumphbögen an der Via Lata in Rom*. Göttingen.

Le Bohec, Y. (1994) *The Imperial Roman Army*. London.

(1998) "Que voulait Onesandros?" In *Claude de Lyon, empereur romain: actes du colloque Paris-Nancy-Lyon, novembre 1992*, ed. Y. Burnand *et al.* Paris: 169–79.

(2000–3) *Les légions de Rome sous le haut-empire: actes du congrès de Lyon (17–19 septembre 1998)*. Lyon.

Le Gall, J. (1953) *Le Tibre, fleuve de Rome dans l'antiquité*. Paris.

Le Guen, B. (2001) *Les associations de technites dionysiaques à l'époque hellénistique*. Nancy.

Leach, E. (1989) "The implied reader and the political argument in Seneca's *Apocolocyntosis* and *De Clementia*," *Arethusa* 22: 197–230.

Lendon, J. (1997) *Empire of Honour: The Art of Government in the Roman World*. Oxford and New York.

(1998) "Three emperors and the Roman imperial regime," *CJ* 94: 87–93.

(2002) "Primitivism and ancient foreign relations," *CJ* 97: 375–84.

(2006) "The legitimacy of the Roman emperor: against Weberian legitimacy and imperial 'strategies of legitimation.'" In *Herrschaftsstrukturen und Herrschaftspraxis: Konzepte, Prinzipien und Strategien der Administration im römischen Kaiserreich*, ed. A. Kolb. Berlin: 53–63.

Lenski, N. (2002) *Failure of Empire: Valens and the Roman State in the Fourth Century AD*. Berkeley and Los Angeles.

Levick, B. (1978) "Antiquarian or revolutionary? Claudius Caesar's conception of his principate," *AJPh* 99: 79–105.

(1990) *Claudius*. New Haven.

(1999a) *Tiberius the Politician*. Revised edn. London and New York.

(1999b) *Vespasian*. London and New York.

Levinskaya, I. (1996) *The Book of Acts in its Diaspora Setting*. Grand Rapids, MI.

Lewis, N. (1954) "On official corruption in Roman Egypt: the edict of Vergilius Capito," *PAPhS* 98 : 153–58.

(1983) *Life in Egypt under Roman Rule*. Oxford and New York.

Lightfoot, J. (2002) "Nothing to do with the *technītai* of Dionysus?" In *Greek and Roman Actors: Aspects of an Ancient Profession*, ed. P. Easterling and E. Hall. Cambridge and New York: 209–24.

Linderski, J. (2007) *Roman Questions II: Selected Papers*. Stuttgart.

Lintott, A. (1993) *Imperium Romanum: Politics and Administration*. London and New York.

(1999). *The Constitution of the Roman Republic*. Oxford and New York.

Lo Cascio, E. (2000) *Il princeps e il suo impero: studi di storia amministrativa e finanziaria romana*. S. Spirito (Bari).

(2007) "The early Roman Empire: the state and the economy." In *The Cambridge Economic History of the Greco-Roman World*, ed. W. Scheidel *et al.* Cambridge and New York: 619–47.

Lozano, F. (2007) "*Divi Augusti* and *Theoi Sebastoi*: Roman initiative and Greek answers," *CQ* 57: 139–52.

Luttwak, E. (1976) *The Grand Strategy of the Roman Empire from the First Century AD to the Third.* Baltimore.

Lyasse, E. (2005) "*Auctis finibus populi Romani?*" *Gerión* 23: 169–87.

MacCormack, S. (1981) *Art and Ceremony in Late Antiquity.* Berkeley.

Mackie, N. (1983) "Augustan colonies in Mauretania," *Historia* 32: 332–58.

MacMullen, R. (1966). "Provincial languages in the Roman empire," *AJPh* 87: 1–17.

(1988) *Corruption and the Decline of Rome.* New Haven.

Magie, D. (1950) *Roman Rule in Asia Minor, to the End of the Third Century after Christ.* Princeton.

Maiuri, A. (1925) *Nuova silloge epigrafica di Rodi e Cos.* Florence.

Malitz, J. (1994) "Claudius (FGrHist 276) – der Princeps als Gelehrter." In *Die Regierungszeit des Kaisers Claudius (41–54 n. Chr.): Umbruch oder Episode?* ed. V. Strocka. Mainz: 133–44.

Malloch, S. (2001) "Gaius on the Channel coast," *CQ* 51: 551–56.

(2004) "The death of Ptolemy of Mauretania," *Historia*: 38–45.

Manning, W. (2004) "The conquest of Wales." In *A Companion to Roman Britain,* ed. M. Todd. Malden, MA and Oxford: 60–74.

Marin, B. and Virlouvet, C. (2004) *Nourrir les cités de Méditerranée: antiquité – temps modernes.* Paris.

Marksteiner, T. and Wörrle, M. (2002) "Ein Altar für Kaiser Claudius auf dem Bonda tepesi zwischen Myra und Limyra," *Chiron* 32: 545–69.

Massner, A.-K. (1982) *Bildnisangleichung: Untersuchungen zur Entstehungs- und Wirkungsgeschichte der Augustusporträts (43 v. Chr.–68 n. Chr.).* Berlin.

(1994) "Zum Stilwandel im Kaiserporträt claudischer Zeit." In *Die Regierungszeit des Kaisers Claudius (41–54 n. Chr.): Umbruch oder Episode?* ed. V. Strocka. Mainz: 159–76.

Mattern, S. (1999) *Rome and the Enemy: Imperial Strategy in the Principate.* Berkeley.

Mattingly, D. (1995) *Tripolitania.* London.

(2006) *An Imperial Possesion: Britain in the Roman Empire.* London.

Mattingly, D. and Hitchner, R. (1995) "Roman Africa: an archaeological review," *JRS* 85: 165–213.

Mayer, R. (1980) "Calpurnius Siculus: technique and date," *JRS* 70: 175–76.

McAlindon, D. (1956) "Senatorial opposition to Claudius and Nero," *AJPh* 77: 112–32.

McKechnie, P. (2005) "Judaean embassies and cases before Roman emperors, AD 44–66," *JThS* 56: 339–61.

McKenzie, J. (2008) *The Architecture of Alexandria and Egypt 300 BC–AD 700.* New Haven.

McLaren, J. (1998) *Turbulent Times? Josephus and Scholarship on Judaea in the First Century CE.* Sheffield.

Meadows, A. and Williams, J. (2001) "Moneta and the monuments: coinage and politics in Republican Rome," *JRS* 91: 27–49.

Meeks, W. (1983) *The First Urban Christians: The Social World of the Apostle Paul.* New Haven.

Megow, W.-R. (1987) *Kameen von Augustus bis Alexander Severus.* Berlin.

Mehl, A. (1974) *Tacitus über Kaiser Claudius: die Ereignisse am Hof.* Munich.

   (1979) "Kaiser Claudius und der Feldherr Corbulo bei Tacitus und Cassius Dio," *Hermes* 107: 220–39.

Meise, E. (1969) *Untersuchungen zur Geschichte der Julisch-Claudischen Dynastie.* Munich.

Melmoux, J. (1990) "L'empereur Claude et la finium Imperii propagatio: l'exemple breton." In *Neronia IV: Alejandro Magno, modelo de los emperadores romanos: actes du IVe colloque international de la SIEN,* ed. J. Croisille. Brussels: 163–82.

Meneghini, R. and Valenzani, R. (2007) *I Fori Imperiali: gli scavi del Comune di Roma (1991–2007).* Rome.

Menichetti, M. (1983/84) "Il ritratto di Claudio," *AFLPer* 21: 181–226.

Meyer, E. (1998) Review of W. Eck *et al., Das senatus consultum de Cn. Pisone patre, CJ* 93: 315–24.

   (2004) *Legitimacy and Law in the Roman World: Tabulae in Roman Belief and Practice.* Cambridge and New York.

Millar, F. (1964) *A Study of Cassius Dio.* Oxford.

   (1966) Review of F. Grosso, *La lotta politica al tempo di Commodo, JRS* 56: 243–45.

   (1967) *The Roman Empire and Its Neighbours.* New York.

   (1977) *The Emperor in the Roman World: 31 BC–AD 337.* London.

   (1992) *The Emperor in the Roman World: 31 BC–AD 337.* Second edn. London.

   (1993) *The Roman Near East, 31 BC–AD 337.* Cambridge, MA.

   (2002) *The Roman Republic and the Augustan Revolution* (*Rome, the Greek World and the East* Vol. 1). Chapel Hill.

   (2004) *Government, Society and Culture in the Roman Empire* (*Rome, the Greek World and the East* Vol. 2). Chapel Hill.

   (2006) *A Greek Roman Empire: Power and Belief under Theodosius II (408–50).* Berkeley.

Milne, H. *et al.* (1928) "Bibliography: Graeco-Roman Egypt. A. Papyri (1926–1927)," *JEA* 14: 131–58.

Milnor, K. (2005) *Gender, Domesticity, and the Age of Augustus: Inventing Private Life.* Oxford and New York.

Mitchell, S. (1976) "Requisitioned transport in the Roman Empire: a new inscription from Pisidia," *JRS* 66: 106–31.

   (1990) "Festivals, games, and civic life in Roman Asia Minor," *JRS* 80: 183–93.

   (1993) *Anatolia: Land, Men, and Gods in Asia Minor.* Oxford and New York.

Mitchell, S. and Waelkens, M. (1998) *Pisidian Antioch: The Site and Its Monuments.* London.

Moatti, C. (1993) *Archives et partage de la terre dans le monde romain (II siècle avant–I siècle après J.-C.).* Rome.

(1997) *La raison de Rome: naissance de l'esprit critique à la fin de la République (IIe–Ier siècle avant Jésus-Christ)*. Paris.

Moatti, C. *et al.* (1998) *La mémoire perdue: recherches sur l'administration romaine.* Rome.

et al. (2000) *La mémoire perdue. 3. MEFRA* 112: 647–779.

Mócsy, A. (1974) *Pannonia and Upper Moesia: A History of the Middle Danube Provinces of the Roman Empire.* London and Boston.

Moltesen, M. and Nielsen, M. (2007) *Agrippina Minor: Life and Afterlife.* Copenhagen.

Momigliano, A. (1934) *Claudius, the Emperor, and His Achievement.* Trans. W. Hogarth. Oxford.

(1990) *The Classical Foundations of Modern Historiography.* Berkeley.

Mommsen, T. (1871–88) *Römisches Staatsrecht.* Leipzig.

(1992) *A History of Rome under the Emperors.* Trans. C. Krojzl. London and New York.

Montevecchi, O. (1970) "Nerone a una polis e ai 6475," *Aegyptus* 50: 5–33.

(1982/3) "La crisi economica sotto Claudio e Nerone: nuove testimonianze," *CRDAC* 12: 139–48.

Morizio, V. (1996) "Le dediche ad Augusto e ai Giulio-Claudi." In *Meta Sudans, I. Un'area sacra in Palatio e la valle del Colosseo prima e dopo Nerone*, ed. C. Panella. Rome: 201–16.

Morris, I. and Scheidel, W. (2009) *The Dynamics of Ancient Empires: State Power from Assyria to Byzantium.* Oxford and New York.

Morris, J. (1964) "Leges annales under the principate," *LF* 87: 316–37.

(1965) "Leges annales under the principate: political effects," *LF* 88: 22–31.

Mrozek, S. (1987) *Les distributions d'argent et de nourriture dans les villes italiennes du Haut-Empire romain.* Brussels.

Murphy, T. (2004) *Pliny the Elder's Natural History: The Empire in the Encyclopedia.* Oxford and New York.

Nauta, R. (1987) "Seneca's *Apocolocyntosis* as Saturnalian literature," *Mnemosyne* 40: 69–96.

Nicolet, C. (1991) *Space, Geography, and Politics in the Early Roman Empire.* Ann Arbor.

(1996) *Financial Documents and Geographical Knowledge in the Roman World.* Oxford.

Nicolet, C. ed. (1994) *La mémoire perdue: à la recherche des archives oubliées, publiques et privées, de la Rome antique.* Paris.

Noreña, C. (2003) "Medium and message in Vespasian's Templum Pacis," *MAAR* 48: 25–43.

Ogilvie, R. (1961) "'Lustrum condere,'" *JRS* 51: 31–39.

O'Gorman, E. (2005) "Citation and authority in Seneca's *Apocolocyntosis*." In *The Cambridge Companion to Roman Satire*, ed. K. Freudenburg. Cambridge and New York: 95–108.

Oost, S. (1958) "The career of M. Antonius Pallas," *AJPh* 79: 113–39.

Osgood, J. (2006a) *Caesar's Legacy: Civil War and the Emergence of the Roman Empire.* Cambridge.

(2006b) Review of J. Højte, *Roman Imperial Statue Bases: from Augustus to Commodus,* AJA Online Reviews 110.4.

(2006c) *"Nuptiae iure civili congruae*: Apuleius's story of Cupid and Psyche and the Roman law of marriage," *TAPhA* 136: 415–41.

(2007a) "The *vox* and *verba* of an emperor: Claudius, Seneca, and *le prince idéal," CJ* 102: 329–54.

(2007b) Review of J. Scheid, *Res gestae divi Augusti. Hauts faits du divin Auguste, BMCR* 2007.10.40.

Pack, R. (1943) "Seneca's evidence on the deaths of Claudius and Narcissus," *CW* 36: 150–51.

Palmer, R. (1980) "Customs on market goods imported into the city of Rome." In *The Seaborne Commerce of Ancient Rome: Studies in Archaeology and History,* ed. J. D'Arms and E. Kopff. Rome: 217–33.

Panciera, S. (1998) "Claudio costruttore *de sua pecunia*! A proposito di una nuova iscrizione templare romana." In *Claude de Lyon, empereur romain: actes du colloque Paris-Nancy-Lyon, novembre 1992,* ed. Y. Burnand *et al.* Paris: 137–60.

Pani, M. (2003) *La corte dei Cesari fra Augusto e Nerone.* Rome.

Parsi, B. (1963) *Désignation et investiture de l'empereur romain: Ier et IIe siécles après J.-C.* Paris.

Parsons, P. (2007) *City of the Sharp-nosed Fish: Greek Lives in Roman Egypt.* London.

Paterson, J. (2007) "Friends in high places: the creation of the court of the Roman emperor." In *The Court and Court Society in Ancient Monarchies,* ed. A. Spawforth. Cambridge and New York: 121–56.

Patterson, J. (1992) "The city of Rome: from Republic to Empire," *JRS* 82: 186–215.

Pavis d'Escurac, H. (1976) *La préfecture de l'annone: service administratif imperial d'Auguste à Constantin.* Rome.

Pavolini, C. (2007) "'L'Agrippina-orante' di Villa Casali e la politica religiosa degli imperatori sul Celio." In *Res bene gestae: ricerche di storia urbana su Roma antica in onore di Eva Margareta Steinby,* ed. A. Leone. Rome: 309–34.

Pekáry, T. (1985) *Das römische Kaiserbildnis in Staat, Kult und Gesellschaft.* Berlin.

Petzl, G. and Schwertheim, E. (2006) *Hadrian und die dionysischen Künstler: drei in Alexandria Troas neugefundene Briefe des Kaisers an die Künstler-Vereinigung.* Bonn.

Pflaum, H.-G. (1950) *Les procurateurs équestres sous le haut empire romain.* Paris.

Piccolo, M. (2003) "Osservazioni ad alcuni papiri dell'archivio di Tryphon," *Aegyptus* 83: 197–213.

Pickard-Cambridge, A. (1968) *The Dramatic Festivals of Athens.* Oxford and New York.

Pighi, G. (1965) *De ludis saecularibus populi romani Quiritium libri sex.* Amsterdam.

Pitts, L. (1989) "Relations between Rome and the German kings on the middle Danube in the first to fourth centuries AD," *JRS* 79: 45–58.

Poe, J. (1984) "The Secular Games, the Aventine, and the pomerium," *ClAnt* 3: 57–81.

Potter, D. (1996) "Emperors, their borders and their neighbors: the scope of imperial mandata." In *The Roman Army in the East*, ed. D. Kennedy. Ann Arbor: 49–66.

(1998) "*Senatus Consultum de Cn. Pisone*," *JRA* 11: 437–57.

Potter, D. and Mattingly, D. (eds.) (1999) *Life, Death, and Entertainment in the Roman Empire*. Ann Arbor.

Price, S. (1984) *Rituals and Power: The Roman Imperial Cult in Asia Minor*. Cambridge and New York.

(1987) "From noble funerals to divine cult: the consecration of the Roman emperors." In *Rituals of Royalty: Power and Ceremonial in Traditional Societies*, ed. D. Cannadine and S. Price. Cambridge: 56–105.

Pucci ben Zeev, M. (1998) *Jewish Rights in the Roman World: The Greek and Roman Documents Quoted by Josephus Flavius*. Tübingen.

Purcell, N. (1986) "Livia and the womanhood of Rome," *PCPhS* 32: 78–105.

(1990a) "The creation of provincial landscape: the Roman impact on Cisalpine Gaul." In *The Early Roman Empire in the West*, ed. T. Blagg and M. Millett. Oxford: 7–29.

(1990b) "Maps, lists, money, order and power," *JRS* 80: 178–82.

(2007) "The *horti* of Rome and the landscape of property." In *Res bene gestae: ricerche di storia urbana su Roma antica in onore di Eva Margareta Steinby*, ed. A. Leone. Rome: 361–77.

Questa, C. (1995) Messalina, meretrix augusta." In *Vicende e figure femminili in Grecia e a Roma: atti del convegno di Pesaro 28–30 aprile 1994*, ed. R. Raffaelli. Ancona: 399–423.

Radin, M. (1925) Review of H. Bell, *Jews and Christian in Egypt*, *CPh* 20: 368–75.

Ramsay, A. (1925). "The speed of the Roman imperial post," *JRS* 15: 60–74.

Ramsey, J. (2006) *Descriptive Catalogue of Greco-Roman Comets from 500 BC to AD 400*. Iowa City, IA.

Rathbone, D. (2001) "PSI XI 1183: record of a Roman census declaration of A.D. 47/8." In *Essays and Texts in Honor of J. David Thomas*, ed. T. Gagos and R. Bagnall. Oakville, CT: 99–113.

Ratté, C. and Smith, R. (2008) "Archaeological research at Aphrodisias in Caria, 2002–2005," *AJA* 112: 713–51.

Raven, S. (1993) *Rome in Africa*. Third edn. London and New York.

Rawson, E. (1985) *Intellectual Life in the Late Roman Republic*. London.

Rebuffat, R. (1998) "'Romana arma primum Claudio principe in Mauretania bellauere.'" In *Claude de Lyon, empereur romain: actes du colloque Paris-Nancy-Lyon, novembre 1992*, ed. Y. Burnand *et al.* Paris: 277–320.

Reynolds, J. (1971) "New boundary stones from the public land of the Roman people in Cyrenaica," *LibAnt* 8: 47–51.

(1986) "Further information on imperial cult at Aphrodisias," *StudClas* 24: 109–19.

Reynolds, J. and Ward Perkins, J. (1952) *The Inscriptions of Roman Tripolitania*. Rome.

Richard, F. (1998) "Les images du triomphe de Claude sur la Bretagne." In *Claude de Lyon, empereur romain: actes du colloque Paris-Nancy-Lyon, novembre 1992*, ed. Y. Burnand *et al.* Paris: 355–71.

Rickman, G. (1980) *The Corn Supply of Ancient Rome*. Oxford and New York.

Rigsby, K. (2004) "Claudius at Delphi," *ZPE* 146: 99–100.

Ritter, B. (2003) *Civic Integration of Jews in the Cities of the Greek East in the First Centuries* BC *and* AD. Ph.D. dissertation University of California, Berkeley.

Ritter, H. (1972) "Cluvius Rufus bei Josephus," *RhM* 115: 85–91.

Rives, J. (1999) *Tacitus: Germania*. Oxford and New York.

(2001) "Imperial cult and native tradition in Roman North Africa," *CJ* 96: 425–36.

Robinson, T. (2005) "In the court of time: the reckoning of a monster in the *Apocolocyntosis* of Seneca," *Arethusa* 38: 223–57.

Rodgers, R. (2004) *Frontinus: De aquaeductu urbis Romae*. Cambridge.

Rogers, G. (1991) *The Sacred Identity of Ephesos: Foundations Myths of a Roman City*. London and New York.

Rogers, R. (1945) "Domitius Afer's defense of Cloatilla," *TAPhA* 76: 264–70.

(1953) "The Neronian comets," *TAPhA* 84: 237–249.

Rolfe, J. (1998) *Suetonius*. Revised by D. Hurley (Loeb Classical Library). Cambridge, MA and London.

Roller, M. (2001) *Constructing Autocracy: Aristocrats and Emperors in Julio-Claudian Rome*. Princeton.

Romer, J. (1998) *Pomponius Mela's Description of the World*. Ann Arbor.

Romm, J. (1992) *The Edges of the Earth in Ancient Thought: Geography, Exploration, and Fiction*. Princeton.

Roncali, R. (2008) "Seneca, *Apocolocyntosis*: 1980–2000," *Lustrum* 50: 303–62.

Rosada, G. (2001) *La Via Claudia Augusta Altinate: ristampa anastatica dell'opera edita nel 1938; con una postfazione di Guido Rosada*. Venice.

Rose, C. (1990) "The supposed Augustan arch at Pavia (Ticinum) and the Einsiedeln 326 manuscript," *JRA* 3: 163–68.

(1997) *Dynastic Commemoration and Imperial Portraiture in the Julio-Claudian Period*. Cambridge and New York.

(2005) "The Parthians in Augustan Rome," *AJA* 109: 21–75.

Rowe, G. (2002) *Princes and Political Cultures: The New Tiberian Senatorial Decrees*. Ann Arbor.

Rowlandson, J. (1998) *Women and Society in Greek and Roman Egypt: A Sourcebook*. Cambridge.

Rudich, V. (1987) "Seneca's palinode: *Consolatio ad Polybium* and *Apokolokyntosis*," *AncW* 15: 105–9.

(1993) *Political Dissidence under Nero: The Price of Dissimulation*. London and New York.

Ruth, T. (1924) *The Problem of Claudius: Some Aspects of a Character Study*. Baltimore.

Rutledge, S. (2001) *Imperial Inquisitions: Prosecutors and Informants from Tiberius to Domitian*. London and New York.

Ryan, F. (1993) "Some observations on the censorship of Claudius and Vitellius, AD 47–48," *AJPh* 114: 611–18.

Ryberg, I. (1955) *Rites of the State Religion in Roman Art.* Rome.

Sabin, P., van Wees, H., and Whitby, M. (2007) *The Cambridge History of Greek and Roman Warfare.* Cambridge and New York.

Sablayrolles, R. (1981) "Espace urbain et propagande politique: l'organisation du centre de Rome par Auguste (*Res gestae*, 19 à 21)," *Pallas* 28: 59–77.

Şahin, S. and Adak, M. (2004) "Stadiasmus Patarensis: ein zweiter Vorbericht über das claudische Strassenbauprogramm in Lykien." In *Siedlung und Verkehr im römischen Reich: Römerstrassen zwischen Herrschaftssicherung und Landschaftsprägung,* ed. R. Frei-Stolba. Bern and Frankfurt: 227–62.

Saller, R. (1980) "Anecdotes as historical evidence for the principate," *G&R* 27: 69–83.

 (1982) *Personal Patronage under the Early Empire.* Cambridge and New York.

 (2005) "Framing the debate over growth in the ancient economy." In *The Ancient Economy,* ed. W. Scheidel and S. von Reden. New York: 251–69.

Sallmann, K. (1987) "Reserved for eternal punishment: the Elder Pliny's view of free Germania (HN 16.1–6)," *AJPh* 108: 108–28.

Scheid, J. (1992) "L'investiture impériale d'après les commentaires des arvales," *CCG* 3: 221–37.

 (1998) *Recherches archéologiques à la Magliana: Commentarii Fratrum Arvalium qui supersunt: les copies épigraphiques des protocoles annuels de la confrérie arvale: 21 av.–304 ap. J.-C.* Rome.

Scheidel, W. (1996) "Finances, figures and fiction," *CQ* 46: 222–38.

 (2007) "Demography." In *The Cambridge Economic History of the Greco-Roman World,* ed. W. Scheidel *et al.* Cambridge and New York: 38–86.

 (2009a) *Rome and China: Comparative Perspectives on Ancient World Empires.* Oxford and New York.

 (2009b) "Introduction." In *Rome and China: Comparative Perspectives on Ancient World Empires,* ed. W. Scheidel. Oxford and New York: 3–10.

 (2009c) "From the 'Great Convergence' to the 'First Great Divergence': Roman and Qin-Han state formation and its aftermath." In *Rome and China: Comparative Perspectives on Ancient World Empires,* ed. W. Scheidel. Oxford and New York: 11–23.

Scheidel, W., Morris, I., and Saller, R. (eds.) (2007) *The Cambridge Economic History of the Greco-Roman World.* Cambridge and New York.

Schmidt, P. (1994) "Claudius als Schriftsteller." In *Die Regierungszeit des Kaisers Claudius (41–54 n. Chr.): Umbruch oder Episode?* ed. V. Strocka. Mainz: 119–31.

Schnegg-Köhler, B. (2002) *Die augusteischen Säkularspiele.* Munich.

Schönberger, H. (1969) "The Roman frontier in Germany: an archaeological survey," *JRS* 59: 144–97.

Schürer, E. (1973–87) *History of the Jewish People in the Age of Jesus Christ (175 BC–AD 135).* Rev. and ed. G. Vermes and F. Millar. Edinburgh.

Schwartz, D. (1990) *Agrippa I: The Last King of Judaea.* Tübingen.

Scramuzza, V. (1940) *The Emperor Claudius*. Cambridge and London.

Seager, R. (2005) *Tiberius*. Second edn. Malden, MA and Oxford.

Segre, M. (1975) "Una lettera di Corbulone ai Coi," *PP* 30: 102–4.

Seif, K. (1973) *Die Claudiusbücher in den Annalen des Tacitus*. Mainz

Severy, B. (2003) *Augustus and the Family at the Birth of the Roman Empire*. New York.

Seymour-Smith, M. (1995) *Robert Graves: His Life and Work*. London.

Shaw, B. (1981) "The elder Pliny's African geography," *Historia* 30: 424–71.

(1982/83) "'Eaters of flesh, drinkers of milk': the ancient Mediterranean ideology of the pastoral nomad," *AncSoc* 13–14: 5–31.

(1989) "Our daily bread," *Social History of Medicine* 2: 205–13.

(2006) *At the Edge of the Corrupting Sea*. Oxford.

Sherk, R. (1988). *The Roman Empire: Augustus to Hadrian*. Translated Documents of Greece & Rome 6. Cambridge and New York.

Sherwin-White, A. (1973) *The Roman Citizenship*. Second edn. Oxford.

Sijpesteijn, P. (1989) "Another οὐσία of D. Valerius Asiaticus in Egypt," *ZPE* 79: 194–96.

Silberman, A. (1988) *Pomponius Méla: Chorographie*. Paris.

Sirks, A. (1991) *Food for Rome: The Legal Structure of the Transportation and Processing of Supplies for the Imperial Distributions in Rome and Constantinople*. Amsterdam.

Slingerland, H. (1997) *Claudian Policymaking and the Early Imperial Repression of Judaism at Rome*. Atlanta.

Small, A. (1996) *Subject and Ruler: The Cult of the Ruling Power in Classical Antiquity*. Ann Arbor.

Smallwood, E. (1961) *Philo: Legatio ad Gaium*. Leiden.

(1967) *Documents Illustrating the Principates of Gaius, Claudius and Nero*. London.

(1976) *The Jews under Roman Rule: From Pompey to Diocletian: A Study in Political Relations*. Leiden.

Smith, M. (1963) "Greek precedents for Claudius' actions in AD 48 and later," *CQ* 13: 139–44.

Smith, R. (1987) "The imperial reliefs from the Sebasteion at Aphrodisias," *JRS* 77: 88–138.

(1988) "Simulacra gentium: the ethne from the Sebasteion at Aphrodisias," *JRS* 78: 50–77.

(1996) "Typology and diversity in the portraits of Augustus," *JRA* 9: 31–47.

(2000) "Nero and the Sun-god: divine accessories and political symbols in Roman imperial images," *JRA* 13: 532–42.

Smith, W. (1849) *Dictionary of Greek and Roman Biography and Mythology*. Boston.

Souris, G. (1992) "The size of the provincial embassies to the emperor under the principate," *ZPE* 48: 235–44.

Spannagel, M. (1999) *Exemplaria principis: Untersuchungen zu Entstehung und Ausstattung des Augustusforums*. Heidelberg.

Speidel, M. A. (2000) "Geld und Macht: die Neuordnung des staatlichen Finanzwesens unter Augustus." In *La révolution romaine après Ronald Syme: bilans et perspectives*, ed. A. Giovannini. Vandoeuvres-Genève: 113–50.

Speidel, M. P. (1994) *Riding for Caesar: The Roman Emperors' Horse Guards.* Cambridge, MA.

Standing, G. (2003) "The Claudian invasion of Britain and the cult of Victoria Britannica," *Britannia* 34: 281–88.

Stevens, C. (1951) "Claudius and the Orcades," *CR* 1: 7–9.

Stewart, P. (2003) *Statues in Roman Society: Representation and Response.* Oxford and New York.

Strocka, V. (1994) *Die Regierungszeit des Kaisers Claudius (41–54 n. Chr.): Umbruch oder Episode?* Mainz.

Stroux, J. (1929) *Eine Gerichtsreform des Kaisers Claudius (BGU 611).* Munich.

Stuart, M. (1938) *The Portraiture of Claudius: Preliminary Studies.* New York.

(1939) "How were imperial portraits distributed throughout the Roman empire?" *AJA* 43: 601–17.

Sullivan, R. (1979) "Thrace in the Eastern dynastic network," *ANRW* 2.7.1: 186–211.

Suolahti, J. (1963) *The Roman Censors: A Study on Social Structure.* Helsinki.

Sutherland, C. (1951) *Coinage in Roman Imperial Policy 31 BC–AD 68.* London.

(1987) *Roman History and Coinage, 44 BC–AD 69: Fifty Points of Relation from Julius Caesar to Vespasian.* Oxford and New York.

Swan, P. (1970) "Josephus, *A.J.* XIX, 251–2: opposition to Gaius and Claudius," *AJPh* 91: 149–64.

(1976) "A consular Epicurean under the early principate," *Phoenix* 30: 54–60.

(2004) *The Augustan Succession: An Historical Commentary on Cassius Dio's Roman History, Books 55–56 (9 BC–AD 14).* New York.

Swift, E. (1923) "Imagines in imperial portraiture," *AJA* 27: 286–301.

Syme, R. (1939) *The Roman Revolution.* Oxford.

(1958) *Tacitus.* Oxford.

(1964) *Sallust.* Berkeley.

(1970) *Ten Studies in Tacitus.* Oxford.

(1971) *Danubian Papers.* Bucharest.

(1986) *The Augustan Aristocracy.* Oxford and New York.

(1995) *Anatolica: Studies in Strabo.* Ed. A. Birley. Oxford and New York.

(1999) *The Provincial at Rome: and, Rome and the Balkans 80 BC–AD 14.* Ed. A. Birley. Exeter.

Tagliafico, M. (1996) "I processi *intra cubiculum*: il caso di Valerio Asiatico." In *Processi e politica nel mondo antico*, ed. M. Sordi. Milan: 249–59.

Talbert, R. (1984) *The Senate of Imperial Rome.* Princeton.

Tandoi, V. (1962) "Il trionfo di Claudio sulla Britannia e il suo cantore (Anth. Lat. 419–426 Riese)," *SIFC* 34: 83–129 and 137–68.

Tatum, W. (2008) *Always I Am Caesar.* Malden, MA and Oxford.

Taylor, J. (2003) *Jewish Women Philosophers of First-Century Alexandria: Philo's "Therapeutae" Reconsidered.* Oxford and New York.

Tcherikover, V. and Fuchs, A. (1957–64) *Corupus papyrorum Judaicarum*. Cambridge, MA.

Temporini-Gräfin Vitzthum, H. (2002) *Die Kaiserinnen Roms: von Livia bis Theodora*. Munich.

Thomas, C. (2004) "Claudius and the Roman army reforms," *Historia* 53: 424–52.

Thomas, E. (2007) *Monumentality and the Roman Empire: Architecture in the Antonine Age*. Oxford and New York.

Thomas, J. (2001) "The administration of Roman Egypt: a survey of recent research and some outstanding problems." In *Atti del XXII Congresso Internazionale di Papirologia*. Florence: 2.1245–54.

Thomas, R. (1982) *Lands and Peoples in Roman Poetry: The Ethnographical Tradition*. Cambridge.

Thornton, J. (2001) "Gli *aristoi*, l'*akriton plethos* e la provincializzazione della Licia nel monumento di Patara," *MediterrAnt* 2001: 427–46.

(2004) "*Pistoì symmachoi*: versioni locali e versione imperiale della provincializzazione della Licia," *MediterrAnt* 7: 247–86.

Thornton, M. and Thornton, R. (1985) "The draining of the Fucine Lake: a quantitative analysis," *AncW* 12: 105–20.

Timpe, D. (1960) "Römische Geschichte bei Flavius Josephus," *Historia* 9: 474–502.

(1962) *Untersuchungen zur Kontinuität des frühen Prinzipats*. Wiesbaden.

Todd, M. (2004a) "The Claudian conquest and its consequences." In *A Companion to Roman Britain*, ed. M. Todd. Malden, MA and Oxford: 42–59.

(2004b) *The Early Germans*. Second edn. Malden, MA.

Torelli, M. (1982) *Typology and Structure of Roman Historical Reliefs*. Ann Arbor.

(1985) "I duodecim populi Etruriae," *AnnFaina* 2: 37–73.

(1994) "Per un'eziologia del cambiamento in epoca claudia: vicende vicine e vicende lontane." In *Die Regierungszeit des Kaisers Claudius (41–54 n. Chr.): Umbruch oder Episode?* ed. V. Strocka. Mainz: 177–90.

Tortoriello, A. (2001) "Gli adlecti inter patricios di Claudio," *AION(archeol)* 8: 183–204.

(2004) *I fasti consolari degli anni di Claudio*. Rome.

Townend, G. (1980) "Calpurnius Siculus and the *munus Neronis*," *JRS* 70: 166–74.

Treggiari, S. (1991) *Roman Marriage: Iusti Coniuges from the Time of Cicero to the Time of Ulpian*. Oxford and New York.

Trillmich, W. (1978) *Familienpropaganda der Kaiser Caligula und Claudius: Agrippina Maior und Antonia Augusta auf Münzen*. Berlin.

Turcan, R. (1987) *Vivre à la cour des Césars, d'Auguste à Dioclétien (I–III siècles ap. J.-C.)*. Paris.

Valente, W. *et al.* (2002) "Caveat cenans!" *The American Journal of Medicine* 112: 392–98.

Valvo, A. (2001) "I diplomi militari e la politica di integrazione dell'imperatore Claudio." In *Integrazione mescolanza e rifiuto*, ed. G. Urso. Rome: 151–67.

Van Der Horst, P. (1984) *Chaeremon, Egyptian Priest and Stoic Philosopher: The Fragments*. Leiden and Boston.

(2003) *Philo's Flaccus: The First Pogrom.* Leiden and Boston.

van Essen, C. (1957) "The Via Valeria from Tivoli to Collarmele," *PBSR* 25: 22–38.

Varner, E. (2004) *Mutilation and Transformation: Damnatio Memoriae and Roman Imperial Portraiture.* Leiden and Boston.

Versnel, H. (1993) "Two carnivalesque princes: Augustus and Claudius and the ambiguity of Saturnalian imagery." In *Karnevaleske Phänomene in antiken und nachantiken Kulturen und Literaturen,* ed. S. Döpp. Trier: 99–122.

Veyne, P. (1976) *Le pain et le cirque: sociologie historique d'un pluralisme politique.* Paris.

(2005) *L'empire gréco-romain.* Paris.

Vierneisel, K. and Zanker, P. (1979) *Die Bildnisse des Augustus: Herrscherbild und Politik im kaiserlichen Rom.* Munich.

Virlouvet, C. (1995) *Tessera frumentaria: les procédures de distribution du blé public à Rome à la fin de la république et au début de l'empire.* Rome.

von Hesberg, H. (1994) "Bogenmonumente und Stadttore in claudischer Zeit." In *Regierungszeit des Kaisers Claudius (41–54 n. Chr.): Umbruch oder Episode?* ed. V. Strocka. Mainz: 245–60.

von Kaenel, H.-M. (1986) *Münzprägung und Münzbildnis des Claudius.* Berlin.

(1994) "Zur 'Prägepolitik' des Kaisers Claudius: Überlegungen zur Funktion von frisch geprägtem Edelmetall in der frühen Kaiserzeit." In *Die Regierungszeit des Kaisers Claudius (41–54 n. Chr.): Umbruch oder Episode?* ed. V. Strocka. Mainz: 45–68.

Vout, C. (2007). *Power and Eroticism in Imperial Rome.* Cambridge and New York.

Wallace-Hadrill, A. (1982) "*Civilis princeps*: between citizen and king," *JRS* 72: 32–48.

(1983) *Suetonius: The Scholar and His Caesars.* London.

(1986) "Image and authority in the coinage of Augustus," *JRS* 76: 66–87.

(1990) "Roman arches and Greek honours: the language of power at Rome," *PCPhS* 36: 143–81.

(1997) "*Mutatio morum:* the idea of a cultural revolution." In *The Roman Cultural Revolution,* ed. T. Habinek and A. Schiesaro. Princeton: 3–22.

(2005) "*Mutatas formas:* the Augustan transformation of Roman knowledge." In *The Cambridge Companion to the Age of Augustus,* ed. K. Galinsky. Cambridge and New York: 55–84.

(2008) *Rome's Cultural Revolution.* Cambridge and New York.

Walser, G. (1980) "Die Strassenbau-Tätigkeit von Kaiser Claudius," *Historia* 29: 438–62.

Wardle, D. (1992a) "Cluvius Rufus and Suetonius," *Hermes* 120: 466–82.

(1992b) "Caligula and the client kings," *CQ* 42: 437–43.

Weaver, P. (1972) *Familia Caesaris: A Social Study of the Emperor's Freedmen and Slaves.* Cambridge.

(2004) "*P. Oxy.* 3312 and joining the household of Caesar," *ZPE* 149: 196–204.

Webster, G. (1998) *The Roman Imperial Army of the First and Second Centuries* AD. Third edn. Norman, OK.

Wellesley, K. (1954) "Can you trust Tacitus?" *G&R* 1: 13–35.

Wells, C. (1972) *The German Policy of Augustus: An Examination of the Archaeological Evidence*. Oxford.
(1992) *The Roman Empire*. Second edn. London.
(1998) "What's new along the Lippe: recent work in North Germany," *Britannia* 29: 457–64.
Wheeler, E. (1993) "Methodological limits and the mirage of Roman strategy," *The Journal of Military History* 57: 7–41 and 215–40.
(1996) "The laxity of Syrian legions." In *The Roman Army in the East*, ed. D. Kennedy. Ann Arbor: 229–76.
Whitehorne, J. (1984) "Tryphon's second marriage (*P.Oxy.* II 267)." In *Atti del XVII congresso internazionale di papirologia* III. Naples: 1267–74.
Whittaker, C. (1994) *Frontiers of the Roman Empire: A Social and Economic Study*. Baltimore.
Wilkes, J. (1972) "Julio-Claudian historians," *CW* 65: 177–92 and 197–203.
(2002) "The legions in the Principate: updating Ritterling," *JRA* 15: 528–35.
Will, W. (1987) "Römische 'Klientel-Randstaaten' am Rhein? Eine Bestandsaufnahme,' *BJ* 187: 1–61.
Williamson, G. (2005) "Mucianus and a touch of the miraculous: pilgrimage and tourism in Roman Asia Minor." In *Pilgrimage in Graeco-Roman and Early Christian Antiquity: Seeing the Gods*, ed. J. Elsner and I. Rutherford. Oxford and New York: 219–52.
Wilson, A. (2007) "The metal supply of the Roman empire." In *Supplying Rome and the Roman Empire*, ed. E. Papi. Portsmouth, RI: 109–25.
Winkes, R. (1995) *Livia, Octavia, Iulia: Porträts und Darstellungen*. Providence and Louvain-la-Neuve.
Winterling, A. (1999) *Aula Caesaris: Studien zur Institutionalisierung des römischen Kaiserhofes in der Zeit von Augustus bis Commodus (31 v. Chr.–192 n. Chr.)*. Munich.
(2003) *Caligula: eine Biographie*. Munich.
(2009) *Caligula: a Biography*. Trans. D. Schneider. Berkeley and London.
Wiseman, T. (1982) "Calpurnius Siculus and the Claudian civil war," *JRS* 72: 57–67.
(1991) *Death of an Emperor*. Exeter.
(2004) *The Myths of Rome*. Exeter.
(2007) "Names remembered, names suppressed," *JRA* 20: 421–27.
(2008) "Rethinking the triumph," *JRA* 21: 389–91.
Wissowa, G. (1912) *Religion und Kultus der Römer*. Second edn. Munich.
Wolf, J. (1994) "Claudius iudex." In *Die Regierungszeit des Kaisers Claudius (41–54 n. Chr.): Umbruch oder Episode?* ed. V. Strocka. Mainz: 145–58.
Wolters, R. (1999) "C. Stertinius Xenophon von Kos und die Grabinschrift des Trimalchio," *Hermes* 127: 47–60.
Wood, S. (1999) *Imperial Women: A Study in Public Images, 40 BC–AD 68*. Leiden and Boston.
Woodman, A. (1988). *Rhetoric in Classical Historiography: Four Studies*. London.
(2004) *Tacitus: The Annals*. Indianapolis.

Woods, D. (2000) "Caligula's seashells," *G&R* 47: 80–87.

Wormersley, D. (1994) *Edward Gibbon: The History of the Decline and Fall of the Roman Empire*. London and New York.

Wörrle, M. (1975) "Zwei neue griechische Inschriften aus Myra zur Verwaltung Lykiens in der Kaiserzeit." In *Myra: eine lykische Metropole in antiker und byzantinischer Zeit*, ed. J. Borchhardt. Berlin: 254–300.

(1988) *Stadt und Fest im kaiserzeitlichen Kleinasien: Studien zu einer agonistischen Stiftung aus Oinoanda*. Munich.

(2004) "Maroneia im Umbruch," *Chiron* 34: 149–67.

Wyke, M. (2002) *The Roman Mistress: Ancient and Modern Representations*. Oxford and New York.

Youtie, H. (1977) "P. Mich. Inv. 855: letter from Herakleides to Nemesion," *ZPE* 24: 147–50.

Zanker, P. (1988) *The Power of Images in the Age of Augustus*. Trans. A. Shapiro. Ann Arbor.

(1997) *Der Kaiser baut fürs Volk*. Opladen.

Ziegler, K.-H. (1964). *Die Beziehungen zwischen Rom und dem Partherreich: ein Beitrag zur Geschichte des Völkerrechts*. Wiesbaden.

Ziethen, G. (1994) *Gesandte vor Kaiser und Senat: Studien zum römischen Gesandschaftswesen zwischen 30 v. Chr. und 117 n. Chr.* St. Katharinen.

Ziolkowski, A. (1992) *The Temples of Mid-Republican Rome and Their Historical and Topographical Context*. Rome.

Index

Note: this index is primarily intended to guide the reader to relevant discussions in *Claudius Caesar*. Individuals are not here identified (though some relations between them are indicated), nor are places located. For Senatorial prosopography in particular, especially useful are the full indices of Syme (1958) and (1986) and also Tortoriello (2004). The entries for some major historical figures are arranged chronologically, as well as thematically.